Desmond Stewart is an Arabist, an authority on the Middle East, and has written widely about the Arab world. Amongst his many books, *The Middle East: Temple of Janus* (1972) and his biography of Theodore Herzl, the founder of modern political Zionism (1974) have received special attention. He has also written several novels, the most recent of which is *The Vampire of Mons*. He divides his time between Norfolk and Cairo.

Desmond Stewart

T. E. Lawrence

PALADIN
GRANADA PUBLISHING
London Toronto Sydney New York

Published by Granada Publishing Limited
in Paladin Books 1979

ISBN 0 586 08306 5

First published in Great Britain by
Hamish Hamilton Ltd 1977

Granada Publishing Limited
Frogmore, St Albans, Herts, AL2 2NF
and
3 Upper James Street, London W1R 4BP
1221 Avenue of the Americas, New York, NY 10020, USA
117 York Street, Sydney, NSW 2000, Australia
100 Skyway Avenue, Toronto, Ontario, Canada M9W 3A6
110 Northpark Centre, 2193 Johannesburg, South Africa
CML Centre, Queen & Wyndham, Auckland 1, New Zealand

Made and printed in Great Britain by
Richard Clay (The Chaucer Press) Ltd
Bungay, Suffolk
Set in Monotype Imprint

To Christopher Sinclair-Stevenson

CONTENTS

Illustrations

Maps drawn by Patrick Leeson

(The spelling of place names on the maps largely follows that of T. E. Lawrence.)

BOOK ONE

1888–1910

An Oxford Scholar Poor

1

BY THE eighties of the last century the green countryside to the north of Oxford had been colonized by red brick and pallid mortar. Angular, castellar villas lining roads dusty from horses looked more intrusive than they do today, when trees have aged and shrubs learnt to sprawl. The roads nearest the university town were settled by Fellows availing themselves of an innovation which permitted them to marry; and then by their widows. Retired tradesmen or lesser members of the university lived in smaller houses further north. Into one such house in one of the less fashionable North Oxford roads[1] moved, in the early autumn of 1896, a couple whose previous eight years recalled the wanderings of classical offenders harried by Furies. Mr. and Mrs. Thomas Lawrence had driven from Oxford station to 2, Polstead Road with their four sons: Bob, a portly boy approaching eleven, Ned eight, Will seven and Frank, the youngest, a stocky child of three. They were accompanied by their nurse-of-all-work, Florence Messham.

2, Polstead Road, like its neighbours, was built of red brick interspersed with stone. Semi-detached, it rose through four storeys from a basement with kitchen, larder, coalstore and cells for servants to a dormitory for the four boys under a red-tiled roof decked with finials. Windows painted with flowers, or, in the case of the door to the hall, with rural themes, provided relief. As acquired from its previous owner, Mr. Glasson, the eight-year-old house still looked raw and new. The apple trees in the small walled garden at the back were not yet full grown. A large ground-floor room would require net curtains if passers in the road were not to peer in. But at the back, entirely private, a drawing-room with marble chimney-piece could be made more substantial by the addition of a glass-and-wood conservatory.

On the 8th October 1896, Mrs. Lawrence bought, in her first recorded action at Oxford, 5d. worth of Hovis bread from a Mr. Cooper. Until exhausted in 1900, an account book complete with Mr. Cooper's telephone number listed in meticulous copperplate Mrs. Lawrence's further purchases along with the periodical addition of her bill and Mr. Cooper's acknowledgement, with thanks, of its payment. She did not buy bread again: instead she bought fine flour—usually by the 7lb bag, its cost one shilling and a penny—to bake her own: an economy, no fad.[2]

Just before the undergraduates returned for the Michaelmas term, an annual festival drew revellers into Oxford from the surrounding villages. Stalls and booths filled St. Giles, the space where Woodstock Road (to which Polstead was tributary) debouched into the city. It was a rowdy occasion. Those of the Lawrences' neighbours who had sauntered past the Bible Stall, its banner bravely protesting that *The Blood of Jesus Christ His Son Cleanseth Us from All Sin*,[3] would not have suspected that a grave social misdemeanour underlay the family's small-scale odyssey, which had conferred a different birthplace on each son. But from the start the parents held aloof. Sarah Lawrence left no cards on neighbours. Thomas Lawrence, a tall, bearded man of fifty, courteously repelled advances. Being unemployed, he had no automatic contacts with colleagues or fellow-workers.

Until almost forty, Thomas Lawrence had lived in County Westmeath, Ireland, a squire among other squires whose roots were in Protestant England but whose tenants were Catholic Celts. Implanted, not indigenous, marrying those of their own derivation, the Anglo-Irish lived on estates whose revenues permitted shooting and yachting, holidays in England and Europe, and sometimes a certain interest in the arts or literature; the adventurous had excelled in army and empire. In Ireland, where his forebears had been sheriffs of their county, Mr. 'Lawrence' had served as a Justice of the Peace. In his Irish days he had borne a surname which required no inverted commas. As Thomas Robert Tighe Chapman of South Hill, outside the village of Delvin, he had bestowed on four daughters—Eva Jane Louisa, Rose Isabel, Florence Lina and Mabel Cecile—his Leicestershire ancestry and Irish status. As Protestant settlers, the Chapmans had owed their first land, in County Kerry, to a powerful kinsman, Sir Walter Raleigh, and their land in County Westmeath (where they lived later) to Oliver Cromwell. In the late eighteenth century, for unrecorded services to the state, Benjamin Chapman, a member of the Irish parliament, was created Baronet. He was the grandson of Robert Tighe of Mitchelstown (also in Westmeath), a kinsman to the Earls (originally Barons) of Howth, whose connection with Ireland went back to the first English invasion under Henry II. The Chapman line, for all its prosperity and connections, was conspicuous for childless males, four of the first six baronets dying without issue. As the nephew of the deceased 4th Baronet and the cousin of the childless 5th and 6th Baronets, Thomas Tighe Chapman could expect to inherit the title and more land. He already had advantageous connections of his own. His mother, Louisa Vansittart, was the grand-daughter of the first Lord Auckland. The cousin whom he married in 1873, Edith Sarah Hamilton

Boyd, was the surviving daughter of George Augustus Rochfort Boyd, in 1843 High Sheriff of Westmeath. Boyd inherited from the Rochforts (originally *De rupe forti*) a name ancient in the English settlement and from his mother, the Countess of Belvedere, large estates. Through such connections by blood or marriage the future 7th Baronet was linked to powerful and eccentric kinsmen in John Bull's major island.

But the match between Thomas Chapman and his cousin proved that happiness does not always result from social compatibility and occupied cradles. Mrs. Chapman frowned on pleasure and ministered to helpless villagers with tracts and treacle. For a trifling childhood mistake she is said to have hung a chamberpot round the neck of one of her daughters.[4] By the early 1890s detestation for his wife propelled this otherwise conventional man into an unconventional action. Formal religious beliefs could not subdue, drink to which he had recourse could only inflame, his passionate attachment to the small, active person of a Miss Sarah 'Maden', a nursemaid imported from Scotland for his daughters. Illegitimate daughter of a Norwegian father and an English mother, Sarah had been sent from Sunderland, her place of birth, to be brought up by a relation whose low-church Episcopalian ministry took him to various parts of Scotland, including the Hebrides.* Her forceful personality linked a shrewd intelligence and manifold household skills with religious principles as stern as Mrs. Chapman's; but as the latter preferred good works to domestic management, Sarah soon became virtual mistress of South Hill. She might have continued so had she not simultaneously become the mistress of her employer.

If, for him, the liaison was a break with convention, for her it involved a sin which oppressed her till she died, aged ninety-eight, in 1959. Nor was it only a sin against the divine law. Her offence, if discovered, would outrage the class which occupied the middle ground between her lover's aristocratic state and her own modest origins. That she agreed to be set up

* According to Somerset House records, Sarah Junner had been born in Sunderland on 31 August 1861. Richard Aldington was the first to link Sarah Maden with Sarah Junner, but he did so tentatively: Mrs. Lawrence was then still living and might have brought an action. Some of his caution survived into Phillip Knightley and Colin Simpson's well-researched study, *The Secret Lives of Lawrence of Arabia*: 'Her background is obscure and even her surname Maden is perhaps not that of her parents.' It is now possible to discard this caution. Aldington had not seen the letter which T. E. Lawrence wrote to his father from Tripoli, on 15 August 1909; the suppression of this letter from *The Letters of T. E. Lawrence* (1939) formed a perplexing lacuna for his biographers. In it, Lawrence referred in passing to his mother's forthcoming birthday. Another letter from Lebanon—dated 30 August 1912—also refers in passing to his mother's birthday. This letter was also excluded from the 1938 *Letters*. Will Lawrence, writing from India on 31 August 1914, begins with characteristic warmth: 'Mother dear, It's been your birthday, and every now and then I have wondered what you were doing, and how you were feeling.' These references (available thanks to Bob Lawrence's edition of the *Home Letters*, 1958) make it possible to identify Sarah Maden with the Sarah Junner born in Sunderland on 31 August 1861.

as common-law second wife in a small Dublin house shows how wildly she had fallen in love. While the upper class would condone a mistress and the lower a love-idyll, the respectable class between was pitiless to unions unsolemnized in church. Yet the illicit bond was made solid in December 1885 when Sarah bore Chapman the first of five sons and the only one to be born in Ireland. An island in which even the Catholic majority had a puritan tinge was far too small and far too gossipy for the sins of the conspicuous to pass unnoticed. Yet Chapman wanted to enjoy conjugal, not furtive, rights with Sarah. One account plausibly suggests that she was rash enough to pass herself off as Mrs. Chapman in a Dublin street before someone who knew better.[5] At any rate, some such gaffe made further Irish residence impossible and in 1888 Thomas Chapman and his mistress embarked on eight years of restless movement. South Hill was left to Edith Chapman who lived on there with her four oppressed and unmarried daughters. The five women enjoyed, if that is the word for so wretched an existence, the bulk of the income from the estate and Thomas Chapman's investments.

Unaware of such public events as Queen Victoria's death, Edith Chapman steadfastly refused to divorce her husband,[6] and he was never free to marry the mother of his sons. Instead, their unmarried status was masked by their joint adoption of a new surname.* The choice of Lawrence may have been influenced in part by reverence for Sir John Lawrence, the hero of Lucknow. But since Thomas Lawrence showed a family loyalty in naming his first son Montague Robert (Montague having been the name of the 3rd Baronet), the choice was probably linked with affection for the 4th Earl of Howth, whose family name was St. Lawrence.† Montagu Robert, or 'Bob', was in his third year when the family sailed from Ireland, Sarah Lawrence again pregnant. They landed in north Wales and because her delivery was near, took refuge in Tremadoc, a town created in the nineteenth century. There, in a boarding house near the main square, their second son, Thomas Edward, was born in the early hours of 16 August 1888. After six weeks the family left Wales and sixteen months later, this time in a rented house on the outskirts of Kirkcudbright in Scotland, a third son, William George, or 'Will', was added to the family barracks. A fourth was born a year later in Jersey: Frank Helier Lawrence recalled, in his middle name, his Channel Island birthplace, St. Helier. His parents had moved there from France, lest their latest son be liable to French conscription.

* Thomas Chapman continued to be listed under his old name in successive editions of Burke's *Peerage and Baronetage*. Although he died in April 1919, as late as the 1921 edition he was named as 7th Baronet, having succeeded his cousin, the 6th Baronet, in 1914. The 1924 edition listed the Chapman baronetage as now extinct.

† William Ulick Tristram St. Lawrence, the 4th and last Earl of Howth, the 30th Baron Howth, was to die, unmarried, on 9 March 1909.

By 1895 the Lawrences were living near Beaulieu in Hampshire, within sight of the Solent. As a former yachtsman Thomas Lawrence may have found in aquatic spectacle and small-scale boating an easement for conscience; Sarah Lawrence derived consolation from caring for him and for her children. But neither parent knew inner peace. Having herself kicked away the basis for her narrow ideals, Sarah Lawrence had even allowed Bob and Ned to attend a Jesuit school when they lived in Dinard and Ned was five.

In classical legends, a deity could halt the wanderings of the guilty. In the case of the Lawrences, relief came from an elderly Evangelical churchman, Canon Alfred Millard William Christopher, then preaching at Ryde in the Isle of Wight. For the Canon, whose kind eyes disputed with bigoted mouth the battlefield of a hair-girt face,[7] Ryde had powerful associations. Long ago, on holiday, he had left his only daughter there, a sick child of four, while fulfilling a preaching engagement elsewhere. Caroline Christopher had died in his absence and now lay buried in St. Thomas's Chapel. Thirty years later, in 1886, he had addressed the Ryde Conference of the World Evangelical Alliance.[8] He could now add a third association. Meeting the Lawrence parents in 1895, the Canon, then in his seventies, convinced them that even they were not beyond divine forgiveness.[9] The Anglo-Catholic practice of confession, re-adopted as this was from Rome, was rejected by the Evangelical Movement. How much Thomas and Sarah Lawrence revealed of their secret is therefore uncertain. A Catholic priest, who would have insisted on hearing all, might have advised them to stay together, for the sake of their sons, but to abstain from conjugal relations.[10] This advice was evidently not given by Christopher. After three miscarriages, Mrs. Lawrence was in 1900 to add a fifth son to her family. But confident that as much of their secret as they had confided to Christopher would be safe, they decided to move to Oxford to be near him.

At first sight their decision might have seemed unwise. Oxford was at the centre of movements very opposed to the form of Christianity which had now become their spiritual sheet-anchor. From the pulpit of the University Church, Newman had launched the Tractarian, or Anglo-Catholic, movement. While they had been hearing Canon Christopher at Ryde, the scandalous ordeal of Oscar Wilde had placed the morals of aesthetically-minded undergraduates under public question. Yet hopeful of Satan's defeat, the resolute Canon had for more than thirty-five years propounded the Gospel from St. Aldate's, a church at the centre of the city. His preaching had borne fruit. And though as he aged the deaf old man attracted smaller congregations, at the height of his powers he had induced a thousand young men, more than a third of the undergraduate body, to attend the final meeting of Moody & Sankey's mission to Oxford.

The section of Oxford society to which the Canon continued to act as spiritual leader belonged to the intellectual and social middle. In one of his contributions to a Church Army report, indicating the gulf between the Evangelicals and the poor, he rejoiced that three Oxford cabmen 'whose honest, manly faces beamed with Christian happiness' had attended one prayer meeting: for 'God is able to use these men to bring in other cabmen, a class not very accessible to clergymen.'[11] His curate had had his coat torn at one St. Giles Fair while on the same occasion his assistants' caps were used as footballs by those resistant to the Word. The resistance of the rich was more polite. If Christian, they admired Pusey or Newman. 'No one will dispute that Oxford is on the whole, a thoroughly High Church place,' the Canon conceded. 'Most of the well-to-do people in Oxford are High Church, if they are Church people at all.'[12] Even so, his influence reached far, and he could congratulate St. Aldate's on having sent more curates into the mission field than any Tractarian church. The Rev. J. W. Tims had gone to the Blackfoot Indians of North West Canada, the Rev. J. J. Bambridge to India, while the Rev. Llewellyn Lloyd had taken the Gospel as far as China.

Canon Christopher was to remain the major spiritual and intellectual influence on the Lawrence family until he died, aged ninety-three, on the eve of the First World War. For Mrs. Lawrence his life was a parable. As a young man in his twenties he had been 'converted' while instructing native boys in India. To the Evangelicals, baptism did not suffice for salvation. Every would-be Christian must give himself in conscious acceptance to Jesus. Copies of Holman Hunt's *Light of the World* hung in many Evangelical homes just as the artist's own copy still hangs in St. Paul's Cathedral. It shows Jesus standing at a latchless door. Only if the heart within opens can He enter and sup.*

In the service of the Saviour's laws the Lawrence family was to worship at St. Aldate's until, after Christopher's retirement in 1905, a new parochial district was formed for the Evangelicals of North Oxford. The routine of the St. Aldate's church council gave Mr. Lawrence a shadow of his former role in Ireland; but at home Sarah Lawrence ruled alone. Her personality overpowered the man to whom with puritan scruple she referred as 'Tom' or 'the boys' father', never as 'my husband',† and to enforce the laws of God she used the rod recommended by King Solomon, applying it with particular frequency to her second son.[14] Projecting her own guilt on to her whole sex, she fostered misogynism. 'We could never be bothered with girls in our house,' she told one inquirer.[15]

* T. E. Lawrence studied the picture closely. He later chose the lamp in Christ's hand as model for 'an elaborately pierced Moorish lantern', which he made from copper.[13]

† These new scruples contrasted with the spirit in which the unmarried pair had entered the false information, that they had been married in St. Peter's Church, Dublin, on the birth certificate of their third son, Will.

To the particular sin of boyhood she shared the attitudes of her generation and class. 'If you do not break yourself of it,' wrote 'The Old Fag', in the Answers to Correspondents corner of *Captain: A Magazine for Boys and Old Boys*,[16] 'you will suffer in after years. It produces consumption, heart disease, and other organic complaints. Take plenty of exercise, avoid alcohol, read pure literature, and seek in prayer that help which only God can give.'

Towards the close of his mission in Oxford, Canon Christopher, now an old man of eighty-three, was to convert Mrs. Lawrence's first-born, Bob, at a confirmation class. Bob was later to be a medical missionary and in old age was to provide a generous subvention to Canon Christopher's biographer. The Canon's simple yet effective creed was to induce the third brother, Will, to go to India immediately after graduation so as to educate Hindu youths on Christian lines. The fourth brother, Frank, addressing boys at an Evangelical camp, displayed a precocious talent for the extended metaphor: 'To steer a straight course the Captain has to refer constantly and carefully to his chart. If we would steer a straight course in our lives we must likewise be in constant touch with our chart, Jesus Christ.'*

This book would hardly have been written if Christopher had succeeded with Ned as he succeeded with Bob, Will and Frank. Lawrence (as we shall henceforth refer to Ned) manifested an independence in not being converted which established his difference from the Lawrence sons born before the move to Oxford and his definite ascendancy; Arnold, born in Oxford in 1900, was to echo Lawrence's development. Yet his break with Evangelical Christianity did not come early. As late as April 1910, Lawrence, by then aged twenty-two, helped Bob to mail the Canon's pamphlets to undergraduates.[17] (The Canon's pamphleteering habits embarrassed his own family. On the occasion of a Governor's party in the Isle of Man they took the precaution of emptying his pockets of tracts, only to find that he stuffed a few packets into his elastic-sided boots and was distributing them to the fashionable throng.)[18] And the moral and unspoken assumptions of the Christopher view of life were to mark Lawrence for life, leaving *sequelae* long after he had rejected the philosophy from which they sprang.

Yet the Lawrence family deviated from that aspect of the puritan tradition which emphasized gainful employment. Thomas Lawrence brought from Ireland and did not discard an aristocratic disdain for business. 'The father's self-appointed exile,' as Lawrence himself put it

* This curious metaphor of the Christian soul as transatlantic liner is to be found, developed in some five hundred words, between pages 610–611 of *The Home Letters of T. E. Lawrence and His Brothers*. Frank himself was only twenty when he addressed the boys at the Whitstandwell Free Church Camp in August 1913.

much later,[19] 'reduced his means to a craftsman's income, which the landowning pride of caste forbade him to increase by labour.' The annual income allowed him from his abandoned estate in Ireland hovered between £300 and £400 throughout Lawrence's boyhood. Although this sum in gold sovereigns (then worth five dollars each) approximated to £1,500 today, it was a scant income on which to put five sons through university.* However, instead of taking paid employment, Thomas Lawrence adapted his tastes to the circumstances of a household which never boasted more than two servants and in which his wife did most of the work. In place of snipe-shooting, yachting and riding, he took up the study of medieval architecture, photography and cycling. These interests —antiquarian, energetic and inexpensive—were his legacies to his sons. After his death, his second son was to confide his belief that his mother had diminished his father and that the discordance between their two natures had ensured that their children's personalities, or at least his own, would be split.[20]

The discord was not between equals. Thomas Lawrence (who, again according to his son, never touched a book nor wrote a cheque) allowed his common-law wife to be minister of education and chancellor of the exchequer. In place of the comparative moderation of Broad Church Ireland she introduced a spirit close to that of the Wee Frees she had known in Calvinist Scotland. For these narrow sectaries, an old joke has it, the Lord will erect in Heaven a silo-shaped enclave, so preserving their illusion (without which Heaven would be something else) that they are the only residents. Something of the shut-off, superior atmosphere of the saved might in any case have enclosed the family at 2, Polstead Road. Because the discovery of their secret might at any time demolish their social respectability, this puritanical though unmarried couple deliberately encouraged their sons to find their outlets in the world of the past, which they explored with their father or in books, or the future, for which their studies would prepare them. Mrs. Lawrence encouraged social contacts only with such trusted friends of Canon Christopher as the distinguished Professor of Arabic, David Samuel Margoliouth, and a few friends they had made in the past, either in France or near Beaulieu.

Such domestic seclusion was to facilitate, when the second son became famous, the proliferation of childhood legend. Those interested in twentieth-century instances of Alexander strangling serpents in his cot may find them in the early biographies or the 1938 *T. E. Lawrence By His Friends*, posthumous reminiscences edited by Lawrence's youngest

* Christopher Hollis, born two years after the last Lawrence, has compared his own poverty as an Eton scholar to that of his contemporary George Orwell: 'My father was at the time the vicar of a Leeds slum parish with an income of a little over £400 a year and four children to educate.' *A Study of George Orwell*, Hollis and Carter, London, 1956, p. 5.

brother and literary executor. Those interested in their demolition may turn to Richard Aldington's *Biographical Inquiry*, wherein, for example, the claim that Lawrence read some 50,000 books in the Oxford Union Library is painstakingly demolished. But however sceptically we read of obstacles surmounted at an unusual age, of trees exceptionally lofty climbed without a fall, of a small boy's turning from the battleships at Spithead to peruse Lord Macaulay's *Introduction to the History of England*, an atmosphere persists which the hagiographer cannot lighten nor the iconoclast disperse. It recalls the gloomy Yorkshire parsonage where another impecunious family with Irish links devised a spiritual nutriment from fantasy and a few stock figures. But while the Brontës of Haworth Parsonage were shut in by moors and illness, the Lawrences were enclosed at Polstead Road by a dogmatic religion and a parental secret. If such a family produced a son whose rebellion took more positive forms than Branwell Brontë's, that son would want to escape from the domestic silo. In the family secret he might find, if he were ruthless, his means.

2

At new year the Lawrence parents measured their sons against the door of a downstairs cupboard: at something over six foot, Will was eventually to push the measure highest. Between 1904 and 1905 (when he was in his sixteenth year) Ned grew 2¾ inches. He was then 5 feet 4½ inches tall. In the following year he added less than an inch to attain a height which Arnold, the youngest brother, was to pass at fourteen.

The door, a rare contemporary source for Lawrence's youth, confirms Mrs. Lawrence's accuracy in matters of which she had first-hand knowledge. Her second son's strength and size dominated her earliest recollections of him. 'He was a big, strong, active child; constantly on the move. He would pull himself up over the nursery gate some months before he could walk.'[1] The example was in itself not particularly remarkable but showed her conviction that physically as well as mentally he had been precocious. The strength was to remain, but the stature was not. Ned's rapid growth, in which she recalled him adding as much as three inches a year, suddenly stopped towards the end of his schooldays.[2]

Lawrence himself, recalling his childhood, was to be less objective than the door. From a manhood of physical trials and inner torments he projected back onto his youth the stigmata of dissatisfaction and rebellion. His friends distorted the record in another spirit. Writing after his death, scratching their memories of his home and boyhood, they either strove to perserve a national icon, or sought to prove their intimacy with a schoolboy who had become a hero.

Bob Lawrence, the eldest brother, had no need to prove his closeness to his subject; his modesty made his tribute to Ned's precocity the more convincing. 'He was remarkably quick at learning and I was slow, so we were more companionable than most brothers.'[3] Bob's career confirms this slowness: matriculating at St. John's, Oxford, in 1904, he was not to complete his medical studies at St. Bartholomew's Hospital, London, until 1915. Photographs show a good-natured young man considerably less alert than his brothers. Bob's claim that Ned 'was for many years a constant worshipper at St. Aldate's Church'[4] bespeaks the future missionary: but it does not conflict with Lawrence's later statement that he had discarded conventional religion and did not notice its loss.[5] And Bob recorded that Lawrence began to hold a Sunday School class while still at school. Since Sunday cycling was condemned, this involved a walk into St. Aldate's twice each Sunday, a total of some five miles. If Lawrence had begun to doubt Christopher's gospel before he stopped teaching it, he found compensation in the company of young people with whom he was popular and successful. According to an Oxford friend, Lawrence lost his Sunday School class through reading the boys a story by Oscar Wilde.[6]

By omitting all shadows his mother and brother produced a flattened portrait. 'He was never idle—brass-rubbing, wood-carving, putting old pottery together, etc.' And in summation: 'he was a most loving son and brother, kind and unselfish, always doing kind deeds in a quiet way; everything that was beautiful in nature or art appealed to him.' Bob wrote in middle age: 'We had a very happy childhood, which was never marred by a single quarrel between any of us. . . . We were always busy and the days were never too long.'[7]

A factor—if a secondary one—in the Lawrence move to Polstead Road had been the existence of the City of Oxford High School. Opened as late as 1881, the school occupied a substantial premises in the centre of Oxford. Possessing a playground but no adjacent playing fields, its excellent scholastic record was attested by the university scholarships won by its pupils. From 1888 to 1925 its headmaster was a brilliant mathematician and Anglo-Catholic, Arthur Wilson Cave. Cave was unfortunately to publish no memoir of T. E. Lawrence, but we know that Lawrence played a leading role in collecting the subscriptions for a watch presented to Cave by the boys after twenty-one years as headmaster. The master who did write a memoir, the Rev. Ernest W. Cox, excelled at the sentimental cliché: 'The Lawrence family were all boys—five of them together. And manly boys they were.' This 'very band of brothers—united, conscientious, strong in character, clean alike in limb and in life,' became in his description virtually indistinguishable. Bob: 'conscientious, solicitous, always kind;' Will: 'one beautiful to look upon; . . . possessed of a certain gravity of mind and character'; Frank (the brother who enjoyed team games): 'a dear boy; lovable and greatly loved; one whose happiness and radiant smile remain an enduring and ever helpful memory.' The Rev. Cox contributed the picturesque story that Mrs. Lawrence dressed her boys in identical blue-and-white striped jerseys and then sent them on their bicycles to school: 'in evenly spaced single file, well in on the near side of the road, and always in that same descending order—the eldest in front and the youngest last.'[8]

Yet even exemplary young men, softened by 'a certain gentleness of disposition which made up for any possible lack of a sister's influence,' must sometimes have disobeyed and quarrelled. Hints that Lawrence was pungent early cannot be excluded. An outhouse at the end of the garden contained a coal-heated copper for Mrs. Lawrence's laundry. There were no drains. A soakaway led the steaming water into the middle of the garden. Lawrence—'one of few words, self-possessed, purposeful, inscrutable'[9]— hammered a nail into a pipe to test its contents. Proving to be scalding water, they drenched his father, and Mr. Lawrence was heard to exclaim: 'Bother take the little brat!' Brass-rubbings of knights hung on the walls of the boys' bedroom. A friend confessed how some were obtained. 'In Waterperry Church there were brasses inaccessible behind some pews. Lawrence, already ruthless, made short work of the obstruction, and I still hear the splintering woodwork and his short laugh, almost sinister to my timorous ears.'[10]

Lawrence's own letters, written in the holidays, tell little of home; but they have the advantage of being contemporary as well as first hand. In the summer holidays of 1905 he joined his father on a cycling tour of East Anglia. From the Fleece Hotel, Colchester on 13th August, he reported on his father's cough (neither of the elder Lawrences enjoyed good health) before expatiating on architecture, butterflies and the stuffed birds in Norwich Castle. Affection intruded towards the end: jocularity kept it cool. 'Kindly take heaps of love from me for yourself; and when you've had enough, divide the remainder into three portions, and give them to the three worms you have with you. . . . Don't forget the Canon's birthday next Sunday. [Canon Christopher's birthday was an annual celebration in the Lawrence family.] We have had one post card from Will, 1 from yourself and one letter from you. Loud snores to all. Love to yourself. Ned.'[11]

Next year Lawrence took his bicycle to France, being joined at St. Malo by C. F. C. Beeson, a schoolfriend one year his junior. In an age when boys tended to conceal their first names, Beeson rejoiced in a hirsute nickname: 'Scroggs'. The friends took a carefully planned minimum of luggage. Over each rear wheel a small basket wrapped in oil cloth, the work of their respective mothers, contained a waterproof cape. So equipped they explored the cathedrals and fortifications of northern France with the aid of Viollet-le-Duc's *Dictionnaire Raisonnée*. Lawrence seemed less interested in warfare and military campaigns than in the purpose for which the architects had built and the extent to which history had justified them. Having no camera that year, he bought picture postcards by the dozen. Beeson sketched the salient features of what they saw, though his main interest lay in plants and trees.[12] When he returned to England at the end of August, Lawrence cycled on his own into Normandy, and then along the chain of châteaux by the Loire.

Next July Lawrence Senior accompanied his son on a new tour to northern France and Lawrence was able to accomplish what he called the dream of years, spending a night at Mont St. Michel, previously visited only by daylight. 'It is a perfect evening; the tide is high and comes some 20 feet up the street. In addition the stars are out most beautifully, and the moon is, they say, just about to rise. The phosphorescence in the water interests me specially: I have only seen it once or twice before, and never so well as tonight. The whole sea, when oars are dipped into it, seems to blaze, for several feet around.'[13]

There is much to smile at in the style of these letters. Describing the Château de Gaillard (in a letter of 11th August 1907) he musters tired adjectives by the squadron. 'I have talked so much about this to you that you must know it all by heart, so I had better content myself with saying that its plan is marvellous, the execution wonderful, and the situation perfect. The whole construction bears the unmistakable stamp of genius.'[14] The remaining eight lines of the passage contain 'great,' or 'greater,' four times, 'fair,' 'exquisite,' 'glorious,' 'magnificent,' 'splendid,' once each. Somewhat more irritating, on top of the grumbles at the quality of picture postcards, is the youthful pose of knowing more than the experts: 'Richard I must have been a far greater man than we usually consider him; he must have been a great strategist and a great engineer, as well as a great man-at-arms.' If the relaying of compliments to himself—'by the way the Chaignons and the Lamballe people complimented me on my wonderful French: I have been asked twice since what part of France I came from'—anticipates later claims, it also creates the unenviable impression of a son who has to strive for his mother's approval. She did not have this effect on the other boys. Frank could write under similar circumstances: 'My French is still ludicrous, & I cannot yet understand what they say, unless they speak very slowly.'[15]

In general, Lawrence's schoolboy letters imply that conversation at 2, Polstead Road revolved round castles and cathedrals, not the normal topics of unsyntactical domestic talk. But despite the straining and the detail, there is still affection. The letters end with the brusque mention of love. Yet together with a batch from Wales when he visited Welsh castles in the spring of 1907 they show little of his developing attitude to life. He describes with unaustere relish a ' "dejeuner" at the Grand Hôtel de Europe in Dinan. Menu was Sardines, Cold Meat, Eggs, Hash, Fowl, Salad, Desert: what will the Dîner be? I had some of everything!'[16] But the letters say nothing of illness and his retarded growth.

In marked contradiction to later reports that Lawrence hated being touched, a school friend has described his fondness for wrestling. 'How often a group of us, absorbed in some discussion of cricket or football, would gradually become conscious of a silent addition to our number, contemplating us with that provocative smile of his, till one of us would seize him and close in friendly wrestling, to feel even then the strength of those iron wrists. One such occasion resulted for him in the accident of a broken leg.'[17] Lawrence's mother attributed his broken leg to a nobler cause. 'When out in the playground one day at 11 o'clock, he saw a small boy being bullied by a bigger one; he went to the rescue. They had a struggle and fell and one of the bones in Ned's leg got broken near the ankle; he was wearing boots that day which helped to support it. He walked into the school, supporting himself by the wall and did his mathematics till 1 o'clock.' His brothers wheeled him back to Polstead Road, and the family doctor, deducing from their description that the leg was broken, brought a splint and set it. The accident, according to his mother, had three results. He lost a term at school. He passed his convalescence in extensive reading relieved by poker work. And most important, 'he never grew much after that—he had grown very fast before (three inches in a year), so evidently the bones were not strong.'[18]

The books he read in bed incited him to change the direction of his studies. This was the first foreshadowing of a clash with his mother's will. Because her father, a shipwright journeyman, had been some sort of engineer, or because science seemed the force likely to mould the new age, the young Lawrence had hitherto concentrated on mathematics, his headmaster's subject. But it was a false start. Lawrence was working against his talents. One of his school friends helped him do his algebra, in return for Lawrence's help with English composition.[19] The obvious change would have been to classics, leading in due time to the prestigious Oxford course of *Litterae Humaniores*. But Lawrence had left the break too late. His claim that Greek accents did not matter would convince no Oxford examiner and to go to the university he needed a scholarship. He therefore switched to History, a subject in which such hobbies as mapping castles, mending broken pottery and taking brass rubbings could be helpful. In abandoning the aseptic symbols of algebra and calculus for studies interwoven with violence and sin, he was entering a world in which Mrs. Lawrence could not pursue him. Despite the literary letters he wrote home, his mother hated writing, he was later to tell a friendly schoolmarm,[20] and found it hard to finish a sentence. 'She reads nothing now, though once she enjoyed it immensely. A Sense gets atrophied by disuse and misuse.'

The change of emphasis (Oxford High School had no history side as such) did not prevent Lawrence's doing well in the Senior Local Examination of the summer of 1906. He was then eighteen. In her recollections of his results his mother erred on the side of modesty. She remembered him coming first, out of all the many thousands, in English Language and Literature. 'He passed in nineteen papers, getting distinction in Scripture

(3rd place) and was placed 13th in the First Class. As far as I can remember there were only 120 got First that year, out of some 10,000.' The Oxford Local Examination Divisions Lists (put out by the Oxford bookseller, Parker and Son, and dated August 1906) showed T. E. Lawrence tying with R. B. Barker and S. C. Morgan for 9th place out of the 81 Candidates given First Class Honours; he tied with two others for first place in English and Literature and took third place in Religious Knowledge.

Lawrence was cycling with 'Scroggs' when his mother's letter brought the news to France. 'The result is on the whole not as good as I had hoped.' he wrote home, 'although I am quite satisfied with the Eng. I wonder whether there is any profession in which a knowledge of one's own tongue is of the slightest use . . . In the Divinity I had hoped for more. Polit. Econ. is not surprising; I expect we both made asses of ourselves.'*[21]

Bob Lawrence was at St. John's, the college past whose façade Lawrence had daily cycled to school; but despite energetic coaching from L. C. Jane, a historian, Lawrence failed to win a scholarship there, though in due course his brother Will was to do so. He was luckier in his second choice, Jesus College in the Turl, the Oxford college which had been founded by a Welsh Elizabethan and over the centuries had maintained particular links with Wales. In 1907 its Principal was Sir John Rhys, a Cardiganshire schoolmaster whose energy of mind had won him the first Oxford chair of Celtic Studies. Jesus had earlier converted moneys funding some otiose scholarships into a series of Meyricke Exhibitions to be awarded to those of Welsh parentage or birth. (Without financial assistance few Welshmen of those days could have afforded Oxford.) The accident that Lawrence had been born in Wales now proved a blessing and in February 1907, Jesus College awarded T. E. Lawrence an Exhibition in history worth £50 a year.†

* C. F. C. Beeson was to win an Exhibition to St. John's and later become Director of the Imperial Forestry Bureau.

† The migrations of the Lawrence parents helped two of their sons. Frank Helier Lawrence, through the accident of having been born in Jersey, was later to benefit from a King Charles Exhibition at Jesus. This was part of a royal bequest intended to furnish the Channel Islands with non-dissenting clergy.

3

FOR LAWRENCE the transition from schoolboy to undergraduate was less abrupt than for those who came up to Oxford from other parts of the British Isles. He already knew from Oxford High School many of the young men he would meet in the university. Of the fourteen Sixth Form boys whom Lawrence photographed, including himself in the 1907 group, twelve went on to Oxford[1] and twenty-six of his generation at school matriculated at Jesus.[2] And because of his family's circumstances, an arrangement was made whereby Lawrence, unlike most undergraduates, would spend only one term—that of summer 1908—in college.[3] For the last term of 1907 and the first term of 1908 he continued to share quarters with his brothers, under their mother's watchful eye.

Yet because the university represented the culmination of eleven years study in the same city, it was to be the more decisive an influence on his intellectual life. The words *Oxford* or *Oxonian* intrude with remarkable regularity into the impressions of those who knew him. T. W. Chaundy, the mathematician who had helped him with his algebra at school, looked back on Lawrence as 'the perfect Oxonian.'[4] By this Chaundy probably meant a certain casualness in the approach to learning, a readiness to challenge accepted opinions, and, naturally, the traditional predilection for lost causes. The references to Oxford were not always complimentary. One friend, admittedly half-Irish, referred to 'the shut-up Oxford face,' which argues that to some, Oxford marred as well as made.[5] Another, impeccably English, observer found 'something clerical, celibate, typically Oxford and pedantic about him,' which balanced the perky schoolboy, an additional constant in a complex nature.[6]

To those outside its walls, Oxford could loom as a mysterious, united fortress, hard to enter. Those who had matriculated, as Lawrence did on 12 October 1907, found the university divided by the traditions and attitudes of its colleges and sets.

Jesus was small and unfashionable. A joke of the time had a visitor coming into the second quadrangle and shouting 'Jones!', only to have every window thrown open. The membership was plebeian rather than aristocratic. The fathers of Lawrence's fellow-matriculants came from a wide professional spectrum: schoolmasters and clergy were offset by a locomotive fitter, a retired spinner, a collier and a stockbroker. The register described Lawrence's father as of 'no occupation. Alive.' Nor was Jesus luxurious. Each undergraduate who lived in had a sitting-room and bedroom; but there were no baths. Inspired by renovations at Christ Church (a college at the other social extreme) a group of Jesus undergraduates reportedly requested Sir John Rhys to install a bath-house. Rhys was shocked that good Welshmen should want to imitate the sybarites of Christ Church. 'And besides, you are only up for eight weeks a term.' In what may be an apocryphal addition, the bursar pushed Rhys towards modernity by congratulating him on his trenchant answer and then insinuating that the bath-house might be installed in the Principal's lodgings. 'But there's no hurry about it,' Rhys is supposed to have replied: 'we'll soon be having the sea-bathing at Aberystwyth.' The tone of Jesus men was earnest, with the Celtic ardour of a Rhys often just beneath the surface.

Lawrence took as little part in college activities as he could manage. He had to attend chapel once a day; he was seen at times in hall, where a portrait of Queen Elizabeth confronted a gallery rebuilt in Jacobean style after a fire; he did his reading in the Bodleian. He took no part in college athletics, later explaining this abstention as due to a detestation for all forms of competition.[7] 'I have known him to lie in wait,' wrote a schoolfriend who had gone on to Jesus, 'day after day, at the college porch while some of us came out, changed for the river or the football field, and then to follow us through the streets, solemnly walking a few paces in the rear, and afterwards to explain to us our merits or deficiencies judged by the Greek standard of physical excellence.'[8]

The range and intensity of his antiquarian interests impressed undergraduates who knew of his presence, initially those who had been with him at school. These interests developed from his hobbies as a townee schoolboy. His primary enthusiasms, for medieval castles, monumental brasses and fourteenth-century pots, involved secondary pursuits. Heraldry helped him to understand, photography to record and cycling to reach, the relics of the Middle Ages. What he described as 'my faculty of making and repairing things'[9] was a valuable aid. Because medieval England had spoken French as much as English, the transition from Chaucer to medieval *chansons de geste* was a natural one.

Lawrence's least sympathetic biographer, Richard Aldington, complained, with some justice, that the accounts of those who knew him at this time, gave an unsatisfactory picture of the youthful Lawrence. 'It is really more a portrait of his interests than him, and the evidence is weakened by the fact that none of it is contemporary while the accounts were mainly written in an atmosphere of posthumous hero-worship heightened by the sense of a loss at his recent death.' Those who recorded his brass-rubbing and castle-measurement were not to blame. Lawrence was himself cat-cautious where it came to self-revelation. It would take years before he would throw even indirect light on his strongest feelings and, having thrown it, would let embarrassment provoke him to further ambiguity and concealment. The strenuous enthusiasms of his youth disguised, in part suppressed, unconventional urges; most of them withered in his later life, the means to them, photography and cycling, outlasting the interests themselves. The contemporary who put him down as a typical Oxonian also recorded that his scholarship-hunting friends felt that Lawrence, while indisputably an intellectual, lacked their narrow devotion to academic interests.[10] Ernest Barker, whose lectures he had attended, felt much the same. He was not interested in historic fact for its own sake, Barker believed. 'He took the Oxford History School because it came in his way, and because it was a hurdle to be jumped on the road that led to action.'[11] He could throw his unrivalled energy into a line of study which constituted for him a phase, an experience, not a lasting concern and Barker included archaeology among such transient studies.

Some indication of interests more powerful and less approved than heraldry is given by the friends Lawrence selected, not those he inherited from Oxford High School. While still a sixteen-year-old schoolboy Lawrence had got to know Leonard M. Green, an undergraduate at St. John's. 'Schoolboys', Green recorded, 'were forbidden to visit undergraduates in their rooms in college and we took a fearful pleasure in disregarding this rule.'[12] The element of the forbidden would always have attracted Lawrence, but some sense of affinity must have assured him that the twenty-year-old Green was his kind of man. Green was an aspirant writer whose style and subject matter Lawrence admired then and later and with Green he first shared a daydream that was to persist under various forms and involve other friends. Green recalled it many years later: 'We decided that we would buy a windmill on a headland that was washed by sea. We would set up a printing press in the lowest storey and live over our shop. We would print only rather "precious" books, an essay or two by Walter Pater, Matthew Arnold's *Scholar-Gipsy*, a trifle of my own of which Lawrence thought highly, worthy things written by our friends. They would not be bound except to suit the temperament of the possible purchaser, and then only in vellum stained with Tyrian dye.'[13]

At this time Lawrence obviously foresaw his future as lying with writers. But Green's account is revealing for the type of man he envisaged as his future partner. While Lawrence was to achieve a fame which would have imposed discretion on the frankest, Green's quieter exploits left him freer for self-expression. First as secretary to an organization striving to improve the conditions of those in the milling trade, then as Chairman of the Save the Children Fund, Green gave his public life to good works. As a writer, published before Lawrence, he was a prominent member of an obscure movement with strong roots in the Oxford of the 1890s which its historian, Timothy d'Arch Smith, has characterized as 'Uranian'. The movement was fostered by Charles Philip Castle Kains Jackson, from 1888 to 1894 the editor of *The Artist and Journal of Home Culture.* Some forty minor poets belonging to it sang for as many years what Lord Alfred Douglas, the most notorious of their roll, accounted 'the love that dare not speak its name.' This love, usually of a middle-aged man for a boy of an inferior social class, inspired prose writers too, the most notable being the Baron Corvo whose employment as amanuensis by E. G. Hardy, a blind Jesus don, had made him a familiar figure to Lawrence.[14] Green (appointed his executor by Kains Jackson) published two books of short stories with an Oxford publisher, *Dream Comrades*, 1916, and *The Youthful Lover*, 1919. These were the prose equivalents of John Gambril Nicholson's *A Garland of Ladslove* (1911). Although the Oxford Uranians sometimes concealed the gender of their beloved, they were less of a persecuted underground than elsewhere. Exeter College, across the Turl from Jesus, produced no fewer than three Uranian poets: John Francis Bloxam, Samuel Elsworth Cottam and Edwin Emmanuel Bradford. Between 1908 and 1930 Bradford was to publish ten volumes of verse with the respected house of Kegan Paul; his admirers included *The Times* poetry reviewer.[15] Such titles as 'Passing the Love of Women' (in his first volume) and 'Boyhood' proclaimed his allegiance.*

Through his friendship with Green, Lawrence thus found himself on the Uranian fringe. Two poems by poets listed as Uranian by Timothy d'Arch Smith remained lifelong favourites: 'Heraclitus' by William Johnson (the Eton master who changed his name to Cory after his sudden dismissal) and 'Night and Death', a sonnet by Joseph Blanco White, who, as editor of *The Studio*, publicized photographs of nude Sicilian boys.[17]

* The first two stanzas of Bradford's poem 'The Call' show him in proselytising vein:

Eros is up and away, away!
Eros is up and away!
The son of Urania born of the sea,
The lover of lads and liberty.
Strong, self-controlled, erect and free,
He is marching along to-day!

He is calling aloud to the men, the men!
He is calling aloud to the men—
'Turn away from the wench, with her powder and paint,
And follow the Boy, who is fair as a saint:'
And the heart of the lover, long fevered and faint,
Beats bravely and boldly again.[16]

The painter of the movement, Henry Scott Tuke, remained one of Lawrence's three favourite painters long after he left Oxford.[18]

There is every reason to assume that the bond between Green and Lawrence was platonic. Particularly in Oxford the Uranians had close affinities with the Anglo-Catholic movement; Bloxam, Cottam and Bradford were all ordained priests of the Church of England. And though at the opposite extreme from the muscular Christianity of 2, Polstead Road, Anglo-Catholicism imposed its own restraints on the expression of physical desire.*

Leonard Green's reference to Matthew Arnold's best known elegiac poem is an important clue towards understanding the first of many mysterious *cruces* in Lawrence's private life.

The 'Scholar-Gipsy's' form derived from Greek pastoral; its mood was described by Arnold himself as 'a pleasing melancholy'. Both form and mood appealed to Lawrence. His antiquarian interests had made him nostalgic for the past and derisive of the present. Arnold's depiction of his contemporaries

> Who fluctuate idly without term or scope,
> Of whom each strives, nor knows for what he strives
> And each half lives a hundred different lives . . .

echoed what Lawrence felt. He will certainly have checked the seventeenth-century account† on which Arnold based

> The story of the Oxford scholar poor,
> Of pregnant parts and quick inventive brain,
> Who tired of knocking at preferment's door,
> One summer-morn forsook
> His friends, and went to learn the gipsy-lore,
> And roamed the world with that wild brotherhood,
> And came, as most men deem'd, to little good,
> But came to Oxford and his friends no more.

The story of a young Oxonian, forced by poverty to forsake professional advance for a life among gipsies, and gaining access to their hearts and

* Worldly prudence was also a cautioning factor. Of the titled Uranians, Lord Henry Somerset had been driven into Italian exile by a scandal involving a male brothel in Cleveland Street; Reginald Baliol Brett, Viscount Esher, had had to publish his *Foam* anonymously; Lord Alfred Douglas was later to prevaricate about the significance of the *Poems* which he had published in Paris the year after the Wilde scandal.

† Joseph Glanvil's *The Vanity of Dogmatizing* (published in 1661) told of 'a lad in the University of Oxford, who was by his poverty forced to leave his studies there; and at last to join himself to a company of vagabond gipsies. Among these extravagant people, by the insinuating subtility of his carriage, he quickly got so much of their love and esteem as that they discovered to him their mystery.'

their secrets, thanks to a skill at dissembling his nature, appealed to something more permanent in Lawrence than love of castles and medieval song. It was soon to inspire a break with his hitherto settled life of outward conformity; in his complex later career it was to play much the same role as a leitmotiv in a Wagnerian opera.

4

THE CRISIS of Lawrence's youth—involving his struggle to break his mother's shackles—took place in late 1908. That summer he had spent his twentieth birthday, 16 August, alone in France, at Chalus in Haute-Vienne: 'the place where Richard I got the wound that caused his death.'[1]* For Lawrence and the area of the world with which he was to be involved 1908 was to prove as fateful as Chalus for Richard. While a major revolution convulsed the Ottoman empire, Lawrence was successfully to challenge parental authority. By Christmas he had achieved a degree of physical separation and, like Stephen Daedalus in *Ulysses*, had taken possession of a substitute father who was to give his life its new direction.

He had had a foretaste of freedom during the summer, or Trinity, term. Moving into Jesus College he was allotted rooms on the first floor of a staircase which overlooked the bustle of Oxford market. His later claim that he had spent most of his three years at Jesus 'reading Provençal poetry, and Mediaeval French chansons de geste'[3] was an exaggeration. Like other colleges, Jesus had a regular tutorial system. There were routine intermediate examinations. But, during his first year at least, Lawrence flaunted what seemed to more earnest undergraduates rather recherché interests. His pursuit of topics only indirectly related to his study of history was more than an extension of his schoolboy preoccupations with pots and brass-rubbings. In both cases Lawrence saw that a path followed by few may lead to greater rewards than a highway pounded by thousands.

Lawrence's interest in pottery had earlier brought him to the notice of those who could give his career a more sudden acceleration than was in prospect for ordinary sloggers at the university curriculum.

In the years immediately following 1905 Oxford underwent a manifold reconstruction, which depended on the pulling down of ancient buildings

* The letter is dated 16 August; its editor, Dr. M. R. Lawrence, his oldest brother, has put in brackets (His twentieth birthday), a date confirmed by his mother.[2] On his matriculation entry he had given 15 August, Napoleon's birthday. The same date survives on the copy of the Kennington bust in Jesus Chapel.

and their replacement by new ones. At the same time the Ashmolean Museum's reports listed annual additions to its collection. The Report for 1906 (which also announced that Mr. C. L. Woolley of New College had been engaged as Junior Assistant Keeper since the beginning of the year) included the following entry: 'During the past year, the considerable disturbance of the ground for the foundations of new buildings in the city, Hertford College, Jesus College, St. John's College (for the new Forestry Laboratory) in High Street (for the new Masonic Hall), and in Cornmarket on the sites of the Civet Cat and Leopold Arms, have produced many remains of pottery and glass of the sixteenth and seventeenth centuries. Owing to the generosity of Mr. E. Lawrence [sic] and Mr. C. E. F. Beeson, who have by incessant watchfulness secured everything of antiquarian value which has been found, the most interesting finds have been added to the local antiquities in the Museum.' Thus, at the age of eighteen, Lawrence had drawn attention to himself in Museum circles as a donor. The report for 1907 recorded (along with the information that Mr. C. Leonard Woolley had resigned at Midsummer) that Mr. E. Lawrence had presented five Nuremberg and three English tradesmen's tokens found in excavations in Oxford. In 1908, now named in full as 'Mr. T. E. Lawrence (Jesus Coll.)', he was to present 'two fine specimens of medieval glazed jugs obtained from excavations on the site of the Civet Cat, in the Cornmarket, and at Pembroke College; also several bottle stamps from the site of the new Forestry Laboratory.'[4]

This persistent support must have been welcome in a Museum going through a financial crisis under a Keeper, Dr. Arthur Evans, who for some time had been fretting to get back to the excavations which he and David Hogarth had initiated at Knossos. Lawrence was no mere donor of objects which the Museum might otherwise have had to purchase.* He had established friendly relations with Leonard Woolley in 1905, and when Will Lawrence wanted to excavate a site in England Ned had written from France, 'Don't dig if Roman. I will consult Woolley on return.' In the careers of his Museum friends abroad he glimpsed tantalizing vistas. Woolley had gone to Sudanese Nubia, assisting Randall MacIver of the University of Pennsylvania Expedition on a site across the Nile from Wadi Halfa. Hogarth, who had described his Anatolian travels in *A Wandering Scholar in the Levant*, was constantly returning to the east, as was the Keeper, Dr. Evans. In 1908 E. T. Leeds, the newly appointed Assistant Keeper, on whom most of the work devolved, enlisted Lawrence's friendship and support. The young man proved more than obliging. He helped produce a Summary Guide to the Museum

* The Museum's annual report for 1905—the year before Lawrence's first gift—recorded the *purchase* of 'three pieces of sixteenth century English pottery, from excavations in Cornmarket Street.'

and volunteered his services (in the words of the next Report) in helping Leeds organize and re-label the somewhat heterogeneous collections of medieval antiquities. In later life Leeds remembered as one of Lawrence's chief characteristics a facility for silent appearance: 'no hammering on the door, no sudden appearance startling out of concentration, but a silent, unassertive presence slipping into one's consciousness, to ask a question, to bring in some new-gathered relic of Oxford's past, or to further towards fulfilment some self-appointed task.'[5]

Leeds will certainly have mentioned Lawrence to Dr. Evans, if the busy Keeper had failed to notice him. For Evans, too, 1908 was a year of crisis. That summer he was to publish (27 May, *The Times*) his remarkable pre-classical discoveries on Crete, an Ottoman island then clamouring for union with Greece. Two generous legacies enabled him to resign from the Ashmolean and attend in affluence to the further excavation of the Palace (as he took it to be) of Minos.[6] For Lawrence, David Hogarth's election to succeed Dr. Evans 'both as Keeper of the Antiquarium and of the Ashmolean Museum as defined by the new Statute' was to prove important. The new statute unified the Museum and the University Picture Galleries and gave Hogarth, as Keeper, an enhanced status and income.

Hogarth had spent most of the 1890s in the eastern Mediterranean. Elected a Research Fellow of Magdalen in 1893, he held for some years the post of Director of the British School in Athens; in 1899 he had added to it the Directorship of the Cretan Exploration Fund. When not excavating at Ephesus or in Crete he travelled in what was then known as the Levant, keeping one eye open for transportable 'antikas', the other on signs of change in the Ottoman Empire. For Hogarth 1908 promised to be the year of decision he had long been awaiting. Because of a general British interest in the moribund empire and a particular interest in its railway system, a number of British archaeologists applied that year for permission to dig in Asiatic Turkey. Professor Garstang of Liverpool obtained permission to excavate at Sakje-Seuz in the Adana vilayet; W. M. Ramsay sought the intervention of Sir Gerard Lowther, newly appointed ambassador in Constantinople, for his daughter to dig at Dorla some forty miles south-east of Konia (which the railway had already reached). But Hogarth was to make the most important request.

On 22 May the Sultan, Abdul Hamid, had ordered the addition of a further 840 kilometres to his existing rail network. His German engineers would soon have to tackle the river Euphrates, the widest water barrier they had so far encountered. It was lucky that a generation earlier the British Museum had obtained part ownership of a great mound on the west bank of the river. Students of the newly recognized Hittite civilization were now convinced that it marked the ancient city of Carchemish. Since the mound lay near possible crossing points for the advancing railway, it and the nearby village of Jerablus had become strategically as well as archaeologically important. The British Museum made moves to reactivate excavations it had abandoned for lack of funds, and as a first step Hogarth was requested to inspect the site in person. On 23rd January 1908, after lecturing for part of the winter in America, he outlined itineraries and suggested likely expenses to Sir Edward Maunde Thompson, then Director of the British Museum. After the Museum* had selected a route going by way of Beirut and Aleppo, the Foreign Office asked Sir Gerard Lowther to obtain permission from the authorities in Constantinople for Hogarth to visit Jerablus. In his travel book, Hogarth had described earlier and fairly extensive visits to Asiatic Turkey. But his horseback itinerary (of which he gave a map) had lain somewhat to the north of the territory through which the railway would push on its way east into Mesopotamia. It was urgent—since Intelligence reports suggested that Ottoman policy might undergo violent shifts—to establish contact with the area. Hogarth got to Jerablus and the Mound just before the Young Turk revolution in Salonika spread to Constantinople and halted his scholarly endeavours.

The Hogarth who knew the Levant knew how any plans to excavate would depend on persons: on his relations with Ottoman officials, on his own assistants. 'The only form of government understood in the Ottoman East,' he had written,[7] 'is immediate personal government.' A change at the top, a revolt, a war, would delay or cancel the best laid plans and make it needful to lay new ones. While Dr. Evans was too busy with his own plans to bother with Lawrence, Hogarth noted in the young man aptitudes that might well be useful. Leeds, Hogarth's Assistant-Keeper, had been struck by Lawrence's mobility as much as by his skill with pots and his silent approach. 'That bicycle—I can see it now;' he recalled thirty years later; 'no petrol-driven fury, it was nevertheless surely sped with wings. Vanishing swiftly and silently down the road, it seemed, almost before one had turned one's back, to come to rest again: Bristol, Hanley, York, Lincoln, Northampton, with an eighty-mile detour thrown in to collect a fragment of information jokingly suggested by a friend.'[8] With a lifelong inclination to gild the lily Lawrence was to claim that the machine had been specially designed for him by Mr. William Morris, later Lord Nuffield.† Richard Aldington, the iconoclast, established that Morris had ceased making cycles by the time concerned. But to Leeds the striking

* In the person of E. A. Wallis Budge, head of the department of Egyptian and Assyrian Antiquities.

† Though dignified by inclusion in Professor A. H. Lawrence's introduction to *Crusader Castles*, (The Golden Cockerel Press, 1936) the legend remains just that; Professor Lawrence had been a boy of but six or seven when the machine was bought.

thing was not the make of machine, but the arduous use to which it was put. On it Lawrence had first tasted freedom from the family silo.

The eight weeks of summer which he spent in college had increased his appetite. In principle his new liberties had their limits; undergraduates were forbidden to drink in public houses, patrolled as these were by a corps of proctors known as 'bulldogs': undergraduates had to be inside the gates by midnight. But such restrictions meant little to Lawrence. He did not drink and could easily master the climbs which traditionally ensured a late return across roofs and walls. But disturbing questions were posed by a new friendship.

On his staircase, immediately over the college kitchens, were the rooms of Vyvyan Warren Richards, an undergraduate who had come up in 1905. His father was a Welsh inventor, his mother an American 'whose childhood had been spent in a home in Utah often barricaded either against Indians or the Mormons.'[9] A self-professed philistine whose classical education had left him scornful of archaeology, architecture and art, Richards was now an established member of the college. He had, he later wrote, heard gossip of 'a queer stranger among us, who walked solitary at all hours of the night in the still quadrangles of the college.'[10] The queer freshman, he ascertained, was the same Thomas Edward Lawrence whose rooms were below his own. Richards, as was common form among undergraduates, decided to call. The oak, that protective outer door which aids Oxbridge study, was unsported, but Lawrence was neither at work nor at home. Richards found in 'a few strange books—of early French poetry chiefly' the only clues to the tenant's personality. Impressed, he left a note inviting Lawrence to return his call. Lawrence did so that night, some hours after dinner, enchanting his host.[11] As the young visitor argued, with undergraduate passion, that the arrival of gunpowder and printing in 1500 had destroyed the real world, Richards was indelibly impressed by Lawrence's long flaxen hair and impish grin. In a city whose traditions wound back to the Middle Ages, where the benefactions of the dead ornamented every turn, Lawrence's nostalgia for the past was not unusual. But the debater, not the debate, captivated Richards. Whether on that occasion or soon after (Lawrence left no record) Richards passionately declared his love. Lawrence's response impressed him by its sheer stolidity: he gave no impression of understanding Richards' emotions. Perhaps to salve his *amour-propre*, Richards formulated a judgement which Lawrence himself was to borrow as a mask: 'He had neither flesh nor carnality of any kind; he just did not understand. He received my affection, my sacrifice, in fact, eventually my total subservience, as though it was his due. He never gave the slightest sign that he understood my motives or fathomed my desire . . . I realize now that he was sexless—at least that he was unaware of sex.'[12]

But Lawrence's stolidity under assault was jaw-deep. His flaxen, Norwegian hair, his eyes blue as his mother's, concealed a mind aware of gulfs deeper than these amorous shallows. And Richards, a future bachelor schoolmaster, was naive if he thought that Lawrence misunderstood his motives. Lawrence had read the poets of the Greek Anthology (widely translated by the Uranians); he knew the sources of Leonard Green's inspiration, he was an early reader of 'Baron Corvo', or Rolfe. But even if the notion of illicit sexual contact had not been condemned by Polstead Road, even if Richards had appealed to Lawrence physically, prudential considerations would have held him in check. He neither accepted nor rebuffed Richards, but instead utilized his devotion. He at once recruited the fervent Welshman into his daydream. At this time a stable building (Lawrence described it as a fourteenth-century hall) was being pulled down at the west end of Jesus to make room for college laboratories, a purpose Lawrence disdained. With the help of Richards he managed to salvage, then store, some of the ancient timbers. Together, one day, they would use the wood for a hall of their own, an ebony tower from which they would issue limited editions of their favourite authors. Two shut-beds, labelled respectively *Meum* and *Tuum*, would soothe separate dreams.

Richards recorded what he remembered as Lawrence's favourite authors. These had as a common quality nostalgia for a better or more colourful past. Closest to his imagination, the greatest influence on his style, was the William Morris whose poetry had striven to exclude words of latinate origin; but Morris had also worked as printer, joiner and painter. Like Morris, Lawrence exalted the craftsman at the expense of the artisan, his modern equivalent. He was to speak when describing his father's means of a craftsman's income, not an artisan's wage.[13] One day Richards cycled with Lawrence to Chipping Campden where a disciple of Morris lived in a converted fourteenth-century chapel. 'There was a copy of the great Morris and Burne-Jones *Chaucer* there, prince of all modern printings, and also most of the other Kelmscott books. So we went on our bicycles one snowy week-end and were gladly taken in to see the Morris treasures. It was a perfect medieval home for them, and there was one which specially delighted us—the actual hand-press that Morris himself had used was housed in one part of this old chapel hall and again in action.'[14]

As well as of a press, Lawrence dreamed of an ideal library which would contain 'some hundred and fifty books, each a paragon of print and binding.' The stress on form could override content. 'I certainly prefer poetry:' he was characteristically to write, 'though prose, in type, makes a neater, blacker page.'[15] Later in life, out of this devotion to the neat black page, he was to scissor words and sentences from his prose.

Some of his subject-matter would have surprised his family. Morris, Malory, the Christina Rossetti who wrote 'Martyrs' Song' were writers he could discuss at home without embarrassment. But among Lawrence's favourite books Richards remembered 'Rolfe's *Don Tarquinio* (for its "fleshiness")'[16], a fleshiness associated with the charms of boys, not maidens. Since Rolfe was not to achieve a large public until long after his Venetian death in 1913, thanks first to a brilliant biography by A. J. Symons, then much later to the dramatization of his novel, *Hadrian VII*, the inclusion of Rolfe's account of adolescents at the Borgia court shows that Lawrence could form his own tastes without regard to fashion.

Perhaps to discourage Richards, or turn his thoughts in a safer direction than himself, Lawrence made a rare move involving females.* Undergraduates were at this time considered so perilous to female students (as it is proper to call them, since they had yet to win the right to graduate) that girls wishing to put on a play did so after the men had left on vacation. That important summer of 1908 Lawrence persuaded Richards to stay in Oxford for an extra day to watch an all-female cast perform Lyly's *Alexander and Campaspe*.

If Lyly staged by girls was to calm his friend, Lawrence used his bicycle, already the key to freedom, to subdue his own flesh.

For the long vacation of 1908—his first as an undergraduate—he planned his most ambitious French expedition. It was to last the best part of two months; except for the final few days, when he would be joined by Will, he would ride alone. He would land at Le Havre, avoid Paris by cycling to the east and then descend the Rhône Valley to the Mediterranean; his return by way of the foothills of the Pyrenees would complete a great loop round the Massif Central up to the Loire and then the Channel. The series of letters to his mother which, in some eleven thousand words, recounted his impressions and finds, remained typically impersonal.[18] But, for the first time, he referred to the east in two emotional outbursts which had no precedent. Their joint occurrence that particular summer gives them significance.

His first reference to the east was prompted by hearing that Frank Lawrence, then fifteen and a pupil at Oxford High School, was writing an essay on *Westward Ho!*, Kingsley's patriotic tale of naval adventure and Jesuit intrigue. Lawrence added in parentheses: ' "Eastward Ho!" is

* In her eighties, Janet Laurie (later married to Guthrie Hallsmith) claimed that she, who had first known the Lawrences when they were her neighbours near Beaulieu, woke the flame of love in Lawrence's breast, but that she rejected him in favour of Will. Her account[17] has an uncanny resemblance to what was long the standard story of Algernon Charles Swinburne's rejection by 'Boo'. Unsubstantiated by any contemporary evidence from the letters of either brother, the story seems to this author to exemplify the unreliability of memory.

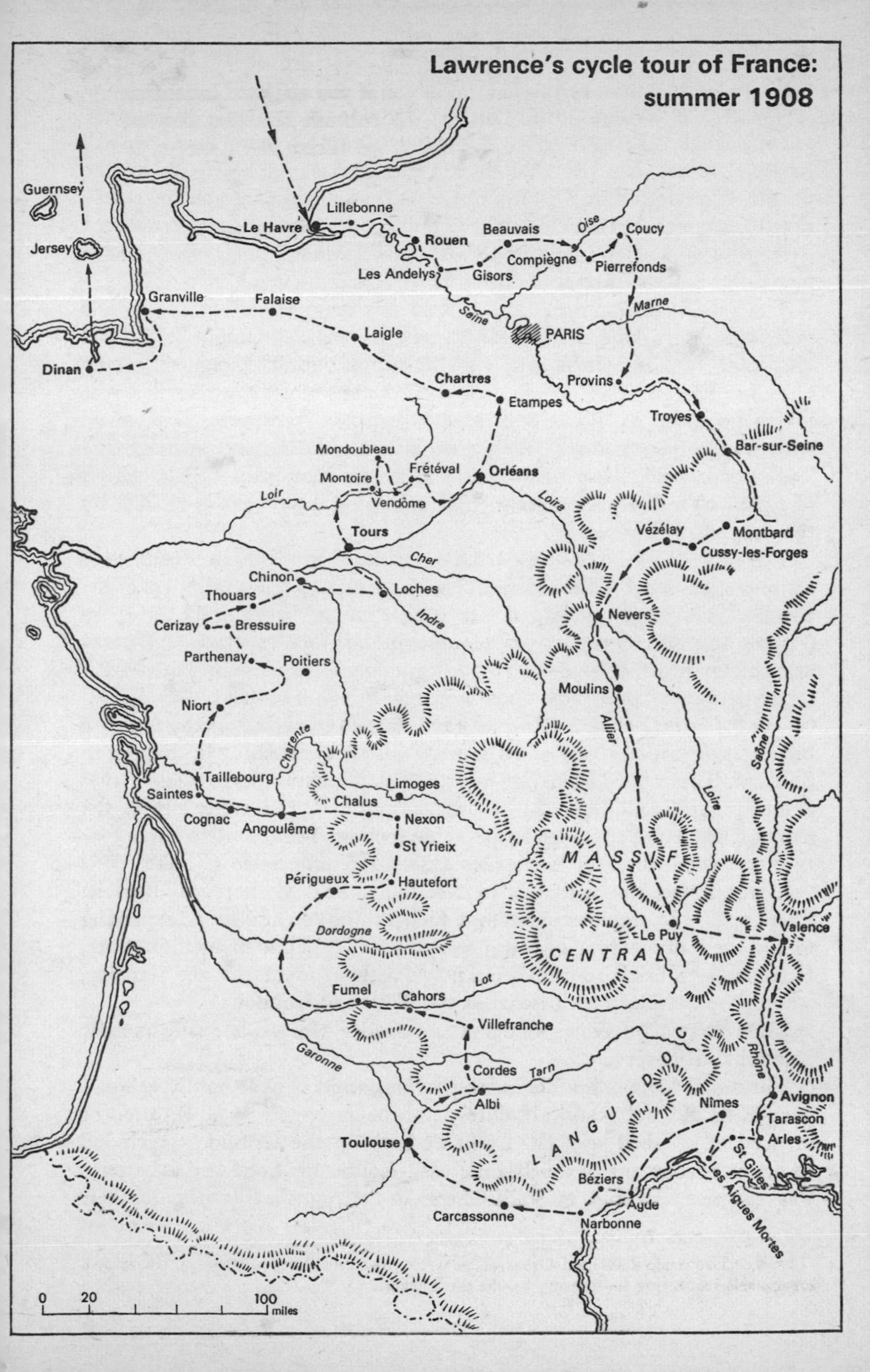

Lawrence's cycle tour of France: summer 1908
Guernsey
Jersey
Granville
Dinan
Falaise
Laigle
Le Havre
Lillebonne
Rouen
Les Andelys
Gisors
Beauvais
Compiègne
Oise
Coucy
Pierrefonds
Seine
PARIS
Marne
Provins
Chartres
Etampes
Troyes
Bar-sur-Seine
Mondoubleau
Montoire
Fréteval
Vendôme
Orléans
Loir
Loire
Tours
Cher
Vézélay
Montbard
Cussy-les-Forges
Chinon
Loches
Thouars
Indre
Cerizay
Bressuire
Nevers
Parthenay
Poitiers
Moulins
Niort
Allier
Charente
Saône
Taillebourg
Saintes
Limoges
Chalus
Cognac
Angoulême
Nexon
Loire
St Yrieix
MASSIF
Périgueux
Hautefort
Dordogne
Le Puy
Valence
CENTRAL
Lot
Fumel
Cahors
Villefranche
Garonne
Cordes
Tarn
Rhône
Albi
LANGUEDOC
Avignon
Nîmes
Tarascon
Arles
Toulouse
St Gilles
Béziers
Les Aigues Mortes
Agde
Carcassonne
Narbonne
0
20
100
miles

all my cry.' A few lines further on: 'Will you if you write to Carcassonne tell me what is happening in Turkey: the rubbish here that they call newspapers say one day that movements are taking place among the people, & a revolution is taking place, or that all is calm, and the sultan drank tea as usual at 6 o'clock on the terrace; I see today he's proclaimed a constitution and his intention to withdraw it: do let me have some solid fact if there is anything in it: it might well be important.'

The July revolt against Abdul Hamid was bound to affect Lawrence's prospects of working in the east. A new government might forbid the reopening of Carchemish; or it could support it. The citizens of the Ottoman Empire were experiencing one of those false dawns when it is joy to be alive. As Turks embraced Greeks, as Armenians fraternized with Kurds, it seemed as though a magician's wand might transform 'the Turk unspeakable' (so Hogarth had subtitled a chapter on the desolation of Anatolia) into a western gentleman, accepted, no longer despoiled, by the concert of Europe.

The Lawrence of more humdrum summers reappeared in the tallies of distances traversed (which were indeed impressive) and reminders of his austerity: he rode strongly and felt fit on a diet of bread, milk and fruit. (At this time and for some years he was an almost total vegetarian.) He was also the Oxford scholar displaying knowledge. On first seeing the Mediterranean: 'then I understood, instinctively burst out with a cry of θαλασσα! θαλασσα!* that echoed down the valley and startled an eagle from the opposite hill; it also startled two French tourists who came rushing up hoping to find another of the disgusting murders that people make such a fuss about I suppose.' The use of archaic phrases, the superlatives, the rhetoric acted as barricades against true feeling. Yet there were two further occasions when the barricades against emotion failed to hold.

'Carcassonne. I'm not going to describe it' he told 'Scroggs' Beeson: ' 'tis impossible, impious to attempt such a thing; go and see it, expecting to find the greatest thing of your life, and you'll find one many times finer. How on earth has it remained unknown with its memories and remains, when people flock to St. Michel or the Tower of London?'

Then on a Mediterranean inlet at Les Aigues Mortes, he made another emotional discovery.

The small town—'huddled along its old streets, with hardly a house outside its old walls, still absolutely unbroken, hardly at all restored or in need of it'—had seen St. Louis embark on the Crusade which led to his imprisonment in the Islamic east. Round his hotel bed Lawrence was surprised to find mosquito nets, or 'curtains'. But despite their

* Since Lawrence disdained Greek accents, he probably shouted thalássa, thalássa: a cry no self-respecting sea-nymph would understand.

protection (or perhaps because he failed to draw them), his body soon seemed an all-devouring bite, only eased when, repeating yet another quotation from Greek tragedy, he bathed in the sea. The bites bequeathed him the malaria which was to affect him periodically throughout his life. But bodily discomfort did not prevent, may even have fostered, the spiritual, or aesthetic, experience which stood out from the inherited ideas which had pervaded previous letters home.

Lawrence often quoted poetry. In one Sunday letter from Dinard two years earlier he had transcribed from memory no less than forty-seven lines from Tennyson's 'Idylls of the King'. They revealed little of an inner self, in part because he did not want to undress before his mother, in part because his selves were still opaque. Action, for its intrinsic excitement and as an escape from perplexities, meant most to him; his inner discoveries would all result from movement. His friend Beeson had noticed how little physical nature, in the sense of plants or trees, meant to Lawrence. Trees were things to be climbed; vegetation was an obstacle course on a strenuous outing. 'I have no time for sight-seeing,' he had written the previous month from Cussy-Les-Forges.

And then, on the same desolate plain that gave him malaria, lines from the opening section of Shelley's 'Julian and Maddalo' (a narrative poem one would not have expected him to memorize) show the authentic working of a soul.

> I love all waste
> And solitary places: where we taste
> The pleasure of believing all we see
> Is boundless, as we wish our souls to be:—

The quotation led him to define, in jerky syntax, a newly found emotion.

'You are all wrong, Mother dear, a mountain may be a great thing, a grand thing, "but if it is better to be peaceful, and quiet, and pure, pacata posse omnia mente tueri,* if that is the best state, than a plain is the best country": the purifying influence is the paramount one in a plain, there one can sit down quietly and think, of anything, or nothing which Wordsworth says is best, one feels the littleness of things, of details, and the great and unbroken level of peacefulness of the whole: no give me a level plain, extending as far as the eye can reach, and there I have enough of beauty to satisfy me, and tranquillity as well! *that* one could never have in mountains: there is always the feeling that one is going up or down: that one will be better, will see clearer from the top than from the valleys; stick to the plains, Mother, all ye little worms, you'll be happiest there.'[19]

* 'To be able to contemplate all things with a pacified mind.'

He had discovered what may be called 'the rapture of the steppe'. The discovery coincided with his recognition that the East (with a capital letter) would be to him what Chapman's Homer had been to Keats. 'I felt that at last I had reached the way to the South, and all the glorious East; Greece, Carthage, Egypt, Tyre, Syria, Italy, Spain, Sicily, Crete . . . they were all there, and all within reach . . . of me.'[20]

The mention of the East may have been, in part, tactical. He was aware that if his proud parents showed his letters to their Oxford friends, his enthusiasm for Hogarth's Levant and Evans's Crete might reach helpful ears. But a new note is unmistakably struck. The injection of 'mother dear' would have been unremarkable from someone less tightly repressed. But struck then, on that August Sunday in 1908, the note of affection is as strong as that of discovery. It was not to last.

The Oxonian on holiday re-appeared as he cycled in a zigzag pattern through the hilly country to the west, chased by dogs, dusty. He could not comfortably walk without a hat; he found an *omelette aux pommes de terre* uncouth. 'This place Cordes is the most picturesque town I have come across in my travels.'[21] But as he rode north, as the emotional magnet of mother and Oxford strengthened, he arrived at Chartres, tired and late, to find his nearest approach to a religious experience. He admitted that superlatives were useless, if unavoidable: 'Chartres is Chartres:—that is, a gallery built by the sculptors to enclose a finer collection than the Elgin Marbles.' Overwhelmed, he concluded: 'and when night came I was absolutely exhausted, drenched to the skin (it had poured all day) and yet with a feeling I had never had before in the same degree—as though I had found a path (a hard one) as far as the gates of Heaven, and had caught a glimpse of the inside, the gate being ajar. You will understand how I felt though I cannot express myself. Certainly Chartres is the sight of a lifetime, a place truly in which to worship God.'

The letter about Chartres had begun *Dear Mother* and had ended with the emphatic, 'We must return there (I would want assistants) and spend a fortnight in pure happiness.'* The postcard which followed it from Dinan (where he had joined Will) announced that he would return to Oxford on the night of the 8th. The postcard's date—4th October—has significance for the east in which Lawrence was beginning to take an interest. Four days before, after suppressing a minor revolt in Arabia, the Young Turks had opened the Hejaz Railway from Damascus to Medina, the city which held the tomb of the Prophet Muhammad. The stations were decked with the watchwords of revolution: Liberty, Equality and Fraternity. The postcard also marks more than a temporal break in

* David Garnett, when editing Lawrence's *Letters*, naturally wished to include this passage, so untypical for its emotional tone. Permission, in 1938, was refused: possibly because Mrs. Lawrence remembered its sequel as distressing.

Lawrence's correspondence: his next letter, from a ship steaming east the following June, would begin and end without endearments.

Between early September and October something occurred to spark the explosion which could have been foreseen as inevitable between one of his independent temper and the constrictions of his mother's household. Since all parties to the domestic crisis were schooled in self-control and practised at keeping secrets, the explosion was contained, kept perhaps even from the other brothers. The cause of the crisis is more obscure than its effects. Possibly the postcard arrived too late to alert his parents that their cat-stealthy son was on his way. The Lawrence who cycled into Polstead Road agog with castles and cathedrals was hardly yet an adolescent and very much a puritan. If, as one acquaintance claimed,[22] the young Lawrence surprised his parents when they were making love, the effect will have been traumatic.

The thought, let alone the sight, of their elders making love often distresses the young and Mrs. Lawrence's disciplinary methods had increased her son's revulsion at the movements of the flesh. But even if nothing so dramatic as has been suggested occurred, it is not hard to imagine a scene in which Mrs. Lawrence's attempts to reimpose control on a son who had spent two months in college and two months alone in France could have inspired hard words and desperate threats. Because Lawrence never completely broke his mother's hold and because of his sense of duty to his family, the precise details have not come to light and are unlikely to do so. He was later to refer vaguely to 'the urge of some private difficulty' and allege that 'he took a sudden turn for military experience . . . and served for a while in the ranks.'[23] But this supposed adventure (for which no solid confirmation has been produced) was set in his schooldays, not the year in which he came of age.

An explosion did occur and the evidence that it did and that its basic motive was Lawrence's desire for greater freedom, is of three kinds: a new living arrangement for him made by his parents at considerable cost; the implications of what some of his friends remembered; and his own new mode of life.

Until the summer of 1908, Lawrence was simply the second of five studious brothers, all either at school or university, sharing the barracklike quarters their parents could afford them. Bob was his senior in years; Will was to win a better scholarship than his at St. John's, a more fashionable college. All this was to change after that fatal September.

We can deduce the seriousness of the conflict from the fact that, as in every impasse, the Lawrence parents appealed to Canon Christopher. Now a very old man indeed, the Canon turned to David Hogarth and Professor Margoliouth, since 1889 the Laudian Professor of Arabic. (It is possible that Lawrence himself may have prompted these approaches.)

The result of them was that Lawrence's demand for physical independence was to find a compromise solution which would give him what he wanted while maintaining the façade of a united family. Meeting on 14 October, the Oxford City Council General Purposes Committee approved plans laid before it by Mr. T. Lawrence, Ned's father, for 'a single storey study/bedroom to be built at 2, Polstead Road.'[24]* The structure which was built following the Committee's approval was described by Sarah Lawrence: '. . . we had a very pretty well-built bungalow of two rooms made for him at the end of the garden. It had a Devon grate, electric light, and water laid on, and a telephone to the house. He hung the walls of the sitting-room with fine green bolton sheeting, which dulled the sounds and made it a very quiet room. There he did all his University work.'[25]

The brilliant second brother enjoyed an ambiguous role: loved, respected, to a degree feared, but always regarded as other. The *Home Letters* convey this impression to those who read them closely. The building of the bungalow gave him a privileged position in the family. It became the equivalent of a shaman's cave in more primitive societies. 'Ned's house' does not seem to have been resented by his brothers, but it conferred advantages at the cost of a certain alienation from the family group. The flight was from his brothers as well as his mother.† (On his side, Canon Christopher may have approved the bungalow, not so much as an aid to Lawrence's studies, but as a place of quarantine.) To Mrs. Lawrence, Ned's independence (however much she tried to belittle it in later statements[27]) was a defeat which she accepted only because the alternative, some Scholar Gipsy gesture, was less tolerable still. (Such gestures were easier for young Englishmen in the days of empire than they are today. Many English families remembered brothers or uncles who had disappeared into the ranks or vanished towards Australia.)

In getting his way, Lawrence, like other adolescents, may have fought foul. If he pried into his father's papers, he will have found, among his accounts, documentation of his Irish connection. Even without such documentation, he could exploit his parents' sense of guilt at an irregular union which he had long inferred. His own disgust needed no feigning. A repugnance for the sexual bond between men and women was a constant in his character, even if, in later years, accompanied by a certain eagerness to hear it described by soldiers. When his youngest brother decided on marriage, Lawrence decried it, only half-humorously, as prostitution à la carte, adding: 'I always thought we wouldn't go in for it

* The bungalow survives, though it has been enlarged since Lawrence's day. In May 1975, it was tenanted by an American student.

† Years later, when he had opted for a barrack life, Lawrence defensively compared its bareness, noise and class, to his boyhood ambience.[26]

in our family.'[28] Nor did getting his way at once dispel what was evident anguish. None of his Oxford friends seems to have been told of his alleged enlistment in the army or of the row which led to the building of the bungalow, which some of them visited. But accounts indicate that he had experienced a season in hell which lasted until after Christmas.

Looking back, many have projected oddities related to this period on to his entire youth, but, examined closely, they can only relate to the months following his return from France. Canon E. F. Hall of Christ Church, for example, remembered that 'there were times when his eyes appeared to burn with the intensity of a soul in pain'. Lawrence came to Hall's rooms at Jesus and fired a revolver into the Turl. 'I was left in doubt whether he was play-acting; but one glance at his eyes left no doubt at all that he told the truth when he said that he had been working for forty-five hours at a stretch without food, to test his powers of endurance.'[29] This period of strain must date from after October 1908, since Hall gave him the use of his rooms in Jesus when Lawrence had moved back to Polstead Road. Vyvyan Richards remembered Lawrence keeping 'Christmas day as a fast alone in his room out of protest against the absurdity of all feasting.'[30] This too can be dated to 1908, since by Christmas 1909 Richards had gone down from Oxford. For Beeson, the same year marked the conclusion of his relationship with Lawrence. 'The last full day in Lawrence's company was in Christmas week of 1908.'

No dramatic event withered this school-based friendship. The friends had outgrown each other, Beeson continuing to be interested in plants and trees, Lawrence in the architecture of the Middle Ages. This dissolution of old friendships, the growth of new, were indeed a normal part of growing up. But the weather in which the friendship with Beeson fizzled out was appropriate to the emerging Lawrence. The two young men met at the bleakest moment of the dying year. In few places has snow a drearier effect than the low-lying valley whose damp abbreviates so many Oxford lives. Conversing in the elliptical fashion open to quick-witted friends whose shared references go back a long way, they climbed Cumnor Hurst by a devious route. Unnoticed while they talked, the day had turned to storm. Snow winds had obscured the familiar landmarks of pine-clump and brick-pit, turning the midland landscape into an icy Sahara of massive snowdunes. To Lawrence, the vile weather acted as spur. He insisted they return to Oxford by a compass-bearing. Up to their thighs in snow, the pair trudged a grim straight line. Taking hedge and fence in their stride, they waded obstructive streams, shallow or deep. Only the lucky accident of striking Folly Bridge at nightfall prevented their attempting the wintry Thames.[31]

5

DAVID HOGARTH became, from the crisis of 1908 until 1922, a substitute father to Lawrence in a sense almost too strong for metaphor. On Hogarth's death in 1927 Lawrence was to describe him as 'the only man I had never to let into my confidence. He would get there naturally.'[1] Hogarth will hardly have been surprised, let alone shocked, by the domestic scandal at 2, Polstead Road. If the social abyss between Thomas and Sarah Lawrence had been as discernible to their son as we know it to have been,[2] to the urbane Hogarth it will have been immediately perceptible. He will also have understood, worldly-wise as he was, that its effect on Lawrence was not one of moral shock. There is, indeed, no reason to doubt Lawrence's own statement[3] that he had known his parents were unmarried since before he was ten. But it is one thing to know a fact theoretically, another to know it in practice and yet another to know its implications. The fact that the puritanical Sarah Lawrence was not even married will, on one level, have made things easier for Lawrence, helping him to break free from the system of ideas to which she had tried to bind him. The fact of illegitimacy would in itself hardly worry someone steeped in the history of the Middle Ages when courtly love was based on a cult of adultery and when some leading knights used the term Bastard in their titles. But the implications of being illegitimate in Edwardian society were not so lightly to be borne. Though Lawrence could later remark that 'bars sinister are rather jolly ornaments,'[4] they were bars to advancement in a stratified society. Hogarth had already discerned the burning ambition in Lawrence; if he had also discerned its obverse, an urge to renunciation, he will have recognized that renunciation requires that you have something to renounce: Lear's gesture is only possible to one who has first been King. If he fulfilled his threats to run away from home, Lawrence would be abandoning a fifth share in a semi-detached house; if his father had begotten him and his brothers legitimately, Lawrence would have been starting life on a level with such cousins, on his Irish side, as Robert Vansittart, educated at Eton and now beginning a diplomatic career. Besides being a city of dreaming spires, Oxford was a microcosm in which the advantages of birth and inherited wealth were plain to see.

In his role of substitute father Hogarth was first and foremost someone whom Lawrence could wholeheartedly respect; because he embodied the powerful qualities which Lawrence admired, this son of a Lincolnshire country clergyman supplanted the Irish aristocrat who had progressively lost such qualities under the influence of Sarah Lawrence. Hogarth had had a patrician education, classical studies at Winchester being completed at Magdalen, the college of Oscar Wilde and the future Edward VIII. Widely travelled, ugly as Socrates, courteous to women and considerate to young men,[5] Hogarth possessed diplomatic talents which made him an acceptable mediator in the family conflict. His solution, while unprising Lawrence from his parents' grip, preserved their secret during Thomas Lawrence's lifetime; Sarah was to be in her mid-eighties when Richard Aldington first saw fit to reveal to a less censorious generation that she had never been married. Hogarth was henceforth to fulfil the practical roles of a father: guiding Lawrence in the choice of a career, paying many of his bills (though if he helped towards the cost of the bungalow he was too much the gentleman to record it), rebuking him when necessary—and at times rousing the resentment hardly separable from a father-son bond.

After the bungalow was built, Lawrence got down in earnest to studies now sharpened by a sense of purpose and assisted by important patrons. Hogarth's close friend and adviser was Professor Margoliouth, another mentor whom the Lawrence parents could trust. The Laudian Professor's apparent acceptance of Protestant doctrine appealed as much as his Hebrew ancestry to the older Lawrences. Margoliouth's father, of Polish-Jewish stock, had been an Anglican missionary to the Jews. Margoliouth, too, had been to Winchester but had been so precocious (unlike Hogarth, who was a late-starter) that even his scholarly headmaster deferred to his erudition. Though his Arabic accent made him unintelligible to most Arabs, his knowledge of their classical literature was hardly rivalled in Europe. In the tradition of Oxford eccentrics, he delighted in rehearsing such quirky topics as how one divergent Muslim sect differed from another or how the name of God might be breathed from the navel. But Margoliouth was also of practical use to Hogarth's protégé. He put Lawrence in touch with an expatriate Syrian clergyman, the Rev. Odeh, who could teach him the rudiments of spoken Arabic. Hogarth himself undertook the rest of his direction.

Although Hogarth's position at the Ashmolean eased his financial situation (he had married the daughter of the local Lincolnshire landlord) and gave him prestige in archaeological circles, he was never, as an archaeologist, to equal such contemporaries as Flinders Petrie or such younger men as Leonard Woolley. However in an age of brilliant amateurs he took a particular interest in the political development of the

Middle East. By temperament an autocrat, he distrusted democracy even in Britain and was entirely sceptical about the possibility of its implantation in the lands of the Sultan-Caliph. He had no illusions about the Young Turks.* His ideas were close to those of the imperialists who saw in Lord Milner their leader and whose later spokesmen were Lionel Curtis and John Buchan. Since to Great Britain the Middle East was richer in threats and promises than any other region, Hogarth's preoccupation with its fate inevitably involved him in Intelligence.

Britain's Intelligence was certainly the best in the Middle East, if not in the world: indeed, so small an island could hardly have amassed so large an empire without it. Founded by Sir Francis Walsingham in 1573, the secret service never depended on those grandiose funds which create huge, self-interested and penetrable networks. It reflected instead the strengths of a small-scale and oligarchical society in which patriotism and good-form worked together. One of the few encyclopaedias which discuss such arcane matters lists the characteristics of British Intelligence as skill at camouflage, malleability of manoeuvre and the absence of a vertical bureaucracy.[7] The graduates of Oxford and Cambridge, army officers, consuls, businessmen and, above all, archaeologists, provided the human material on which men like Hogarth could draw. As a result, British Intelligence (at least during Lawrence's lifetime) had that unity of class and background which, however much condemned, makes for loyalty, scope and resilience. Hogarth recruited Intelligence assistants (many of whom were not paid even their expenses) from friends, Oxford acquaintances and his own relations. The year before he became involved with Lawrence he had, for example, encouraged his kinsman, Harry Pirie-Gordon, to tour the castles of Cyprus and 'Syria'†, accompanied by Harry Luke, later a colonial governor and writer.‡ Pirie-Gordon, whose chief interests were trees and heraldry, composed a useful map.

One of Hogarth's shrewdest moves was to help canalize impulses which could have made Lawrence an Edwardian scholar-gipsy or gentleman ranker. In 1908 military training was as *à la mode* as Dreadnoughts, and against the same prospective foe. At Jesus College, Percival Davies, a year senior to Lawrence, headed a small branch of the Oxford

* Unlike the High Commissioner of the Salvation Army who wrote, that crucial October of 1908, of 'the friendly feeling apparently manifested by all sections of the community towards each other,' in a letter to the British Ambassador in Constantinople.[6]

† Ottoman Syria included, in addition to the modern republic of that name, Lebanon, Israel and Jordan, as well as a portion of southern Turkey.

‡ These two names show how small the world of British Intelligence was, and how ingrown. Pirie-Gordon, like Dr. E. G. Hardy of Jesus, had been a patron of 'Baron Corvo', collaborating with him in literary projects and the Order of Sanctissima Sophia. Sir Harry Luke's son was to dramatize Corvo's *Hadrian VII*.

Officers Training Corps; with contingents from the neighbouring colleges of Lincoln, Exeter and Brasenose, it formed a company commanded by a Brasenose don. In October 1908 Lawrence joined.[8] To the surprise of friends who associated him with Provençal poetry, he was to attend a summer camp and be photographed in sloppy puttees and with tousled hair.[9] The doctrines of 2, Polstead Road saw no contradiction between the Gospel and military service; Christians of Canon Christopher's ilk accepted the Empire as a machinery for bringing untold millions to Christ; they copied St. Paul in using military metaphors for the spiritual life.

Such Christian imperialists were not necessarily racial bigots.* Many felt closer to Jews than to Roman Catholics; some deplored the treatment of the non-white population by the Boers to whom Britain had surrendered South Africa. 'It's not that we're better than the Indians,' Will Lawrence, one such imperialist was to put it, writing from India, 'but that their religions are definitely diabolical at times, and a curse to them.'[11] If such arguments made the O.T.C. acceptable to Polstead Road, Lawrence's motives for joining were less evangelistic. The Corps offered an appealingly masculine environment. Also, military service fitted with the doctrines which activated Hogarth and his influential friends.

Hogarth also suggested a way in which Lawrence could ensure himself a good degree. That same crucial year Professor Firth, Oxford's Regius Professor of History, had obtained permission for candidates for the History School to submit a dissertation in their finals on some topic connected with their special subject.[12] Hogarth advised Lawrence to extend his interests to the medieval architecture of the Middle East. If Lawrence's parents permitted, Hogarth had friends and backers who could help with such necessities as money and an expensive camera. The much travelled Charles Doughty, author of *Arabia Deserta*, could give advice; Pirie-Gordon could lend his map; and the Foreign Secretary, if duly approached through the Principal of Jesus College, could arrange for the *Iradés*, or letters of safe conduct, necessary for travel in Asiatic Turkey.

With these concrete prospects of a career opening before him, Lawrence threw himself into a new mode of life. Apart from his lessons in colloquial Arabic, he learnt to fire a revolver with either hand in hours of practice on the university rifle range. He wrote to Doughty, whose own experience had been of more southerly regions than Lawrence planned to visit, and met Pirie-Gordon at a restaurant in Holborn. More useful than Doughty's warnings of the danger of heat was Pirie-Gordon's map,

* Unlike Milner, who wrote: 'My patriotism knows no geographical but only racial limits. I am an Imperialist and not a Little Englander, because I am a British Race Patriot.'[10] Milner always spoke English with a heavy German accent, acquired in boyhood.

which supplemented the incomplete information in Baedeker; Pirie-Gordon's detailed plans of Levantine castles could also embellish Lawrence's thesis.

In the middle of June 1909, at the start of the long vacation, he sailed from England on the S.S. *Mongolia.* For a journey to the Middle East that was planned as far more than a jaunt, Lawrence prepared his equipment with meticulous care. If it is true that Thomas Lawrence put up £100 (a large slice of the family income), he must have seen the tour as an investment. If not, Hogarth, who saw it as a means of obtaining first-hand information about a vital area in southern Anatolia and as training for a future assistant, will have helped; he certainly paid for the camera which Lawrence selected. Lawrence, who saw his expedition as an opportunity to excel, decided to walk all the way, taking neither horse nor porter. He would thus need stout boots and the minimum of baggage. With his Mauser pistol and Pirie-Gordon's map, his camera and tripod, his Baedeker for *Syria and Palestine*, his rucksack would have space for only one spare pair of socks and a second shirt of thin delaine secured by tiny glove-buttons.[13]

He travelled second-class, sharing a table in the cosmopolitan saloon with a French girl, a German, a Swede, two Spaniards, an Indian, an Italian, a Greek and, most interesting to Lawrence, an Arab from Jerusalem.[14] At meals he chatted with the Arab, endeavouring to improve the smattering of colloquial Arabic he had acquired at Oxford; the Arab's offer to join him on his tour, provided Lawrence paid, was not accepted. On the 22nd June the largely empty ship put in at Gibraltar, Lawrence using the two-hour stop to buy postage stamps for his youngest brother, Arnold. Once in the Mediterranean, the dazzling sea, the narrows between Italy and Sicily, Crete's white, sharp cliffs, the four and a half days of the transit, were constants not soon to alter. Lawrence claimed that he spent six hours a day swotting at his Arabic grammar.

At Port Said he had to change ships. Had he foreseen that a party of Russian pilgrims would monopolize the first vessel to the Holy Land on 1st July, he might have visited Damietta where Egyptians have inherited blue eyes from the Crusaders, or even Cairo, where the early Fatimid fortifications might have modified his developing thesis. But uncertainty as to when he could leave confined him to the city which had sprung to life since the building of the Canal in the 1860s. He was befriended by a young Abyssinian—or 'Ethiopian', as Lawrence was corrected—who had studied at the American school in Beirut,* and spoke eleven languages including English and Arabic. 'Inform Will,' he wrote home, 'that an

* Originally the Syrian Protestant College, it was destined to become the influential American University of Beirut.

Abyssinian looks like a cross between a Greek and Hindu, but with crisp curled hair like a negro.' His cosmopolitan guide showed Lawrence more of Port Said than most tourists saw. Like many cities of the colonial world, it was separated into a European sector for a conglomerate of Greeks, Italians, French, Armenians, Turks, Russians, Germans, Spanish, Portuguese as well as some English,* and a native town whose astonishing vivacity and animation would, more than twenty years later, impress the youthful Evelyn Waugh.[15] If during his five days of excited slumming Lawrence stepped on board a coaling ship, this will have provided the germ for the later legend that 'he took on a checker's job in coaling ships at Port Said.'†[16]

After this brief first visit, Lawrence left Egypt for Beirut on Sunday, 4th July 1909. Despite fears of being quarantined at Jaffa (which the ship reached after an eighteen-hour run), he was inside Beirut harbour soon after dawn on Tuesday, 6th July. Beirut was at this time a city of 150,000 unspoiled by riches or violence. Red-tiled roofs and wrought-iron balconies were interspersed with the greenery of bananas, palms and flowering shrubs. To the north-east, the massive flanks of Kesrouan, the mountains which had given Lebanon its role of refuge, were mauve and blue after the melting of the snows. Mount Lebanon now enjoyed the semi-autonomous status of a separate sanjak inside the Ottoman Empire. After fearsome communal massacres in 1860, Napoleon III had extended a tradition going back to Louis XIV and by forcible intervention left the mountain region more open to foreign influences than the rest of the empire.‡ As residence of the Apostolic Delegate for Syria, of a Maronite archbishop, of a Greek orthodox bishop, and of the patriarch of the Greek Catholics, Beirut had an atmosphere more ecclesiastical than commercial. From the vineyards of Ksara and Musar, through a network of schools and seminaries, French priests extended a beneficent influence. The Jesuit university, in the eastern quarter above the harbour, had faculties ranging from medicine to Oriental literature. On the western reaches of Beirut, the buildings of the American College occupied pine-clad slopes above a brilliant sea. Electric trams had but recently linked the

* They formed a significant enough colony for Lord Kitchener to give a special reception for them: *Egyptian Gazette*, 19 January 1912.

† Liddell Hart asked him: ' "Did you ever work at coaling ships in Port Said before the war?" "Yes: about 1909, for a few days. Checker." '[17] This connection with a coaler can be fitted to no year other than 1909, which is where Lawrence himself locates it. But as he was in Port Said for less than a week engaged in talking, exploring and swimming, the work cannot have been onerous. But it is an interesting instance of how a splinter of truth can provoke a legend.

‡ The sanjak of Lebanon was surrounded on the north and south by the vilayet, or governorate, of Beirut; this included the coastal belt from the mouth of the Orontes in the north to just short of Jaffa in the south, the vilayet itself being sub-divided into the five sanjaks of Latakia, Tripoli, Beirut itself, Acre and Nablus.

dispersed sections of the town; they clattered, bell-ringing, through narrow, congested streets.

Just to the west of the port clustered the few hotels. The oldest, the Orient (now Grand Bassoul) had been visited by most of the famous travellers of the nineteenth century; Pirie-Gordon and Harry Luke had stayed there the year before. But Lawrence chose the Victoria, cheapest of the four listed in Baedeker. A short walk took him to the British Consulate, wedged between the Jesuit university and a large Franciscan convent. Here he learnt that the two *Iradés* requested from Lord Curzon by Sir John Rhys had not yet arrived. But the Consul made light of Lawrence's projected journey, at least of its initial stage south into Palestine: ' "Travelling is as ordinary as in Europe," ' Lawrence quoted him as saying. 'Cook has a permanent camp at Petra, the brute!'[18]

His first afternoon in Asia, Lawrence visited the Common Room at the American College. The young American tutors were in the process of breaking up for the summer. Like the Consul, they made light of Lawrence's trip. Doughty had warned against the insanity of walking in Syria during the summer: these Americans had been spending their summer holidays in this way for years, 'exactly as I propose to do.' Indeed, five of them suggested that he join them two days later for the first week of his southward walk. Amidst this group of young men who knew the country and each other, Lawrence understandably felt shy. He made a deliberate, perhaps nervous, attempt to impress them. Will had luckily inserted a quotation from Theocritus in a recent letter. 'I brought it out,' he wrote home, 'with enormous effect in the College Common Room this afternoon: a reputation as a classical scholar is easily gained.'[19] He left the College to buy a sun-helmet (then considered essential in colonial climes) and a water-bottle.

Either he had impressed his intended companions too much, or one of the young Americans was really taken ill: but Lawrence set off a day late, on Friday, and alone.

This summer walk was to last, in three distinct phases, from 9th July until 24th September. In a fashion we shall come to recognize as typically Lawrentian, these phases were to recede from the known, to the half known, to the mysterious. This first phase—which lasted from 9th to 31st July—took him by way of southern Lebanon into Galilee. 'And that leaves Palestine proper almost untouched,' he admitted in a letter to his father.[20] The second phase—which again began from Beirut, on 6th August, but this time in a northerly direction—lasted thirty-five days. It was to take him into the less trodden highlands of western Syria. The third and last phase began some time after 7th September and took him east from Aleppo into the arid foothills of southern Anatolia, further south than Hogarth had travelled in the 1890s and further east than

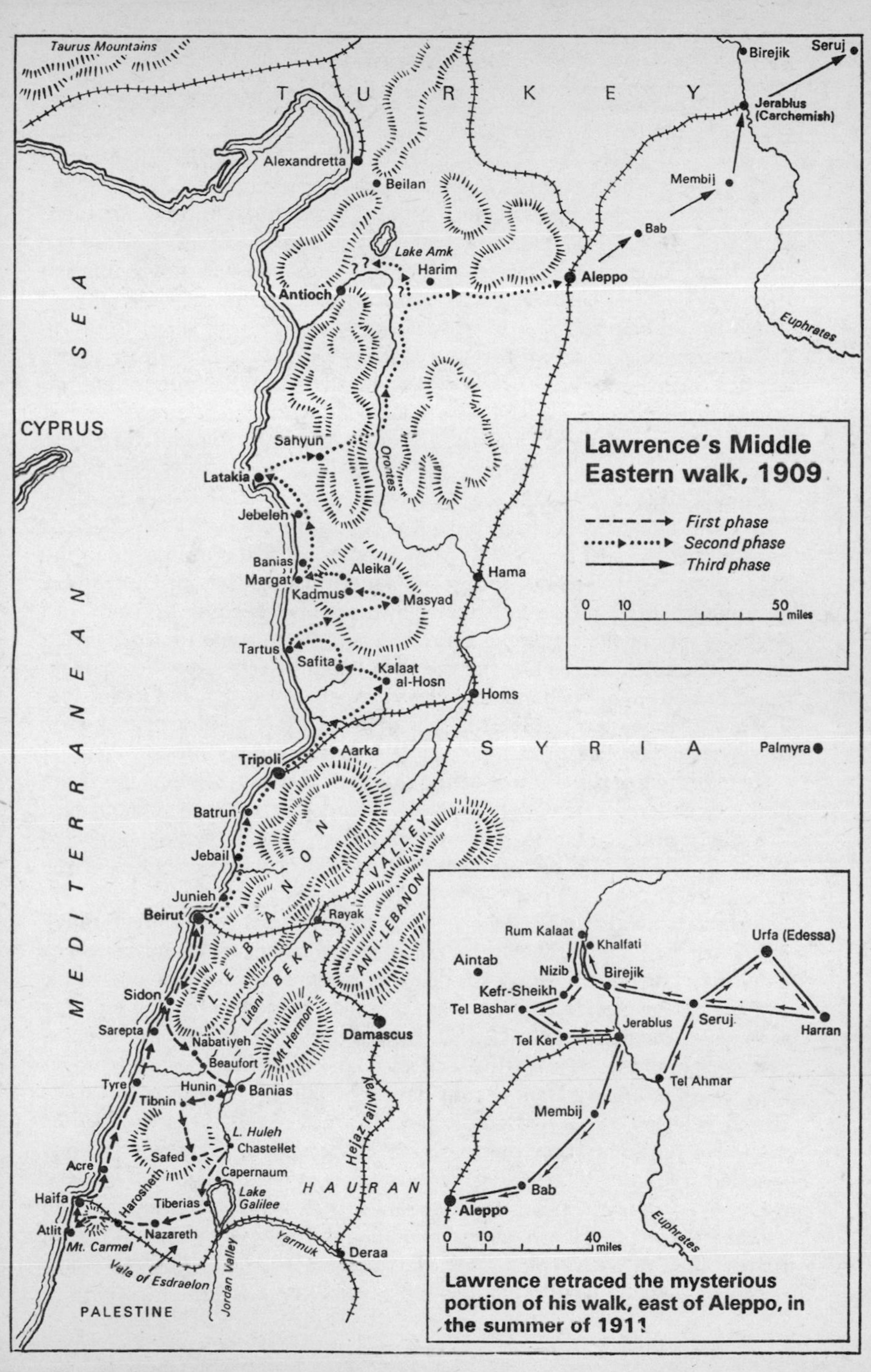

Lawrence's Middle Eastern walk, 1909
First phase
Second phase
Third phase
0 10 50 miles
Taurus Mountains
TURKEY
SYRIA
CYPRUS
MEDITERRANEAN SEA
LEBANON
BEKAA VALLEY
ANTI-LEBANON
HAURAN
PALESTINE
Alexandretta
Beilan
Lake Amk
Harim
Antioch
Aleppo
Bab
Membij
Jerablus (Carchemish)
Birejik
Seruj
Euphrates
Orontes
Sahyun
Latakia
Jebeleh
Banias
Margat
Aleika
Kadmus
Masyad
Hama
Tartus
Safita
Kalaat al-Hosn
Homs
Tripoli
Aarka
Palmyra
Batrun
Jebail
Junieh
Beirut
Rayak
Damascus
Sidon
Sarepta
Nabatiyeh
Beaufort
Litani
Mt Hermon
Tyre
Hunin
Banias
Tibnin
L. Huleh
Chastellet
Safed
Acre
Capernaum
Lake Galilee
Haifa
Harosheth
Tiberias
Atlit
Nazareth
Mt. Carmel
Vale of Esdraelon
Jordan Valley
Yarmuk
Deraa
Hejaz railway
Rum Kalaat
Khalfati
Aintab
Nizib
Urfa (Edessa)
Kefr-Sheikh
Birejik
Tel Bashar
Seruj
Harran
Tel Ker
Jerablus
Tel Ahmar
Membij
Bab
Aleppo
Euphrates
0 10 40 miles
Lawrence retraced the mysterious portion of his walk, east of Aleppo, in the summer of 1911

Pirie-Gordon had gone in 1908.[21] This third phase was fogged from beginning to end with the mystery that still hangs round the clandestine activities controlled by Hogarth. Here Lawrence's academic interests were a pretext not a purpose. About what really happened Lawrence was to relay half a dozen contradictory reports, himself depositing that spore of legend which was to make much of his later career confusing. Although his seventy days on foot were to leave him impoverished and wounded, they also left him entranced with the East and equipped with material which would help secure a First Class degree.

The first stage, a tramp through Galilee, proved, as the young tutors and the British Consul had predicted, hardly more dangerous than an excursion in France. Indeed, the bouts of fever which complicated it almost certainly derived from the mosquitoes at Les Aigues Mortes the year before.

From Beirut he took one day to cover the main coastal road south to Sidon, the ancient Phoenician port. Taking up introductions to American missionaries, he spent Saturday, 10th July, hunting for antiquities in the Sidon shops as well as inspecting the Americans' collection. On Sunday morning he struck inland to Nabatiyeh, the capital of south Lebanon and the chief city of the Lebanese Shiites, whom he mistook for a Christian sect.[22] The town was *en fête* for the corn being conveyed to the coast on camel back from the rich inland valleys of Bashan, Hauran and Esdraelon. There Lawrence secured the services of an escort—'a guide or chaperon or whatever you like to call it (male!)'—to accompany him on the next stage of his journey. After inspecting the great castle of Beaufort, he swam in the oleandered Litani, swift and cold, and the two men then crossed to a village near the top to sleep. On Tuesday, 13th July, they traversed the plain of Huleh, a pleasant contrast to the scrubby declivities of the hills, to reach Banias, once Caesarea Philippi.

Although belittling Baedeker, 'who drivels as usual architecturally,' Lawrence had his copy within reach as he travelled round northern Palestine. Lawrence echoed Baedeker's praise of more than one castle and quoted his measurements. Baedeker also helped to jog his memory as to which incidents of the Old Testament occurred on his route. He was able, for example, to identify Tell el-Kadi with 'the Laish of Judges xviii, & subsequently Dan.' From Banias he and his escort proceeded to Hunin, whose fortress had controlled the ways to the sea in the Middle Ages. He does not seem to have visited Metoullah, the Jewish colony founded in 1896 and at this time populated by more than 300 settlers.

On Wednesday, 14th July, Lawrence paid off his companion and continued alone to Tibnin, and then, taking 'refreshment at the springs of Kades, Barak's native place,'* struck south for Safed. The landscape

* Baedeker: 'It was the native place of Barak, Deborah's general (Judges iv.6).'

impressed him by its lack of level ways. 'The roads are never at rest, indeed climbs & descents of 1500–2000 feet into valleys (usually dry) & up the most scorching hillsides are regular things . . . all day one steps from one sharp rock to another which is not only tiring to the feet but to the brain also for one has to be continually on the alert, to find the best place for the next step, and to guard against slips.'[23] The people he found hospitable; palatable he found their two-foot wide loaves of diaphanous bread. His first week he slept once at the house of a Greek Orthodox priest, three times on the flat roofs of peasant houses, once in the home of a Syrian doctor (in these parts Syrian could mean Lebanese or Palestinian) and twice in the open air.

By the time he reached Safed, a recurrence of fever necessitated a longer halt. He had come to the right place. In this upland township, roadless and a seven hours' ride from Capernaum, the London-based Mission to the Jews (for which Margoliouth's father had worked) ran a hospital. It was directed by a Dr. Anderson from Abingdon, whose wife and four children were with him. To coach one of the daughters for school in England, and to help in the hospital, Dr. Anderson had brought out Miss Nora Harrison, who gave up her bedroom for the young man. 'I remember how we used to question him at every meal about his discoveries. He asked an Arab to let him down into a cavity of the ramparts but he found no treasures, no human bones, only the skeletons of goats and sheep.'[24] Lawrence stayed with the Andersons for four nights. It was a chance to do his laundry (an important chore when you have only two shirts and two pairs of socks) and, when he felt better, to visit Chastellet, now called the Daughters of Jacob, just south of Lake Huleh. From Safed, apparently recovered, he went down to Tiberias on Lake Galilee. This cultivated plain beside the lake was the most pleasing place he had yet struck. He could walk on real grass under trees. The town at this date had a population around 7,500, three-quarters of them being Jews. The two nights he spent at Tiberias he was once more the guest of missionaries. Dr. W. B. T. Torrance, a Presbyterian Scot, was a medical missionary and Christian Zionist,* some of whose enthusiasm seems to have rubbed off on Lawrence, who normally had no interest in botany or agriculture. For as he surveyed the thistles of Chorazin, Lawrence launched into a Pateresque panegyric on the opulence of Galilee in the time of Jesus. 'The Renaissance Painters were right, who drew him and his disciples feasting in a pillared hall, or sunning themselves on marble staircases . . .'[26] and having contrasted the twenty miles

* Will Lawrence, who was to stay with Dr. Torrance in 1913, gives the population as 8,000 and increases the Jewish percentage to nearer 90 per cent. He described Dr. Torrance to his mother as 'just the type of missionary you'd approve of.'[25] Some Christian Zionists wanted the Jews to leave Europe; others believed their Return would precipitate the Second Coming, and consequent millennium.

of thistle behind Capernaum, the dirty, dilapidated tents of the Bedouin, their miserable, snapping curs, he concluded: 'Palestine was a decent country then, and could so easily be made so again. The sooner the Jews farm it all the better: their colonies are bright spots in a desert.'[27]

Lawrence at this time had walked through the scrubby maquis of south Lebanon and north-east Galilee. He was to strike fertility once he left the Jordan Valley for Esdraelon. This valley, destined to be a major area of Jewish settlement,* was at the time farmed by Arabs. 'The plain was very good; so fertile, & all the people of the villages engaged in harvesting & threshing: they take tents out & live in the fields, while strings of camels and asses carry the corn to the threshing floors.' Lawrence was remarking the same abundance which had impressed the British traveller Laurence Oliphant twenty-five years earlier. Then the Arab villagers had produced so much grain that its transport alone to Haifa and Acre had cost their landlord $50,000.[28]

Nazareth, the chief Christian city of Palestine, he found unappealing, liking its fountain only. He remarked on none of the churches in Baedeker, but sent a picture postcard to Canon Christopher (a little late for his birthday). The rest of his Galilean journey involved a rapid tour of castles with his thesis in mind; thanks to Pirie-Gordon's plans, detailed study was not too necessary. After crossing the hump of Carmel from Harosheth (where he remembered Sisera) he reached the sea at Atlit, but neither described its famous Castellum Peregrinorum (which the Templars had fortified in 1218) nor visited the Rothschild colony, founded in 1897 and then numbering five hundred Jewish settlers. From Haifa he took a week to walk to Beirut, arriving there on the last day of July. His Syrian journey, he estimated, had so far cost him around £8, not including what he had spent in Port Said.† In his absence the *Iradés* had reached the Consulate.

The second phase of his journey was to bring worse bouts of fever, scanter food and a brush with danger. A hazier light replaces the lucid sunshine of a Galilee known to every bible student. For one thing, Lawrence was venturing into a swathe of mountainous country unrouted by Baedeker, and on at least one occasion the *Iradés* he had obtained through Lord Curzon were to prove, in Lawrence's own emphasis, *invaluable*.[29]

The one road north from Beirut followed the coast, traversing the rich fruit-growing area around Antalyas until at Dog River the limestone mountains pressed close to the sea. At this defile, on the high cliffside,

* Its absentee landlords, the Sursock family from Beirut, sold it to the Jewish National Trust in the 1920s.

† The fact that he mentions no earnings in Port Said further undermines the likelihood that he had worked on a coaler.

fourteen conquerors from Rameses III, Shalmaneser and Marcus Antoninus to the Arabs and the French had left inscriptions. A few miles further north the horse-shoe bay of Junieh was topped by Harisa, encircled by clifflike hills; the Virgin Mary had supposedly paused here on her flight to Ephesus, but Lawrence made no mention of her shrine to his Protestant family. The next place to claim his attention was Jebail, or Byblos. This small indentation in the Lebanese coast had claims to be the first seaport in history. From it, barques had ferried to Egypt the cedars which were the chief export of Phoenician kings; from the word Byblos derived, thanks to the papyrus which the Egyptians sent in return, the first word for a book, and hence our bible; in medieval times a crusader castle had dominated the little bay. And here in the nineteenth century American Presbyterians had established a school over which a Miss Holmes now presided. Her staff included a Quaker-educated Arab schoolmistress, Fareedah el-Akle. Six years older than Lawrence, Miss el-Akle has described Lawrence's arrival at the mission school.[30] The maid who answered the door misread his dusty boots and bundle on his back as evidence that he was 'one of the German tramps that were going about the town at that time.' Lawrence followed her upstairs to an immediate welcome by Miss Holmes. Delighted by Lawrence's Evangelical connections, she gave him the run of her bookshelves while feeding him on nourishing and punctual meals.

Yet Lawrence had not come east to be cosseted by missionary ladies. After a few days at Jebail he saw several castles on the road to Tripoli, a town of thirty thousand Arabs, mostly Muslims. Here he paused long enough to write two letters home. To his mother he extolled such American missionaries as Miss Holmes, who realized that for the moment the conversion of Muslims was impossible and instead, without engaging directly in politics, sought to mould a generation which would erode those aspects of Islamic civilization objectionable to the New England mind. The presence of such missionary institutions was also encouraging emigration to North America. Within ten years, Lawrence predicted, English would have become the lingua franca of Syria. For it to become so, though he did not say so, would be a striking defeat for the Catholic priests and missionaries who represented France.

The long suppression of the letter he wrote from Tripoli to his father (it was not published until 1954) made it difficult for those interested in Lawrence's walk to understand either its timetable or the emotions to which this first experience of the east was giving rise. There is a perceptible difference in the Lawrence who writes to his father from the more frequent, but less self-revealing correspondent with his mother. To his mother, he is factual, erudite, hard-boiled. Of himself, he projects only his austerities and talents. To his father he writes, more naturally, about the kindness, not only of the missionaries, but 'the common people each one ready to receive one for a night, & allow me to share in their meals: and without a thought of payment from a traveller on foot. It is so pleasant, for they have a very attractive kind of native dignity.'[31] Lawrence then unburdens himself about the challenges ahead and the resources he has to meet them. Three weeks should take him to Aleppo, there being fifteen castles in the first 125 miles. He then allots a week to reaching Urfa (the ancient Edessa) and another ten days to getting south to Damascus. From Damascus he was eager to go further south still to two great castles in the hilly desert east of the Dead Sea. Kerak, the first, had been described by an American archaeologist, Dr. Bliss, as the most interesting castle in Syria; the now functioning Hejaz railway made it easily accessible. Shobek, or Monreal, the second castle, was only two days further. But Lawrence stressed that certain difficulties might force him to change his plans. He had to be back in Oxford for the start of the Michaelmas term; he was short of money. If he visited these two castles, he could not possibly reach Oxford before 20th October; and if he spent this length of time travelling, he would run short of money. 'Mother would have to resign herself to getting only a small packing-case from Damascus.' Sarah Lawrence apparently expected at least a silver teapot. If he got that, he facetiously added, he might have to return steerage. In any case, tea-making was uncommon in the east and Damascus silver was finnicking [*sic*] and hard to clean.

From Tripoli Lawrence took the time he had planned to reach Aleppo. But the journey involved unexpected risks. For a great part of the time he was traversing a mountain region which, though more fertile and less lofty than the Lebanon, had long associations with violence and in Lawrence's time valued firearms as a badge of manhood. Known to the Greeks as Bargylos[32] and to the Arabs as Jebel al-Ansariyah, this highland stretch between Lebanon to the south and the Taurus mountains to the north had provided the Order of Assassins with their twelfth-century stronghold. According to William of Tyre, Lawrence's favourite medieval historian, these fanatical heretics held ten castles, which owed more to geography than architectural skill, and a subject population of sixty thousand. Lawrence spent his first night in this violent region sleeping on a house-roof, his second as the guest of Abdul Karim, a young and pistol-happy Arab noble, who lived in a fortress-like house on top of a mountain.[33] Next the Ottoman kaimmakam, a modern-minded Young Turk, entertained him at Kalaat al-Hosn, or Crac des Chevaliers, and Lawrence spent three days photographing and measuring 'the finest castle in the world'. When he left, the kaimmakam insisted on an escort accompanying him to visit Safita, whose battlements impressed him greatly. From there he looped back to Tartus on the coast, and then walked inland again for Masyad, the only Assassin castle still in fair repair. Not without cause had the kaimmakam worried about his safety. A ruffian took a pot shot at him from two hundred yards. Lawrence returned the shot and the man's horse bolted. The lawlessness of this region evidently had a basis in social discontent: one night the villagers stood armed watch against what Lawrence took to be thieves, but in the morning they told him it was *landlords.*[34]

This first experience of violence, with the concomitant fuss of alerting the authorities, may explain the haze around what remained of his walk. That, and the effects of recurrent fever. According to his account, the next place he visited was Kadmus 'where the "Old Man of the Mountains" himself lived: (I slept in his château.)' Here Lawrence was claiming the impossible. The château had been destroyed eighty years before during an Egyptian occupation of the Levant. One of the river valleys that intersect the hills gave a passable route back to the coast by way of Aleika, still inhabited by the Assassins' descendants, and after visiting 'Margat',* a massive castle by the sea, he had a breather at Latakia. As he took up his pen, once again his mother's distant face had the effect of introducing an artificial note, of stimulating a routine boasting. 'No smoking yet, though here every man woman & child does: Latakia tobacco, which Father knows all grows here: the peasants dry & smoke their own, all in cigarettes: I will have such difficulty in becoming English again, here I am Arab in habits & slip in talking from English to French & Arabic unnoticing: yesterday I was 3 hours with an Orleannais, talking French, & he thought at the end I was a "compatriot"! How's that?!'[36]

His photographs illustrated the rest of his walk to Aleppo better than his letters. Sahyun was the latest recipient of a Lawrentian superlative: 'perhaps the finest castle I have seen in Syria.'[37] He must have then followed the track by the Orontes, since a few days later he noted 'a Crusading castle, too ruined and rebuilt to be valuable' at Harim. But Lawrence's interest had begun to flag with his strength, and his claim to have paid a flying visit to Antioch, to see but not enter its walls, would have involved an unlikely as well as tedious detour.† On foot, he was slower than his mounted escort, and Baedeker (to whose routes Lawrence had now returned) gives the distance from Harim to the walls of Antioch as over five hours on horseback.‡ More probably, he contented himself

* Margat in David Garnett's edition of *The Letters*, 'Nargat' in the *Home Letters* version of the same letter; it has become the more recognizable Markab by 18.2.11 . . . when he again refers to this castle in a letter home.[35]

† Pirie-Gordon had visited Antioch. Lawrence could hardly tell his mother that he had neglected it; it was here that the followers of Jesus had first received the name of Christian. Acts, xi, 26.

‡ In the safer 1920s René Dussaud gave the distance from Harim to Antioch as a day's march each way.[38]

with a glimpse of the city's adjacent lake, visible from afar, before turning with relief towards Aleppo, chief city of northern Syria. At Baron's, the best hotel, he had his first bath, or indeed proper wash, for ten days.

The mysterious third phase of Lawrence's journey began shortly after 7th September (when he wrote from Baron's Hotel) and had plainly ended by 22nd September when, once more in Aleppo, he announced that he had run out of money and was coming home. In his letter of 7th September he wrote, 'I am afraid I have to drive from here to Urfa (Edessa) which is going to cost me about £7.' It would have been out of the question for him to have hiked through the hotter, treeless terrain to the east of Aleppo even if his general health had been less impaired. But Lawrence was surprisingly reticent about what happened between leaving and returning to Aleppo. He had devoted some 11,500 words to his walk through Galilee, a further 4,600 words to north-west Syria; but the mere thousand he gave to the third phase tell us that his boots were 'porous'; that his feet were covered with blisters, and cuts; that though preserved from dysentery by exercise he was tired; that his finances were exhausted—but nothing of his itinerary or what he saw. He did tell his mother, however, that while the coachman had been dozing, his camera had been stolen from his carriage at Seruj, on his way back from Urfa.

Two days after telling his mother this, he wrote a letter to the Principal of his Oxford College which deserves attention as the first documented instance of Lawrence creating a myth about himself.[39] Its pattern is worth analysis.

It is, first, to a person of importance, but Lawrence's opening, *Dear Sir John Rhys* (instead of *Dear Sir John* or *Dear Principal*) shows how new he was to the promotional game. The letter's contents, however, already reveal the potential master. His first and last paragraphs express a flattering appreciation of Sir John's kindness in obtaining the *Iradés* through Lord Curzon. He had had a most delightful tour, though 'the details naturally won't interest you.' He then gives details calculated to excite an appetite far more blasé than Sir John's. He has travelled 'on foot and alone all the time.' He forgets that a paid guide had accompanied him into northern Galilee, that an armed escort had jogged beside him into Aleppo, and that he had travelled towards Urfa in one of the Baedeker carriages at the Baedeker rate.

The blend of truth and untruth which follows is part of a pattern which was to become compulsive. 'I have perhaps, living as an Arab with the Arabs, got a better insight into the daily life of the people than those who travel with caravan and dragomen.' He had certainly obtained a closer view of Levantine life than the ordinary tourist; but he had worn European dress, including a sun-helmet; spoke no more than a smattering of Arabic, and armed with official *Iradés* had been a privileged person whose safety was of concern to the Ottoman authorities. His next addition was calculated to make him the undergraduate of the year: he had seen some thirty-six out of the thirty-seven castles on his proposed route and had made plans, drawings and photographs of many; at Mr. Hogarth's request, he had also bought some thirty Hittite seals, the best of which would go to the Ashmolean. He then arouses pity and wonder. He has been attacked four times by malaria: 'last week I was robbed & rather smashed up.' But the weather (rather than misadventure) is used to explain his failure to go south to Kerak and Shobek. Before he could go walking again the rains would have started. (Yet he had told his father, correctly, that 'the summer is rainless here till early November.'[40]) This was regrettable since, however costly the voyage out, 'the actual travelling, my beggar-fashion, costs practically nothing of course.'

Lawrence concluded this short, packed letter with the shy hope that the loss of a week would not be considered an unpardonable offence.

The effect in Oxford of such a letter, combining as it did a tale of adventure and diligence with disarming flattery, may be imagined. The letter (carefully preserved by Rhys) was widely read. Ernest Barker, then teaching at St. John's, developed a sensational vision of what was without doubt a strenuous vacation. 'He had climbed the old walls barefoot: he had had his troubles with Bedouin, and once (I think he told me) been assaulted and left unconscious.'[41] A seedling had been planted which was to be fed by the nitrates of fact and watered by the dew of legend.

6

TO IMPOSE a straight narrative line on any human existence is an operation as artificial (but often as useful) as a dramatic convention. Even straightforward lives resemble threads in which staples from the past are interwoven with new beginnings. The texture of Lawrence's life makes the attempt all but hopeless. It developed through mysterious episodes which, like knots in a tree, had to be surmounted before the straight timber could proceed.

The episode of his lost camera provides the first instance of what we may term his public mystification. Its forerunner, his challenge to his mother's authority, was essentially private, but in 1909, as an Exhibitioner of Jesus College, travelling on *Iradés* procured for him by the Foreign Secretary, Lawrence already had some public position. Since mystification was often to coincide with crucial moments in his development, this first instance deserves careful scrutiny. We may both hazard a guess as to what really happened and understand how Lawrence used mysteries, and to what end.

Four different versions of what had happened gained currency within two years of the Levantine tour.

The earliest occurred in the letter to Sarah Lawrence of 22nd September 1909. Its complete text was held back until the 1954 publication of *The Home Letters of T. E. Lawrence and his Brothers.* (David Garnett had been allowed to give a twelve-line summary in his earlier *Letters.*) Lawrence in this version stated that he would be needing a new camera: the one he had taken with him had been stolen from the carriage at Seruj on his way back from Urfa. In Urfa he had found the only two beaked towers in all N. Syria; he hoped that his photographs of them would be clear.

The second version was given in the letter to Sir John Rhys which we have just considered, written two days later. Although it said that he had been 'robbed and rather smashed up,' it did not mention the camera.

Harry Pirie-Gordon heard the third version soon after Lawrence's return to England but recorded it much later. Lawrence had returned the borrowed map apologizing for but not explaining bloodstains, which someone had tried to remove from the cover.* 'Later I learned', wrote Pirie-Gordon, probably quoting Hogarth, 'that he had been attacked by Kurds who had beaten him and left him for dead in indignation at finding that the "treasure" which he had been reported to be carrying consisted of no more than his clothes, shabby after his remarkable tramp through Syria in the heat of summer, some Hittite cylinder seals† which he had bought in Aleppo, and a few beshliks [low-denomination Ottoman coins]. They had taken most of his clothes and all the money, but had left the seal and the map as being valueless. He had worked his way to Marseilles, *so I was told*, [this author's emphasis], and landed with enough money to pay his fare back to Oxford.'[1]

Lawrence himself supplied the fourth version more than a year later. In a letter from Lebanon (to be discussed more fully later) he told Leonard Green (who wanted to use some of his photographs): 'My camera was stolen before I could take anything interesting—I really meant to.'[2] This was either an excuse or a prevarication since Lawrence had told his mother that he was robbed on his way back from Urfa, on the final stage of his tramp, having photographed the beaked towers in that last city.

These four accounts are plainly inconsistent with each other. The contradictions suggest that something disturbing underlay what they described. Which account can we believe? It is generally true of legends, as of rivers: the higher we mount towards the source, the purer the element.

Unlike Sir John Rhys, Pirie-Gordon or Green, Mrs. Lawrence, who received the first account, was in a position to check it. She would immediately notice if he returned without the camera secured for him (Vyvyan Richards put the cost at £40[3]) by Hogarth. Later evidence proves that he did indeed return without it. Almost two years after his tramp, when he was working not far from where the robbery had supposedly occurred, his reply to one of his mother's letters indicates that she had been nagging him about the camera: was he doing his best to recover it? had the police in Aleppo found any clues? 'It's two years since I lost that other camera; and it was at Seruj which is miles away. The Aleppo people knew nothing about it.'[4] This makes nonsense of post-war additions to the story in which Lawrence punished the thief and recovered his property—the latter meanwhile metamorphosed into a copper watch.[5]

The claim, in his letter to Rhys, that he had bought thirty Hittite seals

* The map is at present in the possession of Mr. Donald Weeks, author of *Corvo*, who reports that the cover, not the map, is still stained.

† Mr. P. R. S. Moorey of the Ashmolean Museum informs me that at this period archaeologists used the term Hittite more loosely than today. It is likely that these seals were in fact prehistoric North Syrian.

for Mr. Hogarth, could also be easily checked and was evidently true. The section of his tramp which began east of Aleppo had been more on behalf of Hogarth than of his thesis, and he will have seen in whatever confidential charges he was given the equivalent of a test which could affect his career. Lawrence knew from Hogarth's writings, as well as his activities at the Ashmolean, that he was a passionate collector. An addition to the Museum's seal collection would only please.

His claim to Green, that because he had lost his camera he had taken no photographs, makes little sense; it might make more if we still had Green's letter.* It would establish what subjects Green wished to illustrate, and why. From Lawrence's reply we may infer that his friend had been lecturing on a political topic: 'Politics are quite shocking; I would like to have been in your audience tho' . . .'[6] Without Green's letter, we can merely note that on the question of the camera Lawrence had a species of mental block.

In the Aleppo of Lawrence's 1909 visit, a Dr. Altounyan, married to an Irishwoman, ran a first-class hospital. Altounyan's son, also a physician, made friends with Lawrence after 1911 and wrote a memoir of their friendship after his death. He makes no suggestion that Lawrence had needed medical aid in Aleppo in September 1909. A similar silence is manifested by the wife of the British Consul in Aleppo, who met him for the first time in 1911, and also became a friend and memorialist of Lawrence. If Lawrence had been robbed and forced to complain to the Ottoman police, and if the local paper had also reported the murder of a Mr. Edward Lovance killed at Aintab (as he told his mother, adding that the hotel staff received him like a ghost), the consular authorities would certainly have known.

The contradictions in these accounts help us to advance from what we know to what we may suppose. We know that Lawrence arrived in Aleppo on 6 September exhausted by recurrent bouts of malaria and with feet and boots useless for further walking. (They had covered, he estimated, some 1,100 miles.) He was short of cash. He had two things left to do: to buy seals for Hogarth and, again for Hogarth, to make a journey in the direction of the Euphrates.

Marcopoli, an Italian, was the leading Aleppo dealer in seals. (He was to be expelled two years later when Italy invaded Ottoman Libya.) Syrian ploughmen were constantly turning up either bulla-type flat seals or the engraved cylinders which, when rolled across clay or plasticine, could leave a picture. By this time they knew their commercial value. Even more did Marcopoli. A newcomer to the buying game, Lawrence was probably overcharged for the thirty seals he bought for Hogarth,

* Even at this early stage Lawrence's correspondents preserved his letters. Lawrence does not seem to have returned the compliment.

leaving him even shorter of cash. His planned trip to Urfa would take between three and four days and the hire of a carriage would cost between five and eight Turkish pounds; as the Turkish pound was worth about ten per cent less than the British sovereign, this explains his remark to his mother that it would cost him about £7 to drive to Urfa.[7] While calculating costs, he must have noticed the second paragraph in Baedeker's Route No. 48, *From Aleppo to Urfa* (*Edessa*). This warned that at Membij, a village settled by Circassians after the Russo-Turkish War of 1877–8, *the traveller should be on his guard against pilfering.*

On the basis of what he wrote in 1909 we would have to conclude that he nonetheless did go to Urfa and there photographed outstanding features; we would know nothing of any clandestine mission; and we would have to accept that he either lost the camera when the coachman dozed at Seruj (as he told his mother) or when he was beaten up and robbed (as he told Sir John Rhys.) But fortunately we have more evidence to help us. Lawrence was to retrace his steps two summers later, keeping a diary. Written in pencil and in a more carefree style than his letters to his mother, this diary was nevertheless intended for family reading. On the first page he wrote: 'In afternoon walked through liquorice and dust to Seruj. Took room at Khan and inquired fruitlessly about camera.'[8] More significant, when he reached Urfa by carriage on the second day, he wrote about this great Byzantine stronghold as though seeing it for the first time. He photographed the moat from every angle except the north, which did not merit it. After he had photographed the interior from the tall beaked tower at the west end, Lawrence wrote his conclusion: 'almost everything in the place was Arabic except the moat, some straight pieces of wall, and the SW angle tower; with the two Roman pillars.' It is inconceivable that if Lawrence had spent £14 to visit Urfa in 1909, he would have given the castle so cursory a glance that these important conclusions only came to him two years later.

If the 1911 Diary puts in doubt his visit to Urfa in 1909, it confirms that he had reached Seruj. The Diary has him visiting one Nuri Effendi in Seruj, both on his way to Urfa and on his return from Harran, as someone who is already an old acquaintance,[9] and it carries one further reference to the 1909 tour. Lawrence is tramping well to the west of the Euphrates, some distance north-west of Birejik. He visits a village called Kefr-Sheikh: 'the village of Ahmed Effendi, with whom I struck up an acquaintance last time I was out in Syria . . . Ahmed Effendi received me with open arms.'[10]

The implication is clear: Lawrence had been sent east from Aleppo in 1909, not to photograph beaked towers, but to inspect the vicinity of the site where Hogarth planned to dig. As late as 1909 the precise point where the Berlin to Baghdad Railway would cross the Euphrates was still in doubt. Lawrence was to try and discover the intentions of the German engineers and to assess the attitudes of the local people. The Ahmed Effendi whom he visited in 1909 and again in 1911 was plainly a man of some education: he and Lawrence are described as looking over a history of Turkey.

The simplest explanation for the loss of Lawrence's camera is that he and his driver were indeed victims of pilferers. Someone who knew him well was to describe how sensitive he was to ridicule;[11] he might well have concealed his personal carelessness with a good story.

A second explanation might involve the curious introduction of 'Mr. Edvard Lovance' into his letter to his mother and 'my murder near Aïntab (where I didn't go.)'[12] Kefr-Sheikh is much more than half way between Aleppo and Aïntab, in a rough northerly direction, and quite off the north-easterly Baedeker route to Urfa by way of Seruj. If Lawrence had been caught snooping in a sensitive area, and had lost his camera in some scuffle, he might have put a false account in his letter in case the Ottoman authorities opened his mail.

A third explanation would take account of his exhaustion, of his sense that he had done enough research for a 12,000 word undergraduate thesis and, most important, of his lack of cash. 'Bang go my proposed purchases in Damascus,' he had written to his mother on 7 September, contemplating what the journey to Urfa and back would cost him. Yet he put up twice at Aleppo's most expensive hotel and then, according to his brother, Arnold Lawrence, 'hired a carriage to take him back to Beyrout.'* The sale of his camera to some merchant in the Aleppo souq would have been a desperate but understandable step for someone as exhausted as he was, and as poor.

If we consult our own experience, we realize how few of our actions are determined by absolute standards of right and wrong, truth and falsehood. The young man travelling with modest resources who runs out of funds and then pawns or sells whatever he has that is negotiable must indeed be legion. Such an improvisation, or lapse from total probity, is scarcely unprecedented and rarely regarded as reprehensible; no more is the effort to cover up with a 'white lie' the embarrassing or discreditable incident. Much of Lawrence's subsequent manipulations of historic fact can plausibly be ascribed to the internalized notions of right-and-proper, the acceptable and the inadmissable, absorbed from a mother whose own illicit status and lower middle-class code of conduct compelled her to 'live a lie' in the unremitting effort to conform to the

* The quickest and cheapest way back to Beirut would have been by train via Hama, Homs and Rayak, the junction in the Bekaa Valley. Baedeker recommended second-class travel as perfectly acceptable to gentlemen travellers. Even a first-class ticket would have cost only a fraction of the journey by carriage.

strictest canons of respectability. The requirements of Polstead Road propriety and the pattern of Polstead Road deception can hardly have failed to influence a temperament instinctively inclined to shift between the impulse to reveal and the cautionary urge to hide.

But his mother had imposed on him a compulsion to appear a paragon. To her, he could not admit that he had soaked his honourable sores in a bath and then returned normally by second class on ship and train. Fables of working his passage, even the contrivance of stains on a borrowed map, were the paragon's tribute to her exacting demands. None of these mysteries would exist if, even at this early stage of his career, Lawrence could have borne to tell the unvarnished truth.

7

ONE OCTOBER day, early in the Michaelmas term of 1909, Ernest Barker was lecturing on the original authorities for the first three Crusades. After the lecture, an undergraduate whom he failed to recognize—'a man with a very fine face, which seemed thinned to the bone by privation'[1]—came up and spoke to him in a low, quick voice. This proved to be Ned Lawrence, brother to the Will Lawrence who was already Barker's favourite student at St. John's. Lawrence had returned to Oxford soon enough after the beginning of term to have suffered no setback in his academic career.

Except for a short account of his tour in a letter to Charles Doughty of 30th November and an even shorter letter to Leonard Green of February 16th (congratulating him on prose owing nothing to Wilde or Pater), he spent silent, trackless months on the thesis which must secure him a First in Modern History. His efforts bore fruit. 'His First,' Sir Goronwy Edwards was to record, 'was a good one, and some of his papers showed both cleverness and originality; but the outstanding thing about his whole performance was his very remarkable thesis on "The Crusading Castles of Syria".'[2]

Professor Firth, who had sponsored the innovation under which candidates in Modern History could supplement their examination papers with a 12,000 word dissertation, hardly hoped to secure major contributions to knowledge. The purpose of Oxford education was to teach the undergraduate to think for himself. Socrates had found in the asking of awkward questions the beginning of knowledge; it meant the same to Edwardian Oxford. His examiner will not have asked, when he read Lawrence's thesis 'on the castles built by the Crusaders in the Latin kingdom of Jerusalem' whether, as Lawrence claimed, this conclusively proved Sir Charles Oman wrong and established that the soldiers of the Cross had learnt less in the Levant than they brought with them. Still less will he have asked whether the thesis constituted an authoritative and publishable book. Lawrence, who had visited thirty-six out of the fifty castles concerned, had relied heavily on Pirie-Gordon for plans of the castles; his own drawings were often sketchy. To a trained examiner he showed a telltale thinness where he went outside his own experience, as in his discussion of Antioch. We have seen that Lawrence at the time of his tramp claimed only to have reached its walls and had probably contented himself with a distant view. His account of the castle—'It's on a mountain peak and very hard to get at'—is characteristic of a student skating over fragile ice; 'with its long, flimsy wall with the ridiculous buttresses, [it] is evidently residential and not a post of military importance.'[3]

Later, Lawrence pencilled criticisms in the margin of his typewritten thesis. 'In Rum Kalaat,' his text had it, 'another stronghold of Edessa (Urfa) the only sign of Latin occupation is in the form of the grooves for a portcullis. For some reason the Byzantines never used this defence for a gateway with any frequency.' But, after the thesis had been approved, Lawrence pencilled in the margin: 'There are no portcullises in Rum Kalaat. It is all mediaevel Armenian and Arab.' On the map attached to the thesis, places merely mentioned were marked in black, those visited, in red. Rum Kalaat was correctly shown in black, as mentioned, but not visited; Antioch and Urfa in red, as visited.

Important gaps further prevented the thesis from being a definitive study. Lawrence had yet to visit Cairo, where the fortified walls of the Fatimid city, dating from the eleventh century and deriving directly from the Byzantine tradition of northern Syria, embodied features such as the machicoulis—a projecting parapet for the dropping of missiles or lead—unknown in Europe until the end of the following century.

Against such inevitable limitations, the thesis had positive virtues. The willingness to question received opinions—what Lawrence himself termed 'my rather knight-errant style of tilting against all comers in the subject,'—was attractive. An energy that set him apart from armchair students, a diligence which yielded flashes of perception not given by books, were reinforcements. 'The aim in the mind of every architect of the smallest intelligence was to find such a site for his buildings that the waste and weakness of equal accessibility on all sides might be avoided; then he could multiply defences on the one weak face alone.' Lawrence's account of the buildings which the Crusaders had employed to hold down a predominantly Muslim peasantry was counterpointed by Pirie-Gordon's map, which showed that as far north as Sahyun the castles formed a chain, each visible by bonfire to the next. It is true that some of Lawrence's sweeping statements showed racial bias. The Normans 'were not an original race . . .' or 'From France and England come all mediaeval masterpieces in literature and architecture . . . Italy had a hybrid civilization.' But such attitudes were current. Hogarth had undervalued Egyptian art at the expense of Greek under the influence of theories restricting creativity to certain favoured races. Lawrence similarly undervalued the people of the Middle East. 'The Arabs were till Saladin's time contemptible engineers,' would have been untrue, even if by 'Arabs' Lawrence meant those deriving from Arabia. But when two pages later in his thesis he wrote, 'Beibars seems to have been the first Arab sovereign to build respectable fortresses,' the implications had become more sweeping and more wrong. Since the Mameluke sultan Beibars was no more Arab than Saladin, Lawrence was excluding such redoubtable engineers as Ibn Tulun, fragments of whose magnificent aqueduct still remain in Cairo. But such evidence that Lawrence had gone to the east with his mind made up may not have worried his examiner. He was writing in an academic climate still contemptuous of Byzantium. The fluid frescoes of fourteenth-century Constantinople, then hidden behind layers of Ottoman distemper, were yet to explode the legend of an ossified culture.

During the summer of 1910, Lawrence's future hung in doubt. He had obtained his First. He knew what he wanted to do, or at least where he wanted to do it. After Aleppo he had approached a landscape to which Anglo-Saxons were particularly susceptible: not the scrubby hills of south Lebanon and Galilee, in many ways reminiscent of Provence, but the north Syrian steppe which rolled further than eye could reach towards the shimmering depression which was Iraq. He had already felt at Les Aigues Mortes the rapture of the steppe (its archetypal quality surely confirmed by Matthew Arnold's ability to evoke without visiting it the central Asia of Sohrab and Rustum). Added to this was the discovery of a people, simple and direct, and, despite their poverty, good-humoured and hospitable. Lawrence had sensed an alternative society which satisfied levels of his being which in England he repressed. In thus succumbing to the Middle East he was only the latest in a processional frieze of paleface captives whose imaginations had been stifled by the age of reason. Lady Hestor Stanhope and Beckford, Byron and Edward Lane had found inspiration where turbaned heads held ideas close enough to those of Christendom to be readily understood but sufficiently different to intrigue. This attraction was as ancient as the love affair between Antony and Cleopatra. Nor was it a one-sided attraction confined to the Englishman in Mesopotamia or the Frenchman in the Sahara. For every westerner captivated by native bread, baggy trousers and a larger moon, a young Turk or Arab was ready to succumb to the teashops of the west. Since the west was politically stronger, its attractive power would end by destroying the east which soothed, or excited, distraught Europeans. 'Very many of the men in all the mountain villages,' Lawrence had noted with distaste, 'have visited America, and they love to display their English before their fellow-villagers. Once or twice they have tried to overcharge me excessively . . .'[4]

He could not share his mother's pleasure at the prospect of Evangelical values conquering the Levant. But how, before it was too late, could he get back? Even if his family circumstances had been different, he would have disliked the social emphasis of the diplomatic, or the more accessible consular, service. His degree qualified him to teach. But in Syria the educational establishments were French or American. Despite the compliments which he repeated to his mother, he was to admit his brother Frank's French was 'no great success: & I don't like trying to correct him, since I am little better myself.'[5] Besides, both the French and the American colleges had a religious bias. His Protestant background ruled out his working for the Jesuits while his personal independence made it unlikely that he could have long endured Miss Holmes or the American professors in Beirut. He seems not to have contemplated teaching in England or India. His hopes were thus pinned on Hogarth.

In the summer of 1910 the three middle brothers took their bicycles to France. Ned and Frank crossed from Folkestone to Boulogne in early August; Will, who had been staying with their parents in Guernsey, crossed to meet them at Cherbourg at the end of the month. The holiday letters of the three help us to picture some of the preoccupations in Lawrence's head as he relaxed after his finals. Frank Lawrence, in a long letter to their old nurse, confirmed that Ned was thinking of returning to Syria. 'At a little village half-way [to Bayeux] where we stopped to look at the church I bought some flint & steel. It is not a curiosity, it is meant for work, and they use it in the village instead of matches. Ned has been practising a great lot with it for his next Syrian trip. He lit a person's cigarette with it this evening, but failed to get the candle to light.'[6] But Lawrence was also thinking of pottery, the interest which had originally introduced him to the Ashmolean and which might still provide the basis of a career. He paid two visits to Bayeux, first with Frank, then again with Will, who on 4th September wrote to his mother: 'We slept the night at Bayeux. Next day we spent the morning in the Museum. While Ned tried to draw a piece of the tapestry bearing upon his pottery, I acted as decoy in another direction. He got enough notes for him to reconstruct it all right in private. At Caen we separated.'[7]

All three brothers shared one twentieth-century interest: aviation. After leaving Coucy—'the most interesting castle in France, Ned says'—Lawrence and Frank went on to Rheims, 'where all the flying has been. There is not a single aeroplane there now, so we were disappointed.' Will, too, riding through Argentan and Maillebois, refers to 'Latham the aviator'.[8] But as castles balanced the idea of Syria, so Lawrence's old love of books balanced this modern interest. 'Beauvais is finer than ever: & is now marked with a white stone, since there I found worthy French-printed books.' He could at last read Molière, Racine and Corneille. He concluded this same August letter from Le Petit Andelys by exalting the joys of reading: of being in his bedroom at Polstead Road and knowing that nothing, not even the dawn 'can disturb me in my curtains: only the slow crumbling of the coals in the fire: they get so red & throw such splendid glimmerings on the Hypnos* & brass-work.' After spending a night with such medieval knights as Percivale, he rejoices to watch the sun glowering through the valley-mists above the Cherwell. This leads him to expressing confidence in the intelligence at least of Mrs. Lawrence. 'Father won't know all this—but if you can get the right book at the right time you taste joys—not only bodily, physical, but spiritual also, which pass one out above and beyond one's miserable self, as it were through a huge air, following the light of another's man's thought. And you can never be quite the old self again. You have forgotten a little bit: or rather pushed it out with a little of the inspiration of what is immortal in someone who has gone before you.' Still from France, but this time to Vyvyan Richards, he asked about the cost of a first edition of Doughty's *Arabia Deserta*, and of Hogarth's *Wandering Scholar in the Levant*, 'one of the best travel books ever written.' He repeats his need for a good copy of Doughty's masterpiece; but the bookshop at which Richards inquired did not have one in stock. Clearly Lawrence wanted to read the works of Doughty and Hogarth in preparation for achieving something similar himself.

Hogarth had in fact been active while Lawrence had been dawdling, doubting, dreaming. His first year as Keeper had showed a marked increase—from 15,024 to 18,862—in the number of visitors to the Ashmolean. (Lawrence had more than maintained his role of donor, contributing a fragment of glazed jug, part of a candlestick, and a bronze spur, obtained from excavations at the Civet Cat, the Radcliffe Camera and, in the case of the spur, from the site for a ladies' lavatory at the eastern end of St. Mary Magdalene's church.) But Hogarth's chief aim was to proceed with the reopening of the Carchemish dig. This seemed feasible now that the Young Turks had exiled Abdul Hamid to Salonika and installed a tame sultan in his place. By the end of May 1910, Sir Gerard Lowther, British Ambassador to Constantinople, could inform Frederic George Kenyon, director of the British Museum in succession to Sir Edward Maunde Thompson, that the Imperial government had granted a *firman* for the renewal of the dig.[9] The concession was to run from February 1911, for two years. In July 1910, an official letter was forwarded to Kenyon to introduce Hogarth to the British Consul in Aleppo.

With these formalities behind him, Hogarth went to work on behalf of his protégé. Magdalen College, of which Hogarth was a fellow, maintained what were known as Senior Demyships, not exceeding eight in number and not lasting more than four years, for 'such persons, being

* One of Lawrence's treasures was a replica of this well-known bust.

members of the University of Oxford, as shall have passed all the examinations required for the Degree of Bachelor of Arts, and shall satisfy the electors that they intend to enter upon some course of study with a view to taking Holy Orders, or following the profession of Law, Medicine, or Civil Engineering, or to engage in some definite scientific or literary *employment*, and that they may have difficulty in so doing without assistance.' Lawrence, having secured his First, was eligible for such an honour; as Keeper of the Ashmolean and friend of the miscellaneous great, Hogarth was well placed to lobby on his behalf. The Demyship was worth £100 per annum. There were no travel requirements; but if the Demy wanted to travel for his research, he could do so. Lawrence's formal election was to be announced on 14th December. Assured of this income (a third of what his father had used for a household of at least eight persons) Lawrence approached the director of the British Museum. He did so on Hogarth's advice and with Hogarth's endorsement.

Kenyon had the odd habit of dating many of his official letters by the month only. In a letter to the Treasury dated December 1910 Kenyon wrote: 'I have to add that an offer has been received from Mr. T. E. Laurence (an Arabic scholar, acquainted with the country and an expert on the subject of pottery) to join the expedition at Jerablus and to take part in the excavations. Mr. Laurence is willing to give his services without salary, but I would ask your Lordships to sanction the payment of his actual living expenses while engaged on the excavations and of his travelling expenses from Beyrut to Jerablus and back in the same manner as the expenses of Mr. Hogarth and Mr. Thompson.'[10] (Hogarth had engaged Mr. R. Campbell Thompson as Assistant and Surveyor against an emolument of £1 a day, and a similar sum was to cover the daily expenses of Hogarth and Thompson.)

Lawrence repaid Kenyon for misspelling his name by describing himself, or allowing Hogarth to describe him, as an Arabic scholar. Lawrence knew a few nouns and imperatives—he was to put his vocabulary during the Syrian tour at only eighty words[11]—but was in no sense an Arabic scholar. If Hogarth sanctioned the bluff, he will also have warned his protégé that he should improve his Arabic as quickly as possible.

The letter putting Hogarth in charge of the expedition, and attaching Mr. T. E. Lawrence (now spelt correctly) to it, was not signed by Kenyon till the last day of 1910. But Lawrence was prepared to gamble. He had sailed from England in early December, even before the formal announcement of his Magdalen Demyship. He had arranged to spend two months at Miss Holmes's establishment in Lebanon mastering Arabic and there was no time to waste. Excavations at Carchemish were planned to start in February 1911.

BOOK TWO

1910–1914

Bold Qonsolos, Timid Recruit

8

THE LAWRENCE who left England in December 1910 was no longer a mere student with uncertain future. Because his four years at Carchemish would allow him to display facets which he concealed at home, because his new role would gratify a multiple self he named as to Legion,[1] this period proved in retrospect the happiest in his entire existence.[2]

Yet, as he traversed the Mediterranean for the second time, he was still very much the Oxonian making aesthetic apperceptions on the scenery of the classical Grand Tour. The *Saghalien*, one of the less seaworthy vessels of the Messageries Maritimes, had a faulty engine whose troubles gave him a day in Naples—'quite as fine as Beyrout'—and another, once he had fled 'the intolerable cesspit of the Peiraeus', in Athens. His shipboard letters show that the graduate has regained control over the hiker. Very much the donnish Periclean, he reacts to 'the protocathedral of the Hellenes', the Parthenon. 'I only knew that I, a stranger, was walking on the floor of the place I had most desired to see, the greatest temple of Athene, the palace of art, and that I was counting her columns, and finding them what I already knew. The building was familiar, not cold as in the drawings, but complex, irregular, alive with curve and subtlety, and perfectly preserved. Every line of the mouldings, every minutest refinement in the sculptures were evident in that light, and inevitable in their place.'[3]

The ship then passed through the Dardanelles to provoke, at Constantinople, a distinction between the Ottoman capital and Athens which reads bizarrely today: 'Constantinople is as much life as Athens stood for sleep.'[4] But it was an honest observation then, before the departure of Greeks from 'Istanbul' and their influx into Athens reversed the contrast: 'Athens (modern Athens) is the quietest of towns, without trams almost, no motors, no train whistles, no dogs even: so that there is never a sound from the outside to disturb the peace of the rock.'

The streets of Constantinople offered an unsurpassable colour and movement: 'Damascus,' he told Richards, 'is not within a call of it:—and besides there are glorious-coloured mosques, in blue and gold and cream and green tiles, and yellow glazed pottery of *exactly the shapes in England in the xivth cent.*, and a street, a whole street, of the most divine copperware.'[5] He contradicted himself in his next letter home. 'After the walls you have to jump to Turkish xvi century mosques for features of interest. I do not like them much. There seems to me to be a crudeness, an incapacity, a smallness of conception and design about all their art.'[6] As a comment on the massive yet elegant mosques of Sinan this judgment would be hard to defend; but he may have inserted it as a concession to his mother's bigotry.

From Constantinople, where the *Saghalien* had delayed him until 17 December, Lawrence journeyed to Beirut; thence the steam-tram took him to within walking distance of Jebail. He reached the American Mission School on Christmas Eve. Perhaps because Campbell Thompson's specialization was in the cuneiform script of the Assyrians and Babylonians, he had planned 'to settle there for six weeks or so, learning Arabic and Assyrian.'[7] The second project came to nothing. Instead, during the first two months of 1911 he undertook, if we exclude his lessons in colloquial at Oxford, his only systematic study of Arabic with an educated teacher. Fareedah el-Akle, whom he had impressed on his walking-tour two years before, was then in her late twenties. She was later to record that 'notwithstanding the difficulty of the language he made rapid progress; he was able to read, write and speak very simple Arabic in this short time. Lawrence never studied beyond that, although later on when he lived with the Arabs, he could speak their different dialects with ease.'

Counting her friendship with Lawrence one of the greatest privileges of her life, Miss el-Akle's memory inflated his period of study to three months,[8] since the evidence of his letters home clearly established that he had left Jebail by the end of February. And Lawrence himself was to make contradictory claims as to his knowledge of a language whose intrinsic difficulty for the non-Arab is increased by the gap between the spoken language (which differs from region to region) and that used for letter-writing or public speech. To one biographer he put his vocabulary at its fullest at around 12,000 words, to another at around 5,000. He assured both men that he never spoke grammatically and never learned to read or write the Arabic letters.[9] Although he possessed at this time a Koran and a copy of one of the classical odes, as well as 'an Arabic prayer book of 1145 A.D., small but very well written,' bought for 3s 1d, he never read an entire Arabic text and knew Arabic literature only through books about it.[10]

Life at the American Mission School pleasantly combined western comforts (the teachers received the London *Times*) with such amenities of the Levant as oranges picked ripe from the January trees.[11] Jebail was only on the fringe of the Islamic east, although, unlike Junieh to the immediate south, it had many Muslims. Replying to a letter from Leonard Green which was waiting for him at the School, Lawrence used terms that mocked the conventional notion of the east. He is on a divan (translated into English, an American bent-wood chair), inhaling 'haschich' (the effluent of a neighbouring factory), and dreaming of odalisques, which he translates as 'upper-housemaids' and bulbuls, which he does not translate but which were nightingales. Then he tackles Green's inquiries about the Levant. After a résumé of the more useful books available, he skilfully condenses his impressions of the terrain he had tramped through two years before. His prime impression had been of its difficulty. The valleys of Esdraelon and the Bekaa were the only flat places while the coastal plain was a fifty-yard stretch between boulder-covered hills and the sea. His assessment of the region's defensive potential against attack from the east shows a rare fusion of erudition with strategic sense.

It also shows how completely Lawrence still thought of the east in western terms. Although his thesis was now written, he was still seeking evidence for his ideas, not intrinsic interest or inspiration. Instead, the dream of printing beautiful western books beautifully in England seemed about to be accomplished. In a letter of 14 January he requests his parents to send £30, as an advance on his Magdalen Demyship, to Vyvyan Richards, who was already building a hut to house the press and planning to study line-process etching in London, but was short of cash.[12] Lawrence returns to the subject in a letter written ten days later, reporting that to keep their relations elastic, he and his friend have signed no agreement. But Lawrence, for once, sees himself as a businessman. While Richards will have contributed energy, inspiration and design, Lawrence will have put up the capital. Richards should be asked to make a will, guaranteeing the reversion of the money, or the business, to Lawrence, if the money had not been previously repaid. 'We both feel (at present) that printing is the best thing we can do, if we do it the best we can. That means though, (as it is an art), that it will be done only when we feel inclined. Very likely sometimes for long periods I will not touch a press at all. Richards, whose other interests are less militant, will probably do the bulk of the work.'

This description of what sounds an unbusinesslike business introduces a phrase from the Book of Proverbs destined to resound in his later life. Printing, he says, is not a business but a craft; it's no more possible to sit down to it for so many hours a day than to paint a picture on that system: 'And besides such a system would be almost sure to interrupt *The Seven Pillars of Wisdom* or my monumental work on the Crusades.' His work on the Crusades was never to be written; this early *Seven Pillars* was never to be published. He later defined it as a travel-book about Cairo, Smyrna, Constantinople, Beirut, Aleppo, Damascus and

Medina[13], and then, as a book of youthful indiscretion which recounted adventures in these eastern cities and 'arranged their characters into a descending cadence: a moral symphony. It was a queer book, upon whose difficulties I look back with a not ungrateful wryness.'[14] He is said to have burned the manuscript in August 1914[15] and, as by that time he had not visited Baghdad or Medina,* the work must have been in large part a fantasy.

Lawrence's first middle eastern winter was the severest on record. For the first time in forty years snow covered the beach at Jebail. Miss Holmes caught influenza and on 18 February Lawrence accompanied her and Mrs. Rieder (the French teacher, who was to become a favoured correspondent) into Beirut, having said goodbye to Fareedah el-Akle and Omar, her Muslim assistant.† Miss el-Akle's account of his departure shows the impact of a personality that already created myths around it. Apparently the people of Jebail implored him not to risk the journey to Carchemish. 'He would only reply, "I must go, even if I have to cross the snow on sledges or walk in wooden shoes." How he got there will ever remain a mystery to us: Lawrence was the kind of man who could accomplish the apparently impossible, through that unconquerable spirit of his.'[18] In fact, a carriage took him and the two western ladies as far as the terminus; a tram then took them into Beirut where Miss Holmes planned on a few days' rest and Lawrence had to collect new *Iradés* from the British Consulate.

Hogarth was due on the 20th; Campbell Thompson, now engaged to be married, had been shopping for a piano to enliven the dig and had gone ahead to Aleppo. But the weather got worse. Snow blocked the ratchet-railway over the mountain behind Beirut; on one four-mile stretch it lay thirty feet deep. Sunshine over the weekend gave hope that the permanent way might be cleared in time. But it snowed again two days after Hogarth's arrival with Gregori, his sixty-year-old Cypriot headman.‡ Out of consideration for Gregori's health, Hogarth decided not to attempt to cross the mountains but instead to sail to Haifa and that southern spur of the railway which reached Damascus by way of Deraa. Lawrence had paid his own expenses out to Beirut. For the journey to Aleppo, Hogarth, or the British Museum, would now pay.

After a quick visit to the monastery on Mount Carmel, they took their

* When questioned by Liddell Hart, he was uncertain as to whether Medina, a holy city closed to non-Muslims, had been included.[16]

† Lawrence found it impossible to find suitable presents for her and Omar in Beirut. 'Fountain pens one cannot write Arabic with.'[17]

‡ Gregorios Antoniou of Larnaca was known by the vocative form of his name to his English employers. He wore the Ottoman fez and, owing to the technicalities of the British acquisition of Cyprus, retained Ottoman citizenship, which facilitated his travels with Hogarth.

seats in a first-class carriage to follow, in a reverse direction, the route Lawrence had walked in 1909. Nazareth pleased him no better than before. If ever his mother came out, he would let her see it only from some distance: 'it is then no uglier than Basingstoke, or very little, and the view from it, southwards over the plain, is beautiful.'[19] He would take her to the well at dusk, when the parasitic natives had left, and then return her to her tent.

From Beisan, at the head of the Vale of Esdraelon, the train followed the Jordan as far as Samakh at the southern tip of the Sea of Galilee. Here it turned east, to twist and turn up the gorge of a small river which had given its name to a great Arab victory over the Byzantines. The valley of the Yarmouk, where the railway crossed and recrossed savage defiles, was, with the junction at Deraa, to play an important role in Lawrence's later actions and dreams. The railway crossed the old pilgrim route to the Holy Cities of western Arabia, and Lawrence responded to it with characteristic exaggeration. 'Doughty is the only man who had been down it,' he wrote home, 'and written what he saw.' Lawrence was lucky to see the track which had been trodden by countless pilgrims from Anatolia, the Balkans and Syria in dramatic weather: Mount Hermon (likened in Arabic to a Sheikh, or Old Man) was white with snow; every wadi sulked under water. But the sun was shining as they ate lunch at Deraa's modern buffet. Hogarth, who spoke French, German, Italian, Greek and Turkish, showed off his languages.[20] Lawrence was always anxious to emulate, or excel, his heroes. The sight of the pilgrim route had revived the thought of competing with Doughty; Hogarth's performance impressed him so deeply that in later years he convinced many admirers that he was an extraordinary linguist.* This gift of convincing others was perhaps the rarer talent.

From Deraa the train chugged past boulders of black lava scattered on a waste of sand. This landscape, a refuge for outlaws and the western edge of the Jebel Druze, would have stirred his feeling for desolation if he could have seen it, just as the green oasis of Damascus would have been a delightful contrast. But the train arrived after dark and the travellers planned to push on at dawn. Luckily the bad weather held, giving Lawrence his first whole day in Damascus. In the souq he picked up a small blue, red and green Rhodian vase, ridiculously cheap, for his mother's drawing-

* Lionel Curtis, editor of *The Round Table*: 'He could learn a language in a fraction of the time an ordinary mortal would take.' [21] In fact, he was never interested in languages *per se*. He refused to use Urdu when in India on the grounds that it was 'a filthy language'.[22] Of the languages spoken by Hogarth at the Deraa buffet Lawrence knew French best, though his sad desire of 1912, 'I only wish I could speak French without wasting six months trying thereto,' (to Mrs. Rieder, *Letters*, 12.9.1912), was echoed as late as 1934: 'though I can read French readily, I never gained the power of speaking or writing.'[23] Ignorant of written Turkish and spoken German, he could pick out an Italian text with a dictionary. His Greek was literary and depended on cribs.

room.[24] This purchase, like that of the thirty seals bought for Hogarth in 1909, marks an aspect of Lawrence's middle eastern career unrelated to any acquisitive core in himself; from 1911 to 1914, he was repeatedly buying beautiful or unusual objects because Hogarth and the Ashmolean Museum were greedy for them, and on a lesser scale so were his parents.

Next day the archaeologists were again delayed; this time melting snow had washed away a stretch of rail near Homs. They reached Aleppo only on the night of 28 February. Here it took them nine days to assemble stores and the animals necessary to convey them to the site of the dig. As well as the provisions which Hogarth had ordered from England (including nine sorts of jam and three of tea) and those which they now bought in Aleppo, the exiled Oxonians carried with them food for their minds. Thompson had brought a Complete Shakespeare; Hogarth balanced Dante with French novels; Lawrence, influenced perhaps by Doughty's theory that English had deteriorated since *The Faerie Queene* went out of fashion, had a Complete Spenser. Not to be outdone by Thompson, who had arranged for the weekly despatch of a parcel of books, Lawrence decided to order such urgent pabulum as Francis Thompson, in English, Rabelais, in old French, and Virgil and Lucretius in Latin. One of Robert Louis Stevenson's works had already arrived for him at Aleppo.

Though the three men slept at Baron's, their headquarters was the British Consulate, ten minutes walk from the hotel in a diplomatic quarter on Aleppo's north-west outskirts. (The other states with consular representation in the city were France, Germany, Austria-Hungary, Spain, Portugal, Holland, Russia and the United States.) R. A. Fontana, appointed His Britannic Majesty's Consul in the wake of the Young Turk revolution, was, despite his surname and Guido and Tacita, his children, a British national; he was to become in some degree Lawrence's controller while Lawrence was often to use the Consulate as his address. And the Consul's wife, Winifred, became one of the few women to whose femininity Lawrence deferred. Apart from his extreme youthfulness (he looked to her no more than eighteen), he had initially made an unattractive impression: 'something uncouth in Lawrence's manner contrasting with a donnish precision of speech, chilled me.'[25] On that first occasion he had only accompanied his seniors to the Consulate on their insistence, and when they were all three invited to dine next evening, he pleaded his lack of dress clothes (he claimed to have lost them somewhere exotic) as an excuse not to attend. But Hogarth was not one to support such nonsense and in the event Lawrence proved, without being a conversational eunuch, that most agreeable of dinner guests, an attentive listener. His occasional shafts were the more effective for being carefully weighed, disconcerting and sudden and he took care not to aim them at his hostess, who became an admirer for life.

The Consulate was important to Hogarth for more than social relaxation. It was the hub of British Intelligence in northern Syria. After calling there, Hogarth could inform Kenyon on 2 March: 'It seems certain that the Baghdad Railway is going via Jerablus. Could you speak to Sir E. Grey [then Foreign Secretary] about the latter in view of possible complications with the Railway. If the company gets (as usual) a wide strip (10 kilometres or so) on either side of their line, it will include our site. But your rights to excavate it ought to be reserved and it would be easy in any pourparlers Grey may be engaged upon to put in a word to this effect. I think you would be wise to see him officially on the subject at once.' But a postscript shows that the information received from Fontana needed checking: 'Of course I cannot be quite sure of the exact point chosen for bridge-head.'[26]

Technological progress was shortly to revolutionalize travel in the area. A more or less punctual train service would cover the distance from Aleppo to the dig in a matter of six hours. But when the British party left Aleppo on 9th March 1911, they needed eleven baggage horses and ten camels to transport themselves and their supplies. Hogarth drove, walked and rode in turns. Thompson rode and walked. Lawrence walked, except when they had to cross on horseback a tributary of the Euphrates engorged with melting snow. Their journey took two days. All the second afternoon the white summits of the Taurus (that icy barrier between upland Anatolia and the Arab south) were in distant view. The wind which blew from them kept the temperature in the low forties.

Except for these mountains to their left, the scenery was in general monotonous. They were skirting that vast desert which reaches as far as Arabia to the south and which to the south-east becomes the great sump which drains the Anatolian and Iranian plateaux through Euphrates and Tigris into the Persian Gulf. In this steppe the occasional hills, the tells that marked ancient cities, were the more impressive for the general flatness. A shallow plateau dropped slowly, layer by layer, towards the Euphrates, until it reached the new village of Upper Jerablus, a cluster of some forty houses with a clean, fresh spring. The Euphrates, muddy brown from silt mixed with melted snow, flowed half a mile to the east, washing, on its way south, the great mound they had come to dig.

Until the decision to reopen the dig (followed as twin by twin by the arrival of the railway), a Liquorice Company provided the one local industry; its owner, an Arab Christian, was virtual lord of the 200 villagers. Otherwise the Arabs who comprised the population of Upper and Lower Jerablus (the latter just two miles south-east, and on the river bank) grazed their animals on the grassy mound and cultivated private strips of river-watered land. The village headman was the Company's agent. With the hospitality of the east—which is not above noticing that the guests of today may be the employers of tomorrow—he had put the Company's one-storeyed, stone-built house at the archaeologists' disposal. Once Hogarth had approved it (and there was no better alternative), a score of villagers joined the men who had accompanied the caravan from Aleppo in clearing the rooms, choc-a-bloc as they were with camel-hides, corn, poplar poles and lentils. In a week the house had been converted to the simulacrum of a western dwelling. Thompson sowed packets of vegetables and flowers in the yard which surrounded the house on three sides; the smell of liquorice wafted pleasantly through the windows. But the house retained an inconvenience of design. The three bedrooms led off each other in a row. Lawrence occupied the largest, but it was the one in the middle.

Hogarth was pressed to get back to Oxford; he could afford no more than six weeks. On the day following their arrival some hundred diggers were enrolled at a daily wage of eight piastres. The archaeologists then turned to the great mound whose treasures they had come to find.

Known locally as the *Kalaat*, it was a grass-grown citadel some fifteen minutes' walk from the upper village. Most impressive from the river, where it loomed like an acropolis, it had for centuries caught the attention of westerners travelling through Syria. A Fellow of Exeter College, Henry Maundrell, had visited Jerabolus, as he called it, on 20 April 1699, and added a description of what he saw to the third edition of his *Journey from Aleppo to Jerusalem*. Maundrell estimated the circuit of the mound at 2,500 paces and noticed, at the foot of the citadel, 'carved on a large stone a Beast resembling a Lyon with a bridle in his mouth; and I believe anciently a person sitting on it. But the stone is in that part now broken away: and the Tail of the Beast was couped.' Other visitors to describe the site included Sir Henry Layard, the discoverer of Nineveh, who told the British Museum as early as 1850 that 'after the Khabour he hoped to visit Carchemish, "where there are ruins." '[27] But not till the 1870s did Professor A. H. Sayce identify pictographs in a language plainly neither Egyptian nor Babylonian as Hittite. Layard intervened with the Ottoman government, and a *firman* having been secured, Consul Henderson of Aleppo negotiated the purchase of part of the mound. Ambiguities about which portion of the mound had been bought, and on what terms, were later to cause Hogarth's team some problems, but the first frenzied weeks of attacking its surface were untroubled by this kind of worry.

Hogarth's chief experience of excavation had been at Ephesus in western Turkey. The story was told of him—and it was the kind of story that would not have been told of all archaeologists—that having located the site of the Temple of many-breasted Artemis, he had sunk a shaft into the site only to see his most precious discovery slowly sink into a morass. His autobiographical writings, such as the travel book which

Lawrence admired, show him as largely concerned in acquiring portable objects. His present attack was inspired by the desire to find, and find quickly, some exciting antikas, rather than by the more restrained ambition to analyse and understand a site whose lowest stratum had been laid down 2,000 years before the Christian era. This desire was not only promoted by his own approach to archaeology. He knew his patrons. To get further funds he must add to their collections.

As the picks and spades of the Jerablus workmen bit into the mound—two generations earlier the site of their own houses—they first encountered the detritus of the recent past. That meant, in archaeological terms, the centuries since the Ottoman Turks had begun in the fifteenth century to consolidate most of the Near East into their empire. Below this Ottoman layer they could expect to find fragments from the centuries when an Arab caliphate based on Baghdad (in those times reached by the great canal linking Euphrates to Tigris) shared a frontier with menaced Byzantium. Arab pottery and glass were both rare and prized. Beneath these, mosaic floors could be expected then the pillars and naked statues of the Roman Empire. Linking first Hellas with Italy and then Christianity with both, the Romans had secured a long period of stability. Their interest in the Euphrates crossing—which they knew as Europos—was accentuated by the fear that the great threat to the Empire would come, not as it in fact did, from the Germanic north, but the Parthian east. Far below the Roman strata (which, further to confuse the diggers, had cannibalized what went before) the British excavators would reach the provincial Hittite city whose monumental ways, palaces and temples would finally justify their presence. The existence of Hittite civilization had only been recognized in the late nineteenth century and its history was still as obscure as its language. To reach this Hittite layer would take them just over a year.[28]

9

WITH THE start of these labours in March 1911, Lawrence entered on a life as stratified as the mound. The top layers, which displayed his donnish precision of speech and western interests, are unlikely to have been those which later convinced him that 'those days in Carchemish were the best.'[1]

First under David Hogarth (who stayed until 20th April 1911), then under Campbell Thompson (who in July left to get married and was not to return) and finally under Leonard Woolley (who took over in March 1912 and remained in charge of the dig till the outbreak of world war in August 1914 enforced its cessation), Lawrence worked at least formally as assistant archaeologist. For this work he was paid according to the standards of the day. His main source of income was the Demyship payable in gold sovereigns which Hogarth had procured for him from Magdalen. And Hogarth was to continue to look out for his protégé's interests. When the Carchemish results were to be published, he insisted that Lawrence should receive a fifth of the remuneration,[2] and when there was doubt if Magdalen could renew its Demyship after 1914 (there being no precedent for such a renewal), Kenyon, as director of the British Museum, was reminded that 'it will be necessary to raise his salary.' After 1912 Lawrence received fifteen shillings a day while digging.* He thus could count on some £15 a month. This was relatively good pay. (As late as July 1914 Woolley was proposing to engage a Cambridge graduate for as little as five shillings a day besides expenses.)[4] For Hogarth the funding of the excavations was an abiding problem and this need for finance explains the feverish quest for discoveries which could be written up in *The Times*. In fact, only the subvention of an anonymous donor persuaded the British Museum to continue its support.

The digging season was elastic. It could be shorter or longer depending on the weather in a particular year and on the wishes of the man in

* So Lawrence told his biographer Liddell Hart. His recollection is confirmed by an unsigned letter, probably from Kenyon, to the Treasury of 18.10.1913. This puts the terms of employment for Mr. C. L. Woolley and Mr. T. E. Lawrence as '30/- and 15/- a day respectively, in addition to living and travelling expenses. In the interval between autumn and spring seasons they are willing to remain in the East on half pay.'[3]

charge.* It was limited by the demands of the local harvest, which drew off the workers from June to September, and the bad weather customary between November, when the rains started, and March when the snows melted. These factors left the spring (April and May) and the autumn (October and part of November) as the seasons when most work was done.

For the arts graduate of Lawrence's generation, archaeology played much the same role as teaching to the generation of Evelyn Waugh, Isherwood and Auden, and Lawrence was somewhat unwilling to be dubbed an archaeologist. After nearly three years at Carchemish he lamented to Richards his classification as 'an ordinary archaeologist. I fought very hard, at Oxford and after going down, to avoid being labelled: but the insurance people have nailed me down, now.'[5] His interest in the subject was akin to his earlier pursuit of history or the architecture of the Crusades. It was a means to an end. The Hogarth he revered was not on site long; Campbell Thompson was not someone whose shadow eclipsed him and Hogarth had probably confided to Lawrence the opinion of Thompson's judgement he had expressed to Kenyon.† Lawrence, on the other hand, had failed to master cuneiform at the American Mission School in Jebail. 'My eyes got tired easily with the horrible Arabic type in common use: and with the cuneiform on top. So I gave up reading altogether, that they might be fit for the strong sunlight we expect out here . . . it limited my learning of Arabic very seriously.'[7] Except for three weeks in Egypt and a hasty trip through the Negeb on the eve of war, Carchemish was to embody his one serious involvement with the assessment of the past.

In the same way as he valued his trips into the surrounding countryside by the seals he bought from the peasants, he, like his mentor, valued a dig by the objects it produced rather than the light it shed on history, and the urge to impress Hogarth propelled him into the search for small, beautiful and transportable objects. When it was suggested that he might excavate in Bahrein (on the supposition that this Persian Gulf island had acted as a staging-post for the mysterious originators of Pharaonic civilization)‡ he reacted typically: 'as Bahrein is nominally British, I suppose we might carry off the stuff.'[8] The stocking of two Museums in

* In a letter of 20 May 1912, Lawrence wrote hopefully of digging, and therefore earning, for 8 months of the coming year. But these hopes were not even approximately fulfilled. In 1913 digging started on 4th March and broke off on 18th May, to resume around 6th October and to end finally on 4th December.

† Hogarth to Kenyon, Aleppo, 24.4.11: 'He [the Thompson he was leaving in charge] has not much judgement and his editing of results will need assistance.'[6]

‡ Many Egyptologists of that period assumed that the glories of Nilotic civilization must have derived from creative invaders: similarly the rebirth of modern Egypt was attributed to the French, who invaded under Napoleon in 1798, or the British, who occupied the country in 1882.

Britain—the British in Bloomsbury, the Ashmolean at Oxford—was the major aim of his endeavour. A breathless letter to Hogarth at the Ashmolean, dated merely 'End of Feb.,' shows how much Lawrence enjoyed the clandestine side of such an approach to the past. Local tomb-robbers had broken into a necropolis not far from Carchemish. Lawrence, who joined in the fun, describes it as 'a Hittite cemetery of the last period with Roman shaft tombs in between. The Hitt. graves were full of great bronze* spears and axes and swords, that the wretches have broken up and thrown away, because Madame Koch, who is doing the dig, didn't buy such things. I got some good fibulae which are yours, and not Kenyon's this time at all events . . . (18 miles away) much better than the B.M. ones, some bracelets and ear-rings of bronze, a curious pot or two . . . and as a sideline, some Roman glazed bottles, with associated Greek pottery, and a pleasant little lot of miscellanea . . . tomorrow I return there to gather up, I hope, Hittite bronze weapons in sheaves:—unless the police get there first. It is exciting digging: a plunge down a shaft at night, the smashing of a stone door, and the hasty shovelling of all objects into a bag by lamplight.'

Lawrence's study of medieval architecture had not prepared him for the excavation of a provincial city of a little known culture. His schoolboy hobbies, involving the finding and repair of pots, were more useful. The photography which he had learnt from his father and which he had used for his thesis, could be invaluable on a dig. His ability to arouse enthusiasm had been shown in his handling of his Sunday School class at Oxford; his travels showed that he could get on with those of a different background to his own. If he claimed to have been shot at and robbed during his first Syrian journey, he had also endured quilts stuffed with fleas and a meagre diet. In selecting Lawrence the perceptive Hogarth had taken such aptitudes into account and they formed the basis of Lawrence's participation in the dig. His first responsibility was the pottery. 'For most of the day we are not in the least necessary' he wrote that first March,[9] when Gregori was shrieking at the Arab diggers in bad Turkish and Hogarth was controlling where they dug; 'and in those times I play with the pottery, which Mr. Hogarth has handed over to me as my particular preserve.' Lawrence used the word *play* advisedly. Yet however light-hearted, even frivolous, his approach, it did not render his services useless. A poet can intuit what an academic reaches slowly.† Lawrence's remarkable memory could enable him to fit a fragment of a Hittite inscription, jigsaw fashion, to a piece unearthed a year before; or he could

* P. R. S. Moorey, who first published the full text of this letter (*Levant*, VII, 1975), comments: 'This is clearly an error for iron.'

† I owe to the late Dr. Gervase Mathew the observation that in Byzantine studies the intuitive awareness of the poet W. B. Yeats anticipated the work of a generation of scholars.

recall with confident assurance a potsherd which Woolley, not he, had discovered and noted, and recall its stratum and associations. But though Woolley valued this flair, he was to qualify Lawrence's work as 'curiously erratic'. Asked on one occasion to compose a detailed description of a row of sculpted slabs, he duly submitted a notebook. On reading it, Woolley found each slab dismissed with ridicule.[10]

Lawrence's skill as a photographer may have explained his impatience with this particular chore. The value of his instant records was beyond dispute. His letters home were full of accounts of the five cameras he used on the dig—his own new one being the best—as well as requests for new film. 'There is the misfortune that only *Cristoid* films stand heat.'[11]

But Lawrence's influence over the workmen was even more important. There was little to incline the local Arabs to work amicably with moustachioed Kurds or Aleppo riff-raff. When Hogarth and the experienced Gregori left, Thompson and Lawrence immediately ran into labour trouble. They sacked some thirty of the ringleaders, which Lawrence says ' "pacified" the rest.'[12] But stern measures alone could not have maintained a contented dig. Lawrence's power to communicate greater enthusiasm than he personally felt was used on a hundred or more illiterate diggers. They attacked the mound in a Sports Day atmosphere. Discoveries were proclaimed by the firing of revolvers. Finds were rewarded. Lawrence's skill at maintaining excitement on the dig was the more remarkable for his own dislike of competitive games.

Furthermore, whatever his attitude to archaeology, Lawrence had powerful reasons for wishing the excavations at Carchemish to continue. In return for his help with the pottery, the photographic records and the local labour, he lived a more expansive life than he could have afforded in England. As a history teacher in a secondary school, or even as a don, he would have met fewer interesting people and have had less time to himself; he would scarcely have become so swiftly an important figure in his surroundings. The first season at Carchemish (which ended in July 1911) was experimental. Whether it would be followed by a second was all the time in doubt. The finds were still disappointing (however much Lawrence enlarged them in his letters) and a factor in Thompson's decision to resign was the lack of cuneiform inscriptions important enough to make his name.[13]

Living conditions that first year were less pleasant than they were later to be. The Liquorice Company's warehouse was as full of holes as gruyère cheese; at night birds, vermin, even village dogs, invaded the rooms. Only Lawrence, trained by his unusual sleeping habits in the Oxford bungalow, slept, he claimed, through the nightly disturbance. The archaeologists were fed on imported tinned food mixed with badly cooked local produce. Lawrence had watched Miss Holmes's cook at

Jebail and believed that what he had learnt now came in usefully. The thin village bread soon palled. From their English flour Haj Waheed, their village servant, produced something with the texture of rubber sheeting; his cakes were halfway between sponge rubber and custard.[14] The Haj was not to blame. He was trying to bake bread without an oven. Lawrence experimented with constructing one from a giant water jar. But the diplomatic Hogarth, not the inventive Lawrence, solved their problem. The commander of the military garrison at Birejik (the local chief town, some twenty miles upstream on the eastern bank) agreed to supply them with the wholesome bread of the Ottoman soldiers: 'thick, brown, wholemeal stuff, rather like the ideal bread of the Limousin, but darker in colour, and without the very slight sourness of the French stuff.'

At this time the archaeologists had penetrated some ten feet into the gigantic mound. To go deeper they had to clear the rough stone walls of the late Roman town. One early find was an attractive cup of Arab ware; Lawrence gave it a twelfth-century date. But by the time they received their first distinguished visitors—the aged Professor Sayce, pioneer of Hittite studies, in mid-April, and Gertrude Bell in mid-May—they had more to display: slabs of warriors holding captives and chopped off heads; a five-foot-high relief in basalt of lion-headed human figures; a Roman bronze coin. At some eighteen feet into the mound, they struck a basalt pedestal that might have supported a large copper bowl, or a statue. 'Lawrence has identified the right half of the top of the broken basalt sculpture on the West of the stairway and it has been put into place,' Thompson wrote to Kenyon of the British Museum on 3rd May; two weeks later he posted Kenyon two of Lawrence's drawings of lions. Their technique of excavation bore a certain resemblance to children plunging hands in a Christmas bran-tub.

Gertrude Bell—'scholar, poet, historian, archaeologist, art critic, mountaineer, explorer, gardener, naturalist, distinguished servant of the State'[15]—was twenty years older than Lawrence. In this late spring of 1911 (she had hoped to catch Hogarth at Carchemish) she was on her way west from a ride which had taken her to Babylon and Persia. But her arrival was so long delayed that when she reached Birejik the thermometer was pushing towards 90° and the Turkish commandant informed her that Hogarth had been gone a month. Miss Bell made light of the hot, five-hour ride to Jerablus. With Campbell Thompson she found 'a young man called Lawrence,' of whom she prophesied, 'he is going to make a traveller.'[16] The two showed her their diggings and she says she spent a pleasant day with them.

It is doubtful if the respected author of *Between the Desert and The Sown* guessed the effect her arrival would have on the two young men.

The tall, experienced, Miss Bell had recently visited German excavations at Kalaat Shergat where she had found 'great profit from endless talks with Dr. Andrae. His knowledge of Mesopotamian problems is so great and his views so brilliant and comprehensive.'[17] She was outspoken enough to tell Thompson that his archaeological methods were by comparison prehistoric. Lawrence probably exaggerated his account of how he and Thompson counter-attacked. 'We had to squash her with a display of erudition,' he wrote home. 'She was taken (in 5 minutes) over Byzantine, Crusader, Roman, Hittite & French architecture (my part) and over Greek folk-lore, Assyrian architecture, & Mesopotamian Ethnology (by Thompson); prehistoric pottery & telephoto lenses, Bronze Age metal technique, Meredith, Anatole France and the Octobrists (by me): the Young Turk movement, the construct state in Arabic, the price of riding camels, Assyrian burial-customs, and German methods of excavation with the Baghdad railway (by Thompson). This was a kind of hors d'oeuvre: and when it was over (she was getting more respectful) we settled down each to seven or eight subjects & questioned her upon them. She was quite glad to have tea after an hour and a half, & on going told Thompson that he had done wonders in his digging in the time, and that she thought *we* had got everything out of the place that could possibly have been got: she particularly admired the completeness of our note-books. So we did for her.'[18] Anti-feminism and a sense of social inferiority (Miss Bell was the grand-daughter of Sir Lowthian Bell, Bart., iron-master and Fellow of the Royal Society) probably provoked what was hardly a hospitable reception. Even her gift of two volumes of Meredith could not soothe feathers ruffled by a superior female whom Lawrence described to his mother as 'about 36, [she was 43] not beautiful (except with a veil on, perhaps).' Ten years later he was still nursing the episode. The Arabs at Jerablus, he would joke, had thought that Miss Bell had come expressly to marry him. To assuage their wrath if she left without doing so he had explained that Miss Bell was far too plain for his tastes and that, since she was the rebuffed party, she should be allowed to depart discreetly. That Gertrude Bell 'equally enjoyed the joke against herself'[19] shows that she possessed one quality lacking in the jester, but she had probably relished the episode less than she pretended. When she next visited the Middle East, in December 1913, she travelled directly from Beirut and Damascus to Baghdad without calling at Carchemish.[20]*

Lawrence was not in the habit of recording stories against himself. A few survive through posthumous release; his letters, which refer to most

* Lawrence's irritation seems to have survived her death. 'She reminded me,' he wrote after the posthumous publication of her *Letters*, 'in one dress, of a blue jay. Her clothes and colours were always wrong.'[21]

other things, never refer to them.* This was in part the effect of his curious physique, with the junction of massive, high-browed head and small, spare frame, on his personality. Little men rarely like to be laughed at by the tall. But Miss Bell's injudicious remarks gave real cause for worry. Lawrence reported to Hogarth in a way that significantly differs from the account he gave his mother. 'Gerty has gone back to her tents,' he begins, reducing the enemy through flippancy, but then stresses that the thrust of her criticism was at Hogarth. 'She called him [Thompson] prehistoric! (apropos of your digging methods, till she saw their result.)'[23]

Hogarth was vulnerable. His approach to archaeology can be inferred from the three lines about the German diggings which David Garnett struck from his edition of Lawrence's letter home: *where they lay down gravel paths, wherever they want to prove an ancient floor,* & *where they pile up their loose stones into walls of palaces.*[24] The bran-pie approach, in contrast with the reconstructive method which aimed at preserving the ruin as something permanently intelligible, could turn a site into a shambles in its concentration on pretty, transportable objects. Yet the second method had its own perils. Dr. Arthur Evans was so afraid of leaving Knossos a mass of rubble that he reconstructed the mysterious Minoan building in a style reminiscent of twentyish modernism.

A further sentence in the letter to Hogarth—*it would have been most annoying if she had denounced our methods in print*—reveals Lawrence's anxiety. The question of a second season at Carchemish was at issue. In a letter which had arrived on the eve of Miss Bell's visit Hogarth had expressed his confidence that there could be one, unless the first failed to uncover some public building of importance. *The Times* was due to publish his article on Carchemish on 1st July. But if Hogarth's methods came under attack, if the dig ceased, Lawrence would not only be out of work, but cut off from levels of satisfaction he was beginning to savour.

Carchemish was genuine cover for a second activity, references to which spluttered among the squibs with which the two young men had bombarded Miss Bell. Lawrence had mentioned telephoto lenses while Thompson revealed his knowledge of the Baghdad Railway. Lawrence took up the theme of his camera in the same letter which described the visit. 'My camera is proving a good one; and the telephoto has been used several times of late: It acts (at a couple of miles) rather better than the naked eye.'[25] The fragility of bridges, the collapsability of culverts, were fitter subjects for long-distance lenses than excavations.

* There is no reference, for example, to the occasion reported by Leonard Woolley when some Kurdish girls, possibly seeing their first European, immodestly pulled open his shirt to see if his skin was white all over; 'and soon, with shrieks of laughter, they were all about him determined to see more, until he escaped almost stripped. He could not take it as a joke, and would never go that way again; and though he did tell me the story it was only some time afterwards, and then with cold indignation.'[22]

Britain's rulers took the keenest interest in the Berlin to Baghdad Railway. Their empire, the largest the world had seen, no longer seemed invulnerable, the Boer War having exposed its military weakness as well as the political opportunities for determined rivals. In itself Baghdad was unimportant. A sleepy provincial town, its two sides joined by a pontoon bridge, it preserved few relics of its caliphal past. The railway's ultimate destination—Basra, the city of Sinbad the sailor, at the head of the Persian Gulf—mattered more to the British. At this time the existence of the world's richest reservoir of oil was not known to most politicians and clubmen in the Mall and St. James. Instead, their interest was strategic. They, their relations, their friends, had been shaped by the study of the Greek and Roman classics. Thucydides' account of the war which ended the golden age of Hellas held ominous pointers. If Europe was the modern Greece, England, maritime and democratic, stood for the defeated Athens, and Germany, land-based and authoritarian, stood for victorious Sparta. In the slow extension of the railway towards the Gulf, Germany was forging a means to circumvent British sea power and bypass the Suez Canal. It was unlikely that Germany would use Basra to threaten the British position in India; but with its use the Ottoman dominions could become a German equivalent of the Indian Empire. This had been a German aim since the Kaiser in his youth had befriended Sultan Abdul Hamid, and the Kaiser had emphasized it by his 1898 visit to Turkey and Palestine when he had declared himself the protector of Islam and ended his flirtation with Dr. Theodor Herzl and political Zionism. The railway which already linked Berlin with Angora (the future Ankara) and Konya (once the Seljuk capital but now the Canterbury of a dervish order) enforced this diplomacy. An agreement reached in 1902 had settled the route by which the railway should be tunnelled south through the Taurus mountains. From a junction at Aleppo, which became the lynchpin of Turkey's communications south of Anatolia, the railway would push towards the Euphrates and pass by way of Carchemish to Nisibin and Mosul. From Mosul it would follow the Tigris as far as Baghdad, thence to swing south along the Euphrates valley to Basra and the sea. The completed network, with spurs to Adana and Urfa, would comprise some 1,550 miles between Bosphorus and Gulf. The Germans shared the concession with the Imperial Ottoman Bank, a French but not a governmental concern.

The Intelligence work for which Carchemish provided cover had two main concerns, each connected with the possibility of war. (The railway's physical progress, once its route had been published, required no monitoring beyond the competence of a resolute consul.) For Turkey, and whoever happened to be her allies, the railway would represent a vital artery. Conceivably her allies might still be British: even now there were hopes that British influence, symbolized by a naval mission, might be re-established. But should Turkey join Germany in war against Britain, the risks and opportunities would alike be great. The railway thus demanded constant assessment. Captain A. F. Townshend had been seconded from the Scottish Rifles to act as Military Consul in Turkey from 1903 to 1906. A volume of his memoirs published in 1910 described the tour he had made in the spring of 1904 to check on the railway as it approached the Taurus.[26] The Ottoman authorities, as well as the German and Italian engineers, allowed him to be 'the first person, unconnected with the enterprise, to travel on the Baghdad railway,' the new stretch leading towards the mountains. The Military Consul's account clarifies the kind of thing he was exploring. 'The line is constructed in the best and strongest style, the iron sleepers being secured to large pieces of metal buried three or four feet beneath them, so that tearing up sleepers to destroy the line in case of war would be attended with great labour and difficulty.' It was already possible to 'go first class with every comfort from London to Bulgurlu.' As the railway pushed south it would cross vulnerable bridges, penetrate blockable tunnels. Potential enemies would be living near its track. Lawrence's frequent hikes into the country surrounding Jerablus had the same purpose as Townshend's more public journeys. Hogarth's investment in cameras, lenses, film, as well as his insistence that Lawrence should get to know the local inhabitants, was linked with this purpose.

Lawrence's reports and pictures like much Intelligence activity were ultimately futile. War was to break out before the completion of the tunnels through the Taurus. All freight sent south of the mountains had to be laboriously off-loaded and transported by carts, with the same effect as if tunnels had pierced the passes and then been sabotaged. In the event, it was the Pilgrim Railway which ran south to Medina which was to be the subject of harassment, not the commercial railway which ran within whistle cry of Lawrence's Carchemish bedroom.

But an experiment fruitless in one field can be fruitful in another. Lawrence learnt lessons near Jerablus which he was to apply elsewhere. In the vicinity of Jerablus he could study a compost of divisive groups, whose irritations, feuds, and gripes could be fused into a common anti-Ottoman purpose. Jerablus marked indeed a four-point frontier. Running north-south, the Euphrates formed the old boundary between the Roman west and the continental east. Horizontally, Jerablus marked a frontier between the Kurds whom indigence was forcing south-west from Anatolia and the Arabs of the desert south. 'Over this wide tract,' one of the archaeologists was to write, 'wander the Milli-Kurds. Less differentiated than most Kurdish tribes from the old Persian stock, they are newcomers here, whose migration indeed is scarcely ended yet, for they are still by slow degrees pushing before them farther and farther west the Arabs who had held this North Mesopotamian fringe, and villages which but ten years ago were purely Arab are to-day in Kurdish hands.'[27]

Sultan Abdul Hamid, who had used Islam to hold his menaced empire together, gave the Kurds a favoured status, encouraging them to set up vigilante regiments against suspected elements. The Armenians were their prime victims: a Christian nation scattered throughout Anatolia and present in considerable numbers in Lawrence's area. Another mistrusted minority, the Yezidis, believed by their neighbours to worship the Devil in the guise of a Peacock, inhabited an oblong range of hills between Syria and Mesopotamia.

In collecting information, Lawrence had a two-fold mission: to familiarize himself with the territory through which the railway would advance, and to assess the local resentments and passions. His complex nature qualified him for the work: a cast of mind, linked to its owner's aggressive shyness, which thought always in terms of attack and defence; a central core that lacked positive beliefs and so found it easy to assume attitudes not his own; a distaste for self which could find in assimilation to aliens an escape, not a punishment; or if a punishment, then one sought more keenly than pleasure. Lawrence lacked only one skill of the Intelligence operative: he never learnt to be discreet. The traces of Hogarth's secretive career have been all but effaced; Lawrence on the other hand broadcast allusions to what he was doing. Within three weeks of his arrival at Jerablus he told his mother, 'Mr. Hogarth thinks my idea of patronizing the Soleyb, instead of the Arab, promising, both in security, and novelty. They are an interesting people: however no hurry about that, with Carchemish and military architecture and above all the necessary Arabic first.'[28] The Soleyb were metal-working nomads whose skills suggested ideas for their potential use. And another unguarded letter, three months later, established that his interest in Arabic transcended its usefulness in controlling the hired labour. 'I may live in this district through the winter: it strikes me that the strongly-dialectical Arabic of the villagers would be as good as a disguise to me.'[29] A disguise, like a telephoto lens, was of more use to an Intelligence agent than to an archaeologist. A year later, when the railway had arrived at Jerablus, he told his youngest brother how the movements of the German engineers affected his own. 'What more, puffet? The railway is not going to do any more digging for a month or so, and not very much even then for a bit, so I am going into Aleppo, and there will move up to some hill-top, either at Beilan with Mr. Fontana, or in the Lebanon with Miss Holmes and the Beyrout Consul.'[30]

The work of the German engineers did provoke legitimate archaeological concern. In Lawrence's first year at Carchemish an anonymous letter to *The Times* suggested that the Berlin to Baghdad Railway was likely to demolish both Carchemish and Tel Ahmar, another archaeological site near the Euphrates. The German consul in Aleppo protested to his British confrère but from the highest levels of British diplomacy came the suggestion that Mr. Hogarth should maintain a representative on the spot to prevent possible damage.[31] Yet British interests sometimes coincided with German. The excavations produced unsightly and useless masses of rubble. The British wanted to get rid of them, the Germans to use them on their railway. Thus Hogarth could describe Lawrence as 'apparently hobnobby with the Baghdad Railway engineers'[32] a couple of months after Lawrence had reported to him that, although the Germans were locally disliked, they were going to bridge the Euphrates south of the mound, which would not be interfered with. A month later Lawrence himself was describing the Germans as very friendly, 'for we are allowing them to clear away our dump-heaps of last year and this year free of charge . . . The railway is too far away to disturb us.'[33] The higher wages paid by the Germans, with other factors, shaded the picture; the shadows were to be heightened in accounts of the period written after the war; but Lawrence was never to share the dislike of Germans which became widespread among his generation.* When masks could be discarded, he was to be candid about his interest in the Railway and not pretend that it had been prompted by fears of damage to the mound. While stating that his prime purpose for living in Syria had been scholarly, he emphasized that 'incidentally he saw many other things. From Carchemish he had watched the construction of the Baghdad railway with his own eyes, and thus had the keener perception of its potential menace to the outposts of Britain.'[35]

As soon as Thompson had departed, Lawrence set off on a new walking tour. He felt a strong need to do something dramatic, to make important finds. A recent telegram from the British Museum had made plain 'they are so disappointed at our results that there will be no second season.'[36] His walk was to take him from Tel Ahmar (at the confluence of the Sajur with the Euphrates, a short distance south of Jerablus) north-east across the plain to Seruj (where he claims to have asked after his camera) and then by carriage to Urfa. His idiosyncratic methods of travel were justified by their utility for the gathering of information. 'Particularly, my poverty let me learn the masses, from whom the wealthy traveller was cut off by his money and attendants.'[37]† From Urfa he walked south to

* 'Lawrence always, so far as I know, spoke in kindly terms about Germany; often with admiration:' Robert Graves.[34]

† Apart from the obvious dig at those who had travelled the Levant in a more comfortable fashion, the sentence may give the modern reader pause. Influenced by the popularization of Mao Tse Tung's ideas, he may wonder if Lawrence had inadvertently omitted the word *from* from before the *masses*. An Arab writer, Mr. Suleiman Mousa, seems to have read the English in this corrected sense; he refers to Lawrence as attributing his

Harran (the classical Carrhae), then back via Seruj to Birejik for five further days in the hilly region to the west of the Euphrates. The walk could not be compared with his great tramp of 1909 nor with the winter expedition through the Taurus which Mark Sykes had described in *Dar ul-Islam* (1904). But its sixteen days ended in his physical collapse. He had managed to photograph three historical sites—Urfa, Harran and to the west of the Euphrates, Rum Kalaat; he had resumed contact with men he had met during the mysterious last phase of the 1909 journey: he had bought pots and seals; but by 28th July he was back at the village with abscesses, headaches and fainting spells. When early on Saturday, 29 July, he went to measure a floor on the mound, he had a sudden attack of the dysentery he had escaped in 1909. He lay down in a lonely place at about 8 a.m., feeling weak and ill. Sheikh Hamoudi, (or 'the Hoja') one of the senior diggers and acting foreman in Gregori's absences, rescued him after more than six hours. Although Lawrence had described him the day before as 'a terrible bore conversationally,'[39] the Hoja took him into his house and fed him on arrowroot and milk. With some difficulty (and apparently one serious row with his host over the loan of a horse) he caught the train from Aleppo to Damascus and sailed from Beirut for England (after calling on Miss Holmes at Jebail) on the 12th. The July walk had taught him more about the limits of his physique than about archaeology. His dysentery and general exhaustion kept him in Oxford (which he had reached by 26 August) until his doctor reluctantly adjudged him fit, in early December, for a new stage in Hogarth's programme.

---

contentment to his poverty, 'which forced him to mix with the people and learn from them.'[38] But Lawrence meant what he wrote: he had learnt the masses as he might have learnt Turkish or the violin.

10

KITCHENER, A SOLDIER who had studied Arabs as closely as he had studied war, in 1911 succeeded Sir Eldon Gorst as Britain's plenipotentiary in Egypt. The unmarried conqueror of the Sudan was installed at the Residency in Cairo by Christmas Day, when he entertained a party of distinguished British guests.[1] He was in Egypt throughout January; before he left for the Sudan on 12 February, he received in audience Amir Abdullah, the second son of the Sharif of Mecca.[2] Since Lawrence, too, was in Egypt from early in January until 2 February, it is tempting to speculate that an unpublicized reason for Hogarth sending him to Egypt was to introduce him to the most influential Englishman between London and Delhi. But even if Lawrence had come without Hogarth's introduction, Kitchener was the kind of man who would have given a young caller from Syria ten minutes of his time. After Kitchener was dead, Lawrence was twice to claim that he had indeed met him before the War. One account dated their meeting to 1913; in another he claimed to have warned Kitchener of French ambitions in Syria only to have the Field-Marshal end the interview with the prediction that within three years there would be a world war. ' "So run along, young man, and dig before it rains." '[3]*

Ostensibly Lawrence was going to Egypt to acquire new archaeological skills. Hogarth cannot have taken Gertrude Bell's implied criticisms lightly. If Lawrence could pick up something of the approach to excavation of Flinders Petrie (who has been regarded as the originator of systematic Egyptology and who also had links with the Ashmolean Museum), so much the better for his work, open and covert, at Carchemish.

Returning to the Middle East in December, Lawrence had first gone back to Jerablus, travelling by way of Port Said and Beirut. He needed to check on what the Germans were up to as well as to initiate plans for a

* Clement Laar's *Kamp in der Wüste* has a circumstantial account of Lawrence meeting Kitchener, by invitation, at the Army and Navy Club in London in late 1912. The book, which embodies an elaborate attack on International Finance, gives no source for the story. It was published in Berlin by Paul Neff Verlag in 1936.

building to house the expedition since Campbell Thompson had fallen foul of Tonman Brothers, the Liquorice merchants whose warehouse the archaeologists had used their first season.

Lawrence was trying to do too much too quickly. He was overspending. Urgent appeals to his family for £15, or if possible £20, were met: the larger sum was waiting for him at Cook's when he reached Cairo on 6 January. But he was disappointed in his hopes of digging at Heliopolis, just outside the capital. Instead, Petrie, who was himself recovering from an illness and whose wife was due in Alexandria on the 9th,[4] directed him to Kafr Ammar, on the west bank of the Nile some fifty miles south of Cairo. He only had time to glimpse the capital's Arab architecture—he found it 'most glorious'—before catching the train.

Lawrence's letters, from his three weeks' stay on the Petrie dig, project defensive spleen, in the manner of the shy, on to those more experienced than himself.[5] Dismissing Mrs. Petrie as 'a novelty in camp,' he reduces Petrie himself by descriptions intended to make his readers smile. White-haired, grey-bearded, excitable, Petrie is portrayed as a man of rigid systems, knowing the right way to dig a temple, or brush the teeth, the right number of sugar lumps to take with tea, or what jam goes with potted tongue. Lawrence reassured Hogarth that Petrie's methods were slapdash compared with those at Carchemish. But his claim that ' "we" have stumbled on what is probably the richest and largest prehistoric cemetery in Egypt' shows that he learned little Egyptology. 'Prehistoric' can only mean, in Egyptian terms, predynastic, and his excited account of wooden coffins, twenty bedsteads and much bronze must refer to a later period. Egyptian achievements in any case failed to impress him. He found 'very distinct influences of Mesopotamian art in the carvings' while 'the gradual realization of the barrenness of Egyptian art after the Pyramid time has removed all my wish to dig things Egyptian.' He was echoing his mentor. In his travel book Hogarth had belittled the heritage of Memphis and Karnak compared with that of Athens and Rome. 'The thrill which we feel when we credit the Pharaonic architects with lost arts and more than human ingenuity is born of pure fancy; Karnak, impressive and grandiose in an Egyptian twilight, is an agglomeration of architectural absurdities; the familiar pylons of the New Empire and the Ptolemies are the most graceless of all possible structures . . .'[6] Lawrence was no better impressed by the modern Egyptians. He characterized them as 'horribly ugly, very dirty, dull, low-spirited, without any of the vigour or the self-confident independence of our [he meant, Syrian] men.'[7] Yet under the heading *Some Remarkable Finds* Egypt gave him his first mention in a Middle East newspaper: 'The work was carried on by the students of the [British] School. Messrs. Mackay, Wainwright and Engelback, and Mr. Everson, working with Professor Flinders-Petrie.

Mrs. Petrie made the drawings, and during part of the time Mr. Lawrence, from Carchemish, helped with the excavation.'[8]

Before these words appeared Lawrence was back in Syria working with an archaeologist who was to influence his character and style almost as much as Hogarth. Leonard Woolley was eight years his senior at a time in life when such an age-gap is still significant. But because Lawrence already knew Woolley from Oxford, he approached him without the wary, half-humorous hostility which he normally reserved for those in authority or possessed of skills which might challenge his own. Not that the friendship between the two men could be taken for granted. Lawrence was intermittently to condescend—'Woolley is thawing down from his Egyptian aloofness'[9]—and Woolley to annoy.*

Their relationship got off to a bad start when they met in Aleppo on 7 March 1912.† It was on Woolley's orders that Lawrence had gone ahead from Egypt (Woolley himself had been in the Sudan) to see that a house was ready for occupancy by the end of February but Lawrence had to confess that building had not started.

On the eve of departing for Jerablus the two archaeologists bought £35 worth of Marcopoli's 'Hittite' seals just before the dealer was arrested as an Italian: an Italian fleet had recently bombarded Beirut. Otherwise the country showed no signs of disquiet, but if Ottoman officials were more xenophobic than usual, it will not have been surprising.

Travelling in carts, Woolley and Lawrence reached Jerablus on 12 March. The carts were halted by the western slope of the mound. Tents were pitched. Scores of would-be diggers clamoured to be enrolled; many were new to Lawrence, being migrant workers attracted from Aleppo by the railway. Before signing them on, Woolley decided to clear up some minor problems with the authorities. He approached Ottoman complexities in the spirit of an Oxford rag and his imperial audacity impressed his subordinate, even though Lawrence gave it little space in his crowded letters home.

One problem concerned the armed guard which had been placed on the site at the end of the previous summer's excavations. The guard consisted of a platoon of Ottoman soldiers under an *onbashi*, or corporal. Its installation had been a sensible precaution. An increasing flow of

* Lawrence objected strongly when, after the War, Woolley published *Dead Towns and Living Men*, a light-hearted account of Carchemish which Lawrence considered 'a vulgarization of the years which he looked back to as the best in his life.'[10] Writing when Lawrence's own myth was growing like a beanstalk, Woolley portrayed himself as the linguist and man of action, Lawrence almost as his Sancho Panza.

† For once Lawrence, not someone else, supplies the right dates. Woolley, writing from memory, dated his meeting with Lawrence as the end of February. Lawrence gave dates which Woolley himself supported in his letter of 31.3.1912 (British Museum, *Carchemish File*): he arrived in Aleppo on 7 March, Lawrence having arrived from Jerablus the previous day.

tourists as well as the presence of such archaeologists as 'von Oppenheim, the little Jew-German-millionaire who is making excavations out at Tell Halaf in Mesopotamia'*[11] had taught the Syrians the value of antikas. Pilfering was thus one danger. Another was that the German engineers might regard the mound as a convenient quarry. But the *onbashi*'s instructions were rigid; he was to allow only Mr. Hogarth (in whose name the permission to dig had been renewed) to resume operations. Since the *onbashi* was friendly as well as firm, Woolley thought it simplest to send him to Birejik to fix things up with the kaimmakam, or governor. That evening a reply arrived from the kaimmakam. It was addressed, not to Woolley in English or French, but to the *onbashi* in Turkish: the kaimmakam neither knew nor cared who this Woolley was, or was not; in no case was he to touch a stone of the Carchemish mound. For Woolley, who had meanwhile signed on a hundred and twenty men and given them orders when to start, this was his first brush with a bureaucracy whose secret weapon was procrastination.

Since to lose face with his work force would be fatal, Woolley saddled his horse at dawn for the ride up the Euphrates. He took their cook, Haj Waheed, who could translate Turkish into Arabic, a language Woolley understood. He also took Lawrence. Crossing by ferry to the east bank, the little party stabled their horses at a khan on the edge of Birejik and then made their way to the serai, the administrative centre in every Ottoman town of any substance. Woolley sent in his card. Flies buzzed, time passed, and there was no response. Woolley, followed by Lawrence, pushed uninvited into the kaimmakam's office. The official sat facing a pile of papers. Again uninvited, the two Englishmen occupied the divan closest to his desk. The kaimmakam began to speak in a glacial Turkish which their cook struggled to translate. But as his temper rose, the governor himself changed to Arabic.

The kaimmakam was technically in the right. Under Ottoman law digging permits were non-transferable; the permit for Carchemish had been issued in the name of Hogarth; the British Museum should have had the order appointing Woolley as Hogarth's successor issued in due Turkish form. The kaimmakam insisted on sticking to the letter of the law he was employed to uphold, and mocked Woolley's threats. 'I felt,' Woolley wrote later, 'that the whole future of our diggings depended on

* Much in the manner of Hogarth, Freiherr Max von Oppenheim (born Cologne, 1860) combined archaeology with Intelligence work. A traveller who had visited much of Africa and western Asia, a specialist in Arabic and Islam, he founded the German Intelligence Service in the Near East and also the magazine *Neuer Orient*. In 1902 he visited America to study how a railway system had opened up undeveloped country. He was to describe the work which he directed in N.E. Syria from 1911–1913 in *Der Tell Halaf*, 1931. Under Hitler, von Oppenheim appears to have accepted honorary Aryan status; he died at Schloss Ast near Landshut on 15 November 1946.[12]

the result of this interview, and that it was worth risking a lot to get success: if I gave in now, a fresh permit would certainly not be forthcoming that season, and we should have lost all caste with the natives: really to use force was of course out of the question—but would a Turk be sure of that? I looked once more at the kaimmakam, who, with a cold shoulder turned towards us, was again fidgeting with his papers, and I made up my mind that he was not a man who would call a bluff. Taking my revolver out of its holster I got up and walking to the side of his chair put the muzzle against his left ear. "On the contrary," I said, "I shall shoot you here and now unless you give me permission to start work to-morrow." The Turk absolutely collapsed. He leant back in his chair, his hands flat on the desk before him, and tried to turn his head towards me, while his lips twisted into a wintry smile. "Certainly," he said, "I see no reason why you should not start to-morrow." '[13]

Lawrence, not yet twenty-four, had seen no more audacious feat of words. He adverted to it in a short triumphant letter. 'Woolley came out exceedingly well: he explained that he was not declaring war on the Turkish government, but on Biredjik only. We are very well amused.' A few days later Lawrence was back in Birejik buying beams for their sitting-room ceiling. The Turks knew the truth behind his reassuring words to his mother: 'But good heavens don't you know that no Turkish officer or policeman or government official can lay hands on an Englishman or enter his house? Much less imprison him. There would be a warship in Beyrout if anyone in Biredjik only insulted us.'[14] What Lawrence overlooked was that the weak, when insulted, still have weapons. The Turks were to use sloth, litigation, complaint, and finally, when opportunity presented, a vengeful trick. But first they took advantage of the legal problems in which the mound entangled their arrogant guests.

Back in 1878—when, to quote Woolley, 'one dug for plunder wherewith to stock Museum galleries, and was interested in nothing more than that,'[15]—the British Museum, eager to secure its tenure, had wanted the Consul in Aleppo to buy the mound outright. But Ottoman property law was particularly complex. The local people, who still called themselves 'mound-folk', had abdicated their rights on the mound to their chief, Ali Agha, when they came down to the plain. Since Ali Agha refused to sell, the British had waited till he was in an Ottoman gaol. They had then offered to have him freed in return for a third of the mound: or forty out of its 120 dunums. The British area was never precisely delineated. Ali Agha received in payment an embroidered cloak, a pair of black leather boots and a revolver as a toy for his son, Hassan. Hassan Agha was by 1912 a disgruntled old man. He would have happily sold his share for a low price if he had been asked a year earlier. But the sight of

Germans carting off stones convinced him he was being cheated of something valuable.

Hassan Agha's sense of grievance prompted the next round in Woolley's feud with the Turks. The Agha introduced a writ against Lawrence (not Woolley) in the Islamic court at Birejik. All four charges, Woolley wrote to Kenyon, were either false or ridiculous.[16] Under the Capitulations imposed on Turkey, foreigners had the right to consular representation in court; they could not properly be tried in a Sheria court, whose prime function was the application of Islamic law. But perhaps since Birejik was too small to have a secular court, it was thought advisable for Lawrence to attend. Woolley signed a paper assuming all responsibility and provided him with documentary proof that the Germans were getting their rubble free of charge. Lawrence rode back to Birejik, only to learn that the case was adjourned and the papers, encompassing 'a hopeless tangle of unknown boundaries, mortgages, etc.';[17] impounded. Woolley dared not risk their loss, since Hogarth had recently secured further funding for the dig,* and on the day fixed for the second hearing he accompanied Lawrence to Birejik. Once again they found that the date had been changed and the papers impounded. Once again Woolley claims to have drawn his revolver, pointing it at the Cadi (or judge under the religious law) while ordering Lawrence to 'bolt into the next room and hold up the Kaimmakam: I bet the old brute's got the papers himself.' This second forceful move secured the documents but led to a new Turkish riposte. On 19 May, a Sunday, the archaeologists were surprised by the arrival of a procession carrying a document emblazoned with the new Sultan's seal. It declared Woolley in contempt of court and ordered him to pay £30 to Hassan Agha and all the costs. Woolley tore the legal papers into shreds.

Lawrence had come under the influence of someone whose way of doing things was very different from that of Hogarth.† While Woolley brazened his way through problems, Hogarth solved them through personal contacts. On 9 April 1912, he had lunched with the Kaiser on a yacht off Corfu, and the German Emperor, intensely interested by

* Hogarth (according to the Carchemish File in the British Museum) had persuaded Walter Morrison (1836–1921) to put up £5,000 if the Museum found another £2,000. By 15 February 1912 Morrison's contribution had been paid to Hogarth's bankers. Morrison (who, according to the *Dictionary of National Biography*, gave munificently and anonymously to various projects) may have been motivated by patriotic rather than antiquarian considerations.

† Woolley's recollections of events at Carchemish may be regarded as basically truthful, subject to two qualifications. They were published just after Turkey's defeat in a war in which Woolley, an Intelligence agent, was for a while a prisoner. His Turks have something of the farcical quality bestowed, after another world war, on the Colditz Germans. His book was also intended to present the lighter side of an archaeologist's life.

some of the photographs of Carchemish, had promised to safeguard the interests of the British excavators from the demands of the Railway.[18]

In glorious isolation Woolley and Lawrence fashioned a way of life enjoyed by few excavating teams. Their house, once the bureaucratic obstacles were disregarded, was constructed with the economy and haste then possible. By 20 April, the anniversary of Hogarth's departure, Woolley could move in to his bedroom. The house was a low, one-storey structure of rough stone; its roof, except for the timbered sitting-room, was of mud and required flattening with a roller in bad weather. In shape the house resembled a capital Greek *pi*, Π, with the sitting-room, twice the size of any other, taking up most of the top. On the left were a room for Hogarth, a storeroom and, at this stage, a kitchen; on the right, a small museum, a dark-room, Woolley's bedroom, a bathroom, Lawrence's bedroom, and Gregori's. The shape had the advantage that the legs could be extended when new rooms were needed.

The aesthetic focus was a mosaic pavement in nine colours unearthed by the villagers less than a mile from the house. Since the elements would soon destroy it if it were left exposed, Woolley got Lawrence to supervise its removal intact, rather in the manner that gardeners roll cut turf to make a lawn. Once installed, its 144,000 tesserae weighing over a ton (Lawrence's estimate) formed a stone carpet for their sitting-room some twelve feet by twenty-four.[19] It may have been tailored to the room, since Lawrence suggested bringing home 'a little yard-square panel of fishes, if I have time to chisel it up.'[20] By October it was ground smooth; by November it was waxed and complete. The mosaic's lower panel showed what Woolley took to be an orange tree flanked by ducks and gazelles. In the upper panel, a vine thronged with fowl sprang from a vase. Near the apex of the vine perched the Glossy Ibis. In the fifth century A.D. (as believed by Woolley) or the third (as believed by Lawrence) this rare bird had apparently chosen the district of Birejik for its northward flighting point, as it still did in the early twentieth century.[21]

A Morris tapestry, one or two Persian rugs, Damascus tiles, decorated the whitewashed walls; a niche contained two shelves of the European classics. In cold weather, the mosaic was covered with a black goat-hair tent-cloth while a fire with a beaten-copper hood burnt olive-roots ordered by the five-ton boat-load. Pillars and door-mouldings of basalt, as well as 'some nice Kutachia pots'[22] completed a setting in which even the utensils were precious, being 'coffee-cups, sugar bowls, and soap-dishes of the finest Hittite work,' all destined for the British Museum if they survived the season. From Aleppo Lawrence had ordered, to his own design, two armchairs of black wood and white leather. The total cost of the house was £75.[23] Later that year they added separate quarters for Haj Waheed, his wife and children: 'to howl in, at pleasure: for there is a wide space in between as safety zone.'[24]

Their cook was not short of provisions. The Consul's cavass (who had worked for Gertrude Bell) brought up a consignment of loganberry jam, wheatmeal biscuits and shortbread: enough chocolate, asparagus and medicines to stock a ship: not to mention, Lawrence added, eleven pounds of curry-powder and ten tins of Cooper's Oxford marmalade. 'Our jams this year are from eleven firms, and our stores in all from 19 countries: origin has to be given for customs purposes: did you know that rubber sponges were made in Russia: we have those with caviare from that country. Cerebos salt got through this year labelled chemically: salt is here bad, and a government monopoly.' At Bab, half way to Aleppo, Haj Waheed had once contrived a six-course meal of soup, fish, meat, vegetables, omelette, a sweet, over one spirit lamp. At Jerablus he had ampler scope.[25]

Lawrence paid new attention to his clothes. 'As for heat and cold,' he wrote on 6th April, when the weather could still be treacherous, 'I'm always warm, and stalk about the site in a camel-hair cloak like a Sheikh of Baghdad. The colour is red-brown: the texture thick, not very soft: but very pleasant to the touch.' Under this woollen day-cloak which Woolley envied he wore 'a blazer of French grey trimmed with pink, white shorts held up by a gaudy Arab belt with swinging tassels (it was a belt worn only by bachelors, and Lawrence had his tassels made bigger than anyone else's) grey stockings, red Arab slippers and no hat.'[26] The sun-helmet he had worn on his first Syrian walk would have imposed too colonial a motif on what was now an Oxford-aesthetic oasis. His hair was worn long and, in a style that was to be uncommon for half a century, unkempt. 'He used to say that it was too long when it got into his mouth at mealtimes.' For the evening meal he laid aside his day cloak for something yet more dressy. Over his white shirt and shorts he would slip on an Arab waistcoat embroidered in white and gold surmounted by a magnificent cloak of gold and silver thread: he had picked it up cheaply, he told Woolley, from a thief in the Aleppo souq. After the meal, the two men sat on a Bokkara carpet fronting their fire in its copper-and-Hittite grate, the mosaic floor around them and, in their heads, the words of their favourite poets.[27]

To a contemporary, E. H. R. Altounyan, the Carchemish way of life seemed a 'cocoon'; having so described it, he shifted metaphors: it was 'an exquisite temple of culture where learning but slyly intruded and the hobbledehoy from without, not too abashed, could enjoy leisure as he sipped his cups of thin unglazed clay, off the museum shelf.'[28] The service at Carchemish reminded Altounyan of a good hotel.

On 12 May Winifred Fontana became the first woman to dine at the new house. Hogarth had come out to inspect the new finds and she and her husband accompanied him from Aleppo. After dinner, scalding coffee was served in the Hittite cups. 'With lofty unconcern,' Lawrence quieted her fears for her cup, 'saying that should I drop it, the British Museum would be only too thankful to have the pieces.' The men formed a conversation group that attracted the artist in her. 'Although David Hogarth, Leonard Woolley and my husband were present—all of them superb subjects for a painter—it was Lawrence who drew my attention again and again as he sat under the lamp: his fine eyes lost in thought above Doughty's *Arabia*, open across his knees. I thought: "this young man must be a Poet", and quietly fetched my sketch-book.'[29] But the paper proved too rough, or the artist too excited and no adequate sketch preserved the moment.

Women see through the poses of women, men those of men. Altounyan diagnosed the Lawrence of Carchemish as a poseur with a difference. The sheer impenetrability of his pose made it disturbing, disagreeable and impressive in equal measure. 'For here obviously was someone cleaving through life propelled by an almost noiseless engine.'[30] Frictionless, Lawrence sustained the highbrow manner. He never relaxed into light literature, seemed always a Rodinesque reader, his large brow stooped over 'Homer, or Doughty's poems or Blake.'[31]

The engine, however noiseless, was not unpowered.

Carchemish enabled him to support, in a cocoon with hotel-like service, a version of the hierarchic life more interesting than that enjoyed in English country houses. 'We are such kings in the district,'[32] he wrote the summer of his arrival. In a change of metaphor he toyed with the role of Sheikh of Carchemish. England could offer not even a shabby simulacrum of the feudal life for the family of a déclassé Irishman on a meagre income. 'This country, for the foreigner, is too glorious for words: one is the baron of the feudal system.'[33] And Lawrence had the financial resources to back feudal pretensions. As early as 4 July 1911, almost a year before the completion of the new house, he had boasted to Mrs. Rieder that it was a great thing to be an employer of labour. This had been in reference to a young villager, 'our donkey-boy', who was taking lessons from Lawrence. The Syrian adolescent in question was the first person to crack the poses and discover the affectionate, if schoolboyish, soul behind them. But to Mrs. Rieder and others Lawrence was to use jocular evasion to disguise the friendship which gave his Carchemish days their particular lustre.

11

THE TOP LAYERS of Lawrence's personality, his donnishness, his apparent frigidity, concealed deeper and more mysterious deposits, much as the Arab and Roman layers of the mound concealed the solid Hittite temples whose discovery was the purpose of the dig. Two letters of 1912 and 1913, the first to his family, the second to Vyvyan Richards, his Oxford admirer, show with increasing force the extent to which his life in Syria was satisfying these deeper levels. In the first he poohpoohed the idea of an open fellowship at Oxford: 'I don't think anyone who had tasted the East as I have would give it up half-way, for a seat at high table and a chair in the Bodleian.'[1] Yet such a fellowship would have seemed a triumph two years before; it would have still seemed a triumph to Mrs. Lawrence. The second letter killed an earlier day-dream: 'I cannot print with you when you want me. I have felt it coming for a long time, and have funked it. You know I was in England for a fortnight this summer, and actually found myself one afternoon in Liverpool St. coming up to you . . . and then went back again.'[2]

Both these letters display his enjoyment of the east. The first describes a holiday in Lebanon with a particular young Arab; the one to Richards (whose love Lawrence had neither rejected nor reciprocated) is more evasive: 'I have got to like this place very much: and the people here—five or six of them—and the whole manner of living pleases me.' In fact, two 'head-men' (from the two hundred men he had to play with) accompanied Lawrence on the very visit to England when he had funked calling on Richards.

The young Arab who unfroze Lawrence's heart had been known to his family and to Hogarth from letters written as early as his first June at Carchemish. In these letters, Lawrence's schoolboy humour ran through two variants of a single story. He and Campbell Thompson had been mystifying the natives with Seidlitz powders. 'By personal example, and the strictest orders we compelled our two water-boys to take each half a glass, and ever since they have gone about delicately, feeling their limbs, and shaking themselves, in terror lest they be changed to mares or great apes. "I drank some of that sorcery," said Dahoum on the works next day, "it is very dangerous, since by it men are turned suddenly into the forms of animals." (This from a boy of 14 years.)' To Hogarth Lawrence wrote that they had 'forced Ahmed Hassan & Dahum, the two water-boys, to drink each half a glass, under pain of beating and being laughed at.'[3] His next letter home had supplemented his account of Dahoum. He was the only villager (apart from the liquorice-king) who could read a few words of Arabic; he had more intelligence than the rank and file; he talked of going to Aleppo with the money he earned on the dig. This could hardly be accomplished on Dahoum's 45 piastres a week, of which, as late as the following May, he was only getting 15, the rest being extorted from him by his sheikh. Lawrence thought to have him educated on site. The letter to Mrs. Rieder in which Lawrence had boasted of the glory of being an employer also described Dahoum's progress: 'He is beginning to use his reason as well as his instinct: He taught himself to read a little, so I had very exceptional material to work on but I made him read & write more than he ever did before. You know you cannot do much with a piece of stick & a scrap of dusty ground as materials. I am going to ask Miss Fareedah for a few simple books, amusing, for him to begin on. Remember he is to be left a Moslem. If you meet a man worth anything you might be good enough to remember this? A boy of 15 . . . I would be vastly obliged.'[4] Lawrence felt it better for Dahoum to stay in the country, since the temptations were fewer than in a city, but he could not ignore 'the hideous grind of the continual forced labour, and the low level of the village minds.'

Lawrence's growing interest in Dahoum coincided with an increasing disgust at the effect of missionaries on a people whose virtues he increasingly appreciated through his understanding of one individual. 'If only you had seen the ruination caused by the French influence, & to a lesser degree by the American, you would never wish it extended. The perfectly hopeless vulgarity of the half-Europeanized Arab is appalling. Better a thousand times the Arab untouched. The foreigners come out here always to teach, whereas they had much better learn, for in everything but wits and knowledge the Arab is generally the better man of the two.'[5]

Dahoum's job was to bring water from the village spring to the men at the dig. The long hot nights of summer enabled Lawrence to know him better. The village house was mosquito-ridden and stifling. He took to sleeping out, tentless, on the top of the mound. A fresh breeze discouraged insects. Though his references in his letters were jocular—referring to a snapshot, 'the young boy who is turning up his eyes horribly is Dahoum'[6]—he considered spending the winter in Jerablus so as to be near him. To his family, he wrote of boarding with Dahoum's father; he justified his friendship with the son on the grounds that 'the boy can read & write, & so would be the best teacher of Arabic in the district.'[7]

Lawrence had not taken Dahoum on the sixteen-day July walk which precipitated his collapse, but ill as he was he summoned up the energy to write once more to the school at Jebail: 'What I wanted for the donkey boy was a history book or a geography which should be readable and yet Arab. I cannot give him such productions as those Miss Holmes uses, since nothing with a taste of "Frangi" [European] shall enter Jerablus by my means. I have no wish to do more for the boy than give him a chance to help himself: "education" I have had so much of, & it is such rot: saving your presence!'[8]

Dahoum was to be much photographed in the next three years. Lawrence thought that the picture which he took when the boy was ill gave his unusual type of Arab face very well.[9] But being full-face, it does not show the profile which is usually distinctive in an Arab; the lips are parted in pain; a speckled keffia worn against the cold conceals the hair. A picture in the Bodleian Museum, Oxford, shows Dahoum in playful mood with a revolver.[10] Woolley chose another, perhaps the best, showing Dahoum with two villagers standing by a seated Gregori.[11] This gives an impression of quiet strength which finds support in Lawrence's contention: 'Dahoum is strong and I think honest;'[12] Lawrence also claimed that he was the best wrestler in his age group. Stocky, smiling, the Dahoum in Woolley's picture seems more Anatolian than Arab; Lawrence himself accounted him a mixture of Hittite and Arab, with a possible dash of Armenian.[13]

To avoid, or postpone, military service (compulsory for all religious groups in the Ottoman empire and enforced by periodic patrols), fathers kept their sons' ages vague, even when they knew them. It is therefore not surprising that Lawrence refers to Dahoum as fourteen, then fifteen, in letters only a month apart. His father's name is unrecorded; his own correct name* was Ahmed, a name cognate with Muhammad borne by several famous sultans. The significance of Dahoum (or Dahum in Woolley's transliteration) has been disputed, but Woolley was delighted when Lawrence discovered that Dahoum's mother had given him his name because at birth he had been dark; Dahûm meant a dark night when there was no moon. This seemed to prove that pre-Islamic myths had survived into the present and Woolley at once identified Dahûm, the night without a moon, with Tehôm, the ' "darkness" that was on the face of the waters before creation, the Tiamit or Chaos-goddess of Babylonian theology.' Woolley argued that this susceptibility to mythic

* Woolley, more careful about details than Lawrence, refers to him as 'our house-boy, Ahmed' in the book Lawrence resented: *Dead Towns and Living Men*, p. 106.

archetypes fitted with the pride of the 'mound-folk', settled from ancient times on their grass-grown citadel.

On this occasion, as on others, Lawrence may have pulled Woolley's leg. It fits better with the descriptions of Dahoum as unusually fair-skinned that the name simply meant dark, or black, from the root دهم, since 'to give opposite names to people or things is a common Arab custom.'[14] There is a third possibility. Most Englishmen find difficulty in distinguishing the Arabic letter *hay* (ه), which corresponds to the English h, from *hā* (ح), an Arabic consonant found in such words as Muḥammad or Aḥmed and written by orientalists with a dot underneath. Daḥoum could then be a picturesque name used by the Bedouin from the root (دحم), meaning, according to one Arab scholar, a trap laid for foxes.*

Woolley remembered Dahoum as 'not particularly intelligent . . but beautifully built and remarkably handsome.'[16] Certainly his qualities ensnared one of the cleverest human foxes on record. While convalescing at home Lawrence had felt pulled to the east by the youth who stood to him as page to squire and, returning sooner than his doctor wished, he wrote from Aleppo on 13 December 1911: 'here I am in my own Arabic country, and am looking forward immensely to seeing the men again: if only those Germans are neutralized somehow.'[17] Already four or five German engineers had arrived with their twenty tents; workmen were erecting mud huts for others. The representatives of a railway backed by imperial Germany could pay higher wages than a museum. Yet the Jerablus men made their preference plain, downing tools and rushing to greet their English friend. Lawrence was carried off to the Hoja's house where he was delighted to hear the Germans abused for such sins as drinking rakki [a kind of oozo] and meanness. The talk having turned to the supernatural, no one wanted to go out into the dark, and the entire party (Lawrence estimated them as twenty-four) slept together in a tiny house no bigger than an English study. Lawrence snuggled close to Dahoum in 'a most royal heap of quilts, all, wonderful to say, nearly deserted.'

In Lawrence's absence Dahoum had worked for the Germans. Digging had been suspended and Lawrence could not afford to pay the boy himself. 'He was six months table-boy with the Railway Engineers here,' he was to tell his youngest brother.[18] The Germans evidently taught him to wait at table and clear away dishes. But a story, deriving from Lawrence but retailed by Woolley, shows that his emotional involvement with Dahoum made him see the Germans as invaders who had tried to steal his page.[19]

* An Arab officer who fought with Lawrence in the War and wrote about him seems to have understood the name in some such sense. He transliterates it back into Arabic as Dāḥoum (داحوم), not Dahoum.[15]

According to the story, Dahoum, now safely back on the English payroll, had lent some trifling sum to a railway foreman. On his way back from shopping in the village, he asked the foreman to repay the debt. A German engineer, angry that conversation interrupted work, had Dahoum flogged by two soldiers of his guard. Lawrence thereupon acted in a style which would have done credit to Woolley. He stormed into the German camp, found Contzen, the chief engineer, and insisted on confronting the guilty German. The two Germans then talked quickly together (Lawrence knew no German) and Contzen turned triumphantly to Lawrence.

'Herr X never assaulted the man at all. He merely had him flogged.'

'Well, don't you call that an assault?'

'Certainly not,' the Teuton replied. 'You can't use these natives without flogging them. We have men thrashed every day. It's the only method.'

Lawrence thereupon demanded a public apology to Dahoum. Contzen roared with laughter—till an icy Lawrence made it plain he was in earnest. If the engineer refused, he'd take him down to the village and flog him publicly. The engineer then apologized while the villagers smirked.

The incident must be, in David Garnett's phrase, 'apocryphal.'[20] The Germans had formidable guards and were engaged on a project backed by the Ottoman state. Pocket-Hercules Lawrence may have seemed, but karate-hero capable of routing an engineer corps, he was not. In fact, his relations with the Germans were generally good, except over Dahoum. Yet most of Lawrence's tall stories contain a germ of fact. The foreman probably did owe Dahoum some money; an engineer may have cuffed him and told him to be off. Most fantasies make a point, however obliquely. The point in this one is that Lawrence regarded Dahoum as 'his' and felt rage if he were ordered about by others. Such possessiveness is usually part of love. Later Lawrence displayed what Woolley described as 'jealousy' when another European nation, the French, threatened to become large-scale employers of labour in Syria.[21]*

Dahoum's position seemed permanently assured with the completion of the house in spring 1912. And, like his master, he began to work on different levels. He began to be useful to Lawrence in his practical affairs.

In a letter written a month after Woolley's arrival, Lawrence described his new chief as 'getting on very well—goes down with the workmen, is dropping Egyptian hauteur and ruling-race fantasies, likes Syrian cooking and sweetmeats, and (*mirabile dictu*) our dialect! . . Woolley unfortunately has brought two Egyptians with him, to take photographs: he

* In the Contzen story, Lawrence claimed that no Englishman would ever lay hands on a native. This hardly fits his earlier statement that Dahoum had taken the Seidlitz powder under threat of a beating.

refused to believe Mr. Hogarth's assurances that there was not enough work for them: result is that they are loafing, and the men are getting a little disgusted at it. The Egyptians stand very much in awe of them.'[22]

Lawrence's resentment at Woolley's Egyptians was spiced by his protective feeling for Dahoum. Egypt already had a powerful nationalist movement which sought to end the 'temporary' British occupation which had begun in 1882 and still continued. Some nationalists wanted total independence; others an Egypt related to the Ottoman, not the British, empire. The movement had gained impetus since, in 1906, a number of villagers had been hanged and others flogged as the result of a fracas between fellahin and British officers shooting their pigeons. Lawrence saw in Egyptians an influence to be countered at all costs. (An incident of the following year—1913—was to display this determination yet more forcefully.) But apart from protecting the villagers from contamination by Egyptian nationalists, Lawrence wanted the photography for himself and Dahoum, and he was by stages to get his way. By 20 May he could report: 'Woolley has sloughed all his Egyptianity and become enthusiastically Arab . . .' By the following month: 'I told you, I think, that Woolley's Egyptians had run away: so I have the doing of all their sort of thing now, on this very inferior Aleppo paper: the heat makes the surface gelatine melt away, and confuses all the lines of the image. We have decided that we cannot do it all ourselves next year, and so I have the training of a boy—Dahoum, of course—as well to see to. You have no idea how hard it is to instil elementary optics into his head in imperfect Arabic. He will put plates the wrong side out. However all these are little worries, which are working towards my improvement in Arabic: I hope to be fluent—though still incorrect—by Xmas.'[23]

Under Lawrence's supervision Dahoum became a useful photographer for the purposes of the dig. Once trained in the use of a camera, he was ideally equipped to record, inconspicuously, the progress of the railway and other matters that came within Lawrence's competence as a clandestine informant. Dahoum's value in these two roles, as well as Arabic tutor, could also explain an intimacy which might otherwise be misconstrued.

By April 1912, when he proposed bringing Dahoum to England 'for conversation purposes,' Lawrence plainly thought of him as a friend. That scheme had to wait, but in that same summer of 1912 the relationship entered a stage, lasting a year, whose intensity caused discretion to be abandoned and scandal courted. Lawrence's letters give only the barest hints; but since they were written when he only hoped to become famous, candid statements and unpruned images occur. His actions, however, are the more revealing evidence.

One early incident, convincing Lawrence of his spiritual affinity to

Dahoum, inspired an essay which was first published in the *Jesus College Magazine* (of January 1913) and then reappeared in an early passage of his most ambitious book. Whoever in Oxford set the piece in print misread his transcription of Arabic words, so that the published text was full of errors, starting with the title, meaningless as it stands, The Kaer of Ibn Wardani: Kasr was a fortress or palace. Lawrence was impatient to hear that his essay was in print. 'The palace of Ibn Wardani has many strange scents about it, as I wrote: it is famous all over North Syria, and my description is more like the rumour than the reality.'[24]

The passage concerning Dahoum (later developed even further to stress the Arab proneness to renunciation) read in the *Jesus College Magazine* version:

> 'This,' said he, 'is the liwan of silence: it has no taste,' and by some cunning art it was as he said. The mingled scents of all the palace here combined to slay each other, and all that one felt was the desert sharpness of the air as it swept off the huge uncontaminated plains.
>
> 'Among us,' said Dahoum, 'we call this room the sweetest of them all,' therein half-consciously sounding the ideal of the Arab creed, for generations stripping itself of all furniture in the working out of a gospel of simplicity.

The beloved is often a mirror in which the lover can recognize himself. Lawrence discovered through Dahoum aspects of his tight-shut self. Once discovered, they were to affect the direction of his life. He signed his essay with the initials C.J.G. Such incidents as it described re-awakened the rapture which he had first felt at the desolation of Les Aigues Mortes. Others dragged him close to the anguish of the pit.

On Saturday, 1 June 1912 Woolley left Jerablus on leave. Lawrence accompanied him on the drive to Alexandretta, Woolley wishing to avoid Aleppo, under quarantine for cholera. The journey took them six days. They followed the railway track, in poor shape after the departure of the Italian gangers, and then skirted the lake near Antioch. Their route then took them past Beilan, the resort some two thousand feet above the sea where the British Consul passed the summer. Lawrence evidently had to inform Mr. Fontana of his intended movements. 'He was a little astonished at my idea of living the summer in the village, but accepted it as a good one.'

At Alexandretta Woolley boarded the first steamer for Constantinople. The British Ambassador in the Ottoman capital had been told of his high-handed behaviour, and he was to have to do some explaining.

Lawrence drove light-heartedly back by way of Aleppo, disregarding the city's quarantine, 'Woolley is off and I am my own master again, which is a position that speaks for itself and its goodness.'

He had decided to give the teenaged villagers some rudimentary schooling. But a malaria epidemic, which forced him to turn his school into a hospital, at the same time revealed a new side to his character. 'Just now I am in Jerablus,' he wrote to his youngest brother on 21 July, 'and feeling matronly.' The facetious adjective was, in its rough way, appropriate. He was showing for the first time a masculine tenderness to those outside his family circle. Haj Waheed's wife had a child and fell ill; to help her mother-in-law in the kitchen Lawrence brought in Dahoum; but the boy 'ungratefully produced malignant malaria (autumno-aestival) and raved his head off for three days until he nearly died. I had to sit on his chest half one night to keep him in bed.'[25] Then Lawrence had a brief bout of fever himself. Soon the robust Dahoum was convalescent and by 3 August the pair were in Beirut on their way to a holiday in Jebail with Miss Holmes.

Three things had happened, according to Lawrence, after Dahoum's illness in mid-July. First, in a bloodless battle, invading Kurds attacked a group of Arabs digging sand on one of the Euphrates islands. Dating it around 26 July, he exaggerated the fracas to his youngest brother—addressing 'Arnie' as 'Worm', though presumably in a different sense to that used for Woolley's Egyptians.[26] Despite two new attacks of fever, he apparently then visited Birejik, since Hassan Agha was now more willing to sell his share in the mound. But the battle and two more attacks of fever convinced him that it would be prudent, 'in view of the excavations to follow so close, if I rested a bit in the cool before going up to Jerablus again.'* The third event, again according to Lawrence, was a robbery.

On his way through Aleppo with Dahoum he had borrowed £25 from the Consul's dragoman to buy twenty-five seals, including some three or four of the finest Hittite seals he had ever bought.[28] But 'my seals were stolen from my bag in the luggage van of the train between Aleppo & Beyrout on my way to Jebail. Nothing else but a razor, soap and a pair of socks went: no loss and no damages.'[29]

We would hardly pause over this incident if strict truthfulness had been established as one element in Lawrence's complexity. But in the light of other tall tales, and in particular of the contradictory accounts of how he had lost his camera in 1909, pause we must. The loss of the seals for which he had borrowed £25 coincided with the first holiday he had

* These mentions of illness, followed by a later report of two ribs broken in a wrestling-bout with Dahoum, naturally alarmed his family. Lawrence made a somewhat testy rejoinder: 'I am feeling perfectly well, and have always said so: there is a sort of pessimistic fatality which leads you to suppose I am usually ill out here.'[27]

taken with a dependant—a holiday on which he repeatedly asked his family for money. 'I know it is not fair to ask you for such in August, but if you could send me cheque up to £30 I would be exceeding glad: my expenses here in Lebanon will be thrice those at Jerablus: and I don't like debts!'[30] According to Lawrence, the British Museum owed him £10 for work done on its behalf that summer. True, they had now agreed to pay him fifteen shillings a day next season. But he was to spend almost a month at Jebail with Dahoum and was to leave 'in abeyance my question of remuneration to Miss Holmes. I talked to her about it, and she suggested that it be left to you,' he told his father on 30 August; 'you know we have lived very cheaply, perhaps you may feel moved to offer her a something for her work. It was very good of her to come down from the hills to stay with me here, and she has made me very comfortable.'[31]

In the light of his expenses, it seems possible that he had indeed borrowed money at the Consulate (which the Museum would make good) but had in truth not bought the seals at all.

Whether funded by his parents or the British Museum, Jebail provided clean quarters and plain but abundant food. When tired of reading Spenser, Catullus, the poets of the Greek Anthology and the Koran in translation, he spent hours in the sea with Dahoum.[32] Once an Italian fleet sailed past them as they swam. For light relief they dug up near the beach one of the man-shaped pods in which the ancient Phoenicians buried their dead.

His discovery at Jebail of an exciting new pastime was revealed to Mrs. Rieder, though not to his family. Of his three and a half weeks in Lebanon he had spent three in a spare set of Dahoum's long white underpants, voluminous robes, head cloth, agal and cumbrous slippers. From what he told Mrs. Rieder, the village was somewhat sceptical of his excuse that Arab dress eased his convalescence.[33]*

Clothes were as important to Lawrence as they are to more people than they are not. Though dressing in a western, almost dandified fashion at Carchemish, he had taken a keen interest in the local costume. 'There is a splendid dress,' he had told Richards that same summer, 'called "of the seven kings":—long parallel stripes of the most fiery colours from neck to ankle: it looks glorious: and over that they wear a short blue coat, turned up at the cuffs to show a dull red lining, and they gird themselves with a belt of thirteen vari-coloured tassels, and put a black silk & silver weave of Hamath work over their heads under a black goat-hair head-rope.'[34]

* The words in which Lawrence described his adventure to Mrs. Rieder were as follows: '. . . I was three weeks walking about Jebail in Arab dress: Excuse was an illness, which found rest only so: but the village made the most of it!'

But from dress-as-adornment to dress-as-disguise is a giant stride. The dandy embellishes a persona that already exists. The man who disguises himself as an Arab (or in a yet more extreme case, a woman) changes his persona; in so doing he allows a new personality to be assayed; an old, troubling self to be at least briefly put by. In later life Lawrence notably enjoyed the probing attentions of the artist; unlike Virginia Woolf, who recoiled from the sculptor's scrutiny, he was to remain standing for two hours without rest in Arab raiment for a painter.[35] If this was vanity, it was a complex form. In submitting himself as a model, he sought clues as to which of a number of appearances or moods corresponded to his deepest self.[36]

Lawrence was not the first or last Englishman to wear eastern clothes. Lane had dressed as an Egyptian in the Cairo of Muhammad Ali; Doughty had travelled to Arabia, Burton to Mecca itself, in Arab clothes; Lord Cromer's Oriental Secretary, Harry Boyle, had habitually disguised himself as a turbaned Turk when exploring the coffeeshops and hammams of native Cairo. Will Lawrence, setting off with Ramsay MacDonald the following year to a Himalayan school, was to include, 'We'll wear Indian dress there,' as part of the fun.[37] In borrowing Dahoum's clothes, however, Lawrence was identifying with a young Arab whose company he preferred to that of the British Consul at Beilan, and his flaunting the used night-gown (for so it would seem) of a Muslim peasant hardly conformed to the missionary philosophy which his mother approved and Miss Holmes represented. In disguising himself, not merely as an Arab but as Dahoum, he was expressing the wish that what happened to Dahoum would happen to himself; what he would like to have happen to himself would happen to his Arab friend. In this he resembled those 'normal' transvestites who dress as women, not because they want to be loved as women, but because they love women and everything most closely connected with them.

In the illusory stability given by noon, or mid-summer, without forethought or afterthought, Lawrence endeavoured to become someone simple. One photograph shows his enormous, rather ugly grin as he assumes, less elegantly than his younger friend, the clothes of Syria.[38] He was later to adopt personae more august and more drab than that of the gentle and bucolic Dahoum. But with Dahoum's help he had discovered a way to spiritual escape, or in Lawrence's term, to 'rest'.

12

Lawrence in Arab dress had an audience that he seems to have overlooked. In an area with more spies to the square mile than anywhere except the Balkans, colder eyes than those of his Arab friends observed his antics. If 'Turkey in Europe' was likely to provide the world's major explosion, 'Turkey in Asia' would produce the attractive debris.

Jebail was only a few miles north of Junieh, a Maronite town of solid stone houses facing an arc of sea. Red roofs and orange groves were dominated by steeples and clock-towers owing allegiance to a patriarch who lived just above the town at Bkerké. The form of Christianity associated with St. Maron had long been uniate with Rome and allied to France, many Maronites speaking French almost as well as Arabic. French ambitions in the Levant were to depend on the Maronites much in the same way as in North Africa they depended on the Jews, who received French citizenship automatically. What the agents of French Intelligence learnt about the strange little Englishman frolicking in Syrian dress found its way into a secret report dated 20 August 1917. This report[1] had Lawrence two years younger than he really was; it also had him traversing pre-war Syria and Palestine on horseback, on motorcycle or on foot, *costumé en bédouin*. Its description of his appearance —*petit et mince, la machoire imberbe et volontaire, le front très haut, les yeux très clairs illuminés par l'intensité de la pensée, il donne une profonde impression d'énergie et d'intelligence*—shows how closely he had been observed.

The French report includes one curious story five years before Lawrence himself in any way adverted to it. 'It appears that he was conscripted for three weeks by the Turks at Urfa, before managing to escape.'[2]

The mention of Turks reminds us that in the Levant of 1912 the French were not the most interested nor the most nearly omnipresent party. The legal masters of the area were the Turks whom Lawrence and Woolley had mocked and whose feelings as bitter patriots they had ignored.*

* Germans such as von Oppenheim may also have been aware of the annoying little Englishman. Von Oppenheim visited Carchemish more than once. The Railway engineers will have been as frank about Lawrence's defects as he was about theirs.

Once the foremost military power in Europe, the Turks had been losing their empire bit by bit through defects they were powerless to repair: they could not prevent the seduction of non-Turkish elements by the new creed of nationalism; they could not rival Europe's technological and commercial strength. But even at this late hour Turks stubbornly defended their assaulted domains. In Libya volunteers like a young officer, Mustafa Kemal, fought effectively alongside Senussi tribesmen against invaders whose warships gave them access to the North African coast; the Italians would not complete their conquest of Libya until the outbreak of world war, when British armoured cars aided their beleaguered garrisons. The kaimmakam's impotence did not mean that Woolley's revolver was unresented. Like a bullied schoolboy, he must have dreamed of revenge. Lawrence's new penchant for dressing up was to give the Turks their chance. The way they took it was to provide him with an agonizing new insight into his nature.

Lawrence first mentioned 'the Halfati incident' in 1922;[3] since he ignored it in his contemporary letters home, since he made no official complaint and since, on their side, the Turks regarded it as a routine matter, it is impossible to date it precisely.[4] But the fact that a French version existed in cold, if garbled, print as early as 1917 gives the incident a substantiality lacking, for example, in the story of his enlistment in the Artillery as a youth.

The Turks must have sprung their trap some time between 4 November 1912, when Lawrence learned of a mysterious sculpture some distance up river, and the summer of 1913.[5] Woolley had reported that with one obvious exception Lawrence himself 'had no great liking for the individual inhabitants of Jerablus and the Carchemish neighbourhood';[6] his role as employer could as easily induce resentment as feudal loyalty, and some resentful villager seems to have baited the trap by describing to Lawrence a sculpture that looked like a Hittite goddess astride two lions. Lawrence doubted if it could really be Hittite, but to make sure he and Dahoum went up river towards Halfati dressed as Arabs.[7] The pleasure of a jaunt with Dahoum, the possibility of an important discovery, put out of mind the tension then gripping an empire which the Young Turk revolution had failed to rejuvenate and which Europe allowed no respite from attack. Lawrence's letters spoke of government patrols scouring the district for reservists in hiding; he knew of the Balkan Wars. The township of Halfati (near which the sculpture was allegedly located) was as far to the north of Birejik as Jerablus was to the south. At Halfati the two young 'Arabs' were apprehended 'as possible deserters'. Lawrence was to give conflicting accounts of what happened next. In the first (of which he wrote two slightly different versions), he was rough-handled in a manner which anticipated, though in a 'less staining' form, a painful and humiliating ordeal of November 1917;[8] in the second, later, verbal account, Lawrence reported that he and Dahoum had been kicked downstairs into a filthy dungeon and released next morning thanks to a bribe.[9]

The Turks apparently took their revenge for Woolley's intimidation by accepting Lawrence at his face value, as an Arab, and by chastizing him, along with the boy who worked for foreign coin, with Ottoman severity. We know what this could be from the memoirs of an Iranian aristocrat who had enrolled in the Ottoman army. Lawrence and Dahoum were beaten in a mouldering village on the southern flanks of the Taurus; Cadet (later General) Hassan Arfa tasted similar medicine the same year in a military college close to the Bosphorus. 'The discipline was harsh not to say savage, the food so indifferent that even the patient Turkish cadets twice organized a hunger strike to protest against it (for which they were severely punished), and the work, both in the classrooms and the field, hard and exhausting.'[10] When Arfa and some other cadets played truant one Thursday evening: 'we were punished by twenty-five lashes each, administered to us by two sturdy Anatolian soldiers, the officer on duty counting the strokes in a loud voice before the 1,500 cadets of the school. According to the school's tradition, not a groan or even a sigh was to be heard during the operation, the cadets jumping smartly to attention after the punishment and after a smart salute to the officer on duty, rejoining their place in the ranks.' Although for two or three days it was painful to sit on a chair, the son of Prince Mirza Reza Arfa ed-Dovleh did not feel humiliated: he likened his acceptance of a soldierly experience to the spirit in which corporal punishment was accepted in English boarding schools.

It was an experience for which Lawrence's day-school had not prepared him. But what is most surprising about the whole affair is Lawrence's apparent acceptance of physical aggression. Instead of revealing himself for what he was, an Oxford graduate working for the British Museum under an Ottoman *firman*, he seems to have maintained the pretence that he was an Arab and to have accepted alongside Dahoum the rough treatment given to those suspected of deserting, or evading, military service. Judging from his final written version of what happened, he presented himself to the Turkish N.C.O.s, not as an Englishman who could whistle a gunboat into the nearest harbour, but as 'a timid recruit', passively accepting the worst they offered.[11]

One factor may have been his fear of ridicule. If he had complained to his British superiors he would have had to admit that he had been apprehended in fancy dress. The distinctive clothes of the Englishman abroad usually won him the respect commanded by the world's largest fleet and strongest currency. The sun-helmet distinguished the northerner as much as it protected him. For Lawrence to have gone to Mr. Fontana in Aleppo and have complained that he had been mishandled by the Turks when arrayed in Dahoum's second-best *dishdasha* would hardly have fitted his semi-consular role. But probably the strongest motives for his acquiescence involved identification with Dahoum, who could indeed have been a recruit.

Lawrence's enrolment in the Oxford O.T.C., the legend of the Artillery, his commitments in later life, suggest that he indulged in fantasies involving military life. The British Army before 1914 could both attract, and repel, someone of his tangled social and emotional background. Its rankers were largely recruited from men to whom a shilling a day with food and clothing represented something better than they could expect from mean industrial street or impoverished village. Its few 'Gentleman Rankers' (sung in a famous poem by Kipling) were either misfits or those who had dishonoured the middle-class code. British officers were recruited, for the smart regiments, from young men who enjoyed a substantial private income. The public schools, drawing from the professional classes and gentry, provided officers for the other regiments. The Army could briefly appeal to the Lawrence who identified with his Irish father, more permanently, to the Lawrence who sympathized with the illegitimate and the oppressed, to the patriot, to the complex man who hankered after humdrum normality and, as an all-male institution, to the puritan, created by his mother, who had avoided contacts with women and who regarded marriage as a form of sin. As for the military arts, they too interested him on contrasted levels: sometimes he was the scholar-strategist, assessing the penetrability of passes or the impregnability of doctored crags; while in fantasy he intermittently saw himself as the ranker who suffers. The slovenly private in the Jesus contingent at summer camp prefigured the timid recruit.

A second factor will have determined Lawrence's decision to maintain an Arab identity. At Halfati, possibly for the first time, he experienced the irradiation of pleasure through physical pain. He thus approached late, and without rhetoric, the question which Swinburne had repetitiously posed two generations before:

> We shall see whether hell be not heaven,
> Find out whether tares be not grain,
> And the joys of thee seventy times seven,
> Our Lady of Pain.

Lawrence seems to have ignored Swinburne until 1912. While he had discussed the poetry of Morris, Tennyson, Matthew Arnold, Christina Rossetti and had toyed with printing their poems on the press of his dreams, he seems to have appreciated Swinburne only after the Halfati incident. Returning to Syria in 1913 he reported: 'On the way out I came to know the early work of Swinburne better than before. He is quite good after all, though alas, like Browning long-winded to the extent of ultimate boredom. On the steamer however, where all passengers yawn their way along the decks between meals, he was very well.'[12] Writing later, Lawrence had reason to mute his praise: Swinburne, Philhellene, pagan, nostalgic, belonged to the devil's party. Yet the poet of 'Dolores' and 'Anactoria' came closer to understanding some of Lawrence's basic feelings than any other English writer. He, too, was inspired by desolation and sterility; he, too, understood the passionate link between pain and rapture. Lawrence was never to share the poet's desire for surrender to a commanding woman; the Lawrentian masochism was exclusively connected with males, particularly soldiers. Even so, the dungeon (or 'hospital'[13]) of Halfati illuminated affinities between himself and the inspiration of the youthful Swinburne.

Lawrence's dressing up as an Arab (which let him in for the Halfati experience) was to seem in the retrospect of legend the first step in an audacious process but at the time it was more like a mixture of personal revolt and a social gaffe. His family seem to have been shocked that their wayward son had inflicted a native on so estimable a lady as Miss Holmes. 'I don't know what Miss Holmes thought of Dahoum,' he replied on 13 September, when the holiday was over, and, counter-attacking, he belittled Miss Holmes's Arabic and exalted Dahoum's. The Arabic of Jebail was 'one of the ugliest languages on earth: whereas the Jerablus is very like a deep Greek: a Greek without the 4 "e" vowels.' He warned his parents that they might hear that pronunciation for themselves in the coming winter.[14]

Lawrence's links with Jebail were not to be resumed after his August visit. His parents sent Miss Holmes (who had come down from the hills specially to entertain the Englishman and his Arab friend) a cheque for £10, which he characterized as 'abundance'.[15] Early next year he confided to Mrs. Rieder that 'Miss Homes hasn't corresponded with me since the stimulus of your example was withdrawn.'[16] And he did not mention her to his parents until early 1914, when she was said to be lecturing in the United States. The missionary had lost her angelic status; future references to her were, judging by his brother's deletions from published letters, hostile.[17]

Lawrence did reward Dahoum, innocent cause of the rupture with Miss Holmes and his partner at Halfati, with a visit to England. He had talked of inviting an Arab home more than oncc, another candidate for the honour having been Miss el-Akle.[18] Indeed, had linguistic improvement been his aim, she would have been a better instructor than Dahoum. Though Dahoum won, his visit was short and was shared by Sheikh

Hamoudi, 'the Hoja', who had nursed Lawrence on milk and arrowroot in 1911.* Sheikh Hamoudi who acted as foreman at Carchemish in Gregori's absence, was later to accompany Woolley to Ur, where he worked as chief foreman from 1922 to 1934.

The visit took place in the summer of 1913. Woolley left for England on 14 June but Lawrence stayed on at Jerablus hoping to visit Rakka, further south on the Euphrates, around the 18th.[20] But 'a stray English consul turned up' and on 21 June Lawrence was still near Carchemish. At that time he intended to start back on 3 July. The journeys between England and Carchemish usually took around two weeks by way of Beirut and Port Said, and if Lawrence had left on 3 July, he might have reached Oxford by the middle of the month. But if David Garnett is correct and he did not start home until 14 July, he cannot have turned into Polstead Road much before the end of the month.

The Arabs slept in 'Ned's house' at the bottom of the garden and Albert Charles Dodds, a Scottish painter, sketched Dahoum at the Ashmolean. To Sheikh Hamoudi's disappointment, Lawrence prevented them from accepting baksheesh from curious Oxonians: this would have made him 'the showman of two monkeys.'[21] But the most significant incident of the visit involved Will Lawrence, who had just obtained a Second in history. Will was the favourite pupil of Professor Ernest Barker who recorded his admiration for the most handsome Lawrence in Oxonian terms: 'The music and gymnastic which, as Plato thought, could attune the body to harmony with the mind and harmonize all the elements of the mind in a perfect unison had done their work upon him . . . beauty of mind knit to beauty of body, and all informed by a loving spirit of affection, so that his presence was a benediction and a matter for thanksgiving that God had made men after this manner.'[22]

One of Will's friends at St. John's was an Egyptian from the Delta, Ahmed Abdul Ghaffar. Lawrence, according to Barker, 'charged that the Egyptian should on no account be allowed to meet' Dahoum and Sheikh Hamoudi. As in most tales which start with Thou Shalt Not, the order was defied. 'One day, however, the Egyptian came walking up the road . . . and met the two Arabs. He said something which, as I heard it reported afterwards, was understood by them to mean, "Please God the time may soon come when we cut the throats of these infidels." They ran back into the house to T. E. exclaiming "A gun, a gun—there is an Egyptian in the road and we want to shoot him." There was no shooting.'[23]

* E. H. R. Altounyan translated Sheikh Hamoudi's memoir of Lawrence for *T. E. Lawrence by His Friends* into doughty English. For example, 'I was very wrath,' 'Lawrence was very joyful,' when it would have given a less picturesque tone to say, 'I was very angry,' or 'Lawrence enjoyed himself.'[19]

Taken at face value the story would indicate the fanaticism of the Egyptian, the frontier-spirit of Lawrence's loyal companions and his own icy control in preventing violence. But it leaves unanswered the basic question why Lawrence was so anxious to isolate his guests from other Arabs. It was, in effect, a repetition of his attitude to Woolley's Egyptians, but in a sharper key. An exchange of words between the two Syrians and Abdul Ghaffar would have excluded Lawrence and have shown his Arabic to disadvantage. A stronger factor might have been Lawrence's fear that a nationalistic Egyptian could demoralize his friends, giving them second thoughts about the British empire,* which would have undermined his plan in bringing them to Oxford. He had wished to impress them with the benign superiority of British civilization and, possibly through the Ashmolean, to get Dahoum on to some form of payroll. Or perhaps his continuing dislike for Egyptians echoed a fashionable exaltation of the 'pure' Bedouin at the expense of the Nilotic fellahin; though Dahoum's mixed ancestry made talk of ethnic purity in his case absurd.

The end of the Oxford visit can be dated with greater precision than its beginning. Frank Lawrence was away at the Free Church Camp at Whatstandwell in Derbyshire. On 5 August he wrote to his mother: 'I expect you are glad that the Arabs have gone . . . I hope Ned will get back [to Syria] safely.'[25]

After a short visit to London, whose underground railway impressed Dahoum, Lawrence and his guests crossed to the Hook of Holland and took the train to the Austrian port of Trieste, where they embarked on the sea passage via Alexandria and Alexandretta (the port through which the archaeologists imported supplies and exported antikas). They were in Aleppo by 24 August.

The north Syrian town was exhausted by Ramadan. Being a lunar month, Ramadan processes through all four seasons. When it falls in summer it imposes a heavy burden on the faithful. Denied food, water, tobacco smoke, sexual embrace, from the moment before dawn breaks over the desert, the Muslim would join family or friends for an evening breakfast when the gun from the Citadel announced that the sun was safely below the western horizon. Normally the month had something of Christmas as well as Lent, innocent night-time joys balancing the

* The fanaticism attributed to Abdul Ghaffar seems out of character. Back in Egypt he became a prominent conservative politician, serving as King Farouk's minister of agriculture for the third and last time in 1949. Apart from his friendship for Will Lawrence, Oxford seems to have given him pleasant memories. He re-visited St. John's in the years of food-rationing after the Second World War. Distressed by the prevalent dearth, he made it an annual custom to send a couple of turkeys each Christmas to two of the Fellows. One of his grandchildren was to marry into the family of President Sadat.[24]

hardships of day. In a dislocation of routine, children would stay up late; storytellers would fascinate listeners in the lamplit market. But that year Ramadan was darkened by Turkey's military struggles with covetous neighbours. There were rumours of further conscription once the holy month was over. There was no point in lingering in Aleppo. Dahoum and Sheikh Hamoudi went back to the village; Lawrence joined them there by the 29th to find the two travellers enthralling the village with tales of Europe. 'They declare to all the world,' Lawrence reported to Hogarth, 'that Syria is a mere flea-bite in public worth . . . and the Arabs too few in number to matter much.'[26]

He had one month of lotus-eating liberty before Woolley returned on 1 October. He invited Dahoum to stay at the archaeologists' house. He dabbled in excavation. He also entertained.

Will was the first and last member of his family to accept an invitation to visit Carchemish. On his way east to a teaching-post in India, he bought his sun-helmet at Port Said and caught an Austrian Lloyd steamer to Beirut. The sun-dried mountains, which he traversed by railway, recalled the Pyrenees; Damascus seemed the most beautiful city he had seen. Near Baalbek's Roman ruins Will compared the natives with Ned's visitors to Oxford and decided that Sheikh Hamoudi, not Dahoum, was more typically Arab. But it was Dahoum who was standing by Lawrence's side when Will alighted from the train at Aleppo. After escorting him to Baron's Hotel, the pair showed him the sights.

'I'm with Ned now, he's very well and a great lord in this place.'[27] Will's excited account shows how Lawrence, early in his career and with someone as close as a brother, impressively blended information with myth, diffusing a smoke in which fact and fantasy could cohabit and in which genii could co-exist with sun-helmets and Oxford boots. 'Ned is known by everyone,' Will wrote, 'and their enthusiasm over him is quite amusing.' His brother had led him through stone-paved, stone-roofed bazaars to meet Busrawi Agha of the Milli Kurds, who was on a visit to Aleppo: 'a marvellously-dressed and dignified person who's invited me to go over to his tribe to see some horse-racing and dancing.' Despite his training in history, Will retailed an extraordinary tale about this Kurdish ruffian and Lawrence. 'Busrawi is the man who carried out the massacres at Urfa, 8,000 people, and Adana, and Nezib just four months ago. At the last my brother was actually on the spot in disguise.'[28]

The Urfa atrocities were a lamentable fact, but they dated from early 1909, when Sultan Abdul Hamid was in his final struggle with the Young Turks. Lawrence had at that time not visited the Middle East and was several years from his first experiments with Arab dress. But this was not the only tall tale which Will believed. Another involved Lawrence and a Kurd in contingency plans to sack Aleppo: 'actually arranging which should have the loot of which house, and apportioning two bankers' houses, great collectors of objets d'art to Ned.' These plans had been temporarily frustrated by the Bulgarian failure to capture Constantinople.

Ned was too busy, or ill, for Will to see much of him at Carchemish. He was visited successively by the Altounyans, an American missionary returning to Lake Van, a professional soldier on leave and an attack of fever. The fever prevented him from joining Will on the planned visit to Busrawi's encampment. Instead, Will rode to the distant tents with the soldier, Lieutenant Hubert Young; they spent two nights there. 'I rode the best Arab mare in Mesopotamia for days, riding by night in the moonlight with summer lightning playing all the time.' In addition to Lawrence's mythopoeia, Will picked up a stomach infection from the Kurdish feasts just before he caught the Aleppo train. 'You must not think of Ned as leading an uncivilized existence,' he told his parents. 'When I saw him last as the train left the station he was wearing white flannels, socks and red slippers, with a white Magdalen blazer, and was talking to the governor of Biredjik in lordly fashion.'[29]

Will visited the Holy Land while Lieutenant Young stayed on. Three years older than Lawrence, Young achieved a surprising rapport with someone who was to dislike army officers as much as he did English public schools and their products.[30] Lawrence later told Young that he remembered his visit for Young's confession, laudable from a regular soldier, that he sometimes felt afraid.[31] At the time Young was preoccupied with everything associated with his military career, yet he remembered that nothing to do with war was discussed. Instead, the two young men dabbled at sculpture.

The long low house with its bare exterior needed, Lawrence had decided, a few gargoyles. Young executed an idealized female head, Lawrence 'a squatting demon of the Notre Dame style' for which Dahoum had posed naked. The figure which Lawrence worked from the soft local sandstone embellished the roof edge.

Lawrence's gargoyle proved the epicentre of a local scandal. Reared in the Muslim suspicion of all representational art, the villagers took Lawrence's sculpture of a naked youth as proof of a guilty passion. 'The scandal about Lawrence was widely spread and firmly believed', Woolley wrote later.[32] 'The charge was quite unfounded. Lawrence had in his make-up a very strong vein of sentiment, but he was in no sense a pervert; in fact, he had a remarkably clean mind.' But Woolley evidently thought that the relationship needed defending. 'He knew quite well what the Arabs said about himself and Dahoum and so far from resenting it was amused, and I think that he courted misunderstanding rather than tried to avoid it; it appealed to his sense of humour, which was broad and schoolboyish. He liked to shock.' Woolley added that Lawrence took a detached interest in the homosexuality of the ancient Greeks.

Islam has been less hostile than Christianity to homophily, because less hostile to sex in general. Muslim theologians never recommended celibacy nor imagined that the ordinary man could live without satisfying his bodily desires. The Koran pronounced penalties for such sexual misdemeanours as adultery and fornication (which could cause social havoc) but passed over in silence what men did with men or women with women.[33] Even so, an unwritten law, deriving possibly from Bedouin prejudice, condemned the passive partner in sexual activities between males—common as such activities could become in situations where the sexes were kept apart. The relationship between Lawrence and Dahoum would not provoke the question, Is this relationship sexual, but the question, Which is the active partner? The honour of a village family would repose in the manliness of its men as much as in the chastity of its women. Anyone who tried to adapt the morals of the Greek Anthology to village boys could expect trouble with their fathers.

The sculpture certainly embarrassed Dahoum, although his courage in posing, his readiness to disregard the smiles or sneers of the village, proved that he had more than a winning smile and a wrestler's build. The drawing of him done by Dodds now hung on the sitting-room wall beside the Morris tapestry. 'A really beautiful piece of work,' was Lawrence's comment, 'which gets more pleasant with familiarity: he [Dahoum] has never summoned up, himself, enough courage to show it to his people.'[34] But though Dahoum, too, benefited from the friendship, learning from the Englishman new skills and attitudes, Lawrence was the chief beneficiary. His easy, affectionate relationship with Dahoum helped him develop into someone very different from the eccentric who had walked the midnight quadrangles of Jesus College.

Will seems to have visited Carchemish in part to assess whether his family had been right to give Lawrence a privileged position, to build him a bungalow, to advance him loans and to accept his native friends. In his first reactions Will was cautiously enthusiastic about Ned's life at Jerablus. 'His is certainly a very jolly position, and a responsible one. Although there was no work doing when I was there, I only saw him read at meal-times: all other times he was either having to arrange village land-quarrels, or discuss the question of desertion from the army, or entertain the native visitors who kept dropping in for advice or out of courtesy.' So he summed up his first impressions in a letter from Port Said.[35]

But the enigma of his brother continued to puzzle him. Will's experience was almost as wide as Ned's. He, too, had cycled and walked in western Europe. At Cowes he had surveyed the assembled yachts of

Europe where the Kaiser, the Czar and assorted kings arrayed themselves as admirals, while elsewhere their ministers sailed their different countries on a course to war. Will had frequented scholars such as Ernest Barker, writers such as Corvo and Ezra Pound. He was now to teach Indians in Delhi, whose viceroy ruled more men and women than any other potentate on earth. On 24 January 1914, the *Illustrated London News* devoted four pages to the discoveries at Carchemish. When the magazine reached India it incited Will's muse. A short poem, dedicated 'to T.E.L.' was dated 18 February 1914.

I've talked with counsellors and lords
Whose words were as no blunted swords,
Watched two Emperors and five Kings
And three who had men's worshippings,
Ridden with horsemen of the East
And sat with scholars at their feast,
Known some the masters of their hours,
Some to whom years were as pressed flowers:
Still as I go this thought endures
No place too great to be made yours.[36]

Lines inspired by the sight of his brother's work written up in a leading periodical, by the recollection of his own moonlit rides, were also an answer to the family's question about their most unusual member. If by citing the men of power Ned would demand as peers Will correctly intuited his brother's ambition, the reference to someone very old—'to whom years were as pressed flowers'—is an assertion that in his own way Lawrence was spiritually on a level with Canon Christopher, who had died aged ninety-three the previous year. But the words, *as I go*, were sadly prophetic. Before the end of 1914, the yachtsmen of Europe were to be at war. The catastrophe which would give Lawrence the opportunity to fulfil the prediction of greatness would end Will's life.

BOOK THREE

1914–1918

Whitemantle

13

WOOLLEY AND LAWRENCE worked through the last months of 1913 as though their blend of excavation and fine living might endure forever. But just before Christmas a telegram arrived from the British Museum instructing them to assume the archaeological duties in a survey being undertaken, between Gaza and Petra, by the Palestine Exploration Fund, an organization with biblical leanings.[1] Accompanied by Dahoum they at once caught the train to Aleppo where they found a letter with a second telegram waiting for them at the Consulate which clarified their unexpected instructions. As they caught an Egyptian steamer from Beirut for Jaffa none of the three can have foreseen in their sudden new venture the shadow of events which would make Woolley a prisoner-of-war, Carchemish inaccessible on a new frontier, Lawrence internationally famous and Dahoum a ghost. But Lawrence saw through the pretence behind their expedition: 'We are obviously only meant as red herrings, to give an archaeological colour to a political job.'[2]

Lawrence was right. Their assignment represented the result of some eight months of secret negotiations between Britain's Director of Military Operations and the Foreign Office. The problem was logistically simple but politically complex. In 1872, when Kitchener had been a young lieutenant in the Royal Engineers, he had, with another lieutenant, executed a survey of Palestine for the same Palestine Exploration Fund which was nominally to sponsor Woolley and Lawrence now. After occupying Egypt, the British had been able to survey the Egyptian side of the Sinai frontier, but the Director of Military Operations now pointed out to the Under-Secretary of State for Foreign Affairs the existence of a blank space between Kitchener's old Palestine survey and the newer survey of Sinai. 'The only knowledge of this area is that obtained from unreliable sketches and reports of travellers, and it is considered desirable, from a military point of view, that a survey should be made of this district, the area of which is about 400 square miles.'[3]

Southern Palestine, the triangular Negeb, was under Ottoman control as well as sovereignty.* To allay Turkish suspicions, the survey which

* Although Egyptian Sinai remained under Ottoman sovereignty until Turkey's entry into the War in 1914, the British were in effective control.

was finally authorized, would be ostensibly concerned with the wanderings of the Hebrews. It would be conducted by Captain Stewart Newcombe (then in Egyptian Sinai), who would be assisted by two lance-corporals in mufti of whose military rank it would be needless to inform the Turkish authorities. The presence of two *bona fide* archaeologists would further whitewash the expedition. A letter from the Director of Military Operations of 17 December 1913, misnaming Woolley's companion as 'G. E. Laurence' shows that he was still little known in official quarters.

From Jaffa Lawrence, Woolley and Dahoum drove south in a carriage between hedges of acacia and eucalyptus dividing Arab-owned orange groves. After passing Ashdod, Askelon and Gaza (where they picked up further instructions) they turned inland to meet Newcombe at Beersheba, the bedouin town on the desert's northern fringe. Newcombe, a regular soldier, had been expecting intellectuals laden with fifteen tons of baggage. He was relieved to find that his civilian helpers were travelling light: with two tents, one cook and enough luggage for a single donkey.

In a quick look at Beersheba they found some twenty inscriptions, including one in Hebrew. They had had no time to mug up books previously published on the region. As they travelled south, camping on sites of long abandoned Byzantine cities, they merely speculated on the route of the ancient Israelites. Lawrence and Dahoum spent one day at Akaba, where the desert met a coral-filled inlet of sea between barren mountains. (Woolley, to save time, had gone off in another direction.) When the Turks, suspicious of their motives, had Lawrence and his Arab friend followed by a lieutenant and a platoon, Lawrence infected Dahoum with his delight in the excitement of outwitting their watchers.

The risks were greater for Dahoum than for Lawrence. As an archaeologist working under an Ottoman *firman*, Lawrence merely risked his job if he were suspected of spying; as an Ottoman subject, soon liable for military service, Dahoum could lose much more if the relations between Turkey and Britain deteriorated to the point of war. But Dahoum had found in Lawrence a friend whose heroic qualities blinded him to risk. 'We respect him and greatly admire his courage and bravery'; he had told Miss el-Akle, 'we love him, because he loves us and would lay down our lives for him.'[4] He would have dismissed the perils of his situation, if he bothered to foresee them, with the comforting *Mashallah*! (As God wills!) of the Muslim peasant. Lawrence, too, thought only of the moment. A carefree mood, a tang of cops and robbers, pervades his letters from what he and Woolley called The Wilderness of Zin in the hasty, rather amateurish book which recorded their journey. But one problem beset him. By the time he and Dahoum reached the gorges of Petra he had run out of money. Fortunately they discovered encamped there a rich English tourist, Lady Evelyn Cobbold, whose annual practice it was to leave her villa in the south of France to winter in Egypt and the countries near it. All over a world which they controlled Europeans were working, or taking time off, as though the sunshine of their *belle époque* would last forever. Lady Evelyn lent the friends enough money for the train which now ran north from Maan near Petra. On 28 February, they reached Damascus and went on to Carchemish, where, after some further weeks of normal spring excavation, Lawrence left Dahoum for Oxford. Neither friend can have foreseen that their farewell was final. Lawrence was in England when a Serbian assassin killed the Austrian Archduke in Sarajevo, and at 2, Polstead Road when on 4 August the British Empire declared war on Germany.

When war was declared Frank Lawrence was at a boys' camp in Yorkshire. With his love of team games, he was the most conventionally normal of the five brothers. An undergraduate at Jesus, a member of the O.T.C., he shared the mood of exhilaration which swept an empire protected for a century by the world's strongest fleet. His patriotism was tinged with an Evangelical sense of responsibility. 'I have filled up the form for the Special Reserve not lightly nor without thought,' he wrote to his mother from camp. 'Please get it taken at once to 9, Alfred Street. If there is anything you want to say about it please wire.'[5] (Mrs. Lawrence's ill health throughout the early months of the war implies that the role of stoic mother did not come easily.) By September he had been commissioned as a Second Lieutenant in the 3rd Gloucesters. His affectionate letters from various barracks and camps remained unchauvinistic and even happy. But he was depressed by the soldiers' language and fondness for drink. 'The Adjutant said an interesting thing the other day. Speaking about drink, he said that if he had the power he would make it a penal offence to bring drink into England, and would hang anyone trying to do so.'[6] Frank's battalion moved to France and, like other officers, he had the duty of censoring his men's letters. 'Many when writing home say how they would like some beer or spirits. It is much more sad, I think, than all the deaths in this war.'[7]

Will Lawrence, older and more sophisticated, foresaw from India 'an awful prospect of a world-struggle,' in which Britain's position, fortunately, seemed better than that of any other belligerent. 'Just at the moment though the personal aspect is what I feel most. What will Ned have to do, stop at home or go East again and steer his country into safe waters?'[8] A week later he showed as deep a Christian feeling as Frank, planning to write a letter to a German friend in Jerusalem, to show that he felt no personal animus.[9] But his detachment wilted as letters from England named friends already at war. He became impatient, he told his father, 'to sprint at once and get in with Frank. I wonder what you and Mother would think if I left here for a year next May? Whether you think the country [England] or the education of India on Christian lines the more important. Because I'm sorry that I'm here at the moment.'[10] It astonished Will that Ned spoke of returning as a civilian to Carchemish. 'Turkey has mobilized through Syria and digging will be absurd.'

Lawrence had greeted the war with a humorous detachment which marked the distance he had travelled from certainties unquestioned by his brothers. For some months the clash between France and Germany failed to involve the country—'his country' as Will perceptively named it—where Dahoum was awaiting his annual return. Meanwhile he had work to finish. Kitchener, recalled from his return journey to Cairo to become Secretary of State for War, wanted the previous winter's jaunt rendered as quickly as possible into a book. If Turkey stayed neutral, it would allay suspicions; if Turkey joined the Central Powers against Britain, the maps would be useful. Mrs. Rieder was now in America. On 18 September Lawrence told her: 'I am writing a learned work on Moses and his wanderings: for the Egyptian people say they want me but not yet, and the War Office won't accept me till the Egyptian W.O. [i.e. the British military authority in Egypt] has finished with me.' With thousands of others, including Will's local commander in India, Lawrence shared the feeling that 'it will all be over with Germany in six weeks'; but he expressed a particular 'horrible fear that the Turks do not intend to go to war: for it would be an improvement to have them reduced to Asia Minor.'[11] He ridiculed the British females whose needles were turning out 'Balaclava helmets'. The wearing of such things, he told Mrs. Rieder, by deafening the troops would render them liable to slaughter as they slept.

In 1914 Lawrence's talents and experience were known to an appreciative, influential but tiny circle. When, later, he became famous, some of his admirers, and in certain moods himself, would feel pressed to explain his admission that 'I did not try to enlist'[12] by invoking a diminutive stature that, according to the never confirmed story of his own telling, had not prevented his joining the Artillery when smaller and younger.* Yet Lawrence's activities during the early stages of the war must have seemed valuable to those prosecuting the war from London and Cairo. Once he had helped produce the maps for the strategic area linking British-occupied Sinai with Palestine, his four years' experience of Asiatic

* Sir Mark Sykes, destined to play an alternative role in the war to Lawrence's, was overtly accused of cowardice; so much so that his sons had to be removed from one school to another to avoid the malice of war hysteria.[13] Yet Sykes—Catholic, aristocratic, a Member of Parliament, married—had travelled more widley in the Middle East than Lawrence and become, in his own way, captivated by it. Like Lawrence he felt he could best contribute to his country's cause in the area he knew; not in the anonymous maelstrom of the Western Front.

Turkey could be utilized in other, related fields. British Intelligence linked a network of men trusted by their controllers; the network had the attendant weakness of being small. Their experts on the Levant might have formed two cricket teams, with Gertrude Bell, the only woman, thrown in as umpire. All were known personally to David Hogarth who later defined his own 1914 convictions: 'unless everyone in the country who had any special qualification put it at the service of the country, we couldn't get through, and I put mine with one sole object—to beat the Bosche! and keep Britain where she was before the war.'[14] As Hogarth knew that one of two British plans envisaged an assault on the Syrian port of Alexandretta,[15] he could recommend Lawrence wholeheartedly as one who knew that particular region well.

A technical problem for those in Intelligence was to procure titular ranks which could disguise their actual functions while enabling them to enjoy such authority or facilities as their tasks demanded. Hogarth, land-traveller and antiquarian, was by 1915 to appear metamorphosed in the bulging whites of a Lieutenant-Commander in the Royal Naval Reserve. T. E. Lawrence, his protégé since 1909, was officially gazetted as 'Temp. 2nd Lieut-Interpreter' under the date of 23 October 1914. There would later be a conflict of evidence as to how Lawrence had secured His Majesty's commission. Lawrence himself said that Hogarth had intervened with an official of the Royal Geographical Society 'who got [Sir Coote] Hedley to take me. The interview with Hedley [War Office head of the Geographical Section of the General Staff] was by Hogarth's appointment.'[16] Sir Coote, when Hogarth was no longer alive, disputed this account, alleging that Lawrence called on his own initiative. He remembered him looking about eighteen, wearing grey flannels but no hat and claiming to have been turned down as too small for Army service.[17] The conflict is unimportant. Sir Coote probably denied the link with Hogarth from loyalty to the practice that connections with Intelligence should be concealed. However introduced, Lawrence was taken into Sir Coote's office while still a civilian to help finish the Sinai maps and was then commissioned.

Except for his brief spell in the Oxford O.T.C., Lawrence never underwent even rudimentary military training. He was recruited to serve as an Intelligence operative in the Middle East, an area of vital importance to the British Empire. Although the Turks had recently done badly in war, Constantinople's claim to the Caliphate of Islam posed an ideological threat to Britain, ruler of millions of Muslims in India and elsewhere. The territories controlled by the Turks, at the hinge of the three continents of the Old World, were strategically important to an empire whose lifeline was the Suez Canal. If such dangers were worrying, the possibilities were tempting. Should the Sick Man of Europe at last die, he would leave a rich legacy to be disputed. That the legacy included oil-wells was already known.

Lawrence's patriotism lacked the old-fashioned simplicity of his brothers'. As an idea, he valued it as a reinforcement to a man's identity; it need imply no preference for the values of one society over another. 'It is a very good thing to have a country to grumble over or praise as one wishes: it doesn't matter much which country I fancy!'[18] Writing this two years before, he had used the exclamation mark to admit that he was being heterodox. 'His' country, the Euphrates-side landscape in which he had seen himself as baron and Dahoum as his devoted page, was still not at war. But it was on his mind. 'Turkey', he wrote on 19 October to Winifred Fontana, who had just left Alexandretta in a cattleboat with her children, 'seems at last to have made up its mind to lie down and be at peace with all the world. I'm sorry, because I wanted to root them out of Syria, and now their blight will be more enduring than ever. You have no news of Carchemish I suppose?'[19]

On 29 October units of the Turkish fleet bombarded ports in southern Russia, Turkey's traditional enemy but Britain's ally in the struggle against Germany. When the Italian invasion of Libya had shown the Turks their desperate need of modern warships, two battleships had been ordered from Britain and paid for by public subscription. But in August, on the orders of Winston Churchill, the completed ships were summarily transferred to the Royal Navy. Germany had immediately ordered two cruisers, the *Goeben* and *Breslau*, then in the Mediterranean, to proceed to Constantinople, where, to public enthusiasm, their crews changed the flat German cap for the Ottoman fez. Secret agreements at the governmental level had earlier ensured Turkish participation in the war; on the popular level, German exploitation of the British blunder made it popular.

Turkey's entry into the war made Dahoum an enemy alien and forced Consul Fontana to leave Aleppo. Before he did so, Lawrence had urged him to try and persuade the Turks to allow Dahoum and the other 'head men' to do their military service on the dig as guards. 'I wonder', he asked Winifred Fontana in a second letter, 'if he got this through, before he left. I hope the men will carry off everything from the house before any Turk can sack it. It would grieve me if any Turk shot me with my own revolver. However I asked Haj Wahid & Dahoum to see to them. Between them they can dispose of all things cunningly in the village.'[20] Not for the first time he used jocularity to hide his feelings. For it was as desperate as it was naive to suppose that the Turks would allow a Syrian who had worked with foreigners to choose the form and place of his military service. And it was doubtless Dahoum's new situation which made Lawrence reverse his attitude to Turkey's initial neutrality. 'Will is consumed with a wild patriotism,' he was to write four months after Turkey had entered the war and he himself had become a Lieutenant. 'I am afraid that I don't feel strongly enough. So far as Syria is concerned it is France & not Turkey that is the enemy . . . but I wish I could give it to Germany in some way, for the shameless way in which she dragged Turkey into the war.'[21] Love made Lawrence, like most men, inconsistent.

By early December Lawrence and Newcombe had completed their work on the text and maps for *The Wilderness of Zin*. They then crossed France by train to embark at Marseilles for Alexandria and by 14 December Lawrence was installed at the Grand Continental Hotel in Cairo. His immediate chief was Ernest Dowson, Director-General of the Survey of Egypt. In retrospect Dowson, who met hundreds of Englishmen during his years of service, got the date of their first meeting wrong; ascribing it to the beginning of the 1913–1914 season 'when he [Lawrence] came on Newcombe's instructions . . . to report for duty and to collect field equipment and field staff.'[22] But Dowson clearly remembered his first reaction to the short, boyish figure who insinuated himself with a half apologetic grin into his Giza office: 'Whoever can this extraordinary little pipsqueak be?' Lawrence certainly seemed unremarkable compared with the distinguished, in some cases aristocratic, additions to British Intelligence soon to arrive. By 17 December Leonard Woolley (recalled from the Artillery for which he had volunteered) had already reached Cairo along with two Members of Parliament, George Lloyd and Aubrey Herbert.

The Egyptian capital was to be the physical link between the two halves, as neatly contrasted as the elements within himself, into which Lawrence's wartime experience was to fall. Until October 1916, except for a side-visit to Athens in 1915 and a longer trip to Mesopotamia in early 1916, he was engaged in varied but humdrum desk-work at the Cairo hub of British Intelligence; from 16 October 1918, he was still attached to Cairo by the thread of command as in the fringe of western Asia he took part in the Revolt which was to inspire his legend and provide the matter for a major book.

Lawrence was to sleep more nights in Cairo than in the Jerablus which had made him happy or the Arabia which was to make him famous. Yet although he had come at a superb moment to explore the richest sequence of Islamic monuments in the world, as well as military architecture closely related to the subject of his thesis, he was never to like the Egyptian capital. For one thing, it showed the impress of the west. In the wake of Napoleon's 1798 invasion, a dynasty of Balkan origin, descendants of Muhammad Ali Pasha, had ruled first as vassals of the Ottoman sultan and then, after the British occupation, as virtual puppets of the British. Though in theory the Khedive, up till 1914, owed his appointment to the

Sultan-Caliph, in whose name Friday prayers were offered in Egyptian mosques, His Britannic Majesty's Consul-General controlled the country through a network of British advisers in all departments of state. The summer preceding the outbreak of war the reigning Khedive, Abbas Hilmi, had been holidaying in Constantinople when an attempt was made on his life by an Egyptian student. Wounded, he stayed on in the Ottoman capital, giving the British a chance to turn Egypt into a protectorate, to abolish the title of Khedive and to install Abbas Hilmi's uncle as 'sultan', a term which the French in Morocco and the British in Malaya had found innocuous.

These measures left a residue of hostility of which Lawrence was conscious, though he did not sympathize with Egyptian aspirations.* He simply did not like the results of Europeans sharing a city with orientals. The Cairo of the war years was still spacious; its future congested suburbs were still villages scattered on a plain between tawny cliffs to the east, dominated by Saladin's citadel and Muhammad Ali's Stamboul-style mosque, and the escarpment to the west with its clusters of pyramids. One dramatic change had happened to Cairo within recent memory. Previously each summer the flooding Nile had turned the fertile plain between the Giza plateau and the city huddling below the Citadel to the same annual lake which the Pharaohs had used when ferrying giant limestone blocks to build their pyramids. Cairo had been bounded by its 'Canal', a large ditch encircling inwoven cities of successive rulers and filled with water once the earth-dikes holding back the flood were broken. But when European engineers succeeded in damming the river upstream, the Nile flooded no longer and it became possible to colonize what had been vegetable gardens and orchards. The Khedive had presented the new dry land to those who could build to certain standards. This meant, in effect, the south Europeans who had progressively poured into the country throughout the nineteenth century. Thus, when Lawrence settled in Cairo, two cities, different in spirit and appearance, faced each other where the filled-in Canal formed a boulevard for traffic. To the east, the labyrinthine lanes of the *beledi* city twined between the stern façades of ancient schools or mosques and small shops which sold curios, gold or perfume. Here the ordinary Egyptians, dark-hued and stalwart, wore the traditional gallabya, bathed, not at home, but in the city's domed hammams, gossiped in innumerable coffeeshops and prayed in the yet more numerous mosques. Their veiled wives stayed at home rearing the children, who, through tiny schools where they learned the Koran,

* 'In the Cairo Mosques,' after the deposition of the Khedive, 'the prayer for the Moslem *Khalīfa* was repeated three times in succession and each time response was general and loud, whereas that to the prayers for the Sultan of Egypt was feeble or inaudible. The students of the Law School appeared wearing black ties and lugubrious expressions; many girls in the Government Secondary Schools sported black rosettes.'[23]

would progress to the great university mosque of al-Azhar, keeping alive the faith which, despite repeated foreign domination, gave them a sense of peace and potential dignity.

The other, *frangi*, Cairo, dating from the nineteenth century, was built largely in a south European style and inhabited either by immigrants from abroad or by Egyptians who could afford a western way of life. Neapolitan-style palazzi, tenements with art nouveau additions, branches of western banks, agencies for western companies, were thronged and tended by Greeks, Italians, Jews, Maltese, French, British and Christian Syrians. On an island in the Nile former plantations had been cleared to make a Sporting Club complete with race-course. A high British official was embarrassed by the way other members looked at him when he invited an Egyptian guest, later destined to be prime minister. Although physical power was based on the great British barracks by the Nile (later the site of a Hilton hotel), 'apart from the officials and the Army, Cairo was still mainly French-speaking-thinking-and-living, just as Alexandria was Italian and Greek.'[24]*

Lawrence was attracted to neither city. He could not, among suspicious or servile Egyptians, find a substitute for the friendliness he had enjoyed with the villagers at Jerablus, even if it had been possible for a commissioned officer to make friends with 'natives'. Nor was Lawrence attracted to the pleasures of the western city, where race-meetings attracted punters throughout the war, where tennis-courts were overcrowded and 'You cannot get a table at the Club!' was the common cry. Although he was pleased when Lady Evelyn Cobbold 'turned up, on her usual winter visit to Egypt,'[25] he disliked a wealthy society in which he was too poor to impress the Levantines and too obscure to impress the British. He poured his hatred for the conjoined cities into a letter to Hogarth: 'Anything fouler than the town buildings, or its beastly people, can't be.' After six months' exile from England and Carchemish, the latter seemed 'a village inhabited by the cleanest & most intelligent angels.'[26]

Yet Lawrence reacted with characteristic energy to the sour reversals whereby a pastiche metropolis of clubs and tennis courts supplanted the barren yet haunting steppe; a mixed population regarded the British as occupiers or catered to tastes which he despised; British officers, with their conventional code, displaced Dahoum. He sealed off the layers of his personality which Carchemish had fulfilled and gave all his energy to his official work. But, as always, he disdained discretion, disregarding censors as he corresponded with his family and Hogarth. When asked what his daily cycle rides to Giza involved, he described himself as

* The writer showed by his use of 'Cairo' how little the Egyptian city, where everyone spoke Arabic, entered his calculations.

'drawing, and overseeing the drawing of maps: overseeing printing & packing of same: sitting in an office coding and decoding telegrams, interviewing prisoners, writing reports, & giving information from 9 a.m. till 7 p.m. After that feed and read, & then go to bed. I'm sick of pens, ink & paper: & have no wish ever to send off another telegram.' He and his colleagues were studying each far-flung tentacle of an octopoid empire. 'We do daily wires to Athens, Gallipoli, & Petrograd; & receive five times what we send, all in cypher, which is slow work, though we have a good staff dealing with them.'[27] His war work involved European Turkey, Asia Minor, Syria, Mesopotamia, Arabia, Sinai and Tripoli. The last referred to Libya whose tribesmen were still resisting Italian occupation of the coast.

At Carchemish, one of two Englishmen in a Euphrates village, Lawrence had seen himself as an unofficial Qonsolos, mediating quarrels or chastizing those who dynamited fish. In Cairo he was a junior officer working with the élite of an empire that still controlled a fifth of the world and aimed to control more. 'Newcombe, one Macdonnell and myself are Intelligence, Captain Cosens, Lord Anglesey, Lord Hartington & Prince Alexander of Battenburg do the ciphering & deciphering with us: that's all we are:—with a Colonel Clayton who does Egyptian Foreign Politics in command of us.'[28] The Turks had recently made a sortie against the Suez Canal. Except when interviewing Arabic-speaking prisoners, Lawrence avoided speaking Arabic lest he pick up the Egyptian accent and vocabulary.[29]

Bearing authentic names, educated at famous schools, only a few of his military seniors—W. F. Stirling was one[30]—found his humour refreshing for saying things that conventional upbringing forbade. His contemporaries, many of whom found him pretentious, invariably referred to 'little Lawrence'; that he lacked social position as well as inches pushed him to excel, not just in sly humour, but in the hours he devoted to his work, in his expositions of stratego-political problems or in the precision of detail he could display when he wished. The memoranda, then the reports, which he composed for his superiors were designed to promote his own reputation as much as imperial interests. They reveal no emotional involvement with any particular subject race or people.

Two obsessions ruled his thoughts: that the British should get into Syria before the French and that they should do this by occupying Alexandretta. He probably pushed these notions in conversations with his superiors; he certainly did so in letters which he sent to Hogarth *en clair* and which could have harmed Britain's relations with her most important ally if they had fallen into the wrong hands. That so youthful a lieutenant should argue such grandiose ideas to men old enough to be his father could seem, to the critical, pipsqueakism or fantasy. Yet

Intelligence services that wish to thrive need to be more open to ideas than a Guards battalion. In London, before sailing for Egypt, his colleague, George Lloyd, a banker as well as an M.P., had also discussed the policies planned for the Middle East. 'The line on which the W.O. [War Office] appear to be working (and they are calling the tune at present) is that all the Territory south of a line drawn approximately from Haifa to the north of Baghdad and thence east to the Persian frontier should be a British sphere. Arabia and the Holy Places would be left practically independent and their integrity guaranteed against external aggression, but it would give Britain the complete control of the Euphrates valley and secures the "all red" overland route to India.'[31] This policy would leave Jerablus out of the British zone, but not, presumably, leave it to Turkey.

The letters Lawrence wrote to Hogarth in 1915 not only show the intellectual accessibility of the older to the younger man; at times they give the impression that the correspondents were at war with France. The French were insisting on Syria, he wrote on 18 March, and this Britain would have to concede: 'there remains Alexandretta, which is the key of the whole place as you know. It's going to be the head of the Baghdad line, & ∴ the natural outlet for N. Syria & N. Mesopotamia.'[32] In a further letter from Port Said he projected using an anti-Turkish amir in north Yemen so that 'we can rush right up to Damascus, & biff the French out of all hope of Syria. It's a big game, and at last one worth playing.'[33] Alexandretta was, of course, the port of access to 'his' country. A British occupation of the port and its hinterland could rescue the villagers of Jerablus from the Turks without handing them over to new French masters.

Lawrence was not the first Englishman to press for a landing at Alexandretta. Three months earlier, his chief, Colonel Clayton, had pointed out that such an operation would strike 'at a most vital point and would cut the only line of communication, not only with Syria but also with Baghdad and even the Caucasus, provided the Black Sea route is closed.' Clayton had learnt from reliable sources that German commanders in Syria dreaded nothing so much as a British landing in north Syria: 'they say themselves that this would be followed by a general defection of their Arab troops.'[34] Clayton's idea was supported by a high-ranking British agent: 'Alexandretta offers facilities for something like a decisive blow over half Turkey . . . a comparatively small force, from 10,000 to 20,000 men, depending on the opposition, could hold the line Ayas-Alexandretta-Beilan.' This agent added that the force would need to advance either to Jerablus, where the Euphrates was being bridged, or west to the pass in the Taurus Mountains known as the Cilician Gates, if Turkish communications were to be properly cut.[35]

Lawrence took practical steps to prepare for such an operation. He asked a British businessman who had recently left Alexandretta for Cyprus for help with maps of the port and the Beilan pass above it.[36] In April Hogarth suggested that the British might occupy the cotton-growing plain immediately to the south of the Cilician Gates. 'By all means Cilicia,' Lawrence replied. 'I was only afraid of asking too much. And Alex. [-andretta] as the naval base is the crux of the whole show.'[37] In naming eminent supporters of the scheme Lawrence showed the partiality for the famous common to clergymen, actors and spies. 'The High Commissioner [Sir Henry McMahon] is strongly of the same opinion, & General Maxwell [Commander-in-Chief in Egypt] also . . . K. [Kitchener] has pressed it on us: Winston [Churchill] seems uncertain, & Someone—not Grey [the British Foreign Secretary]—perhaps Parker in the F.O. is blocking it entirely . . .'[38] Lawrence's suggestion, that the 'uncertain' Churchill (who had recently sponsored a disastrous alternative in the Dardanelles) should be told of imaginary oil wells on the beach and of iron deposits nearby, is certainly a joke. Yet Churchill became a convert. As late as July 1917 he was described by the Secretary to the British Cabinet as being 'hot for an expedition to Alexandretta.'[39]

In advocating such an expedition Lawrence had better arguments than imaginary minerals or fears that a French fleet might use the port to menace Egypt. A German officer who fought on the Middle Eastern front was to discuss, in a post-war book, the puzzle of why 'England never attempted to cut the rear communications line from the sea through a landing in the Gulf of Alexandretta, thus severing at one blow the life-line of the Turkish armies in Mesopotamia and Syria-Palestine. The Anatolian railway there comes close to the sea and the coast was thinly guarded. Ayas Bay offered a favourable point for a landing. Nothing explains the non-action of the English who could have dealt Turkey a death-blow in that theatre of war. A glance at the coast shows how convenient Cyprus was as a base, its north-east peninsula seeming to indicate the way.'[40]*

Hogarth was able to answer the puzzle only when the war was over: France had stubbornly refused to sanction any operation in Syria in which her own troops could not take part and as, at the time, she was hard-pressed at home, her veto was accepted. Hogarth believed that their subsequent harsh treatment of the Syrian Arabs sprang from the Turk's realization that the British were not, after all, going to land at Alexandretta, as well as from the British weaknesses revealed at Gallipoli.[41]

Lawrence's attitude to France seems at first sight the betrayal of a boyhood love. Yet he had loved medieval France only. In the twentieth century two Frances existed in an uneasy partnership which a second German War would sunder, and neither appealed to Lawrence. His

* Cyprus had the disadvantage, as a base, of lacking good harbours.

protestant background made him distrust the Catholic France whose focus was the Army and his conservative upbringing made him suspicious of the secular France inspired by the Revolution. Catholic missionaries as much as teachers in state-backed lycées could turn simple Arabs into fake Europeans. And philosophical bias was underpinned by personal factors. The French report on Lawrence circulated in the war[42] was evidence of how closely his antics with Dahoum had been observed. Someone who feared ridicule could fear it most deeply from the witty yet acerbic French.

War's abstract monomania, the fantasy of being a general and knighted before he was thirty,[43] carried him through two private griefs. His brother Frank was killed on 9 May 1915, as he prepared to lead his men in one of the myriad unsuccessful assaults in a war of stagnation. Frank left two letters, written at different dates, to be opened after his death. The first was more confident than the second; both were informed by an acceptance of God's inscrutable will and the certainty that any parting from his family would be 'for an infinitesimal space of time out of eternity . . . In these last three months, I have gone through indescribable depths of infamy, living in the midst of it, and if I had been accustomed to going to theatres, music halls etc. in the seemingly harmless way other boys go I should have found it trebly hard to have kept myself clean.'[44]

Lawrence concealed his grief behind a formal manner.

'Today I got Father's two letters. They are very comfortable reading:—and I hope that when I die there will be nothing more to regret. The only thing I feel a little is, that there was no need surely to go into mourning for him? I cannot see any cause at all—in any case to die for one's country is a sort of privilege.'[45]

Will Lawrence had hurried home from India to share this privilege. In January he had assured Lawrence that he would forego inviting Abdul Ghaffar, his Egyptian friend, to meet them, as he transited the Suez Canal, 'in case of awkwardness with the three of us possibly together.' Abdul Ghaffar, 'settled, married and quiet in his home out of Cairo,' had not rallied to the Allied cause. The brothers themselves met briefly at Port Said in March. But skirmishing by the Canal delayed the ship and Lawrence had to go back to Cairo.[46] Will, obviously quoting his brother, described Egypt 'as quiet as a mouse' and spoke of the Egyptian Army being used against the Turks. (This, and the later conscription of fellahin into labour battalions was to increase Egyptian resentment of British rule.) On board Will met Lady Evelyn Cobbold, 'a strange person', who invited him to lunch at her villa outside Marseilles on 28 March. It was a last social pleasure. On 23 October, an observer in the Royal Flying Corps, Will was shot down after only a few days in France. At Christmas, Lawrence urged his parents to 'Look forward all the time.'[47]

Though Cairo could not replace his brothers or reunite him with Dahoum,* in the person of the Hon. Aubrey Nigel Henry Herbert it produced one of those impressive personalities from whom, throughout his life, Lawrence admiringly borrowed attitudes, conceptions and, in one case, a surname.

The son of an earl, an Etonian and a Balliol scholar, Herbert had packed impressive achievements into the eight years by which he was senior to Lawrence. In defence, Lawrence wrote of him somewhat patronizingly: 'Then there is Aubrey Herbert, who is a joke, but a very nice one: he is too short-sighted to read or recognize anyone: speaks Turkish well, Albanian, French, Italian, Arabic, German . . . was for a time chairman of the Balkan League, of the Committee of Union and Progress, and of the Albanian Revolution Committee. He fought through the Yemen wars, and the Balkan wars with the Turks, & is friends with them all.'[49] In the words of a less complex admirer, Herbert had already established 'a fantastic record in various terrains of the War. He was taken prisoner in the retreat from Mons, when, armed with an alpenstock, he must have presented a figure like Don Quixote's; and, knowing Turkish, during a truce at Gallipoli, he is said to have taken command of a Turkish unit and escorted it back to its trenches.'[50]

In Cairo Lawrence had known Herbert superficially. He was to learn more of Herbert's ideas, in particular of how Islam could be exploited by the British Empire, when in the spring of 1916 both he and Herbert were entrusted with one of the strangest missions of the war: the attempt, by last-minute bribery, to avert the surrender into Turkish captivity of some 13,000 British and Indian troops besieged in the Tigris-side town of Kut al-Amara.

* Lawrence's last reference to Dahoum in his correspondence dates from January 1916: 'I can get no news of Dahoum: indeed I am afraid to send & ask. Most of the men (and boys) from that district have been sent to Constantinople, where they still are.'[48] At least one of Lawrence's agents, a Christian Arab, travelled backwards and forwards between Cairo and Haifa; but Lawrence knew that if he asked detailed questions about Dahoum, this might bring his friend to the closer attention of the Turks, who had already marked Dahoum's connections with Lawrence and Woolley and knew of his link with British Intelligence.

14

LATE IN MARCH 1916, a converted Canadian liner, the *Royal George,* carried Lawrence through the Red Sea south from Suez. The journey round the vast Arabian peninsula to Mesopotamia afforded an opportunity for him to ponder an area which he so far knew only from the written word. Since his Oxford days he had admired Doughty's *Travels in Arabia Deserta*; Hogarth had written on the penetration of Arabia although without visiting it himself; Gertrude Bell had given useful accounts of the tribes; Intelligence reports had reached his desk.

To starboard, Egypt's coastal mountains soared like the serrated spine of some stone armadillo, the hundred-foot sand drifts mocking the glaciers of northern ranges. Behind this waterless barrier a railway followed the Nile up-river to the first cataract. South of that Sir Reginald Wingate ruled, as Governor-General, the immense Sudan. A generation earlier the dervish army of the Mahdi and his Khalifa had shown the power of an idea working on simple minds. But the Sudan was now quiet and the Gothic buildings of Gordon College formed a memorial to the murdered Scot.

More challenging, far more mysterious, were the massifs on the eastern side of the Red Sea. Bare, gully-broken, pre-Cambrian, these mountains marked the western limits of the Arabian desert, much of it still untraversed by Europeans. Unlike the Arabian interior, the coastal province was under Ottoman control. The Hejaz, as this region was known, was the Holy Land of Islam, associated as intimately with the life of the Prophet Muhammad as Palestine with the life of Jesus. In the Mecca of his birth and then in the Medina of his rule, death and burial, Muhammad had received the revelations which his followers regarded as the final utterance of God. Muhammad's role as Prophet was unique and died with him but his role as leader of the Muslim community had passed to a series of successors, or caliphs. Although, unlike Medina, Damascus and Baghdad, Mecca had never been the centre of a caliphate, its prestige was immense, depending both on the fact that it had been the city of Muhammad's tribe, the Koreish, and that the central object of its ancient pagan shrine, the Kaaba, a cube-shaped building incorporating a black meteorite, remained the focus of Islam. Every Muslim was supposed to pray five times daily towards the Kaaba; every Muslim was supposed once in his life to go on pilgrimage to the place where the Angel Gabriel had called the Prophet. Mecca also contained a site of particular importance to Arabs: the well of Zemzem, in the same precinct as the Kaaba, was believed to be the well at which Hagar had sat with Ishmael; it thus linked the last of the three monotheistic faiths with the first.

Until the sixteenth century, it had been undisputed that a caliph must derive, however tenuously, from the Prophet's tribe, the Koreish. When the Turks, history's toughest converts to Islam, took over and reunited the Arab provinces which had been ravaged by the Mongols, they at first deferred to a caliph without power who based his claims on his descent from the Prophet's uncle, Abbas, and who reigned as a kind of hereditary pope in Cairo. But when in 1517 Selim the Grim conquered Egypt for the Ottoman Empire he took the last Abbasid caliph to Constantinople, the new capital of Islam at the junction of Europe and Asia.

The Ottoman Empire was then at its height and its rulers could afford to dispense with the fripperies of caliphal awe. But as Constantinople found itself threatened by the nations of a once impotent west, its sultans, eager for any reinforcement, began to claim that the caliphate had passed to them, as the House of Osman. Many Muslims, aware that the Ottomans had no blood connection with the Koreish, nevertheless accepted the claim in the context of an Islamic world threatened by greedy neighbours while the Ottomans were morally strengthened by their possession of the three holiest cities in Islam: Mecca, where Muhammad had been born and received his first revelation; Jerusalem where he was rapt into Heaven on a mystical journey; and Medina where he was entombed. The pilgrimage to Mecca was an annual institution which emphasized the unity of Islam in the world. Each year, at seasons processing according to the lunar calendar, scores of thousands of weary, often robbed yet exultant pilgrims approached the dust-bowl city forbidden to non-Muslims and hidden behind the treeless mountains which Lawrence observed from the deck of his liner. In a custom first started by a Mameluke queen, each year a black, embroidered covering had been sent from Egypt to deck the Kaaba. But for the last two years the covering had not come to Jidda, the port for Mecca, since a British blockade of the Red Sea restricted the pilgrimage to those who could come from Arabia itself or by the new railway which linked Medina with the north.

Yet many Arabs remembered the days when the rulers of Islam had been Koreishi Arabs, and none remembered them more keenly than Mecca's paramount family. Known as Hashemites, from an ancestor of the Prophet, they claimed descent from Hassan, one of Muhammad's two grandsons, although since Hassan sired many children, their honorary title of Sharif (or 'Noble') was shared with many others.

Like most Arab families, the Hashemites were divided; the head of the clan, known to Europeans as the Grand Sharif, was a local potentate appointed by the Ottoman government. Ottoman policy had been to favour now one feuding Sharif and now another. The present Grand Sharif, Hussein, had passed fifteen years of respected captivity in Constantinople, where the last great Sultan, Abdul Hamid, had given him a post similar to that of a British Privy Counsellor. Hussein's four sons—Ali, Abdullah, Feisal and Zeid—had been brought up in Constantinople. This city, with a mixture of east and west similar to that of Cairo, was dazzling to young men from the backward Hejaz.* It made them aware of a challenging world outside Arabic Islam. The same challenge had inspired the Ottomans, conscious of their technological weakness, to introduce such amenities as railways, bridges and telegraph offices, all useful in centralizing their widespread empire and the Turks had also improved their armed forces by importing military advisers from Germany and naval advisers from Britain.

Hussein and his sons looked on this modernized Turkish capital with the same mixture of admiration and distrust as the Turks themselves projected towards Europe. The new Pilgrim Railway which was planned to link Constantinople with Mecca symbolized their twofold response. On the one hand, they, like the Turks, wanted Islam to be again what it had been in the past—an innovatory, vigorous society, not a shabby fossil—and this purpose would be served by the Railway. On the other hand, the Railway enabled the Turks to move troops quickly to an area whose remoteness had hitherto given it a certain security. While their bedouin subjects disliked the Railway because it made looting harder, the sons of Sharif Hussein saw it as a further threat to their local autonomy, already threatened by the evident growth of a purely Turkish nationalism.

This Turkish nationalism was in turn encouraging some Arab Muslims to consider the new idea of Arab nationalism. Ironically, both Turkish and Arab nationalism derived from non-Turks and non-Arabs: Turkish nationalism was propounded largely by Ottoman Jews, influenced by western ideas, while Arab nationalism was the invention of Lebanese Christians, similarly open to the west. At the outbreak of war the French consul in Beirut, Georges-Picot, had foolishly left his correspondence files unburned and the Turkish authorities had thus discovered evidence of a breakaway movement which, in the light of their experiences in Greece and the Balkans, they could not tolerate. Muslim and Christian Arabs had paid for their indiscretion on the scaffolds of Jemal Pasha, the ruthless governor of Syria.

* Mark Sykes had suddenly understood, when visiting Delhi in 1914, why Indian Muslims saw in Constantinople something externally more efficient than they could find at home.[1]

All this was known to Lawrence, both from his reading and from friendship with Ronald Storrs, the second most important civilian in Egypt. Two years of office warfare in Cairo had enforced a lesson Lawrence already knew instinctively: to promote yourself or your ideas, there is no substitute for the man at the top. If the man at the very top, Sir Henry McMahon, the High Commissioner, was a step out of reach, Ronald Storrs, his Oriental Secretary, was not.

Storrs knew more about the situation in the Hejaz than any other Englishman. He believed that the Oriental Secretary should incarnate the political, diplomatic and social tradition at the British Agency; he had to be 'the eyes, ears, interpretation and Intelligence (in the military sense) of his Chief, and might become much more.'[2] Storrs defined the Agency, which in theory ranked alongside other Consulates General, as combining, for Egyptians and foreigners alike, the roles of 10 Downing Street and Buckingham Palace.[3] More than something of a snob, Storrs had not heard of Lawrence in his Carchemish days and would probably not have remembered if he had. But the two men met after Lawrence's arrival in Egypt the first winter of the war. A shared love of the Greco-Roman classics (not common even then among wartime personnel) drew them together. Lawrence, in Storrs' words, gulped down all Storrs could shed for him of Arabic knowledge, till then bounded for Lawrence by the western bank of the Suez Canal.[4]

Storrs was not as good an Arabist as he pretended; but he was playing a pivotal role in a plot concerned with Arabs in the Hejaz. In April 1914, when Kitchener had been the British plenipotentiary in Egypt, Sharif Hussein's second and favourite son, Abdullah, had paid a second call at the Agency: 'he appeared to have something to say but somehow did not reach the point of saying it.'[5] Abdullah was staying in Cairo as the Khedive's guest, and since the Turks were suspicious of such contacts with the Grand Sharif's sons, Kitchener did not receive Abdullah again. Instead, he deputed Storrs to call on him at Abdin Palace, where the home-comforts available to a British puppet must have impressed the Amir. After much literary talk, Abdullah had come to the point: would Britain provide guns for an anti-Turkish revolt? Under instructions from Kitchener, Storrs delivered a sanctimonious answer: the British could not possibly contemplate supplying arms for use against a friendly power. But Turkey's entry into the war had ripped off the fig-leaf and Storrs became the medium for telegrams from Kitchener at the War Office encouraging precisely what Abdullah had proposed.

The advantages to Britain of a revolt in the Hejaz were manifold. The Grand Sharif had already withheld active support for a *jihad*, that supernumerary article of the faith enjoining Muslims to fight for Islam. If he went further and revolted against the Sultan, he could shatter the political unity of the Turkish Empire. Strategic effects could be equally important. In early 1916 Germany planned to send a mission under Major Freiherr von Stotzingen to establish an information post, or *Nachrichtenstelle*, at Hodeida in Yemen to link Berlin with German East Africa. Since the British controlled the Red Sea, and since Christians were forbidden to pass through Medina and Mecca, the German mission planned to travel south with a Turkish escort by way of the Hejaz coast. A revolt could thwart such dangerous ambitions. And, politically, an Arab revolt under British sponsorship would help to offset the Gallipoli disaster.

In this context, Sir Henry McMahon had conducted an ambiguous, convoluted correspondence with the Grand Sharif. His letters were not the clearer for being written by a Persian employee at the Agency and for being vetted by Storrs, who had a limited knowledge of written Arabic. But to their Sharifian recipients the letters seemed to reach a positive climax in an apparent promise, dated 24 October 1915, that Britain would recognize Arab independence, not in Egypt, which was not then considered an Arab state, nor in North Africa, already shared out between France, Italy and Spain, but in those areas of Asiatic Turkey wherein speakers of Arabic comprised the majority. This was the culmination of an interchange of demands and answers in which Sharif Hussein spoke for the Arabs (who had not elected him to do so) and the High Commissioner probably exceeded his instructions from London. The boundaries that McMahon seemed to accept were the Taurus mountains in the north, the Iranian plateau in the east and the Mediterranean in the west. The only area specifically excluded, out of deference to France's traditional patronage of the Maronites, was a somewhat vaguely delineated Lebanon, and the ports of Alexandretta and Mersin.

Lawrence at the time was far from seeing in such undertakings the charter for the freeing of a people he particularly esteemed. In January 1916, he had written a secret report, *The Politics of Mecca*, which concluded that an Arab revolt would be beneficial to the British Empire 'because it marches with our immediate aims, the break up of the Islamic "bloc" and the defeat and disruption of the Ottoman empire, and because the states he [Sharif Hussein] would set up to succeed the Turks would be as harmless to ourselves as Turkey was before she became a tool in German hands. The Arabs are even less stable than the Turks. If properly handled they would remain in a state of political mosaic, a tissue of small jealous principalities incapable of cohesion, and yet always ready to combine against an outside force.'[6]

In the light of Britain's decision not to invade Syria by way of Alexandretta and the difficulty of getting arms, or even letters, to the Hejaz, the revolt remained for some time a project merely. Ironically, it was the German plan[7] to send their mission through the Hejaz which was to stir the Sharif and his family to desperate decisions. They knew from experience what scores could be settled, what rebels could be punished, by a Turkish column moving through their territory.

As the *Royal George* steamed south and the arid Hejaz yielded to the higher, greener fastnesses of Asir and Yemen, the departure of the German expedition from Damascus was still six weeks in the future. From Aden, where Britain had built a small coaling port round an extinct crater, the ship followed the mountainous southern coast of Arabia, where Arab traders with the east had created strange, near skyscraper towns. Beyond, inside, rolled the wastes of the Empty Quarter whose shifting sands, scant wells and unmapped ruins occupied an area larger than most European states. Passing the straits of Hormuz (Lawrence knew the region so little he misnamed them Bab el-Mandab after the narrows between South Yemen and Africa,[8]) the *Royal George* steamed past fishing villages linked to Britain by treaty and concealing riches beyond a pearl-diver's dreams. The ship dropped anchor at Kuwait, a part of the Ottoman empire surreptitiously acquired by Britain, a mud-walled, dhow-building home for divers and a mart for camels.

Transhipping to the *Elephanta*, a fast mail-steamer, Lawrence approached through date-groves the Ottoman province which showed the most vivid contrast between past glory, present squalor and future hope. Known to the Greeks as Mesopotamia, to the Arabs as Iraq, the wide valley where Euphrates and Tigris blended the rains and snows of the Anatolian and Persian plateaux had been the site of Sumer, Ur and Babylon. From a billiard-table plain the stumps of eroded ziggurats, a child's idea of mountains, astounded the eye. Little else did. With a culture older than Egypt's, the land of Haroun al-Rashid was now a sullen, sallow flatland where, he noticed, 'the palm-trees get flooded every day, with a mixture of salt and fresh water which seems to agree with them.'[9] Lawrence had ignored the vegetable wealth produced by Egypt's fellahin, who filled each precious inch of watered land with emerald clover or the white gold of cotton but he could not help noticing the dereliction of Iraq. The great irrigation systems of the Middle Ages were long since abandoned; the prairies of the caliphs had become a wilderness coruscating with salt on which half-settled tribesmen planted sporadic patches of green. Basra, in medieval times a city of poets and mystics, the home port of Sinbad, now boasted a shabby bazaar in which Lawrence's eye found nothing native to appeal. West of Basra's creeks and waterways began the upland steppe of Arabia proper.

At Basra men propelled strange craft with gondola-like prows six feet above the water: on the muddy land British and Indian soldiers had deposited the impedimenta of modern war. The only faces familiar to Lawrence were those of Campbell Thompson, his first chief at

Carchemish, and Gertrude Bell, his first woman visitor. They made him welcome.

After three days (loaded with gifts of bully beef and biscuits), he boarded a paddle-steamer. The craft's provenance—it had served as a ferry on Burma's Irrawaddy—symbolized the diversity of imperial politics. The government of India, one of whose fiefdoms was Burma, had mounted the invasion of Iraq for purposes of its own. A blow to the Ottoman caliphate (whose appeal to India's Muslims could still be feared) could also mean new territory for surplus Indians, sizeable colonies of which had already been settled in British Guiana, Uganda, Mauritius and South Africa.

The up-river journey was no tourist cruise. There being no cabin, Lawrence slept on deck; he used a valise as pillow. The steamer pulled hundred-foot steel barges, one each side, laden with forage and firewood, as padding against the treacherous mud-banks. The weather did not fit the Arabian Nights. As the river veered east, the summits of the Iranian mountains gleamed bleakly white. Wind and rain drubbed the deck and the soldiers joined their waterproof capes into makeshift tents. The first night they anchored near Gurna, the palm-girt village where the two rivers swirled together for the last joint push towards the sea. Diminished by irrigation on its long journey south, the Euphrates retained the colour Lawrence remembered from his Jerablus home. The steamer then veered east to enter the swifter and more violent of Iraq's two rivers. The Tigris twisted, changing course and width, through a landscape of date palms, salt flats and the occasional meadow. Since the alluvial soil lacked stone, the sparse houses were formed of soft mud bricks produced in the kilns whose chimneys interrupted the general flatness. The most elaborate edifice between Basra and the whalebacked banqueting hall at Ctesiphon (the highest point reached before the British had been forced back to Kut) was Ezra's Tomb, a domed mosque and a courtyard wherein dark-glazed brick imposed green patterns on a general saffron. Five miles further upstream the Turkish gunboat *Marmaris* lay on its side, fired by its crew to prevent its re-use by the British.

Watching the Iraqis, Lawrence thought of his 'own' country further north. 'The Arabs here are wonderfully hard, much rougher and poorer than our Jerablus men, but merry, and full of talk. They are in the water all their lives, and seem hardly to notice it.' The hundred or so British soldiers on the steamer were less adapted to this aquatic world. Standing at attention for their army tea, they were flung by collision with a mud-bank into a hot and sugary confusion.*

* Lawrence obviously paid little attention to his compatriots. He described them at the time as 'Cumberland territorials'; three years later they had become 'one hundred Devon Territorials, young, clean, delightful fellows, full of the power of happiness and of making women and children glad.'[10]

After six days they reached the river-boat, complete with a saloon and awnings, which constituted British headquarters. A few miles north, more than 13,000 British and Indians, including non-combatants, along with 6,000 townsmen, were under siege by the Turks inside the small town of Kut. Incompetent and aloof, the British commander, General Townshend had conceived a plan, endorsed by Kitchener, to bribe the Turkish commander, Khalil Pasha, nephew of the Young Turk triumvir, Enver Pasha, who had been sent south to restore a reputation damaged by the loss to the Russians of Erzerum in eastern Turkey. Townshend proposed a bribe of a million gold sovereigns if Khalil would let the British depart on parole, an unprecedented scheme which the regular officers considered dishonourable and foredoomed. German accounts suggest that he might have accepted the bribe, had not his pro-German uncle sternly ordered its rejection, even when doubled to two million.

Basing themselves on the steamer, Lawrence, Aubrey Herbert and Colonel Beach, head of Military Intelligence in Iraq, took three weeks in attempting to carry out this scheme. The superficially westernized Khalil entertained them to a lavish banquet; in the end he agreed to the release of some thousand British wounded; nothing more. The humiliating details of the negotiations (the British officers were led blindfold for long distances) and their aim gave the Turks a propaganda success. Editorials and cartoons mocked mercenary Britain. 'Enver Pasha's refusal of money was held up as a noble gesture; England's hour had struck; English gold coin could no longer prevail where English arms had failed.'[11] Kut's surrender on 29 April 1916 involved a death-march for sick, half starving troops, seventy per cent of whom never reached home. Many Arabs of Kut were hanged.

For Lawrence the trip was useful despite its failure. Besides offering a peripheral insight into what was going on inside the Turkish empire and a break in his Cairo routine, it inspired a private report which revealed, without overstating, his superior talents. It scathingly put down Britain's Intelligence operatives in the field. 'They do all their examination of agents, prisoners and refugees, through interpreters. They have never learnt or read anything of the manners of Turk or Arab, or of their customs. They know nothing of the country beyond them: they cannot test an agent by cross questioning . . .'[12] The report emphasized the practical importance of the Arab Bureau which Lieutenant-Commander Hogarth had come out to Cairo to head, under the general supervision of Colonel Clayton.

At Kut Lawrence again met the Hubert Young with whom he had dabbled in sculpting at Carchemish. Young was disenchanted. 'He [Lawrence] seemed to me thoroughly spoilt, and posing in a way that was quite unlike what I remembered of him at Carchemish . . . I . . . noticed his anti-regular soldier complex, and, perhaps not unnaturally, resented it hotly.'[13] But at Carchemish Lawrence had been happy in the company of Dahoum. In Iraq, he was forcing his psyche into the drive, antithetical to Eros and Apollo, which is concerned with power.

Lawrence's thrust to power found nourishment in the company of Aubrey Herbert, whose influence on his life he was later to compare to Hogarth's.[14] By coincidence, while Lawrence and Herbert parleyed with the Turkish general who had been discredited at Erzerum, in distant London the temporarily invalid John Buchan was writing *Greenmantle*, a fictional fantasy scaffolded round Erzerum and Herbert.

Buchan's hero, Sandy Arbuthnot, passes for a Turkish dervish and at Erzerum engenders a pro-Allied revolt inside Islam. Because of resemblances between the later Lawrence and Arbuthnot, a link between Lawrence and the capture of Erzerum was later to be made. The connection was supplied by Lawrence himself who, with the contempt for regular soldiers which nettled Young, pulled the leg of the most respected military theorist of his day, Captain Liddell Hart. Hart, on hints from Lawrence, was to write of him: 'In the spring of 1916 he had a long-range hand in a more important matter, the "capture" of Erzerum by the Russian Caucasus Army after a curiously half-hearted defence—readers of John Buchan's subsequent novel, *Greenmantle*, may find it worth while to remember that fiction has often a basis of fact.'[15]

Buchan, who first met Lawrence after the war, has established the source of his inspiration. His autobiography refers to Sandy Arbuthnot as 'reminiscent of Aubrey'; a book of reminiscences by his wife and friends quotes him as saying: 'I drew Sandy in *Greenmantle* from him [Aubrey Herbert].'[16] The novel was published in October 1916: the month in which Lawrence was to set foot in the Hejaz.

Even so, between Lawrence and the real-life Herbert there was the living exchange between a young man peculiarly responsive to heroic models and a figure who had already inspired a mythopoeic novelist. Impressed by Herbert's lineage (he was the second son of the 4th Earl of Carnarvon), Buchan had portrayed Sandy as 'Ludovick Gustavus Arbuthnot, commonly called the Honourable, etc.,' son of the fifteenth Baron Clanroyden. He evoked the farflung connections of an adventurer who on any pilgramage to Mecca was likely to be the intimate friend of half a dozen pilgrims. 'In shepherds' huts in the Caucasus you will find bits of his cast-off clothing, for he has a knack of shedding garments as he goes. In the caravanserais of Bokhara and Samarkand he is known, and there are shikaris in the Pamirs who still speak of him round their fires.'[17]

Above all Buchan recorded Herbert's ideas on the qualities desirable in a new Muslim leader. 'The Turk and the Persian wouldn't follow the ordinary new theology game. He must be of the Blood. Your Mahdis and Mullahs and Imams were nobodies, but they had only a local prestige. To capture all Islam . . . the man must be of the Koreish, the tribe of the Prophet himself.'[18] In other words: a Sharif.

Back in Cairo before the end of May, Lawrence found Storrs and Hogarth packing for an expedition of their own. The High Commissioner had received a cable, sent from the Hejaz by way of Port Sudan, inviting Storrs to meet Sharif Hussein's son, Abdullah, on the Arabian coast. Storrs, Hogarth, and Captain Cornwallis left Cairo on the 28th with a modest £10,000 in gold coin. On 6 June, after some cross-sailing in the Red Sea, the party went ashore on a beach near Jidda expecting to learn from Abdullah the planned date for the revolt. Instead, they were met by the youngest brother, Zeid. He reported that the preparations in Medina for the von Stotzingen expedition had convinced the family that if their father 'could not rise now, he would probably not get another chance.'[19] Ali had therefore attacked Medina the previous day while Abdullah was at that moment besieging Mecca. Having taken the plunge, the family were now apprehensive about the Turkish response. Cheering Zeid with a present of his gold watch, Storrs returned to Cairo to be met by an atmosphere of universal gloom. While the Arabs had been firing off their guns in the hot Hejaz, in the icy Arctic Kitchener had drowned on his way to Russia.

In Cairo a desk-bound Lawrence followed the news of the Revolt. Jidda, the chief port, surrendered on 16 June; the last Turkish fortress in Mecca hoisted the white flag on 9 July; two smaller ports, Yanbo and Rabegh, were captured on 27 July. In their successes the Sharifians had been helped by the Royal Navy along the coast and inland by Egyptian artillery sent by Wingate's orders from Sudan. At this juncture Storrs showed his friendship for Lawrence by interventions which were to ensure his involvement in the Arab Revolt.

For more than twenty years the Germans had worked to secure the friendship of Islam in general and of the Turks in particular. The efforts of men like von Oppenheim had been rewarded when, in November 1914, the Sultan-Caliph had proclaimed a *jihad*, so arousing justifiable apprehension in the British, who ruled more Muslims than the Turks and who faced the Senussi on Egypt's western border. The Kaiser's dream of placing 'the forces of Mohammedanism to the fullest extent—under Prussian leadership—at my disposal'[20] seemed fulfilled. The defection of the Sharif of Mecca was thus a bitter blow to the Germans, the more so because it followed the collapse of the Irish rebellion they had supported in their own attempt to subvert an enemy empire. Langwerth, the German consul in Beirut, could still report that by the end of July no general revolt had taken place, but his report referred to Beirut and Lebanon only.[21] From Constantinople Liman von Sanders, the German commander of the Turkish 5th Army, was less reassuring: 'The position in the Hejaz is very unfavourable for Turkey. We Germans should take the situation much more seriously than we are doing. By his betrayal, the very clever influential Amir of Mecca, with his large scale rebellion, has seriously disturbed the religious interests of all the Mohammedans in the region. These could endanger the very existence of the present Government.'[22]

The Germans were perplexed about what to do. Enver Pasha told von Falkenhayn, recently appointed to command a new Turkish army intended to drive the British from Iraq, that only money could put down the rebellion. How much? At least £50,000—and if possible in gold. 'There is no need to underline the extreme desirability of mastering the revolt in the Hejaz,' von Falkenhayn told his German superiors. 'It threatens permanently to disable Turkey as an ally.'[23]

Because of the Revolt's religious and political implications, the Germans deemed it vital to hold Medina as a counterweight to Mecca, and the Turks installed there Sharif Ali Haidar, a rival Hashemite, with the title of Vizir. At the same time the Germans used their considerable influence in the neutral press to minimize the significance of Sharif Hussein's action. As a countermeasure, Storrs decided to issue a set of postage stamps for the new state, which would prove to the world that independent, pro-Allied Arabs controlled the Hejaz.

Lawrence, who had collected stamps as a boy, and, in Storrs' words, 'had a complete working technique of philatelic and three-colour reproduction,'[24] was the ideal assistant in this project. He had lately shown a capacity for finnicky exactitude in a disingenuous clash with an official charged with transliterating Arabic place-names for the Survey of Egypt. He was later to dismiss that problem crisply: 'Arabic names won't go into English, exactly, for their consonants are not the same as ours, and their vowels, like ours, vary from district to district. There are some "scientific systems" of transliteration, helpful to people who know enough Arabic not to need helping, but a wash-out for the world. I spell my names anyhow, to show what rot the systems are.'[25] He had nevertheless used his supposedly superior knowledge to confute a rival. Now he was to show that he had philatelic taste also.

Together Storrs and Lawrence visited Cairo's Islamic Museum in search of suitable motifs. From London, Hogarth, home for consultations, informed Clayton that King George V, a keen philatelist, was anxiously awaiting the Hejazi stamps.[26] By 24 September (two days after the Turkish garrison surrendered the hill resort of Taif near Mecca) Lawrence was able to send his youngest brother 'a few 1 piastre stamps at last. In the middle is Mekka el Mukerrama,* (Mecca the Blessed, a regular phrase, without which Mecca is not mentioned) on top is Hejaz post, and underneath 1 piastre. Date 1334 which is the Sharif's revolt.† The half-piastre looks Chinese, and the quarter-piastre Egyptian. This is pure Arabic, and I like it rather.'[27]

The stamps completed, Storrs, not Hogarth, arranged for Lawrence to visit the new theatre of war. In August the notion of sending some young officer to organize the Arabs had already been broached in London; instead of proposing Lawrence, Hogarth had written to Clayton stressing the complexity of the problem and dismissing Cornwallis (who had gone on the first trip to Arabia and was later to take over the Arab Bureau in Hogarth's absences) as 'too young and not equipped with sufficient guns for the job.' It might be wiser, Hogarth suggested, to employ a civilian.[28] Storrs had meanwhile paid a second visit to the Hejaz in September. Now that the Red Sea was no longer blockaded, the Holy Covering could be sent to Mecca and he escorted it as far as Jidda on a British warship. The courtesy enabled him to meet Abdullah's elder brother, Ali. Storrs was unimpressed: Ali's Charles I-like beard seemed to mask a weak chin. But Storrs took a useful step towards organizing the Arabs. So far he was dissatisfied with the Sharifian showing: 'The wick is as yet far from burning with that hard gem-like flame I could have desired. The Arabs . . . are naked, unarmed, and more esurient than the Greek himself; further they have not one *bobbo* to their name.'[29] By telephoning 'Mecca 1' he contacted Sharif Hussein and induced him to appoint a brilliant ex-Ottoman officer, Aziz al-Masri, to command and train his forces.

In October Storrs decided to go once again to Jidda. Abdullah had been cabling for *bobbos* and the British were afraid that the Revolt might collapse. Lawrence was due some local leave. Storrs enjoyed his company and knew of his arduous travels; his experience of Intelligence work could be urged against those who criticized his long hair and his practice of carrying, not wearing, his belt. Storrs obtained permission to take 'little Lawrence, my super-cerebral companion,' with him and Lawrence was later to repay the debt, and mildly chastise Hogarth, by acclaiming Storrs as 'the most brilliant Englishman in the Near East.'[30] The two Englishmen and the half-Circassian, half-Arab al-Masri boarded the *Lama*, a small converted liner, at Suez. Two English vets were also going to Jidda to buy camels for the Egyptian Camel Corps and Lawrence shared a cabin with one of them.

'We had the accustomed calm run to Jidda,' he was later to write, 'in

* Lawrence here follows the Franco-Egyptian system of transliterating the Arabic definite article as *el*; English systems usually prefer *al*. *Mukerrama* is closer to 'dignified' than 'blessed'; it had been given dignity by the Prophet's birth there.

† The Islamic calendar, based on a lunar year, dates from Muhammad's migration from Mecca to Medina in A.D. 622.

Above 1906-1907 Sixth Form of the City of Oxford High School taken by T E Lawrence who appears on the far right

Below Dahoum (on left) and head men at Carchemish

Above The Little Shrine, Carchemish

Below Carchemish digs in 1913

Above left Richard Meinertzhagen

Above right Amir Feisal

Left Sharif Ali by Eric Kennington

Above Azrak, interior of the main gate. Lawrence's room is above the arch

Below Lawrence on a balcony in Damascus, 2 October 1918

Left Sir Ronald Storrs

Below Sir Reginald Wingate in 1899

Left Charlotte and George Bernard Shaw

Below T E Lawrence on a motorcycle

Right Moreton House

Below right Clouds Hill

Overleaf T E Lawrence in 1935

the delightful Red Sea climate, never too hot while the ship was moving. By day we lay in shadow; and for great part of the glorious nights we would tramp up and down the wet decks under the stars in the steaming breath of the southern wind. But when at last we anchored in the outer harbour, off the white town hung between the blazing sky and its reflection in the mirage which swept and rolled over the wide lagoon, then the heat of Arabia came out like a drawn sword and struck us speechless.'[31]

Lawrence's response to the bare, the barren, the bleak, had been confirmed, not prompted, by his April talks with Aubrey Herbert. The arrogant desolation of the Arabian hills—the rock floors of barren wadis, the rare and therefore astonishing vegetation—made immediate impact. It re-evoked the mood in which Dahoum had exalted the odour of nothingness, a mood which Buchan's *Greenmantle* was conveying that month to the patrons of English bookshops. The West had failed to understand that the East was austere and hostile to pleasure; misled by false pictures, it imagined the Oriental as 'lapped in colour and idleness and luxury and gorgeous dreams. But it is all wrong . . . It is the austerity of the East that is its beauty and its terror . . . The Turk and the Arab came out of big spaces, and they have the desire of them in their bones. They settle down and stagnate, and by the by they degenerate into that appalling subtlety which is their ruling passion gone crooked. And then comes a new revelation and a great simplifying. They want to live face to face with God without a screen of ritual and images and priestcraft. They want to prune life of its foolish fringes and get back to the noble bareness of the desert. Remember, it is always the empty desert and the empty sky that cast their spell over them—these, and the hot, strong, antiseptic sunlight which burns up all rot and decay . . . It isn't inhuman. It's the humanity of one part of the human race. It isn't ours, it isn't as good as ours, but it's jolly good all the same.'[32]

Independently of Buchan and Herbert, but in tune with them, Lawrence had formed an equation between his puritan self and this emptied landscape.

The steamer carrying Lawrence, Storrs and al-Masri had anchored some distance off the humid town. They were transferred ashore by a yacht flying the British flag and at the service of Colonel C. E. Wilson, the Governor of the Red Sea Province of Sudan. The Governor-General, General Sir Reginald Wingate, who was in basic charge of British involvement in the Hejaz and held the important second post of Sirdar, or Commander-in-Chief of the Egyptian Army, had been tactful enough to name Wilson as his representative in Jidda and not as the city's Governor.[33] Colonel Edouard Brémond had been appointed as Wilson's theoretical French equivalent.

On shore, a ragtaggle guard of Syrian defectors to the Sharifian cause presented arms to al-Masri, their new commander. Lawrence followed Storrs through the shabby food market, noticing the flies which moved from dates to meat to men in the dazzling sun-shafts which penetrated the dark booths through torn places in the wood and sack-cloth roofs.[34] He also observed—and despite his debt to Storrs, his pencil later recorded—a visual joke against the Oriental Secretary. Aboard the *Lama*, Storrs had occupied a red-leather armchair while discoursing on Wagner and Debussy to al-Masri in a mixture of French, English and the German which al-Masri had learnt during his military studies in Constantinople. The effusion of sweat on the hot leather had turned the great man's trouser-seat a vivid scarlet.

Jidda was the water-gate to the Hejaz. It was also the portal through which Lawrence entered a new phase of his life, the phase which was to win him unrivalled fame.

15

The exploits of Lawrence's next two years were to be shadowed by puzzles of a kind whose stencil he had cut at Oxford and Carchemish. Like those earlier enigmas, they were prompted in part by love of mystification, in part by the wish to compensate for obscurity or smallness, in part by the need to conceal emotions or actions which contravened his family's values or his own vision of himself. Throughout his life his character contained elements which contradicted one another and which a weaker personality could not have held in equilibrium. But whereas in England or Syria the satisfaction of one or other of these had depended on himself, his Arabian experience involved him directly in public events and later in the attempt to describe that involvement in prose. He was no longer an Oxonian dilettante, posing for his own amusement as a consul one day, as a villager the next. A commissioned officer, he was now fusing his own wishes with the larger wishes of an empire at war. His scope was greater; so were the constraints on his freedom. A sequence of fact, legend and interpretation stratified his two years in Arabia; the layers have to be distinguished if we are to understand his life.

The stratum of fact, made up of Lawrence's movements and actions between his arrival at Jidda on 16 October 1916, and his departure from a freed Damascus two Octobers later, needs approaching first. It corresponds to the bedrock which in a landscape dictates the vegetation and even the architecture which occurs or is built on top. We can isolate this layer of fact, which includes the question of why, where and when he did what he did, with the help of contemporary documentation. Apart from his own letters and reports (which require to be construed with a certain caution), there are the letters and reports of his British superiors; the reports of his Turkish or German adversaries; the records and memoirs of British, French and Arab soldiers who fought on his side.

No sooner had this stratum of fact been laid down than an American publicist, responding to the element of fantasy in Lawrence himself, superimposed upon it a layer of legend; he did so in lectures, magazine articles and books. Fragments of this legend, sometimes incandescent, often tawdry, were to become embedded in later accounts. But however

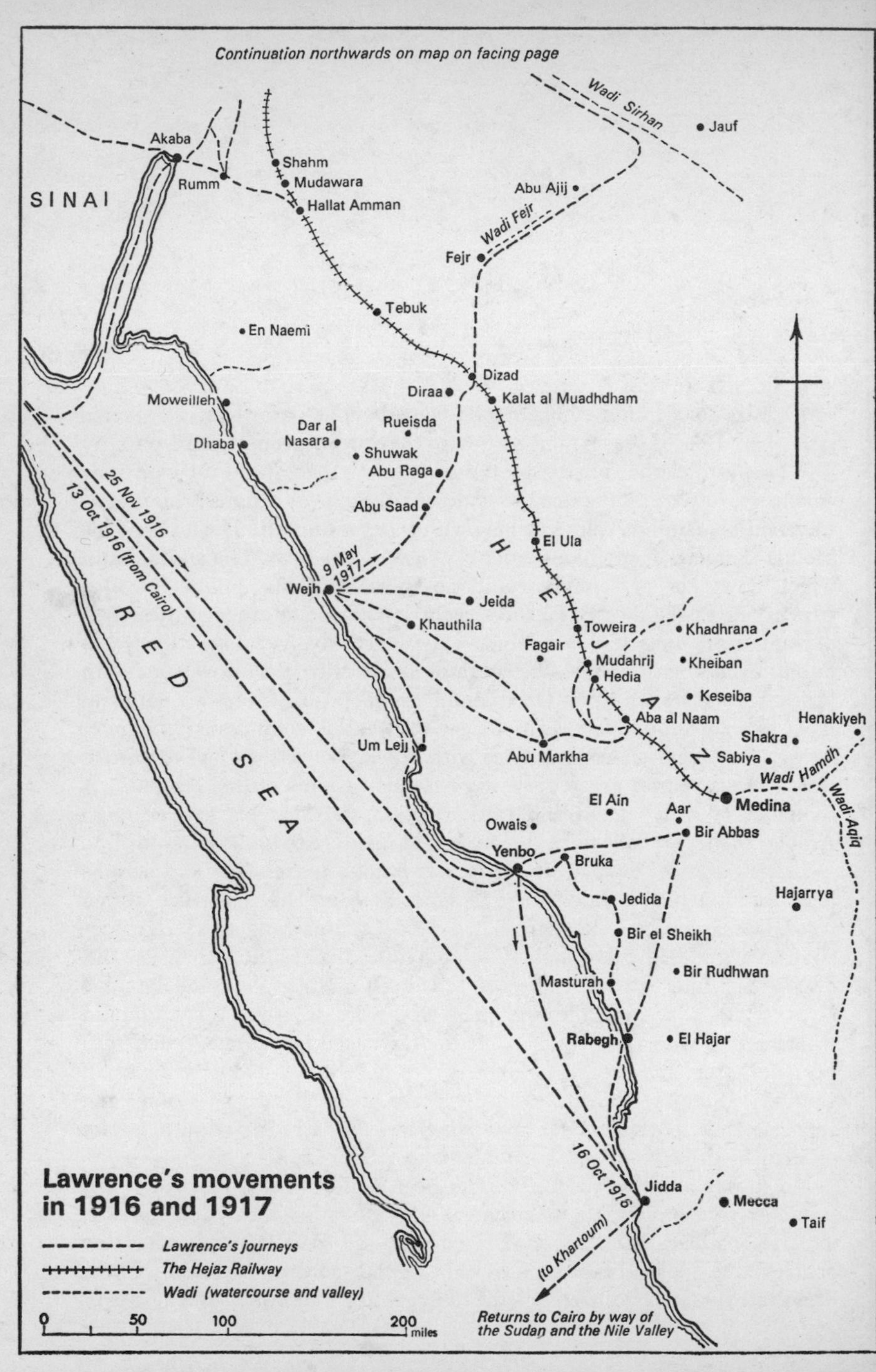

Continuation northwards on map on facing page
Wadi Sirhan
Jauf
Akaba
Rumm
SINAI
Shahm
Mudawara
Hallat Amman
Abu Ajij
Wadi Fejr
Fejr
Tebuk
En Naemi
Dizad
Diraa
Kalat al Muadhdham
Moweilleh
Rueisda
Dar al Nasara
Dhaba
Shuwak
Abu Raga
Abu Saad
25 Nov 1916
13 Oct 1916 (from Cairo)
H E J A Z
El Ula
9 May 1917
Wejh
Jeida
Khauthila
Toweira
Khadhrana
Fagair
Mudahrij
Kheiban
Hedia
Keseiba
Aba al Naam
Henakiyeh
Shakra
Um Lejj
Abu Markha
Sabiya
Wadi Hamdh
R E D S E A
Medina
Wadi Aqiq
El Ain
Aar
Owais
Bir Abbas
Yenbo
Bruka
Jedida
Hajarrya
Bir el Sheikh
Bir Rudhwan
Masturah
Rabegh
El Hajar
16 Oct 1916
Lawrence's movements in 1916 and 1917
Jidda
Mecca
Taif
(to Khartoum)
Lawrence's journeys
The Hejaz Railway
Wadi (watercourse and valley)
0 50 100 200 miles
Returns to Cairo by way of the Sudan and the Nile Valley

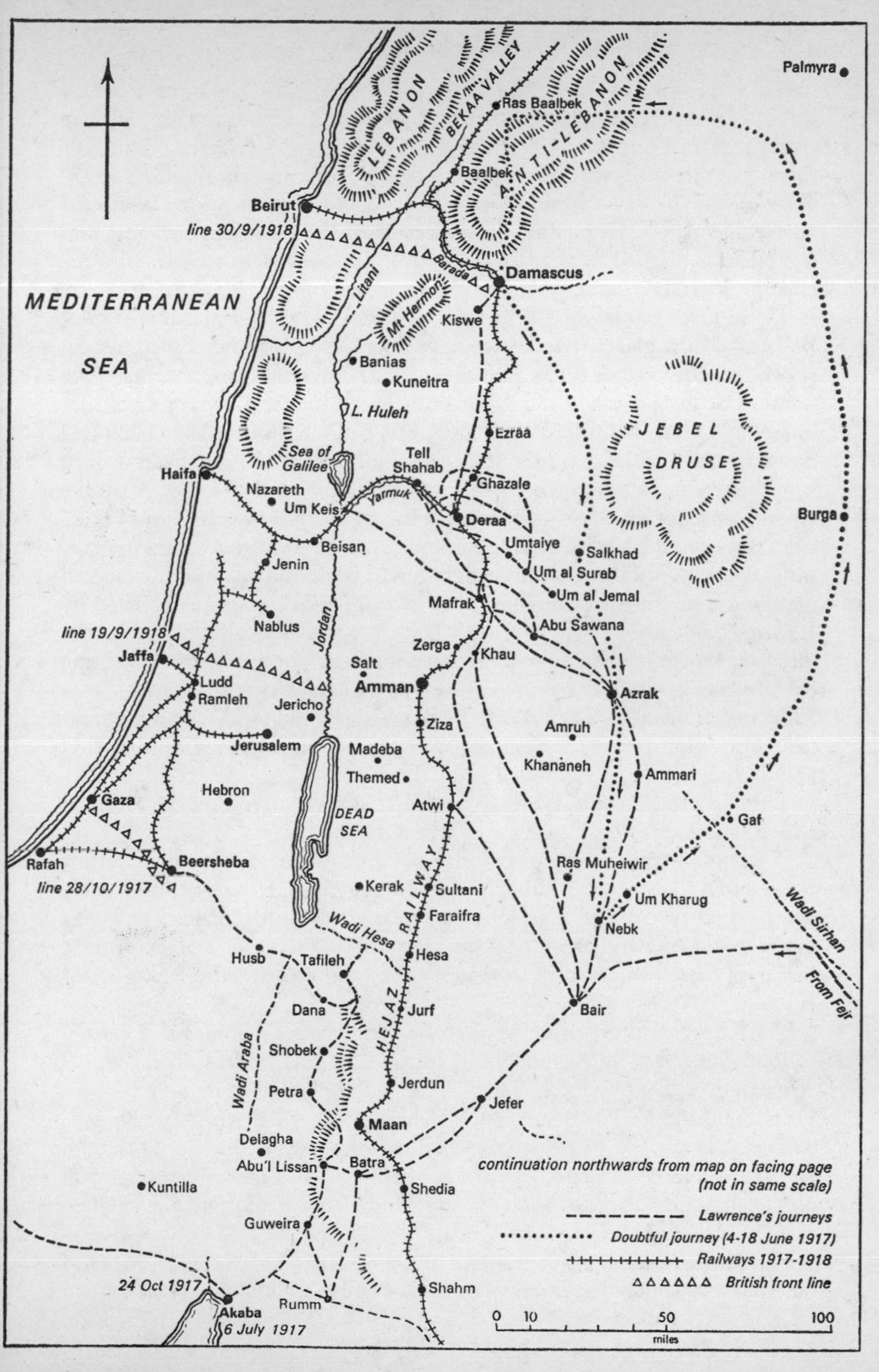
MEDITERRANEAN
SEA
LEBANON
BEKAA VALLEY
ANTI-LEBANON
Palmyra
Ras Baalbek
Baalbek
Beirut
line 30/9/1918
Barada
Damascus
Litani
Mt Hermon
Kiswe
Banias
Kuneitra
L. Huleh
JEBEL
DRUSE
Ezraa
Sea of Galilee
Tell Shahab
Haifa
Nazareth
Ghazale
Um Keis
Yarmuk
Deraa
Burga
Beisan
Umtaiye
Salkhad
Jenin
Um al Surab
Um al Jemal
Mafrak
Nablus
Abu Sawana
line 19/9/1918
Jordan
Zerga
Khau
Jaffa
Salt
Ludd
Amman
Azrak
Ramleh
Jericho
Ziza
Amruh
Jerusalem
Madeba
Khananeh
Themed
Ammari
Hebron
Gaza
Atwi
DEAD SEA
Gaf
Rafah
Beersheba
Ras Muheiwir
line 28/10/1917
Kerak
Sultani
Um Kharug
Faraifra
Wadi Sirhan
Wadi Hesa
Nebk
Hesa
Husb
Tafileh
From Feir
Bair
Dana
Jurf
HEJAZ RAILWAY
Wadi Araba
Shobek
Jerdun
Petra
Jefer
Maan
Delagha
Abu'l Lissan
Batra
continuation northwards from map on facing page
(not in same scale)
Kuntilla
Shedia
Lawrence's journeys
Guweira
Doubtful journey (4-18 June 1917)
Railways 1917-1918
British front line
24 Oct 1917
Shahm
Rumm
Akaba
6 July 1917
0 10 50 100
miles

much a nuisance to those interested in truth, the legend as a whole cannot be ignored. It established Lawrence's reputation in all five continents and inevitably it affected his own view of himself. Thus the third, last stratum—the use of his Arabian experiences in *Seven Pillars of Wisdom*, the book he started writing in 1919 and produced for a restricted readership seven years later—is the result of the interaction of fact and legend in the crucible of his imagination, influenced as this was by his existing legend.

These three strata cannot simply be lifted apart like mattresses on a Balkan bed. In places, two layers have been fused together by emotional shock; embarrassment has played one role, mystification another. The stratum of legend could not have been laid down if Lawrence had not done highly unusual things in Arabia; but neither could it have been laid down in the form it assumed if Lawrence himself had not been a born romancer. The fact that his legend was being boomed as far as Australia when Lawrence sat down to write inevitably affected the stratum of creation. But even the legend could illuminate, as well as obscure, and the fantasies of which it was made threw light on deep promptings and unresolved conflicts. The third stratum—*Seven Pillars of Wisdom*—was admitted by Lawrence not to be 'strictly truth'. But though bad on dates and elastic on facts, Lawrence had a good memory for detail, and, like many serving officers, he ignored the ban on keeping wartime diaries. Thus *Seven Pillars of Wisdom* can brilliantly light up states of mind, though sometimes the illumination is indirect, reflected from myths we must first comprehend.

That Lawrence could be terse and factual was proved by the letter in which he compressed his first two weeks in the Hejaz:

'I left on October 13 from Cairo, reached Jidda on October 16, left there on October 19, for Rabegh. Left Rabegh on October 21, by camel; went up to Sharif Feisal's H.Q. at a place called Bir Abbas, half-way between Medina and the sea, about 100 miles North of Rabegh. After a few days there returned by road to Yenbo, and embarked on Nov. 1 for Jidda.'[1]

The letter was not written until 18 November, as Lawrence had chosen to return to Cairo by a roundabout route. The new address at the top—Arab Bureau, Savoy Hotel, Cairo—reflected a change in his official role. Until then, the Commander-in-Chief had preferred that no Intelligence officers should be officially attached to the Arab Bureau, although Lawrence had co-operated with the Bureau all summer. Instead it had remained under the direction of the High Commissioner, the civilian responsible for Arabian affairs.

For all the lack of colour in his letter, Lawrence's initial experience of the Hejaz was almost as strenuous as his Galilee walk and he was later to use even more words to describe it. This first letter omitted to mention his voyage with Storrs and al-Masri to Rabegh and al-Masri's original ideas on how the Sharifians should fight their war; it did not name Nuri al-Said, the Baghdad-born officer, his own age, who had deserted the Ottoman cause as early as 1914; it said nothing of his first glimpse of the young Arab who was to capture his imagination in a way that even Dahoum had failed to do. His single mention of Feisal, the third of Sharif Hussein's sons, all four of whom he met, was thus more striking.

Storrs was still a civilian, and Lawrence's visit to the Hejaz, although sponsored by Storrs, had required the sanction of Lawrence's military chief, Brigadier-General Clayton, as he now was. Clayton filled several roles in the military hierarchy of wartime Egypt. As head of Military Intelligence, he exercised a general supervision over the Arab Bureau. He held, with some friction, the post of Staff Officer at the headquarters of General Sir Archibald Murray, commander of an Egyptian Expeditionary Force engorged with troops evacuated from Gallipoli. Most important, he was Wingate's Agent in Cairo.

Storrs had prompted, Clayton permitted, Lawrence's entry to Arabia. A more important patron was needed to perpetuate his involvement and Lawrence knew who this must be. From Jidda, he persuaded Admiral Sir Rosslyn Wemyss to take him across the Red Sea to Port Sudan, the base, linked to Khartoum by a railway, which had been built by Wingate, who had recently used it to send British arms and Egyptian troops to the Hejaz. On 4 November Wemyss cabled Wingate that he was bringing with him 'Captain Lawrence who is desirous of seeing you.' Wingate had already read Lawrence's report on his first days in Jidda. He wrote to Wilson of his 'delight' that Wemyss was bringing Lawrence to Khartoum. 'They are due this afternoon and a good talk over the whole situation with them should clear the atmosphere considerably. Lawrence strikes me as a man who has thoroughly grasped the situation and I was much interested in his brief but pithy report of 21 October.'[2]

A Lowland Scot in his late fifties, Wingate had spent seventeen years restoring order and bringing a measure of prosperity to a million square miles of north-east Africa. He had achieved this as the British representative of an Anglo-Egyptian condominium. Under this makeshift constitutional contrivance British expatriates (many the pick of Oxford and Cambridge) administered the re-conquered Sudan while Egyptians provided most of the manpower and all the money: the British and Egyptian flags flew as equal. The formative event of Wingate's youth had been the Mahdi's victory over General Gordon. What had seemed to some a successful anti-colonial revolution had seemed to Wingate the triumph of barbarism over comparative civilization. It had impressed on him for life the dangerous potency of an aroused Islam. Earlier in 1916 he had energetically put down Ali Dinar, a Sudanese supporter of the Turkish *jihad*. He was now haunted by fears that the revolt in the Hejaz might collapse through inefficiency, or take a wrong direction. Believing that Gordon's ignorance of Arabic had been his undoing, Wingate had learnt to read as well as speak the language of the men he ruled. He had also seen early the need for copious and accurate information, and since becoming Assistant Adjutant General for Intelligence in 1887, he directed the best informed service in the Middle East. Hard-working and honest, a liberal-minded Freemason, Wingate lacked that subtle blend of the forceful and the feminine which gave Kitchener his mysterious attraction. He also had one major weakness: he was easily influenced. Slatin Pasha, for example, an Austrian Jew in the Egyptian service, had imposed his virulent hostility to the Mahdi and his followers on his British friend. Fortunately when Austria's entry into the war forced Slatin to resign his position of Inspector-General of the Sudan, Wingate had begun to adopt a more conciliatory approach to that important segment who still revered the Mahdi.[3]

Lawrence impressed Wingate. In the presence of Admiral Wemyss, the 28-year-old newly created captain urged the conclusions he had reached after visiting the Hejaz. Two of these, which had first been advanced by al-Masri, showed his facility for adopting other people's arguments as his own; the third and most important was indeed his.

At Jidda a few weeks earlier, al-Masri had forcefully argued in conference with Amir Abdullah, Storrs, Wilson and Lawrence that the introduction into the Hejaz of a British brigade would be imprudent and unnecessary. Abdullah took the opposite view: he feared that without some foreign presence on the coast, the Turkish commander in Medina, Fakhry Pasha, would surge south at the head of fourteen thousand Turks and annihilate the Sharifian forces.[4] But al-Masri had cogent reasons for not wanting Christian soldiers in the Hejaz. The townsfolk of Mecca and Jidda (many of them non-Arabs) distrusted the bedouin and opposed the Revolt. The Hejaz was by tradition closed to non-Muslims. The arrival of troops from Britain or France (colonial powers) would undermine Sharif Hussein's moral position beyond repair. At the same time, al-Masri had proposed a strategy for the individualistic, ill-armed, untrained Arabs. The rebels should organize two types of force. A regular army of Muslim Egyptians or captured Iraqis should be officered by defectors or prisoners from the Ottoman army. In tandem, a lightly-armed, fast-moving force of irregulars could raid deep into Syria, terrorizing and paralysing Ottoman positions. Such a guerilla force could then retire to inaccessible desert bases to be reinforced and resupplied. This paraphrase of al-Masri's strategic ideas, which Lawrence presented to Wingate, derives from Nuri al-Said, whom Cornwallis had cultivated when Nuri was living as a friendly alien near Cairo.[5] Lawrence had made little impression on Nuri in Cairo. But after crossing to the Hejaz in July and having seen the Arabs' desperate need for artillery, Nuri had been glad to meet an officer with direct access to the British in Egypt. Lawrence had promised to press the need for weapons to match those of the Turks.

Wingate showed his vacillating nature over Lawrence's first recommendation. On 22 November he cabled to the British Foreign Secretary explicitly backing Lawrence's argument that it would be unwise to land troops at Rabegh; 'views which are those he expressed at meeting held in Khartoum when Admiral Wemyss was also present.'[6] But less than a month later Wingate was concurring with Colonel Brémond in the opposite view: that it was essential for French and British contingents to be rushed to Rabegh.[7]*

Lawrence had meanwhile left Khartoum for Egypt. He had *Morte d'Arthur* to read and an additional proposal to ponder as he journeyed by rail, Nile and then again rail to Cairo. As for Wingate, he may have heard towards the end of November an opinion calculated to make him reconsider his judgment. 'Lawrence', Colonel Wilson wrote to Clayton from Jidda, 'wants kicking and kicking *hard* at that, then he would improve. At present I look upon him as a bumptious young ass who spoils his undoubted knowledge of Syrian Arabs etc. by making himself out to be the only authority on war, engineering, manning H.M.'s ships and everything else. He put every single person's back up I've met, from the Admiral down to the most junior fellow on the Red Sea.'[9]

But Lawrence had been wise to visit Khartoum. He had won Wingate's basic support and in contacting him had shown a flair for sniffing out the important who were to become more so. During his few days in the Sudan the British Government suddenly recalled the High Commissioner, Sir Henry McMahon (whose approach to the Egyptian protectorate, derived from his experience in the Indian Empire, had alienated Egyptians from the pro-British Sultan down) and replaced him by Wingate. Thus the Arab Bureau and Lawrence had in Cairo a powerful new ally in promoting the Sharifian revolt. Wingate had made early contacts with the Sharif from the summer resort of Erkowit near the Red Sea and had ordered the first delivery of arms. Even before the war he had instructed his agents to assess the vulnerability of the Hejaz Railway.

Lawrence's final and most important recommendation involved a basic political question.

Assuming the Revolt survived, who could best inspire and lead it? British money provided its chief incentive, the Royal Navy its lifeline,

* Colonel Wilson told Wingate that in his private opinion 'Brémond does not wish to train Arabs who may later be a nuisance in Syria.'[8]

British ordnance its weapons. For Britain the ideal leader should be someone capable of fanning the flame of revolt while in no way conflicting with Allied aims.

No British, still less French, adviser recommended the selection of local leaders through democratic process. Experience had shown both allies that sultans or rajahs were more amenable to 'advice' than the committees or parties which troubled India and Indochina.

Lawrence did not at this stage attempt to meet the sexagenarian Sharif Hussein. Hussein's capital, Mecca—in which he was 'crowned' later that year—was banned to Christians, and Hussein neither suggested coming down to the coast nor was he invited. He was too old, had shown too much independence, was too little a soldier, to suit British needs, though Storrs admired him and Wilson became a faithful ally. For Lawrence's purposes seniority in age posed no problem: the European principle of primogeniture was not generally accepted in Islamic states. To have it adopted in his family, the Khedive Ismail of Egypt had paid a large sum to the Sultan, who had not adopted the principle himself. Hussein's mantle, or Blood, could descend equally to Ali, Abdullah, Feisal or Zeid. Lawrence considered each of the four in turn as potential leaders, and instruments.

The obvious claimant was Abdullah, Hussein's favourite son, whom Lawrence met first with Storrs at Jidda. Abdullah had carried out Hussein's most important missions; as, in Storrs' phrase, a 'Senator' in the Ottoman parliament, he had first established links with Kitchener, while his brother Feisal, more reluctant to defy the Sultan-Caliph, had been sounding Arab nationalists in Syria. Wingate addressed Abdullah as the 'General Officer Commanding the Hejazi troops'; Storrs found him possessed of 'intelligence, energy and charm', while Clayton had described him, when Storrs and Lawrence left Egypt to meet him, as 'the mainspring of action . . . clever and judicious.'[10]

But Lawrence disliked Abdullah on sight. His reaction blended rational and emotional factors. A skilled chess-player, Abdullah was certainly wily. But his request for the presence of Christian soldiers in the Hejaz was both imprudent in itself and could lead to that 'frangification' which Lawrence had detested in Syria. Further, Abdullah's liking for handsome young men approached areas in Lawrence's own psyche which Lawrence kept hidden. Abdullah spoke Arabic brilliantly but no English or French. Impressed (as he was meant to be) by his British visitor's knowledge of Turkish troop dispositions, the Amir probably smiled at the rustic expressions which Lawrence had remembered from Dahoum; worse, may have corrected his grammar.*

* Writing when Lawrence and his two oldest brothers were dead, Abdullah got his own back: 'Lawrence appeared only to require people who had no views of their own,

Abdullah rejected, Lawrence disembarked at Rabegh further north of Jidda. This would be the key-point in any Turkish advance on Mecca by the watered, coastal route. At Rabegh he found Abdullah's eldest and youngest brothers. Neither impressed him. Ali was a sickly thirty-seven, a man of piety more than action. While Zeid was too juvenile and the son of a Turkish mother. (In fact, the nationality or even religion of a man's mother harmed him little in Islam.) For the journey inland to meet the last brother, Ali lent him a splendidly arrayed camel. Lawrence would have to pretend to be a Syrian defector from the Ottoman army and therefore wore an Arab head-dress with his khaki. Since Syrians were sometimes ruddy-complexioned, the pretence would not be impossible if he held his tongue; nor would a few words betray him, as the Hejazis knew that the Syrian dialect differed from theirs; but for him to utter more than a sentence would now and always betray him as an Englishman. A tribal guide would remind him to be silent.

The camel journey to Feisal's camp introduced like some sombre overture the swelling act. Their first morning Lawrence and his guide halted at a desert well. There he chanced to see, though not to meet, a handsome and athletic young Sharif. Sharif Ali ibn al-Hussein al-Harithi* wore rich Cashmere robes while, to deceive Turkish spies, his cousin, a Sharif, too, acted as his servant. Sharif Ali happily sustained the pretence by ordering his cousin about and striking him on head and shoulders with a riding stick.

The journey to Bir Abbas, painful to one unused to camels, pleased the side of Lawrence that liked discomfort. When they finally arrived, his first sight of Feisal came as a revelation. The guerilla prince stood tense and white-robed in a black doorway, a spirit both noble and tragic infusing his wan flesh. Lawrence's response to Feisal was not eccentric. Two years later Feisal was to remind the conventional Hubert Young of 'some beautiful thoroughbred quivering at the starting-gate.'[12] A British general was to inform his wife: 'You would like Feisal. He is a keen, slim, highly strung man. He has beautiful hands like a woman's, and his fingers are always moving nervously when he talks. But he is strong in will and straight in principle.'[13] He, not Abdullah, had elected to lead the flying-column of al-Masri's double army and Storrs found him 'blunt and outspoken' compared to Abdullah.[14] Besides appealing to the freelance in

---

that he might impress his personal ideas upon them.' Abdullah had by then disproved fears that he might be too independent. In his role of British puppet he was praised by Winston Churchill as ' "a very agreeable, intelligent and civilized Arab prince" who, in return for his kingdom and his subsidy, had agreed to maintain order in Transjordan, and to restrain his subjects from both anti-French and anti-British activity.'[11]

* Because Sharif Ali ibn al-Hussein had the same name as King Hussein's eldest son—who could be described as Sharif Ali or Amir Ali—he has been confused with him. Cf. Index to *The Letters of T. E. Lawrence*, ed. David Garnett, 1938, p. 877.

Lawrence, Feisal had a practical advantage over his elder brother. When the family had lived in Constantinople under Sultan Abdul Hamid, Feisal had taken lessons in English,[15] so that if Lawrence wished to tell Feisal something confidential, or if he did not know the correct Arabic expression, he could use English; if he made mistakes in his Arabic, Feisal would not care, provided Lawrence's meaning came across.

Lawrence imposed his choice of Feisal on his British superiors. A few days after his visit to Khartoum Wingate verbally demoted Abdullah to Minister of Foreign Affairs, no longer calling him General Officer Commanding. The same day Wingate wrote to Wilson (whose criticism of Lawrence had not yet reached him) that 'clearly everything that is possible must be done to keep Feisal in good fettle.'[16] In Cairo Lawrence had as quickly convinced his colleagues at the Arab Bureau. To Clayton (eager to establish an Intelligence Section in the Hejaz) he stressed that Feisal was most unlikely to grant a non-Arab such a facility. Clayton quoted Lawrence: 'He [Feisal] has his own agents and would probably impart their information if Lawrence was sitting in his camp. He might take advice as to their direction, but he is *very* difficult to advise.'[17] Four days before Wingate had told Wilson in Jidda: 'Instructions have been wired to Clayton to send Lawrence to Yenbo as soon as possible; it is vitally important that an officer with knowledge of Arabs should be there to keep in touch with Feisal and arrange for his supplies.'[18] But Wingate intended that Newcombe should replace Lawrence as soon as possible since his services would be invaluable to the Arab Bureau in Cairo.

The men directing British policy had accepted Feisal thanks to Lawrence; his forceful personality was to subvert Wingate's hopes (which Clayton shared) of recapturing Lawrence himself for the Arab Bureau. Leaving Cairo on 25 November, by early December he was acting as political officer to his chosen Amir.

The next seven weeks Lawrence spent between ship and shore assessing the potential of Feisal's forces and at first still posing as a Syrian deserter. Feisal's headquarters were at Yenbo, a small harbour almost on the same line of longitude with Medina. Soon after landing Lawrence reported to Wilson: 'Feisal treats me very well, and lets me ask hear and see everything, including his agents.'[19] Feisal's agents were, at second hand, British: Turkey, obliged to use silver and, finally, a debased paper currency, found it hard to compete with Britain's gold sovereigns.

Rich though Britain then was, Wingate needed all the assistance of such banker friends as George Lloyd before securing 'a more or less free hand from the Foreign Office to make advances, recoverable from subsequent monthly settlements, in an emergency.'[20] Clayton acknowledged the power of finance: after a summer visit to England, he noted that the Jews were 'an increasing power as the war becomes more and more a question of who has the deepest pocket and the longest credit';[21] and Storrs was later to estimate that Britain spent £11,000,000 on the Arab Revolt: a heavy price when it is remembered that it had cost Egypt only £1,600,000 to reconquer the Sudan and Britain half that sum.[22] Again to quote Wingate, 'The main essential is funds for liberal payment to tribesmen.'[23] No more than two per cent of the Hejazi population, in Lawrence's view, supported the Revolt: for these, money represented incentives when they flagged and rewards when they won. For the majority who still considered the Sultan their Caliph, the money helped soothe consciences which might otherwise have jibbed. In December 1916 Lawrence had only £50 in gold; by May the following year the sum at his disposal had swollen to some £20,000; by August these funds had multiplied tenfold. The gold sovereigns at his disposal, with their equestrian image of St. George, gave him an authenticated nickname, *Abu Khayyal*, or Father of the Horseman.*

By 8 January 1917, Lawrence could send Wilson detailed observations of the Turks so far captured and of Feisal's forces. In addition to Feisal's irregulars, Amir Ali commanded some 8,000 men to the south of Medina while Amir Abdullah commanded some 4,000 to its east and north-east.[24] Since Feisal's camps were widely dispersed, Lawrence could not precisely confirm his Amir's estimate of over 6,000 Arabs.[25] He could, however, assess their quality: 'They still preserve their tribal instinct for independence of order, but they are curbing their habit of wasting ammunition, have achieved a sort of routine in matters of camping and marching, and when the Sharif approaches near they fall into line and make the low bow and sweep of the arm to the lips which is the official salute. They do not oil their guns—they say because they then clog with sand, and they have no oil handy—but the guns are most of them in fair order, and some of the men know how to shoot.'[26] He entitled a section of his report *Feisal's Table Talk*. His quips had a Lawrentian ring: 'Feisal says that Abdullah, though quick when he does move, is rather luxurious in taste and inclined to be lazy;' in reporting that his old rival in Syria, von Oppenheim, had offered Feisal the Egyptian crown if he backed the Germans: 'Feisal quoted the *Koran* to the disparagement of the Egyptians, and said that he had lately been in Egypt, and had been offered the crown by the Nationalist party. Egyptians were weather-cocks, with no political principle except dissatisfactions, and intent only on pleasure and money getting.'†[27]

Amidst this medley of military information and political gossip there are

* Sir Herbert Todd told the author in Baghdad 1955 that he had so heard Lawrence hailed by a crowd of enthusiastic Arabs. The 'al-Urens' (in its many variants an anticipation of the 'Issyvoo' of Mr. Isherwood's Berlin stories) seems fanciful. 'Lawrence' presents no particular difficulties to the Arab tongue.

† The story is unconvincing; Feisal had not been recently in Egypt and the Egyptian Umma Party in general supported the Ottoman cause and the deposed Abbas Hilmi.

hints that what had happened to Lawrence in Carchemish was now happening, on a grander scale, in the Hejaz. He described an Arabian cavalcade to Colonel Wilson: 'The order of march was rather splendid and barbaric. Feisal in front, in white: Sharaf [a proper name, not a title] on his right in red headcloth and henna dyed tunic and cloak; myself on his left in white and red; behind us three banners of purple silk, with gold spikes; behind them three drummers playing a march, and behind them again, a wild bouncing mass of 1,200 camels of the bodyguard, all packed as closely as they could move, the men in every variety of coloured clothes, and the camels nearly as brilliant in their trappings, and the whole crowd singing at the tops of their voices a warsong in honour of Feisal and his family.'[28] One can hear Wilson snorting.

Counselling an Arab noble of ancient lineage and impressive demeanour, Lawrence could see himself as vizir to some medieval caliph. He was not the only Englishman to be impressed by ancestry. In October 1914 Kitchener had concluded a telegram with the pious hope: 'that one of Arab race will assume Califate at Mecca or Medina and so good may come by help of God out of all the evil which is now occurring.'[29] Lawrence had soon discarded khaki for Arab robes, according to him, at Feisal's suggestion; but as the clothes he wore—the 'splendid white silk and gold-embroidered wedding garments' of a Sharif—made him conspicuous, the suggestion was probably prompted by Lawrence. (The regular Sharifian forces, who did most of the serious fighting, wore khaki uniforms with the Arab head-dress.) Writing home, Lawrence described Feisal as 'about 31, tall, slight, lively, well-educated. He is charming towards me, and we get on perfectly together. He has a tremendous reputation in the Arab world as a leader of men, and a diplomat. His strong point is handling tribes: he has the manner that gets on perfectly with tribesmen, and they all love him.'[30] To Newcombe, his chief on the Negeb expedition, he evoked another self, the warrior sportsman; in describing Feisal as 'an absolute ripper,' he used a phrase appropriate to an army officer of those days.

'This show is splendid: you cannot imagine greater fun for us, greater fury and vexation for the Turks. We win hands down if we keep the Arabs simple . . . and to add to them heavy luxuries will only wreck this show, and guerilla does it. It's a sort of guerre de course, with the courses all reversed. But the life and fun and movement of it are extreme.'[31]

The same letter adverted to the next Sharifian operation. 'Boyle [Captain William Boyle of the Red Sea Patrol] is good—proud of his profession, but white and itching for a show. Try and get him a little game at Wejh. I'd like him to land north of the town, and work along the sandhills into the camp.' Vickery (an officer on Newcombe's staff whom Lawrence disliked) had been complaining that nothing important had yet been achieved. Lawrence counselled a British self-effacement that left as much as possible to the Arabs. 'After all, it's an Arab war, and we are only contributing materials—and the Arabs have the right to go their own way and run things as they please. We are only guests.' As an instance of such independence, King Hussein, as the Grand Sharif was now recognized by the British, had dismissed al-Masri (the advocate of guerilla war) and replaced him by Jaafar al-Askari, a relative of Nuri al-Said's, whom the British had taken prisoner on the Libyan front.

The essential next step in Sharifian strategy was clear. The Arabs must complete their hold on the coast before envisaging operations outside the Hejaz or deciding whether to risk another attack on Medina. The Royal Navy's control of the Red Sea could then secure Arab links with the outside world. To the ports the Arabs had already taken they must first add Wejh, opposite al-Kusair on the Egyptian coast, and then Akaba, at the head of the gulf dividing the Hejaz from the Sinai peninsula. Lawrence's role was to ginger up the Sharifian forces in their landward advance on Wejh. But now that he was briefly happy, he allowed the lotophagous inertia he had indulged at Carchemish to affect his role as Feisal's adviser. If his superiors expected him to impose western punctuality on eastern irregulars, they were disappointed. At dawn on 23 January H.M.S. *Hardinge* would be disembarking at Wejh 400 Arab regulars under Captain Bray with a support party of 200 British seamen, and Feisal's troops should have arrived from the south at the same moment. But Feisal's picturesque army took its time. Wejh had been captured and looted before Feisal, Lawrence and the tribesmen turned up on the 25th. At the end of the month Lawrence was on leave in Cairo. When by 12 February he was back in the Hejaz, Wejh had been established as the northern Sharifian base. In a letter home he summed up the capabilities of the tribal guerillas, and predicted that railway sabotage was next on the agenda.

The bedouin were rebellious by instinct but unwilling to obey anyone's orders, he wrote; they were thus condemned to form 'a mob of snipers or guerilla-fighters.'[32] They were active, 'quite intelligent' and did what they did fairly well. They were not—and German military reports, as well as events, confirm Lawrence in this—fit to meet disciplined troops in the open, and it would be long before they were. The Arab movement itself he termed 'a curious thing'. Small and weak in its beginning, it could easily be suppressed by anyone who controlled the sea. But though the sparse, impoverished populations of the desert condemned the movement to be widespread rather than deep, its smallness gave it much of its strength: 'for they are perhaps the most elusive enemy an army ever had, and inhabit one of the most trying countries in the world for civilized warfare.' The Turkish flag might reasonably be expected to vanish from

Arabia. 'It is indiscreet only to ask what Arabia is. It has an East and a West and a South border—but where or what it is on the top no man knoweth. I fancy myself it is up to the Arabs to find out! Talk about Palestine or Syria or Mesopotamia is not opportune, when these three countries—with every chance—have made no effort towards freedom for themselves.'

Lawrence here revealed the assumptions underlying his political thought. An Arab's right to freedom depended on the extent to which he helped the Allies. That an Arab might want freedom, yet believe that collaboration with the colonizers of Algeria and Egypt was the wrong way to win it, did not occur to him. Syria (where many educated Arabs had perished on the scaffold) was no longer his magnetic north.

Within a month the conflict between the interests of the Arab rebels and their British allies had come into the open.

During the winter of 1916–17 the Commander-in-Chief of the Expeditionary Force in Egypt, General Sir Archibald Murray, had used Egyptian labour to push a railway across Mediterranean Sinai to the Turkish frontier south-west of Gaza. The aim was initially defensive, to prevent further Turkish attacks on the Canal; but a railway could also be used for the conquest of Palestine. However, as later wars were to show, moves into Sinai from Egypt are vulnerable. Murray was to suffer two serious reverses, on 26 March and 19 April respectively, when the Turkish garrison repulsed British attacks on Gaza. A false report that the Turks had decided to evacuate Medina led to a shift in British thinking against all-out support of the Arab cause.

As recently as November Wingate had reported a divergence with his French allies on the question of the Hejazi city still in Turkish hands. 'We should welcome the capture of Medina by the Sharif whereas the French, in view of their future Syrian policy, seem to me to regard with some alarm the great acquisition of strength which the Sharif's cause would immediately obtain by the active support of all the Arab tribes in the Syrian hinterland who have sworn to rise in the Sharif's favour immediately Medina is in his hands.'[33] If the Turks had withdrawn from Medina, they could have greatly strengthened their Palestine front. But because of Medina's religious importance, Enver Pasha, the Turkish strong man, vetoed the move. 'The sacrifices necessarily involved in providing the garrisons in Medina and Maan with food and ammunition,' the Ottoman governor-general of Syria later admitted, 'compelled us to halve the supplies provided for Palestine and Sinai and prevented us from reinforcing our Sinai front when and how we liked.'[34]

Yet the Arabs, for whom the capture of Medina was important, could not take it without much heavier arms than their allies were prepared to give them. The vacillating Wingate had veered to the French policy of keeping the Turks in Medina. At a conference in Khartoum before Christmas 1916, he and Lloyd concurred with Brémond's argument that it would be imprudent to allow the Arabs to capture Medina (at least before the British armies in Palestine and Iraq had effected a junction) lest it give the notion of Arab unity a dangerous fillip. (We shall see that as late as 1918 British statesmen were to consider a deal with the Ottoman Government at the expense of the Arabs.) The capture of Medina might also dispose the Arabs to seek a separate peace: Ben Gabrit, the leader of the French pilgrimage to Mecca in 1916, had reported Hussein's conviction that the Turks would make him a generous offer.[35] Behind its fortified entrenchment Medina was to hold out until after the war had ended elsewhere.

Lawrence was instructed in early March to press the strategy which suited British interests: to leave the Turks in Medina, but harry their communications. A demolition school had been set up at Wejh under Newcombe and another British officer, Major Garland. Its alumni were now to damage the Railway in order to prevent an orderly Turkish evacuation to the north. A first attack had been made as early as November 1916; but the sabotage campaign started in earnest under Newcombe and Hornby in March, 1917. Among the Arabs recruited for this work was the personable young Sharif, Ali ibn al-Hussein, whom Lawrence had seen at the well his first day in the desert.[36]

The Khartoum conference had set as first priority the capture of Akaba. The port had interested Wingate for some time. As early as 1912 he had sent a British agent there along with two other spies disguised as his chef and butler. The agent had found it 'a miserable sort of village hidden in a large date palm grove', its buildings knocked about by an Italian bombardment.[37] Akaba now became a focus of Anglo-French rivalry.[38]

Akaba, like other ports, could be attacked in one of three ways: by naval bombardment followed by a marine landing; by assault from inland; or by a combination of these two approaches. Lawrence later claimed that his pre-war day in Akaba had convinced him that the gulfhead village could not be taken from the sea. *Could not* was perhaps an exaggeration; but recent experience in the Dardanelles, where floating mines and coastal batteries had worked havoc on a fleet trying to force the narrows, had induced a wary mood. Wingate argued that a landing was 'open to grave objections on military grounds,' since the Railway could bring Turkish reinforcements close to the coast. 'One mobile division would be the smallest force consistent with safety. To detach such a force would seriously affect operations on the Sinai front.'[39]

The authorship of the plan to take Akaba solely from inland was later disputed between Lawrence,[40] Feisal and Auda abu Tayi, the desert

Ajax whom Lawrence first met in April at Feisal's headquarters at Wejh.[41] Complicated discoveries can be made simultaneously in different laboratories: the comparatively simple choice of one of the three approaches to Akaba may have occurred (with variants of tactic) to all three men. Feisal, the representative of King Hussein, took the political decision to carry the war this stage further into Ottoman domains. Auda (his brain oiled by a £10,000 gift from Feisal[42]) may have remembered how the seventh-century hero, Khalid ibn-Walid, had won victories by unexpected appearances across vast distances of desert. He in any case was to provide, from his Howeitat tribe, the manpower necessary to take on the three hundred Turks at Akaba with whatever other troops might be found en route. On 9 May the expedition struck north-east from Wejh towards the grazing grounds where the impromptu force could be put together. Lawrence's saddlebags contained £20,000 in gold sovereigns.

The two months following the departure from Wejh enfold, like the flanges of an oyster, one of the major puzzles of Lawrence's war. The first flange was the slow, dangerous ride north-east under the command of Sharif Nasir of Medina. Crossing the Railway, avoiding the Turks, the Sharifian forces rejoined Auda at his oasis of Nebk on 2 June. The second flange began two weeks later on 19 June. By this time the Arabs were ready to strike south-west towards Akaba: they would fight their one battle on the limestone ridge dominated by Abu'l Lissan; overwhelming raw Turkish recruits they would then ride down a high-walled wadi to accept the surrender of Akaba's small garrison on 6 July. The pearl of puzzlement lies in the period when Auda and Nasir were mustering their forces, between 4 and 18 June. Arabs who took part in the venture have insisted to an Arab historian that throughout these two weeks Lawrence was with them at Nebk. Lawrence for his part claimed to have accomplished an unrivalled camel ride. According to this claim (embodied in the official report he sent to General Clayton after the capture of Akaba) he left Auda's force on 4 June to ride north with two bedouin companions. Having arrived within a short distance of ancient Palmyra, the small party swung west to Ras Baalbek on the other side of the Anti-Lebanon range and then moved east to the outskirts of Damascus 'where on June 13th I met Ali Riza Pasha Rehabi, G.O.C. Damascus.'[43]

Lawrence recorded his movements or positions-at-night from 1 January 1917 until 8 October 1918 in what he termed a 'skeleton diary'.[44] The hundreds of listed places compose the odyssey of a human flea. Yet for this period of two weeks the skeleton diary has the laconic entry: *Nebk, etc.* Arab memories apart, what makes it difficult to accept the veridicity of Lawrence's report to Clayton (apart from his later evasions about the journey and the improbabilities in the distances covered) is his claim to have met *Ali Riza Rehabi, G.O.C. Damascus* outside that city on 13 June. Apart from the lack of precision about detail—Ali Ridha al-Rikabi, one of the few Arab officers to become an Ottoman general, was at this time civil mayor of Damascus, not General Officer Commanding—the secret meeting seems never to have taken place. Lawrence deliberately falsified some of the names in his subsequent book, but al-Rikabi was a historical personage whose career was to become intimately linked with the Sharifian cause. When he met Lawrence after the liberation of Damascus, Lawrence reminded him of their previous meeting, not at or near Damascus during the war, but at Carchemish where, in peacetime, al-Rikabi had visited the excavations.*

Conceivably, despite the recollections of those Arabs who remembered Lawrence remaining with them in camp, he may have ridden off to the north, in a search for news of Dahoum. Possibly the insertion into his report of outlandish names, the suggestion that he blew a small bridge here or healed a vendetta there, could then be kin to his previous defensive tales of lost camera or stolen seals. What seems impossible is that he met al-Rikabi near Damascus. When after the War al-Rikabi denied this meeting, such an association with an emissary of Feisal could not have harmed al-Rikabi's reputation: Abdullah was then king of Transjordan and Feisal's dynasty established in Iraq. Al-Rikabi was a truthful man who denied the meeting because it had not occurred.

British officers, for all the faults which Lawrence attributed to them, campaigned in an atmosphere of trust. They neither told fibs themselves nor thought to be fibbed to by others. They no more expected a brother officer to romance in an official report than to embezzle mess funds. Even those who disliked Lawrence's manner or dress thus took what he wrote at face value and his report on the expedition from Wejh went unquestioned, particularly when on 13 July H.M.S. *Dufferin* sailed to Akaba and confirmed that the hungry town (for which it had brought food) was indeed in Arab hands. Two days later Wingate informed Colonel Wilson (who generously praised 'a very fine feat by all accounts') that he had strongly recommended Lawrence for the Victoria Cross, the most coveted British military honour. 'For obvious reasons I have of course been obliged to curtail the official communique and have confined the scope of his reconnaissance—in public—to the Maan-Akaba neighbourhood.' Next day Wingate followed up his recommendation by writing

* Feisal was to appoint al-Rikabi military governor of the eastern liberated region in October 1918; he then made him his first prime minister after being proclaimed King of Syria. Amir Abdullah later nominated al-Rikabi as his first prime minister in Transjordan. Al-Rikabi denied that he had met Lawrence during the war to the late Akram al-Rikabi, who stated this to Suleiman Mousa, the Arab historian. His second son, Ali-Haidar al-Rikabi, confirmed the same denial, in detail, to the present writer in Baghdad, 1974.

to Sir Mark Sykes, 'His exploit in the Syrian Hinterland was really splendid.'[45] He suggested that Sykes put in a helpful word as well. But two months later Hogarth explained to his wife that Lawrence had not been given the V.C. 'because of the proviso in the Charter of the Order that there must be British officers witnesses of the deed. The C.B. was given instead and the H.C. [High Commissioner] thinks it is really a higher honour at his age and implies more for the future.'[46]

Apart from his alleged bedouin companions, Lawrence was the only witness of his great ride north, but he had indeed taken part in Auda's charge at Abu'l Lissan. However, in the excitement he had shot his camel through the head and been catapulted to earth. At the decisive moment of the decisive battle the only British officer on the field had been unconscious.

16

THE FOUR months from March to early July 1917, constituted Lawrence's longest unbroken stay in Arabia. The last two months of this period, from when the Sharifian expedition left Wejh to the day in early July when he and his camel carried the news of Akaba's capture to Suez, constituted his longest single absence from a British base. These four months also established his reputation with his superiors, who, as we have seen, were particularly impressed by what he claimed to have accomplished on his long ride north. As early as March Wingate had described his services with Feisal as 'enormous'; Storrs, too, was now speaking of 'my little genius';[1] while the terms in which Clayton wrote to the Commander of the Imperial General Staff showed that the remote Field-Marshal was expected to identify this one captain out of fifty thousand. Sir Mark Sykes, who had done so much to shape British policy towards the Middle East, considered Lawrence's march of six hundred miles epochal, while George Lloyd, destined to be a peer and High Commissioner for Egypt, wrote that Lawrence had done 'wonderfully well and will some day be able to write a unique book.'[2]

In the desert Lawrence was isolated from 'a khaki crowd very intent on banker and parades and lunch.'[3] Communications with Arabia were in fact so bad that in November the Arab Bureau suggested that it might be desirable to introduce carrier pigeons for linking Yenbo with Feisal.[4] In the more congenial desert atmosphere Lawrence could excel and romance. But the same isolation meant that when he reached the banks of the Suez Canal with his exciting news about Akaba he knew nothing about events important to himself and the Arab movement which had occurred in his absence. In Iraq General Maude had atoned for the squalor of Kut by capturing Baghdad. In London the bellicose prime minister Lloyd George had sent a new general to the Middle East with orders to replace the luckless Murray and capture Jerusalem 'as a Christmas present for the British nation.'[5] Also in London, and at the same season, Colonel John Buchan, 'one of the mysterious high priests of the Ministry of Information,' advised an American publicist and his photographer to search the Middle East for war stories more uplifting than any to be found in the Flanders quagmire.

Lawrence saw one new development for himself while he waited on Ismailia station for the Port Said to Cairo express. Out of an opulent carriage stepped, deferentially attended, the imposing figure of General Edmund Allenby. Nicknamed 'the Bull', Allenby had assumed command of the Egyptian Expeditionary Force from Murray at the end of June. An ornithologist and strict disciplinarian, he had at once toured the Palestinian front. Between the outskirts of Gaza on the sea and the defences of Beersheba on the edge of the desert, he noted with equal sharpness flamingoes at the mouths of wadis and the shortcomings of the soldiers now under his command.

Lawrence was introduced to the new commander a few days later in Cairo, and Allenby proved one of the few figures in Lawrence's life to arouse strong yet contradictory emotions: usually a man was either ripping or a rotter. Although in his letters home Lawrence referred to Allenby in flat, unemotional, yet dutiful terms, in later writings he bestowed on him admiring superlatives. Yet some years after Allenby's triumphs Lawrence was to denounce, in important company, the once 'morally great' commander as unprincipled and weak.[6]

Allenby provoked this ambivalence by incarnating qualities the opposite of Lawrence's own. He was tall, conventionally married and a former public-school prefect. He assumed authority as naturally as an overcoat. Lawrence, who was small, celibate and socially undistinguished, had had to sidle into positions of influence. As a member of Lawrence's least liked profession, Allenby exemplified those stodgy virtues which are missed when they are gone. Decent, fair, capable of explosions of temper but (unlike the much flogging Kitchener) not given to brutal punishments, he was neither a gifted writer nor an inspiring leader. He had the characteristic limits of the professional soldier. 'Executive skill is the fruit of practice; and constant practice, or repetition, tends inevitably to deaden originality and elasticity of mind.'[7] Yet this rather humdrum man, who left neither interesting letters nor revealing papers, who inspired no cult among disciples or the general public, was to achieve the one decisive victory in a war of indecisive slaughter. The private side to Allenby's character, his delight in birds and shrubs, his concept of happiness as growing roses in a garden of one's own, showed affinities with his only son, killed in France a month after his father's arrival in Egypt. (Just before his death the twenty-year-old Lieutenant Michael Allenby had startled brother officers by advancing 'socialistic' ideas and defending conscientious objection.) Allenby's public side responded neither to Lawrence's personality nor his undisciplined Arab irregulars but he was willing to use both (just as he used a Staff Officer with a genius for military ruses) as tools for victory.

At their first Cairo meeting Allenby looked sideways at Lawrence as if unsure 'how much was genuine performer and how much charlatan.'* In a recent report Lawrence had suggested that the eastern tribes of Syria, who had played a vital role in Saladin's victories against the Crusaders, could be similarly useful in a new attack on the Holy Land. This idea interested the scholar in Allenby. But he was perturbed by 'a little bare-footed silk-skirted man,' as Lawrence described himself, 'offering to hobble the enemy by his preaching if given stores and arms and a fund of two hundred thousand sovereigns to convince and control his converts.' Allenby could, when studying the routes taken by ancient invaders of Sinai, construe a page of Strabo's Greek without a lexicon. He may have wondered what the scruffy little man in Arab dress could preach to Muslim tribesmen, or what preaching needed such quick link with coin.† But Allenby was a man of his word. His parting promise, 'Well, I will do for you what I can', meant what it said. It also meant that Lawrence and the Arabs must do the same for him.

A new situation was immediately evident at the port of Akaba. A cluster of dusty palm trees and mud huts had become the bustling forward base of Britain's Arab allies. The Royal Navy, no longer threatened by mines, supplied Akaba with food, gold, armoured cars and limited munitions. We have seen that for political reasons the Arabs were never given arms in sufficient quantities for them to attack fortified positions with success. (On the same day that Lawrence brought his exciting news of the capture of Akaba to Egypt, the *Arab Bulletin* had recommended to its restricted readership that it might do no harm if the Sharif Hussein suffered a mild check. 'He will be more modest and accommodating if he realizes more closely that he is dependent on our help for success.'[10]) Since Akaba symbolized the opposite of a check, the occasional squeeze became the more needful. The stores, on the other hand, arrived in such quantities and were so difficult to guard that Akaba was soon a black-market emporium; flour, rice and sugar found their way, at exorbitant prices, to the empty Damascus markets and the hungry Turks. This black-market was an irritation to Germans and Allies alike. 'There is a regular communication,' a German report complained, 'both commercial and personal, between Akaba and Damascus. In this way the Druses let the Germans down, having instituted a black-market in corn.'[11]‡ A British officer complained of the same thing but admitted that Feisal could do little to stop the trading. If this Arab 'Lieutenant-

* His biographer, Sir Archibald Wavell, says Allenby never resolved the conundrum, 'but always suspected a strong streak of the charlatan in Lawrence.'[8]

† It was probably at this time Lawrence invested £60 of the gold in having a new circlet for his white Arab head-dress fashioned in Cairo.[9]

‡ The semi-autonomous Druses lived both in the Lebanon and Jebel Druse south of Damascus; they could muster, according to the same German report, 30,000 well-armed warriors. The trade passed through their territory.

General' in a Christian army had taken a strong moral line, the inland tribes would have harassed his communications.[12] In this context gold became more and more essential.

Armoured cars were an innovation in Arabia. Former Royal Army Service Corps driver S. C. Rolls has described how in the late summer of 1917 he and his comrades of the Duke of Westminster's Brigade escorted eight armoured cars and two Rolls-Royce tenders, 'Blast and Bloodhound', by way of Alexandria and the Egyptian railway system to Suez. Thence the monstrous cargo was ferried round the point of Sinai to Akaba, from which the desert uplands could be reached by the pass of Itm, a narrow, steep-walled corridor blocked by giant boulders. Lawrence suddenly appeared out of the blue with 'a group of dishevelled Arabs, mounted on richly harnessed camels, who were riding slowly down the pass, picking their way between the stones.' Rolls, an unsophisticated and slightly bolshie Englishman, had been soldiering since 1915; he had not yet heard of Lawrence, nor had his comrades. Next morning their captain told them that they were there 'to serve Colonel* Lawrence, and that his commands must be obeyed smartly and in a soldier-like manner. I suppose he thought that because Lawrence was dressed in Arab clothes he might find it difficult to exact prompt obedience; in the army a man's clothes are so often the only sign of his authority . . . In our corps, as in others, orders were snapped out iike curses, and salutes to officers were exacted in the fullest manner. The orders were passively obeyed, the salutes were yielded. Lawrence's orders were directions, and he cared nothing about saluting, except that he preferred to dispense with it. Instead of an order, he usually seemed to raise, first of all, a question for discussion; giving the impression, a true one, that he wanted to have one's opinion of what was best, before he decided on the course to be followed.'[13]

It took two weeks to clear the road to the interior through the twenty-mile gorge. Speed was urgent as Auda and some six hundred tribesmen were holding the other side of the gorge against the Turks. But Turkish attacks could be political as well as military, and the armoured cars which would use the road, while dramatizing to the Arabs the power of their British ally, raised doubts about its true intentions. Since Christmas 1915 Blast, Bloodhound and their armoured pups had been busy aiding the Italians, British allies since May 1915, in suppressing the last efforts of the Senussi Arabs.

The ambiguities of Sharif Hussein's position as a rebel became daily plainer.

In July 1917 Feisal was still the commander of the northern Sharifian army; his headquarters were still at Wejh, though he had planned to

* Lawrence was at this time a Major.

transfer them north to Akaba. Lawrence's new duty was to induce Feisal, and if possible his father, to accept a change in the status of the northern army and in the nature of the Revolt.

From the start, the Revolt's coincidence with British interests had aroused the suspicions of most educated Muslims. The principle of nationalism which Hussein invoked as a pretext for attacking the Sultan's forces was a weaker bond to Muslims than was religion. The Ottoman Empire had been a plural society in which a man's loyalty was either to the Empire as a whole or to his *millet*, or religious group. Nationalism had worked with Greeks and Bulgarians, because, being Christian, they had a different religion as well as culture from the Turks. The Arabs shared the same religion with the Turks; their two cultures had much in common. Most Arabs desirous of a change thought of decentralization rather than independence: in a formula discussed in August 1918, something akin to Bavaria's existence as a separate kingdom inside the German empire.[14] The nationalism espoused by Christian Arabs as a means for escaping their minority status derived from the ideology which had been the blight of nineteenth-century Europe. It meant nothing to the tribesmen of Arabia, most of whom had never come under a Turkish governor or a European schoolmaster. The nomad felt loyalty to his tribe and to Islam. Even urban Arabs knew an Islamic loyalty that superseded attachment to their linguistic group, and many memoirs attest the crises of conscience which young Arabs went through before deciding to enlist in the Sharifian ranks. This was less the case with aspiring politicians such as Nuri al-Said or his relative, Jaafar al-Askari (it was he who after being captured in Libya had changed sides and replaced al-Masri) than with the young idealists who made their way from the cities of Syria and Iraq to join Feisal and his brothers. The ruthless treatment of dissidents by Jemal Pasha, the Ottoman governor-general of Syria, was the decisive factor with such recruits, who were of a different temper from the bedouin tribesmen who enjoyed a bloodless scrap and welcomed gold from whatever source.

On his new mission of persuasion Lawrence returned to Wejh, and then rode inland in search of Feisal, who was busy directing operations against the Railway. Feisal was persuaded by Lawrence's argument that, since Akaba was only a hundred miles from Suez but eight hundred from Mecca, it made sense for the northern army to come under Allenby's command. His acceptance of this advice was the most fatal single decision in a family history no stranger to wrong choices.

Feisal's agreement secured, the *Dufferin* conveyed Lawrence south to Jidda. Here he met for the first time the architect of the Revolt. In referring to King Hussein as 'a pious old gentleman with a strong tendency to swollen head', Driver Rolls undoubtedly echoed Lawrence

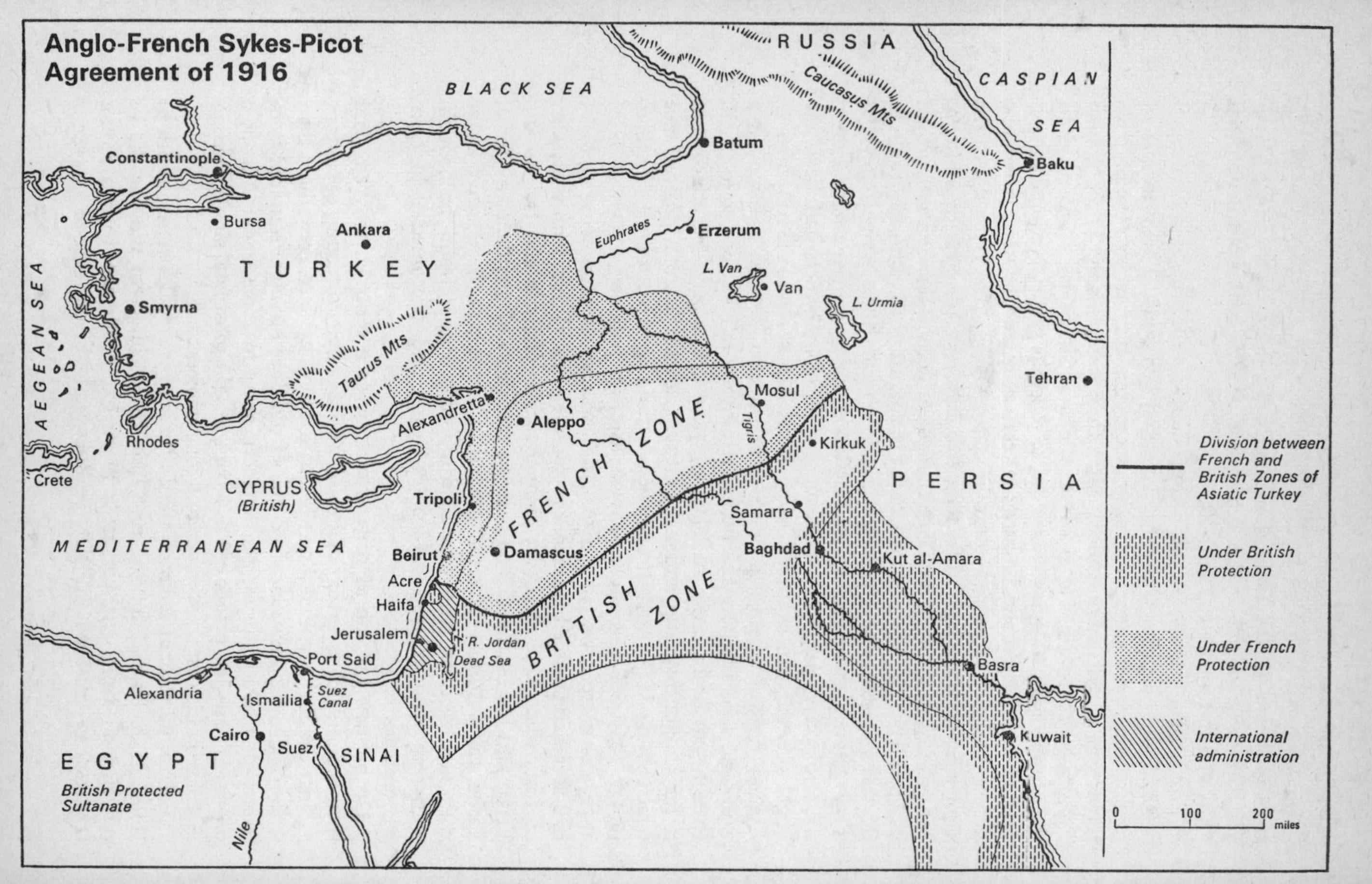
Anglo-French Sykes-Picot
Agreement of 1916
RUSSIA
BLACK SEA
CASPIAN SEA
Caucasus Mts
Batum
Baku
Constantinople
Bursa
Ankara
Erzerum
Euphrates
TURKEY
L. Van
Van
L. Urmia
AEGEAN SEA
Smyrna
Taurus Mts
Tehran
Mosul
Alexandretta
Aleppo
FRENCH ZONE
Tigris
Kirkuk
Rhodes
Crete
CYPRUS
(British)
Tripoli
PERSIA
Samarra
MEDITERRANEAN SEA
Beirut
Damascus
Baghdad
Kut al-Amara
Acre
Haifa
BRITISH ZONE
Jerusalem
R. Jordan
Dead Sea
Port Said
Basra
Alexandria
Ismailia
Suez Canal
Cairo
Suez
SINAI
Kuwait
EGYPT
British Protected
Sultanate
Nile
Division between
French and
British Zones of
Asiatic Turkey
Under British
Protection
Under French
Protection
International
administration
0
100
200
miles

who in turn knew Wingate's opinion that Feisal, not his father, should receive British funds, lest 'Hussein secure a preponderating voice in regard to the future settlement of the Syrian problem.'[15]

Hussein was under no illusions as to Feisal's shrewdness. He nevertheless concurred in his son's decision. Two recent encounters had given him premonitory shudders. In May (when Lawrence had been on the Akaba expedition) first Sir Mark Sykes alone, then Sykes with Georges-Picot, the former French consul in Beirut, had visited Jidda. As co-authors of a secret 1916 agreement, defining the basis on which Britain, France and Tsarist Russia would divide the Middle East, the two men have won places in Arab demonology only a notch above Balfour. Yet probably they were no more anti-Arab than many British officers in the Sharifian forces—indeed Sykes, a Catholic, was fond of the Middle East—but simply accepted more openly the imperialist nostrum that all backward peoples needed western tutelage. The agreement they had concocted divided the Mediterranean littoral and Iraq between France and Britain, leaving autonomy to the inland desert areas; Russia was to get Constantinople in the north.

Sykes and Picot had come to the Middle East, immediately after the first, Kerensky stage in the Russian Revolution, to allay Arab fears that the Allies might be planning what they were indeed planning. In Cairo, Sykes was introduced to three representative Syrians, selected by the British, whom he endeavoured to convince that nothing sinister was being prepared. But, as he reported to London, it had not been easy 'to manoeuvre the delegates without showing them a map or letting them know that there was an actual geographical or detailed agreement.'[16] Wingate had then sent him on a tour of the Hejaz arranged by the Arab Bureau, in the course of which Sykes was obliged to be as evasive with Feisal, whom he met at Wejh, and with Hussein, in Jidda, as he had been with the Syrians in Cairo. Sykes, who had a humorous pen, scribbled a caricature of himself sweating in the suspicious old king's company: although he sketched the thermometer at 120 degrees fahrenheit on 5 May, his perspiration was morally induced.[17] Once more he produced no map, though this was the key to the agreement's jigsaw; once more, he gave no official account of the agreement, or even admitted its existence.*

Colonel Wilson, who attended a conference between Sykes, Picot and Feisal (with Fuad al-Khatib translating) was so disgusted by the way in which Hussein was 'being led down the garden path', that he threatened to resign. Wilson told Wingate that the old man's trust in Britain was implicit. 'It will be ruined. He was brought to agree to the Arab kingdom

* Wingate was to confirm a year later that Hussein had not been officially informed of an agreement so deeply affecting the Arab future and in such blatant contradiction with previous undertakings.[18]

having the same status in Syria as in Iraq.' What the King had not been told, Wilson stressed, was what he himself had learned from Lloyd—that Baghdad was intended 'to be practically British'. Wilson quoted Feisal as saying that 'he can't urge Syrians to rise against the Turks if France is to have the country and if he did, he would be a "despicable traitor" to people who trust him.'[19] Hussein now assured Lawrence that he had refused to approve French annexation of either the Lebanon or the largely Muslim city of Beirut. 'If you want to take the Christians from us and leave the Moslems to us, you are creating divisions among the people and fostering bigotry. Lebanon need not be ours or yours either. Let it be as its people wish but I do not want outside people to interfere.'[20] This was 29 July 1917.

At least as early as March 1915 Lawrence had known of the French determination to get hold of Syria. His own essays for the *Arab Bulletin* employed a cynical tone that would not have been condoned by Sykes. The French determination was now sanctified, he knew as he spoke to King Hussein, by Britain's agreement with this ally who was all the more important to her after Russia's virtual collapse. The British members of the Arab Bureau, in particular Hogarth, opposed the agreement and believe it would lapse; but their opposition, at this stage, sprang from hopes of gaining more for Britain rather than from any romantic support for King Hussein. During his talks with Hussein, who reiterated his belief that Great Britain could not be lying, Lawrence may have perspired as much as Sykes, though he left no cartoon of himself so doing. Normally the imp in him might have smiled at the turbaned old man's comic gullibility. But he could not forget that King Hussein was Feisal's father.

A generalized guilt was to pervade Lawrence's later life and prompt, at least in part, some of his strangest decisions. His book about his Arabian experience was to link this guilt with the sense that he had played a dishonest role in the war: 'had I been an honest adviser of the Arabs I would have advised them to go home and not risk their lives fighting for such stuff [as British promises].'[21] But he wrote these words after the war when Hogarth, too, had become disillusioned. To weigh the extent to which his sense of guilt sprang from his Arabian experiences two extremes must be avoided: on one side, believing that Lawrence had dreamed since boyhood of freeing the Arab race; on the other, concluding that his cynical essays in the *Arab Bulletin* expressed his feelings in their entirety.

Lawrence approached the Arabs rather as a naturalist approaches a species in its native habitat. He studies what differentiates it from other species, rather than valuing it for intrinsic virtues or potential ability to readapt. This scientific approach, with undertones of affection and exasperation, contrasted with the approach of Middle Eastern reformers, both Turkish and Arab. These wished to modernize their societies so that they could play as effective a role in the twentieth century as they had in the ninth or sixteenth. Ready to imitate the west if progress required this, some Turks found a model in independent Bulgaria (once an Ottoman province) while some Arabs admired an Egypt modernized by contact with France and Britain. Since Napoleon's arrival in the Delta, Egypt had constructed a railway system only twenty years later than Britain, opened schools for girls as well as boys, abolished forced labour, appointed some honest judges, and produced, as early as the 1860s, a press which satirized the ruler in words and cartoons. The contrast between Egyptian progress and Ottoman stagnation had particularly impressed Syrian Christians. The Khedive created Christian beys and pashas; Lebanese immigrants grew rich from businesses as well as newspapers. But such Egyptian progress was repulsive to Lawrence; it exemplified the corruption from which he had wished to shield Dahoum. Thus he was as suspicious of the young, educated nationalists in the Sharifian army as they were of him. They dismissed him as a British agent when the alliance was useful and denounced him as an anti-Arab pervert when it curdled.* Their spiritual progeny were to slaughter Feisal's grandson, brother, nephew, chief-of-staff and prime minister.†

Lawrence for his part doubted the ability of the Arabs to build a united state, was largely ignorant of their classical literature and often disparaged their music and art. Yet he could be fiercely loyal to Arab superiors or subordinates chosen by himself. Into a world of Hotchkiss guns and Rolls-Royce tenders he introduced medieval allegiances. He could feel guilty if, by deceiving King Hussein, he might be deceiving Feisal, or fearful if his links with Intelligence might endanger Dahoum. He cared nothing for an Arab freedom based on the ballot-box or a critical press.

In his official position as political adviser to 'Lieut.-General' Feisal, Lawrence received indefinite—and also definite—assignments from Allenby. An indefinite assignment was to encourage, through Feisal, the mosquito-like harassment of the Ottoman left flank. The aim was to make the region between the Jordan river and the inner desert (where Ottoman jurisdiction ceased to run) as perilous as possible for the Turkish army and its German allies. Allenby also gave Lawrence two specific assignments. These were linked with the two offensives by which Allenby

* One Sharifian officer, in a chapter of his memoirs entitled 'Perversion', accused Lawrence of unnatural practices, not only with Dahoum, but others of the Jerablus villagers.[22]

† 1. Feisal II of Iraq, son of Feisal's son, Ghazi (himself killed in a mysterious car-crash), was shot in Baghdad on 14 July 1958.

2. Abdullah, at the time King of Jordan, was assassinated in Jerusalem in 1951.

3. Amir Abdul Ilah, son of Feisal's eldest brother Ali, died with Feisal II.

4. Jaafar al-Askari was assassinated in Baghdad in 1936.

5. Nuri al-Said was killed immediately after the Royal Family in Baghdad, July 1958.

was to defeat Turkish power. The first offensive, of November 1917, led to the capture of Jerusalem; the second, of October 1918, drove the last Turkish forces north of the Taurus.

Lawrence threw his formidable energies into the assignment of harassing Turkish communications. Activities such as train-bashing and camel-riding silenced doubts and stifled guilt by giving vent to the impulses of a wanton schoolboy. In the excitement of train-bashing Lawrence could temporarily forget about politics. Because destruction excited that juvenile side of his character which had enjoyed apple-bobbing and practical jokes, and because when excited he could write unforgettably, he established himself as the train-basher par excellence: stealing a fame which belonged more properly to Newcombe and Hornby.

The supplies which Wingate had sent to Jidda at the start of the Revolt had included dynamite. But since no one in the Hejaz knew how to use it, Hussein returned it to Port Sudan. This situation had been put right by Garland, an expert on demolition. Since March 1917, Newcombe and Hornby had been blowing up stretches of the line between Medina and Maan, the station where Lawrence and Dahoum had caught the train from Petra to Damascus in 1914. Lawrence had spent his time obeying his own dicta: 'The beginning and ending of the secret of handling Arabs is unremitting study of them. Keep always on your guard: never say any unconsidered thing . . . watch yourself and your companions all the time: hear all that passes, search out what is going on beneath the surface, read their characters, discover their tastes and their weaknesses, and keep everything you find out to yourself.'[23]

In fact, while he was inducing Feisal and King Hussein to put their northern army under Allenby's command, Lawrence had discovered that doubts about British intentions were ominously widespread. Not only Auda, the desert warrior, but most of the Arab leaders, Feisal included, were, during the year of fighting which remained, to consider the advantages of a separate peace with the Turks.[24]

One train-bash, except to the insatiable, is much like another. But Lawrence's attitude to a successful raid of mid-September 1917—just before he left on his first definite assignment from Allenby—was typically layered. His first account went to his family on 24 September:

'I'm now back in Akaba, after having had a little trip up country to the Railway, for the last fortnight. We met all sorts of difficulties, *mostly political*, but in the end bagged two locomotives and blew them up, after driving out the troops behind them. It was the usual Arab show, *done at no cost to us*, expensive for the Turks, but not decisive in any way, as it is a raid and not a sustained operation.'[25] The emphasized passages (this author's italics) illustrate Lawrence's true preoccupations and his chronic inaccuracy.

Next day he composed two other versions of the incident. The first was to Major Stirling, a regular officer whom he had met in Egypt. Stirling was to join him as special Staff Officer early the following summer 'with instructions to bring up a big green Vauxhall car for the use of the Amir Feisal.'[26] Stirling was to become an almost idolatrous admirer, though never an intimate, of the younger man he served; he was the posthumous son of a Scotch naval captain who had died in one of the great sea mysteries of British history. An overmothered child, he was self-effacing rather than aggressive.[27] The schoolboy language which Lawrence thought appropriate for use with a regular soldier needs no emphasis:

'The last stunt was the hold up of a train. It had two locomotives, and we gutted one with an electric mine. This rather jumbled up the trucks, which were full of Turks, shooting at us. We had a Lewis, and flung bullets through the sides. So they hopped out and took cover behind the embankment, and shot at us between the wheels, at 50 yards. Then we tried a Stokes gun, and two beautiful shots dropped right in the middle of them. They couldn't stand that (12 died on the spot) and bolted away to the East across a 100 yard belt of open sand into some scrub. Unfortunately for them, the Lewis covered the open stretch. The whole job took ten minutes, and they lost 70 killed, 30 wounded, 80 prisoners, and about 25 got away. Of my hundred Howeitat and two British NCO's there was one (Arab) killed, and four (Arab) wounded.

'The Turks then nearly cut us off as we looted the train, and I lost some baggage, and nearly myself. My loot is a superfine red Baluch prayer-rug. I hope this sounds the fun it is. The only pity is the sweat to work them up and the wild scramble while it lasts.'[28]

More than the language bespeaks the schoolboy. One sensitive, secretly scared adolescent impresses another, equally scared, with his boasts of a 'Buffalo-Billy sort of performance'.

The recipient of the second letter—E. T. Leeds—was long concealed under the title 'Anonymous Friend'. (Leeds may have refused to have his identity revealed because of the somewhat collusive references to Dahoum in Lawrence's letters from the Wilderness of Zin and the somewhat intimate terms, neither hearty nor happy, in which Lawrence now described the raid.) After an elaborate introduction he compressed the incident into one extended sentence:

'The last stunt has been a few days on the Hejaz Railway, in which I potted a train with two engines (oh, the Gods were kind) and we killed superior numbers, and I got a good Baluch prayer-rug and lost all my kit, and nearly my little self.'

Lawrence abandoned to this scholarly friend the martial pose he had assumed to Stirling.

'I'm not going to last out this game much longer: nerves going and temper wearing thin . . .' His occupation was so 'narrow and voracious' that he had lost his balance and become hopelessly centred on himself. 'I hope when the nightmare ends that I will wake up and become alive again. This killing and killing of Turks is horrible. When you charge in at the finish and find them all over the place in bits, and still alive many of them, and know that you have done hundreds in the same way before and must do hundreds more if you can.'[29]

Few paramilitary historians can have written so variously about one experience. But his next operation was to make the affair of two potted trains and attendant casualties seem harmonious and simple.

17

THE EXPEDITION which was to inspire Lawrence's most tormented pages and lead to his strangest post-war actions took place during a month which changed the history of the world. November 1917, which saw the Bolsheviks establish their power in Russia, also marked a turning-point for the zone that had cradled the three monotheistic religions, Judaism, Christianity and Islam. No people of the Middle East, or connected with it, was unaffected by the events of this one month.

For the Turks, a military defeat marked the doom of four centuries of empire south of the Taurus. Deceived by Allenby's feint towards Gaza, massively bombarded from the sea, they had lost Beersheba, the eastern strong-point of their fortified line, by 31 October. Between the first and second days of the new month Allenby stormed Gaza, thus opening the way to the capture of Jerusalem. The loss of the second of the three holy cities of Islam was to destroy what was left of Ottoman awe, though another seven years would elapse before the caliphate was formally abolished by the Turks themselves.*

For the British Empire, Allenby's breach of the Beersheba-Gaza line won forty years of Middle Eastern hegemony. But a simultaneous declaration by the Foreign Secretary, Arthur Balfour, followed three weeks later by Trotsky's disclosure of the secret Sykes-Picot terms, ensured that Arab nationalists would resist this hegemony from the beginning and terminate it as soon as they had the power.

The Jews had been absent politically from the Middle East for nearly two millennia and they would not normally have welcomed the replacement of Muslim rule in Palestine by Christian. They had suffered as badly as the Muslims during the Crusades, and when forced to take sides, the followers of Moses had more often supported the Crescent than the Cross. But Balfour's declaration (its terms arranged between British and American Zionists) that His Majesty's Government viewed with favour

* Although no caliph of Arab stock had ruled from Constantinople, the Ottoman caliphate was recognized even by such Arabs as the Amir Abdullah. His *Memoirs* refer to Constantinople as 'the traditional seat of the Caliphate'.[1]

'the establishment in Palestine of a national home for the Jewish people, and will use its best endeavours to facilitate the achievement of this object,' enraptured those Jews, still a minority, who accepted Theodor Herzl's secularized version of the Messianic return. The Declaration was balanced by provisos—'it being clearly understood that nothing shall be done which may prejudice the civil and religious rights of existing non-Jewish communities in Palestine'—which Balfour in private discounted and as to which the Staff Officer responsible for Allenby's ruses admitted frankly: 'I cannot see how a Jewish state can ever be established which would not prejudice the civil and religious rights of the Arabs.'[2]

For Arabs fighting the Turks the events of 1917 meant, even if this was not at once apparent, that they were fighting alongside allies whose political decisions would involve them, over the coming decades, in an oceanic expense of property, money and blood.

And for Lawrence this crucial month blended physical and psychological extremes which were to remould his life. Danger and physical hardship, failure and remorse, a last lonely delight in empty space, love for one Arab, corrosive hatred for another, cruelty imposed and accepted, were the ingredients of his last and most mysterious wartime adventure. After November 1917 the flutes of excitement and fun were to be drowned by the drums of guilt and self-distrust.

Lawrence had learnt of his assignment in mid-October when he was flown to Allenby's Canalside headquarters. Allenby was now under pressure from London not merely to capture Jerusalem for Christmas but to knock Turkey out of the war. This would release reinforcements for the all-important Western Front where Haig's soldiers had been involved in two months of inconclusive slaughter. To defeat Turkey, Allenby needed more men himself. Somewhat irritably he needled Lawrence on his Arabs and the value of their hit-and-run raids. Dynamiting the Railway south of Amman was like putting a flea inside a chess-opponent's shirt: it might distract him but it could not guarantee a quick checkmate. In conversation with Allenby, a scheme was born—Lawrence claimed it as his—which would amount to the obstruction of an opponent's windpipe. The chess-player, to continue the metaphor, was von Falkenhayn, the German general originally sent east to command the new Turkish army planned for the re-conquest of Iraq. With his headquarters in Jerusalem, von Falkenhayn now depended for supplies and reinforcements on that vital spur of the Hejaz Railway which pushed into Palestine through the twisting, east-west gorge of the Yarmuk River. If Lawrence and his Arabs, assisted by Indian Army engineers, could cut the line somewhere near Deraa, not by destroying a reparable culvert or a replaceable stretch of track, but by dynamiting a high-arched viaduct, the Turks who, Allenby predicted, would then be in retreat, might face catastrophe. Lawrence was requested to interrupt rail traffic between 5 and 8 November.

The expedition charged with this mission left Akaba on 24 October. It was to be away from the Sharifian base for thirty-four days and to cover four hundred miles. Hogarth described it as a risky venture which, if successful, would finally win Lawrence his V.C.[3] It was also to be Lawrence's last major operation before the Transjordanian desert became frequented by Allied officers in armoured cars and journalists armed with passes. Even so, this time he was not the only Englishman attached to the raiding Arabs. Captain George Lloyd accompanied him for the first four days, eager to see Wadi Rumm, a spectacular stretch of sand where, beneath red sandstone cliffs, the tents of nomads stood out like ticks on some spotless fleece. Lloyd left the party at Jefer, Auda's base, and rode back to Akaba. But a second Englishman, Lieutenant Wood of the Royal Engineers, was to be with Lawrence for the next two weeks.

Feisal was still local commander. As his father's deputy, he had devised a purpose for this northern expedition that fitted Hussein's belief that victory would be worthless unless it produced the pan-Arab state which he understood McMahon and the British to have accepted. Syria would be this state's most important province.* On its way north the expedition would pass by Azrak, an oasis fifty miles east of Amman; with the trackless desert at its back, it would be an ideal base for the penetration of Syria. Feisal attached two Arabs to the expedition who could help make the oasis a centre for recruitment and Intelligence. This aim was more important to Feisal than the blowing of the bridge.

The two Arabs were to be all-important to Lawrence in contradictory ways. The first—Sharif Ali ibn al-Hussein, the enthusiast who had already tried his hand at dynamiting rail—was named by Feisal as head of the expedition, since, contrary to myth, no English Christian could lead a bedouin force through tribal lands. A young man of outstanding good looks, his eyes like peeled almonds in a harsh, swarthy face, Ali was the desert's equivalent of the athletes whom Pindar celebrated in his odes. He could, according to Lawrence, outstrip a trotting camel on his bare feet, keep up with it for half a mile and then leap into the saddle with his rifle. In another feat he would kneel down with his palms upwards, then rise to his feet hoisting a man on each hand. He was ruthless. In Syria he had suggested to Feisal that they should murder two important Turkish guests: an outrage to desert morality at which Feisal had shuddered. The young Sharif came honestly by his nimble feet, his lack of scruple, his delight in action and blood, for his tribe, the Harith, were by tradition

* In the sense then current, Syria included, besides the modern republic of Syria, Lebanon, Palestine (or Israel) and Transjordan.

robbers. In a landscape where, apart from poetry, the *ghazu*, or raid, was the prized activity, this tradition was less horrendous than it might have seemed elsewhere. Feisal instructed Ali first to help Lawrence dynamite one of the two bridges and then to attract recruits from Syria and the surrounding desert to the Azrak oasis.

The second important Arab attached to the expedition was an exiled prince. Amir Abdel Kadar al-Jezairi ('the Algerian') was the grandson of a legendary warrior who had long resisted, from the Kabyle mountains, the French occupation of Algeria. Eventually the heroic old man had led his followers into Ottoman exile; Louis-Napoleon gave him a pension while the Sultan allowed the Algerian newcomers to farm along the northern, wooded slopes of the Yarmuk river. Handsome, swashbuckling and impetuous, Abdel Kader had experienced colonialism in its European and Turkish forms. Algeria, heavily settled by the French, was marked for total integration into metropolitan France; its cultural tradition had been attacked and its language reduced to a forbidden patois. But recently the family had suffered from the Ottomans. One of Abdel Kader's uncles had been hanged by Jemal Pasha, who had banished the family to Bursa, the first and loveliest of the three Ottoman capitals, its mosque-tombs set among poplars under snow-topped Uludağ. Managing to go on pilgrimage, Abdel Kader had met King Hussein in Mecca and at once accepted his vision of a pan-Arab state along with the gift of a red banner which he swore to raise in Syria. But Abdel Kader had jibbed at Feisal's new status as Allenby's subordinate. When he had protested at the sight of a little Englishman disguised as a Sharif flitting in and out of Feisal's one-storey Akaba headquarters, Feisal had answered:

'We are compelled to go along with these people because we depend on their money and arms in order to fight.'[4]

Feisal envisaged Abdel Kader's role more in terms of agitation from Azrak (close as it was to the quasi-independent Druse highland) than bridge-blowing on the Yarmuk. For one thing, the prince's Algerian retainers lived on the wrong side of the gorge to give much aid to an expedition coming from the south, and for them to become openly involved in anti-Ottoman activities would have invited dire reprisals. Unlike the Druse highlands, the region around Deraa and the Yarmuk was under close surveillance.

The raiding party moved north from Rumm, slipping across the Railway just south of Maan, which held the last major Turkish garrison between Amman and Medina. The raiders then rode north-east in an arc that swung far enough from the Railway to escape Turkish notice.

Outwardly the expedition seemed well-balanced. Sharif Ali was a natural leader and enjoyed the backing of Feisal. Abdel Kader had grown up in Syria and was trusted by King Hussein. Wood and his Indians were trained professionals, even if they were less accustomed to forcing their camels than the Arabs. Lawrence had travelled the Yarmuk line with Hogarth in 1911. Besides knowing the art of train-bashing, he carried in his saddle-bags gold coins to ease the expedition through the territory of hesitant or hostile tribes and then to reward success. He had a proved ability to keep volatile Arabs on a chosen course.

But strains between the three leading figures were immediately evident. Lawrence was possessively attached to Sharif Ali and jealous of Abdel Kader; Abdel Kader was suspicious of Lawrence and could make eloquent Arabic asides to Ali. By 3 November, when the party encamped just east of Azrak, the tensions had become explosive. While Lawrence smiled at the nineteen-year-old Ali's first experience of grass—the young Sharif showed elegant calfs as he gambolled through the alien softness—Abdel Kader and his seven retainers suddenly disappeared into the stony uplands which lay immediately to the north of Azrak, the realm of the Druses, toughest and healthiest of Syrian Arabs. Ironically, in view of Lawrence's later strictures, these adherents of a heretical version of Islam had been traditionally backed by Britain, just as the Maronites of Lebanon were backed by France.*

The rift between Abdel Kader and Lawrence signified a split in Sharifian policy; it also signified contrasted notions of loyalty. From now on Abdel Kader regarded himself as exclusively the representative of King Hussein; he saw the Revolt, not as a campaign complementing British action, but as a phase in a long-lasting anti-colonial movement. He was loyal to Hussein not for his Blood or royal position but as leader of a movement. He was thus closer in spirit than other Sharifians to later generations of Arab revolutionaries: to his own Algerians, who would bury his grandfather's remains in North African soil after achieving independence; and to the eastern Arabs who would clash repeatedly with Britain and France and, above all, with the beneficiaries of the Balfour Declaration. Lawrence, on the other hand, served Feisal because through him Britain could increase her Middle Eastern estate but he also felt personal, feudal loyalties. Dahoum had been his page; Feisal was now his liege-lord in a desert setting; Ali ibn al-Hussein was Feisal's vassal and Lawrence's peer; Allenby was The Old Man who had given him a chance to play a greater role than Kim in Kipling's Great Game.

In November 1917 his feelings for Abdel Kader had not yet frozen into hatred. But he asked Colonel Joyce, the British commander at Akaba, to inform Feisal that Abdel Kader had shown fear: 'much talk, and little doing, in his way. Neither Ali nor myself gave any offence.'

* German reports stressed their unreliability; the princely Atrash family had conferred with the British resident in Cyprus just before the War.[5]

Although Lawrence was to stress by way of contrast 'the consistent loyalty and assistance' of Ali ibn al-Hussein, he did not suggest that Abdel Kader had gone off to betray them to the Turks.[6]

Moving north-west from Azrak, the reduced party crossed the Railway from east to west near Mafrak. On 7 November it approached the Yarmuk gorge from the south over level ground. Besides Wood and six Indians with Vickers machine-guns, it now comprised Sharif Ali and a handful of bedouin followers along with Lawrence and a mixed force of some sixty guerillas from the Serahin and Beni Sakhr tribes. According to an Arab whom Lawrence praised at the time and who survived into the 1960s, the raiders should have rushed the Tell Shahab bridge: the nearby cascade was deafening and would have drowned the noise of their approach, allowing them to overwhelm the small Turkish guard-post and blow the pillars.[7] Instead, Sheikh Mifleh, father of Turki, Sharif Ali's seventeen-year-old favourite, couched his camel by the edge of the dim ravine and the others followed suit. The raiders then set off on foot through the dark. They carried the necessary dynamite in fifteen sacks. As they made the slithery descent into the ravine, an Indian dropped his rifle. The clatter alerted the Turkish sentry. As he fired into the dark, his comrades rushed from their tent and bullets spattered the ravine. The bedouin knew from report what happened when a bullet hit dynamite. Abandoning their explosives in the gorge, the party fled.

On their long ride north the raiders had heard, from far to the west, the thunder of Allenby's guns attacking Beersheba. Lawrence understood their message: how vital it was at that moment for the Railway to be cut. His failure was a grief so bitter that, like his grief for his brothers, he never put it into words. But a report sent from the German Embassy in Constantinople to Berlin indirectly indicated its degree. Summing up the problems of Germany's Turkish ally in the Palestine of 1917, the report put the Railway on a level with shortages of food, men and material. 'The Railway's inefficiency is due in part to corruption, in part, too, to passive resistance by Levantine railway officials, but also to lack of rolling stock and fuel.'[8] A demolition on the Yarmuk would have dwarfed such strictures. But owing to bad tactics or bad luck, the crucial viaduct remained intact.

Sharif Ali took the failure in a light-hearted spirit; for him, the chance to do something destructive had merely been postponed. He and Lawrence could demolish something else. While Wood and the Indians returned to Azrak, he, Lawrence and the tribesmen looked for a train to dynamite on the line to Amman. After hungry waits and disappointments they succeeded on 11 November. But with no strategic gain. The beflagged train which they attacked carried one distinguished passenger, Mehmet Jemal Pasha, commander of the Turkish Eighth Army Corps, and four hundred troops. But the Pasha escaped unhurt and the soldiers on the train were also too many for the raiders; they did manage to save Lawrence, who had been slightly injured by the exploding boiler, at the cost of seven lives. With little but a boost to their morale Lawrence and Ali rode back, the next day, to Azrak.

Pink oleander flowers in a drought-brown wadi: white clouds of aromatic broom hiding a camel and its rider in Rumm's sandstone gorge: such sights predicted in little the surprise of an oasis.

To Azrak's south, the immense low wadi of Sirhan stretched through shimmering dust and mirage to the upland domain of Ibn Saud and his puritanical Ikhwan, a warrior brotherhood ready to slaughter for infractions of their code. To the north, the desert was black with jagged lava. Yet in the oasis itself men had contrived, for thousands of years, not merely to subsist but to know delight. A black basalt fortress commanded a chain of wells, palm groves and bird-thronged marshes. Fragments of a Greco-Roman altar, inscriptions of the Emperor Jovian and a Mameluke governor, attested the variety of its passing tenants. Its newest were to be Sharif Ali and Lawrence. Lawrence's servants used brushwood and palm-fronds to repair the leaking roof of the northern gate-tower. Ali, as commander, occupied the corner tower to the south-east. For the first time in many months Lawrence could spend as long as ten days in a single place. He needed to come to terms with his failure to carry out Allenby's assignment; his camels needed rest.

Lawrence later wove into this brief rest—from 12 November to 22 November 1917—the most harrowing experience of his life. It is therefore important to be clear about the dates. They alone make it possible to sift fiction from fact. His skeleton diary followed the entry *Nov. 12, Azrak, etc.*, with *Nov. 23, Wadi Butm*, on the return ride back south to Akaba. Lawrence's *etc.*, as his fictional claim of meeting with Ali Ridha al-Rikabi showed, could mean anything or nothing. To Lawrentian mysteries, the earliest documentation always provides the best key. Lawrence wrote two letters to his father at the time. The first, written from Azrak itself on 14 November, told of living in 'an old fort with stone roofs and floors, and stone doors of the sort they used in Bashan.'[9] He was making, he reported, daily improvements to the fort and planned to stay a few days at Azrak, resting his camels. The second letter (unavailable to earlier writers on Lawrence) was written a month later. Lawrence was then staying as Wingate's guest at the Nile-side Residency in Cairo. 'I wrote to you last from Azrak,' he told his father, 'about the time we blew up Jemal Pasha, and let him slip away from us. After that I stayed for ten days or so there, and then rode down to Akaba in 3 days: good going, tell Arnie: none of his old horses would do so much as my old camel.'[10] Neither the information in these documents, nor in the letters which Hogarth was writing at the time to his wife in Oxford, nor in the official reports on Lawrence's movements, fit with the later account of a strenuous return ride to Deraa nor with the chapter of humiliation which was to form the spiritual climax of his post-war book.[11]

The only link between the events of 12 to 22 November and the episode he created in his book (which will be discussed in due course) was one of mood. He metamorphosed guilt and failure into a myth of degradation and torture and transferred its site from Azrak to Deraa.

Even if Sharif Ali had been the kind of Arab who wrote books, prudery would have deterred him from recording behaviour contrary to Islamic norms. (Even Cairo's vigorous novelists have produced little confessional writing: no author has, for example, admitted to sexual or other vice.) So that, apart from Lawrence's own letters, no contemporary accounts describe the stay at Azrak on which Lawrence later imposed the myth of Deraa. Sharif Ali was ten years younger than Lawrence. He had none of the Englishman's sense of failure. On the contrary, for the first time in his life, the young Arab was enjoying the exercise of authority. The fiasco at the Yarmuk viaduct was for him eclipsed by the triumph of outraging a Turkish general. Ali's master was Feisal, whose instructions he was carrying out with success. In his refurbished Azrak tower he received potential recruits with a generosity made possible by English gold. Reporting to von Oppenheim in French as late as May 1918, a pro-German Druse wrote of an 'Amir* Ali' established within range of the Jebel Druse and subverting the people.[12]

Lawrence's dejection at letting down Allenby, his clearsighted recognition that his promise to cut the enemy's supply-route had not been kept, led to a desire for punishment. This is not surprising in one of his upbringing. As a boy in Polstead Road misdemeanours had been followed by 'humiliating whippings with the trousers pulled down,'[13] indelibly implanting the necessary link between crime, punishment and spiritual relief; as we have seen with Dahoum at Halfati he had learnt that the plenitude of pain could bring physical relief as well. Sharif Ali, the most attractive man he had met in Arabia, the formal commander of the expedition, could be seen as Allenby's representative at Azrak.

Lawrence's urge to blurt out fusions of fact and fantasy has left two clear indications that, with Ali, he underwent a ritual involving token imprisonment and punishment. The punishment left scars and accorded with the savagery Lawrence repeatedly cited as characteristic of Ali's actions.[14] His acceptance of it accorded with what was to become a dominant feature of his post-war behaviour.

The first indication dates from the following summer. In September 1918 the war was nearing its end. Machines increasingly dominated the

* The word can mean commander, or prince.

desert; Lawrence's claim to have spent 2,000 hours in the air was certainly exaggerated but nevertheless attests the new mechanical element in which war was waged. Driver Rolls had chauffeured Lawrence north to Azrak, now Feisal's forward base for the final advance on Deraa and Damascus. There Lawrence showed him round the black fortress in which he had lodged with Sharif Ali. 'He beckoned me to him and, pointing to what looked like the crumbled mouth of an old well, bade me look into it. It appeared to lead into a sort of cellar, but all was black down there, and I could see nothing. I looked at him inquiringly. He said to me, "Once I was kept a prisoner in that dungeon for months." I was amazed to hear this, but there was more to come yet. He leaned down and pointed to the inside of the hole, at a place where the light just reached, and said, "Do you see those scratchings?" I looked, and saw something which appeared as though the decaying surface of the stone had recently been scraped away. I looked at him again without speaking. "Those are some of my attempts to escape," he said.'

The story is incorrect in detail. There are no lost 'months' which Lawrence could have spent in prison and before the war he had not visited this part of the desert. The only possible occasion for even a mock imprisonment was thus the crucial period of November 1917, in which he later set the myth of Deraa.

The second indication of what really happened came a year after the first. In 1919, under circumstances to be detailed later, a brother officer saw Lawrence naked in the bath. He was horrified by the sight of red weals across Lawrence's ribs, as prominent as tattoos. Lawrence passed them off as due to 'a camel accident at Azrak; dragged across barbed wire.'[16]

Azrak, not Deraa, was the place where Lawrence made the deepest discoveries about his basic nature. The discoveries resulted, not from a Turkish pasha's lust, but from the compliance of a sturdy young Arab whom he respected and loved.

18

'TO-DAY I ENTERED Jerusalem on foot'; Allenby wrote to his wife on 11 December 1917. Along with the French and Italian Commanders of the Allied detachments in his Army, walked Lawrence in the role of General Clayton's Staff Officer for the day. He had laid aside the white silken robes in which he had flown up from Akaba and borrowed the red tabs and brass-bound hat of a major in the British army. The procession entered the Holy City at the Jaffa gate and Allenby, after issuing a proclamation in many languages from the Citadel, received the notables of the Holy City as well as the heads of the numerous Churches. 'After this we re-formed our procession and returned to our horses—which we had left outside the walls.'[1] A cable from Sir Mark Sykes, recalling how the Kaiser's prancing entry had contrasted with the modest arrival of One greater, seems to have prompted the modest celebration. The presence of the two Allied commanders, in particular the French, constituted a Pyrrhic victory for the co-author of the Sykes-Picot Agreement. Sykes had discovered in the Hejaz that French officials were 'without exception anti-Arab . . . their line is to crab British operations to the Arabs, throw cold water on all Arab actions . . . They do not attempt to disguise that they desire Arab failure.'[2]

Lawrence later claimed that the entry into Jerusalem was for him the supreme moment of the war.[3] This could have been a last bow to the values of Canon Christopher; more likely, it implied that his own later triumph at Damascus was flawed. In the capture of Jerusalem he had taken no part; he had failed in the assignment which might have enlarged the victory's scope; and, unlike Newcombe whom the Turks had captured near Hebron, he was safe if scathed.

Lawrence had gone to Jerusalem by way of Gaza. He had there met Hogarth, his oldest mentor.

Hogarth had anxiously followed Lawrence's movements from the Arab Bureau. He, like Lawrence's father, had received a letter from Azrak dated 14 November. While relieving some fears, it brought the bad news that Lawrence's main venture had failed: 'as I feared it must, but without involving him in the worst fate.'[4] Hogarth asked his wife

Laura to tell her friend, Mrs. Lawrence, that the French government had awarded her son the *Croix de Guerre*; Hogarth had 'news of him up to about the 20th' and knew his future plans. In Gaza he was now relieved to find Lawrence 'looking much fitter and better than when I saw him last. He still looks absurdly boyish for twenty-nine.'[5]

Yet behind the mask of youth Lawrence was changing; as was Hogarth, though, in his case, behind what he ruefully characterized as 'over-developed age and underdeveloped attractions, streaky past and dubious future.'[6] The naive imperialism of his youth—when he had written that 'the vices of the worst Moslem ruffian are at least those of a conquering race'[7]—was dead. The intrigue and double-dealing he witnessed had sickened him to the point where he yearned to abandon foreign policy, and get back to his museum. Hogarth's influence still eclipsed Lawrence's later obligations to Storrs, Clayton, and Wingate. A month after their meeting in Gaza, Hogarth was awarded the C.M.G. 'It leaves me cold,' he told Laura, 'and if I'd been a civilian when it was offered I'd have declined the honour.'[8] Lawrence was to imitate this attitude in regard to his own decorations.

Not being a civilian, Hogarth was reluctantly committed to new British policies which conflicted with earlier undertakings made to King Hussein. He was hotly to deny his son's charge that he advocated an imperialist policy towards Iraq. 'I am against imperialism,' he wrote, 'and not for it, and I want to see some settlement there as in Palestine which does not entail an addition to our already overgrown empire. But it is very hard in both places to devise an alternative which will secure them from occupation by someone else that we do not, and they do not want.'[9]

While still in Gaza Lawrence had met a man who was to be a counterweight to David Hogarth, influencing him in another direction. Colonel Richard Meinertzhagen, a massive eccentric of Danish origin, was the British staff officer responsible for many of the ruses which had thrown the Turks off guard at Beersheba. He was also, like Allenby, a keen ornithologist. On the night of 9 December Meinertzhagen was working in his tent when: 'in walked an Arab boy dressed in spotless white, white headdress with gold circlet; for the moment I thought the boy was somebody's pleasure-boy but it soon dawned on me that it must be Lawrence whom I knew to be in camp. I just stared at the very beautiful apparition which I suppose was what was intended. He then said in a soft voice, "I am Lawrence, Dalmeny sent me over to see you." I said, "Boy or girl?" He smiled and blushed, saying "Boy".'[10]

Meinertzhagen, a gentile, was as chief political officer in Palestine to become an enthusiastic Zionist. An old man at the end of the British Mandate, he claims to have borrowed a Coldstream guardsman's uniform and gun and gone ashore at Haifa to kill three Arabs in the fighting for the port. Lawrence was similarly to borrow Meinertzhagen's Zionist ideas in his post-war efforts to outwit the French.

But ten months were to pass after the capture of Jerusalem before the Sharifian forces entered Damascus and set in motion a conflict which the French were to win. In this period of waiting, interrupted only by sporadic fighting, Lawrence no longer knew the zest of which he had earlier written to Newcombe. A bitterness more complex than Hogarth's prosy recognition of 'the shackles into which the highest placed officials abroad are put and the despicable things they are set to say and do,' poisoned exploits which to the world seemed heroic and finally triumphant.[11] Fear of betrayal and Messianic self-identification were important ingredients.

Betrayal was a constant possibility now that suspicion of British motives was increasingly widespread. Just before the fall of Jerusalem, Jemal Pasha had given in a speech details of the Sykes-Picot Agreement, already revealed by Trotsky. Published in an Arabic newspaper, *Mostakbil*, they came to the eyes of King Hussein. Lest the old man abdicate or make peace with the Turks, the Foreign Office advised Wingate 'as an immediate and opportunist policy,' to prevaricate.[12] But within twelve months Hussein's suspicions had become certainties. In September 1918 British Intelligence intercepted one of the King's telegrams. It contained the telltale sentence: 'Living under the orders of a disobedient son and a traitor has burdened my shoulders with this misery.'[13] The outburst was occasioned by a dispute with Feisal over the King's right to demote Jaafar al-Askari from his position as Commander-in-Chief of the Sharifian army. But it exemplified the general distrust of Britain which was to lead to violence in places as far apart as Egypt, Palestine and Iraq. Arab soldiers had begun to show their resentment of British advisers early in 1918. Young, whose mastery of the problem of supply helped the Arab forces to reach Damascus, noted an amusing exchange which nevertheless typified a situation in which 'British officers were not in executive command, and could give no direct orders, even to a camel-herd.'

MYSELF: Good morning, Ali Bey. Are the camels ready to go up to Abu'l Lissan?

ALI BEY: Good morning, my brother, I fear not.

MYSELF: How is that, my friend? They were to be ready at nine o'clock and it is now eleven.

ALI BEY: I have employed them in carrying some supplies which were required by Sheikh So-and-So.

To Young's protests Ali Bey snorts:

I am an Arab. I am working for Arab *Istiqlal* [Independence]. I take orders from no one.[14]

The legend that the Turks had put up posters offering £20,000 for Lawrence alive or £10,000 dead* reflects a fact: he was personally at risk in an army not all of whose soldiers fought for money. Some hothead, persuaded that Lawrence's policy implied European or even Jewish rule over Arabs, might make his point with dagger or bullet. Nor were all bedouin politically ignorant. Philby, travelling through inner Arabia in 1917, found that 'even in remote valleys, people knew the pattern of the war—that the Turks and the British were enemies; that the Sharif of Mecca was a suspect Muslim because he was fighting alongside Christians.'[15]

Lawrence was not the only British officer to face this situation. But his solution, which combined practical and aesthetic elements, was characteristic. He recruited a bodyguard of handsome desperadoes, men who having violated some aspect of the bedouin code could without conscience (since conscience had gone) sell their allegiance to the Christian spy in their midst. *Sell* was the right word. Lawrence paid his bodyguards six gold sovereigns a month, a fortune by the standards of those days. Their numbers increased during 1918. 'My bodyguard of servants,' as he described them to his family on 8 March,[16] 'is about 25'; while on 15 July to Vyvyan Richards, who could appreciate the decorative side: 'my bodyguard of fifty Arab tribesmen, picked riders from the young men of the deserts, are more splendid than a tulip garden.'[17] (They wore every colour except his own Sharifian white.) Stirling, who joined Lawrence in May, estimated the guard as just under 100.[18] It had a high rate of wastage, not so much from fighting as desertion: even Feisal's irregulars, when sated with booty, awarded themselves periods of leave, or an honourable discharge.

The readiness for treachery existed on both sides. A contemporary source, of unimpeachable veracity, indicates that at least one important member of the Lloyd George government considered the abandonment of the Arabs, not to the French or the Zionists, but to the Turks. On 26 February 1918, the British Ambassador in Paris, Sir Francis Bertie, dined at the Ritz in the company of Winston Churchill, Minister of Munitions since July 1917. Bertie noted in his diary that 'Winston' had declared 'that the war is a European war and the result must be European. I suggested that what he meant was that the decision of the war would

* The story, which Hogarth derived from Lawrence, has no confirmation in the writings of Jemal Pasha, the Turk, or Liman von Sanders, the German who commanded on the Palestine front in the last phase of the War: they both omit his name from their published memoirs. The German military archives for the First World War were bombed at Freiburg in the Second. But before their destruction they had been carefully worked through by Carl Mühlmann. His authoritative *Das Deutsche-Türkische Waffenbündis im Weltkriege*, Leipzig, 1940, does not confirm the story; nor do the German diplomatic archives which survive in Bonn.

be in Europe. To this he said Yes, but added that nothing outside Europe *mattered*. He then went on to say that if Germany breaks up Russia, we must break up Turkey. The inverse of this is that, if Germany lets go her hold of portions of Russia seized, we will give up Palestine and Mesopotamia and *desert the Arabs of Arabia and leave them to settle accounts with Turkey* [this author's emphasis] . . .'[19]

The Sharifians, too, considered deserting allies whose double, or triple, intentions were now appearing through the fog of words. The vast German offensive in France forced Allenby to delay his final assault until after the summer. But knowing it was coming, General Ludendorff read with the greatest interest an August report from Major von Papen, Chief of the General Staff of the Ottoman army, that 'Sharif Feisal, supreme commander of the Sharifian forces as also of the Anglo-Egyptian forces in the northern Hejaz, has declared himself ready, to the leader of the 4th Ottoman army, to restart negotiations towards an agreement.'[20] The tentative negotiations which had started some weeks before had foundered on Turkish reluctance to grant the requisite concessions. Ludendorff saw the utmost desirability of an agreement with Feisal. 'An English attack can only have any prospect of success if the Sharifian forces, further reinforced by English troops passing through Akaba, really attack the Hejaz railway. Preparations for this attack are under way. If this attack results in the taking of Amman, the Haurani tribes are certain to join the English, and Deraa, the branch station for the 7th and 8th armies, will find itself in enemy hands.' Ludendorff concluded his telegram by stressing the importance of an understanding with Sharif Feisal to relieve the Turkish 4th Army of pressure in its rear. It would also benefit the relations between the Haurani tribes and the Ottoman government and would allow the harvest (vital against a background of starvation) to be gathered. The German Ambassador in Constantinople was asked to exert the strongest possible pressure on the Turks to make the concessions required. Only the obstinacy of Enver Pasha and his associates aborted these last-minute German efforts.

But Lawrence knew of both the English and the Arab moves.[21] He knew of the distrust for Britain now widespread in the Sharifian ranks, particularly among educated Syrians and Iraqis. An unsigned note, of 16 June 1918, bears the stamp of his thought. (Lawrence was on that date in conference with Hogarth and others in Alexandria.) 'As soon as Feisal is in possession of this area [Syria], the effendi class, the educated class, the Christian and the foreign elements will turn against him. His movement is a popular one, and his supporters are the peasants under the village sheikhs, the tribes under the tribal sheikhs, and the poor Moslems of the towns.'[22]

And yet (except in inner Arabia) the educated Arabs were, for better or worse, to shape the future.

'There took part in the Revolt a number of educated civilians, some of whom found their way to the battle-front by way of the tribes, others of whom went first to Iraq and from there to Egypt and so to the front. Others had lived in Egypt and went directly from there. For the most part they were Syrians because of Syria's proximity to the area of revolt. They threw whatever skills they had into the struggle.'[23]

The Damascus-born author of these lines—Subhi al-Umari—fought with the Arab force to which Lawrence was attached. Al-Umari had enrolled at the Ottoman military college in Beirut a few weeks before Turkey entered the war. After a year's study he stayed on at the college as instructor but in the autumn of 1917 Jemal Pasha's savage measures against dissident Arabs persuaded him, aged nineteen, to adhere to Feisal. Al-Umari was to record his wartime experiences in an Arabic book, *Lawrence As I Knew Him*. His final judgment was harsh: that Lawrence deceived the Arabs in his actions and maligned them in his writings.

Al-Umari first set eyes on Lawrence as the Englishman picked lice from his undergarments. The scene was Tafileh, a highland village south-east of the Dead Sea which King Hussein's youngest son, Zeid, had recently occupied. The time, January 1918, marked a new stage in the development of the Arab army. Only a few days later a column of a thousand Turks left Kerak to retake Tafileh. The Arabs still lacked sufficient artillery and could not yet take a major fortified position, but the battle of 24–25 January proved that regular Arab forces co-operating with bedouin irregulars and village partisans could effectively resist. The retreating Turks left behind many prisoners, guns and the body of their commander.

Lawrence and al-Umari both described the battle of Tafileh. Lawrence's three thousand words presented himself, somewhat implausibly, as all-commanding and omnipresent. Al-Umari, who by chance was at the battle's decisive position, wrote a shorter, less coloured, version.

Tafileh lay at the southern end of a low plateau corrugated by four hillocks. The Turks had to approach from the north down a twenty-mile wadi. Overconfident, overburdened by equipment, food and fodder, they advanced till they had occupied the third hillock. From it, after resting, they planned to descend on the dissident village. They were opposed, to cite al-Umari's figures, by a mule company of eighty soldiers under Ismail Namiq; two Indian mountain guns under Hussein al-Madfai; a detachment of infantry under Lieut. Abdullah; a company of sixty volunteers under Suliman al-Jenawi; a demolition squad; a machine-gun detachment commanded by al-Umari himself; a few bedouin (though most had gone south with Auda because of the cold); and Lawrence with five of his guards. The discipline of Zeid's regular officers, the fears and passions of the Tafileh villagers, the raid-lust of the bedouin, produced an ordered confusion closer to a partisan skirmish than a text-book battle. The Turks, first held up by a section of Zeid's regulars, were then harassed by the villagers, who, like their counterparts in Lebanon, were accustomed to arms. Al-Umari struck the final blow. Acting without instructions, he and his men scaled the hillock on which the Turks were established and attacked them with machine-guns. Their flank attack played a decisive role, but it was haphazard. Zeid had not been in touch with al-Umari; Lawrence had only five men under his direct command. At first Zeid intended to have al-Umari punished, but when his initiative succeeded, punishment was changed to promotion. Al-Umari claims to have divided two thousand of Lawrence's gold sovereigns among his men. Lawrence blamed Zeid for squandering so much gold on the local tribesmen and villagers, and soon afterwards the Turks re-entered Tafileh. Even so, this impermanent triumph suggested that the skills which had won the Arabs their seventh-century empire might still be latent.

Shortly after the battle of Tafileh, Lawrence was enabled by the new mobility conferred by car and plane to visit Storrs, now Military Governor of Jerusalem with the temporary rank of a Lieutenant-General. The visit had incalculable results. At the moment when Lawrence was catching Hogarth's disillusion, when his exploits linked failure with exasperation, he became entangled with the awesome new power of public relations.

The fall of Jerusalem had made him aware of the Middle East campaign's propaganda potential. Before Christmas he had predicted that his parents would soon be reading about the Arab conflict. The war in the Hejaz had been kept hush-hush while its outcome was in doubt; the capture of Akaba had eased the stress. 'As public sympathy is desirable, we must try and enlist on our side a favourable press.'[24] Pirie-Gordon, Hogarth's kinsman, Corvo's patron and the man who had lent Lawrence his crusader map, was coming out to write articles.

Meanwhile a publicist more heavily backed and, incidentally, longer-lived than Pirie-Gordon was on his way.* An American journalist, Lowell Thomas, with his camera-man Harry Chase, had received orders from Washington (and financial backing from twenty Chicago financiers) 'to cover the Allied campaigns on all fronts, obtain all the interesting material available, rush back to America, and tell what I had seen in as optimistic a vein as might be. The idea was, of course, to chant hallelujahs for the gallant pitch of belligerent frenzy and thus stimulate a popular demand

* As late as 1975 Mr. Lowell Thomas was still performing as a TV news-analyst.

by the voters and taxpayers that Uncle Sam throw his full weight into the war.'[25]

Dispirited by the European fronts, the two Americans had been directed by Colonel John Buchan to the Middle East. Thanks to military bureaucracy they reached Palestine by a tediously roundabout route, by way of Egypt, the Upper Nile, Sudan and the Red Sea. But the sight of Lawrence in Jerusalem arrayed as a Sharif of Mecca made the long trip worthwhile. And Lawrence was a co-operative subject. Thomas later dismissed as 'bunk' the suggestion that Lawrence avoided his shorthand or Chase's lens. 'Along with his other magnificent talents,' Thomas recorded, 'he had a rare gift for "backing into the limelight." He arranged for my jaunt to Arabia.'[26]

It was indeed Lawrence who secured Allenby's consent for Thomas to visit Akaba. Thomas, in the manner of many journalists, later exaggerated both his own participation in the Arab campaign and the time he spent with Lawrence, and sometimes his pencil moved too fast; he reported, for example, that Lawrence absented himself from Oxford, not for the summer of 1909, but for two years, and that his brother Frank tramped the Near East with him. Absurdities such as Lawrence's descent from the crusading Sir Robert Lawrence, or his connection with Sir Henry and Sir John Lawrence of India may have resulted from Lawrence's own romancing.

Lawrence later took pains to minimize his links with Thomas, who agreed to insert a disclaimer in his book that Lawrence was the source of his material. An American admirer was told by Lawrence: 'Lowell Thomas was ten days in Arabia. He saw me for two of those; and again one day in Jerusalem: and afterwards I breakfasted with him once or twice in London. His book is silly and inaccurate: sometimes deliberately inaccurate. He meant well.'[27]

But in the first articles which Thomas published* there are passages of extreme importance for an understanding of Lawrence's state of mind in early 1918. One confirms the displacement of Jerablus and its villagers from his affections in a sentence which has implications for Dahoum's disappearance from Lawrence's life as well as suggesting the inspiration of his major book. 'The nomad is a poet, a sportsman, and a lover of personal liberty. The villager is indolent, dirty, untrustworthy, and absolutely mercenary.'

More significant still is a passage purportedly quoting Auda, the victor of Akaba, on the subject of Lawrence. Thomas knew no Arabic; the 'translator' was almost certainly Lawrence.

' "By the beard of the Prophet," he roared, "this fair-haired son of

* In January 1920 issue of the *Strand Magazine*; unfortunately no text of his 1919 lectures survives.

Allah can do everything that we do even better than we do it ourselves. He has the face and hair of a Circassian beauty, the physique of an oryx [Arabian ibex], the courage of Abu Bakr, and the wisdom of Omar." '

Apart from the slightly odd inversion of characteristics attributed to the first two caliphs* the passage contains a phrase which would have choked Auda had he seen and understood it.

The fundamental contradiction between Islam and Christianity (which otherwise have much in common) is the Koranic rejection of the Incarnation. The chapter which has been called the Essence of the Koran† states emphatically of Allah: 'He begetteth not nor was He begotten.' An Arab could refer to a man as a son of Adam or a creature of God; the Arabic names beginning '*Abd*—or 'slave'—stress the abyss between man and his creator. For Auda to have called Lawrence a 'Son of Allah' would have been as blasphemous as the advertising copy in the *Strand Magazine* which published Thomas's articles. The copywriter claimed that Lawrence 'became a great white god. At twenty-six he was the uncrowned King of the Hejaz, Prince of Mecca.'[28]

In some westerners the desert undoubtedly induces a Messianic mood; some westerners with a Messianic tendency are drawn to the desert. Hogarth argued that Charles Doughty (whom Lawrence so revered) portrayed 'Khalil'—the name Doughty went by when travelling in Arabia Deserta—'not only as Man but with something about him of the Son of Man; reading, one is haunted by the familiar words, "He was despised and he was rejected, a man of sorrows and acquainted with grief." '[29]‡ The phrase 'Son of Allah', impossibly ascribed to Auda, testifies to the delusions of grandeur which can accompany a sense of being betrayed or persecuted. Captain Hubert Young, describing the last month of a largely uneventful summer, reported: 'I found out afterwards that he thought we were all under his orders, but I did not know this at the time, and still regarded him more as Feisal's liaison officer with General Allenby than as a real Colonel in the army, a position which he gave the impression of holding in great contempt.'[30] Lawrence had gained his colonelcy as a result of his report of what had happened at Tafileh on 25 January; the same report led to his being awarded the Distinguished Service Order.

Allenby's plans, on which the Arabs waited after Tafileh, were deflected by events in France. At the end of March a meeting of the War Cabinet in London had linked the situation on the western front with a decision

* Abu Bakr, Muhammad's father-in-law and first caliph, is generally remembered for his wisdom, while Omar, the second caliph and conqueror, is remembered for his moral and physical courage.

† Sura CXII.

‡ Into his next sentence, also significantly, Hogarth introduces the name of Lawrence.

to order Allenby to attack in Palestine. 'We are advancing side by side up the two sides of the Jordan,' Hogarth could tell his wife on 10 April. But early in May, as the consequence of German successes in France and Turco-German counter-attacks in the Jordan region, he had dropped this theme. Lawrence spent the next two or three months travelling between Palestine, Akaba and Egypt; in June he spent some days by the sea at Alexandria. In July he dined in Cairo with Hogarth, Clayton and Cornwallis. He was then expecting to go to England for high level discussions.

When Allenby eventually launched his offensive, the convergence of an Arab force on the Turkish lines of retreat would (as Ludendorff had predicted) be an important factor and Young played a major role in enabling the Arabs to be where Allenby required them. From Akaba, he tackled the problem of transporting some six hundred Arab regulars across a desert relieved by only three oases—Jefer, Auda's headquarters, Bair and Azrak—to within striking distance of Deraa. For Feisal, the arrival in Syria of these Arabs under men he could trust was politically essential. Despite the attempts of Lawrence and an embarrassed Hogarth to reassure him, he knew of the French intentions and feared that unless he and his army were on the spot, the French would easily take control. Another danger was that Syrians who wanted independence, but not under Sharifian rule, might head the resistance, first to the Turks and then to the French.

Despite the ferocity of the last German offensive, American participation in the war made it increasingly safe to predict an Allied victory. Diplomatic wrangling, not fighting, dominated the summer. The Zionist leader Chaim Weizmann (whom Meinertzhagen's diary described as 'naturally a violent enemy of the Arabs') met Arab notables in Jerusalem in an attempt to appear something else. In Cairo, Britain made yet another promise, this time to a group of seven Syrian notables: those Arab territories which were free and independent before the war—i.e. which were so backward or hard to subdue that no one had made the effort—would remain so. Elsewhere the British government would recognize the 'complete and sovereign independence of the inhabitants' in those Arab areas freed by the Arabs themselves. This declaration signally failed to reassure Arabs apprehensive at the implications of the Sykes-Picot Agreement and the Balfour Declaration. Such Arabs had welcomed President Wilson's publication on 8 January of his Fourteen Points, the Eighth of which stipulated 'unmolested opportunity of autonomous development' for the non-Turkish nations in the Ottoman Empire. The British Declaration to the Seven marked an ominous retreat from Wilsonian principle.

Lawrence's mood, in which Messianic delusion was one component, that last summer of war accounts for surprising actions soon to follow. Writing to Vyvyan Richards in mid-July, while two thousand camels were assembling to transport the Arab strike force north, he specified another component—a sense of unreality. 'I have been so violently uprooted and plunged so deeply into a job too big for me, that everything feels unreal. I have dropped everything I ever did, and live only as a thief of opportunity, snatching chances of the moment when and where I see them . . . I hate being in front, and I hate being in back and I don't like responsibility, and I don't obey orders.'[31] But while he focused his mind on the practical problems of getting money for Feisal, Lewis-guns and camels for himself,[32] the Arabs still appealed to his imagination. They symbolized a civilization which had discarded household gods and unnecessary trappings. 'The gospel of bareness in materials is a good one, and it involves apparently a sort of moral bareness too. They think for the moment, and endeavour to slip through life without turning corners or climbing hills. In part it is a mental and moral fatigue, a race trained out, and to avoid difficulties they have to jettison so much that we think honourable and grave: and yet without in any way sharing their point of view, I think I can understand it enough to look at myself and other foreigners from their direction, and without condemning it. I know I'm a stranger to them, and always will be: but I cannot believe them worse, any more than I could change to their ways.'[33]

Between the writing of this letter, and the capture of Damascus three months later, something happened to deflate his admiration. In August the plans for the Arab army to move north across the desert were suddenly advanced: if Arab raids around Deraa were to affect that nodal point of Turkish communications, they must do so by 16 September. In 1933, when Lawrence's fame was at its peak but before post-mortem reverence imposed its censorship, Young was to publish his account of how, in a desert marathon, the Arabs reached Deraa on time. Young plainly admired Lawrence's dash. Equally plainly he was exasperated at the impracticality of some of his notions and amused by some of his pretensions. But Young's book was most valuable for giving a day-by-day account of Lawrence's movements in the month leading up to the capture of Damascus. This record enables us to dismiss one explanation subsequently offered for the change of mood which Lawrence himself described when, near Azrak, 'I went off down the valley to our remote Ain el Essad and lay there all day in my old lair among the tamarisk, where the wind in the dusty green branches played with such sounds as it made in English trees. It told me I was tired to death of these Arabs; petty incarnate Semites who attained heights and depths beyond our reach, though not beyond our sight . . . My nerve had broken; and I would be lucky if the ruin of it could be hidden . . .'[34]

Gunner T. W. Beaumont has pictured Lawrence tripping across the lines to contact Dahoum, apparently still conveying important information to his friend and spymaster. Beaumont places this curious activity at Umtaiye in September 1918. 'One day Lawrence told us, "Don't worry, I'll be away for a few days. I'm going to see Salim." [According to Beaumont, this is how Lawrence now referred to Dahoum.] When Lawrence came back I said to him, "Did you see Salim?" and he said, "He's finished. He's dying. He's got typhoid." I'm sure it was typhoid because we all got emergency typhoid shots afterwards. Lawrence turned away and pulled his keffieh over his face and I heard him say, "I loved that boy." When he turned back I could see that he had been weeping. I overheard the bodyguards talking and I caught the Arabic word for death and I saw them make gestures like Lawrence holding Salim in his arms.'[35]

Lawrence's September movements, recorded by himself and confirmed by Young, leave no possible time for this sad story. Umtaiye was a ruined settlement more than half way from Azrak to Deraa. Lawrence did stay there on three occasions that fateful month. With Driver Rolls acting as his chauffeur, he had driven north to Azrak, the Sharifian mustering point, on 6 September. His first visit to Umtaiye was for the two nights of 14 and 15 September. He left it on the morning of the 16th for a four-day foray in the company of Young, Winterton and Nuri al-Said. His aim was to disrupt the railway running from Deraa south to Amman: Young was eyewitness of his almost foolhardy attack on a culvert. For the night of 18 September, Lawrence was back at Umtaiye where he and Young directed the clearing of a landing-strip for British planes. The Turco-German planes based on Deraa had local mastery of the air and put the Anglo-Arab forces at constant risk.

When Lawrence left Umtaiye after this second visit he did so in a south-easterly direction, reporting to Feisal at Azrak before flying, on the 20th, to Allenby's headquarters at Ramleh in Palestine. On the 22nd he flew back to Azrak to inform Feisal that the Allies had entered Nazareth and Beisan after routing the last Ottoman forces in Palestine. His final night at Umtaiye was that of 24 September. On the morning of the 25th the Arab army moved north in an alternation of demolition and advance which was to take them into Damascus by 1 October.

The company at Azrak, not Dahoum's death, explains Lawrence's sudden black mood. Just before his description of this mood, he listed an almost Homeric assembly of fighting men: Feisal himself, 'Nuri Said the spick and span,' 'Jemil the gunner,' 'Pisani's coster-like Algerians,' Nuri Shaalan with Trad and Khalid, Faris, Durzi and the Khaffaji; Auda abu Tayi with Mohammed el Dheilan; also Fahad and Adhub, the Zebn leaders, etc. In the glut of names the absence of 'the greatest asset of

Feisal's cause in this work up North'—Sharif Ali ibn al-Hussein— 'the lunatic competitor of the wilder tribesmen in their wildest feats'[36]— is conspicuous but unexplained. Sharif Ali's shadow lies across the intrusion of 'our' remote Ain el Essad, where the mood fell.

It is not hard to understand why Ali ibn al-Hussein was absent from that Azrak roll. Since vanishing in November 1917, Abdel Kader the Algerian had recruited a paramilitary force from southern Syria ostensibly to back the Ottoman cause but in fact to defend his own vision of resistance. Sharif Ali had been converted to Abdel Kader's view that Feisal's cause was his own or Britain's; not that of the Arabs. And, like other bedouin fighters, he had gone back to the desert.

Sharif Ali absent, Dahoum a ghost, two violent emotions propelled Lawrence on the road to Damascus: one was, in his own words, 'to restore Feisal's supremacy,'[37] the other was to seek revenge.

Military events were now nearing a climax. Of the two forces converging on Damascus, Feisal's, to the east, was much smaller than Allenby's to the west. On 25 September, the day the Arab army started north, at a conference in the Palestinian township of Jenin Allenby appointed an Australian, General Henry Chauvel, to direct the capture of the city. Chauvel then sent a division under General Barrow to join the Arabs east of the Jordan and appointed Lawrence liaison-officer between Chauvel (or his deputy Barrow) and Feisal.

Lawrence was irked by the slowness of Barrow's horses; they required more regular watering than the Arabs' camels. Further, his eagerness to reach Damascus was now obsessional. It allowed him to condone atrocities, to accept tactical risks, and, on the last day, to desert his British commander in his haste to press ahead.

That there would be brutalities became almost inevitable once the order for a general Turkish withdrawal was given. 'We know what Turkish troops in retreat are like,' Liman von Sanders wrote of his allies. 'And this time they are hungry, ill clad and ill shod.'[38] The Turks felt betrayed by their fellow-Muslims. On 27 September Young learned of terrible atrocities committed by the Turks at a village three miles north-west of Deraa, and of Arab reprisals. An Iraqi officer told him that he and Lawrence had tried in vain to save a batch of prisoners from massacre by the bedouin, whose latent savagery had been aroused by the sight of butchered women and children.[39] Lawrence gave a starker version in his last contribution to the *Arab Bulletin*. After reporting the massacre of some twenty small children and sixty women—'I noticed particularly one pregnant woman, who had been forced down on a saw-bayonet'—he wrote: 'We ordered "no prisoners" and the men obeyed, except that the reserve company took two hundred and fifty men (including many German Army Service Corps) alive. Later, however, they found one of our men with a fractured thigh who had been afterwards pinned to the ground by two mortal thrusts with German bayonets. Then we turned our Hotchkiss on the prisoners and made an end of them, they saying nothing.'[40] A British cavalry commander confirmed that Auda and his tribesmen had slaughtered survivors of a charge by the Middlesex Yeomanry when, the morning after the action, he sent an officer's patrol to inquire into their fate. 'Not a soul had survived. Every atrocity and mutilation had been perpetrated on the unfortunates.'[41] Hans Guhr, German commander of a Turkish division, saw Turkish corpses which had been stripped and mutilated by the bedouin. By contrast, the local peasantry, equally eager for loot and vengeance, released their victims after beating them up and taking their clothes.[42]

19

Already ancient in biblical times, Damascus had been the capital of the first Arab empire. Although the ninety years of its caliphate were eclipsed by Baghdad's five centuries, its appeal to Arabs was unique. The men who made it an imperial city, ruling from the Atlantic to central Asia, were the astute, worldly Omayyads, relatives of Muhammad who had first opposed and then taken over the expansion of Islam. Conquerors, they ruled half the Byzantine and all the Persian empire in a spirit still more Arab than Islamic.

Damascus was also unforgettably beautiful for its geographical setting. From whatever side the traveller approached, down the Barada gorge leafy with pomegranates and vines, from the saffron ridge of the anti-Lebanon, across the lava-black deserts to the south, his eye was conquered by poplar-rustling green, his parched throat refreshed in anticipation by its streams. The Prophet Muhammad, according to report, had declined to enter the delectable oasis, remarking that a man should enter Paradise but once. It was believed that the Prophet Jesus would alight, at his second coming, on a minaret of the main mosque.

In his Carchemish years, Lawrence had known cosmopolitan Aleppo better than Damascus, though in its main bazaar (roofed with corrugated iron after a fire) he had bought presents for his family. Now Damascus, a medieval city with additions from the age of railways and hotels, was the power-centre for the Syrian province he wished to secure for Feisal—and indirectly for Britain—against other contenders.

Syria, in which he had spent his happiest years, was the emotional Ithaca to whose repossession he had consecrated the fatigues and the wiles of an Odysseus. To ride in triumph beside Ali ibn al-Hussein, one Sharif by another, would have obliterated the failure at the Yarmuk: to find among the rejoicing crowds a smiling Dahoum would have cancelled nightmare. But such dreams were dead. Ali had been absent from the warriors crowded at Azrak. Dahoum, a known agent of British Intelligence, could hardly have survived a famine in which the Turks themselves were often starving and in which missionaries reported that a third of south Lebanon's population had died of hunger.[1] (Richards was to understand that Dahoum had died of typhus, a disease common in crowded prisons.[2]) Now Lawrence concentrated his will on getting Feisal's representatives into Damascus before Allied officialdom. Early on the morning of 1 October, without warning Major-General Sir George Barrow, to whom he was officially attached, he drove ahead with Colonel Stirling. Their car was soon flagged down. An officious N.C.O. in charge of an Indian platoon arrested the officers, Stirling in his Arab headdress and Lawrence in Sharifian white, as runaway Turks. After talking their way free, they drove undramatically into Damascus.

Even so, they were beaten to it by William Yale. This State Department observer and former Near East employee of Standard Oil of New York had simply walked into the city at sunrise. No liberating troops had yet appeared. But the streets were already crammed with shouting, laughing crowds, exultant round Arab warriors on horses and camels. Yale found that the Muslims were as mad with joy as the Christians, though the latter were reassured that British troops were in the offing. 'We were invited into people's homes and had wines and sweetmeats urged upon us.'[3] Among the mounted Arabs seen by Yale was the twenty-year-old al-Umari, acclaimed as liberator by relations and friends.

Lawrence's prime fear had been that the Arabs might clash with a British high command committed to working with the French. He had not foreseen another danger: that a third force would already control Damascus: a force that acknowledged King Hussein, not his son Feisal, as leader of the Revolt: a force that envisaged a unified Arab state independent of foreign tutelage. This third force, being in place, had indeed won the first round. Although the British and Arab armies had created the conditions for its liberation, Damascus had been freed, without fighting, around noon on 30 September.[4]

This peaceful transition to Arab rule was the result of an accommodation between departing Turks and resident Arabs. Far from seeing their conflict as an absolute, both sides shared the bond of Islam and a respect for Damascus. Both wished to reconstruct societies that had proved unable to resist external threats. One of the departing Turkish officers—Mustafa Kemal, victor of Gallipoli and the future Atatürk—was destined to create a secularist Turkey. Arabs such as Subhi al-Umari felt more affinity to such reforming Turks than to Lawrence or Allenby.

On the morning of 30 September, the Ottoman commander-in-chief in Syria, Jemal Pasha the Lesser (to distinguish him from his ruthless predecessor) had sought out Damascene Arabs who could help prevent a collapse of order. He would probably have accepted Feisal's nominee, Ali Ridha al-Rikabi, if he had been available, since al-Rikabi had remained publicly loyal to the Ottomans throughout the war although, like many

Arabs with torn minds, he had resented, not so much the Sultan Caliphate, as the chauvinistic nationalism of the Young Turks. In the last weeks of the war al-Rikabi had been reposted to a military command outside the city. There, Hubert Young recorded, 'I was summoned . . . to interview a mysterious visitor who demanded to see the G.O.C. This turned out to be an Arab general in the Turkish Army who had been entrusted by the Turks with the organization and command of their last line of defence south of Damascus. He told me with glee that he had purposely disposed his troops in an indefensible position, and had then secretly left them to place himself at the disposal of the British Army.'[5]

In al-Rikabi's absence, Shukry Pasha al-Ayoubi, a reputed descendant of Saladin, was another possibility. But Shukry was still in the gaol where the Turks had detained him. The Algerian princes, Abdel Kader and his less flamboyant brother, Said, were the two obvious leaders, and Jemal Pasha ordered five hundred rifles to be issued to the force which Abdel Kader had raised north of Azrak (and which he had claimed was for local defence). At the same time Jemal Pasha entrusted Said (who lived to write his memoirs) with responsibility for public order since rowdy demonstrations could be predicted once the last Turkish forces left. Indeed, one such demonstration soon rescued Shukry Pasha from his prison, and, according to one account, the last Ottoman official to leave, Brigadier-General Behjet Bey, the deputy *wali* of Syria, handed over to him.[6] At noon on 30 September (at the start of the popular fervour witnessed by Yale) the Algerians acted in concert with Shukry. Said telegraphed to all cities of Syria, including Beirut, announcing that an independent Arab nation under King Hussein had come into being. Abdel Kader hoisted King Hussein's banner over the Serai, or governmental building. Shukry ordered the immediate liberation of four thousand prisoners. Surprisingly, there was no looting or disturbance. Lawrence himself was to acclaim this Arab discipline[7] but he did not mention that it had been enforced by Abdel Kader.

At 7.30 on the morning of 1 October, British airmen saw the first Allied troops—Australian cavalry who had spent the night outside the city's north-west outskirts—gallop into Damascus. The first Sharifian regulars had entered a little earlier, led by Feisal's political representative, Sharif Nasir. Irregular units included such tribal sheikhs as Auda abu Tayi, Nuri Shaalan and the Druse sultan al-Atrash. To these the city's welcome was not untempered. Culturally the bedouin were as alien to the Damascenes as the highlanders had been to the Edinburgh citizens of 1745. To prevent disorder, various sections of the army quickly took over the city's various regions. Subhi al-Umari's machine-gunners were given the important central zone, including the two main bazaars.

After the Australians and after Sharif Nasir and his Arabs, Lawrence and Stirling entered Damascus, accompanied by Nuri al-Said. Nuri was an ideal assistant for Lawrence in his immediate purpose and, in his subsequent career as intermittent dictator of Iraq, would prove a consistent, subtle and occasionally ruthless servant of British interests. In the Second World War he helped reimpose an unpopular Regent (Hussein's grandson and Feisal's nephew) after a pro-Axis revolt; after the war he hanged communists in Baghdad squares. By urging Sir Anthony Eden to strike at Egypt in 1956, he signed his own death warrant later than many observers had predicted. He died, in July 1958, as Lawrence had enjoyed living, in clothes not his own. Having escaped the soldiers who slaughtered most of the royal family he was gunned down in a Baghdad street when his shoes betrayed his female disguise. But in the early days of October 1918 Nuri was at the height of his powers, and, in the interval before Allenby and Feisal reached Damascus on the 3rd, he helped Lawrence to execute a swift political coup.

Lawrence and Nuri entered the Serai together and, in the overfurnished Ottoman salon, came upon a disturbing sight. Sharif Nasir was seated amicably on the same sofa as Shukry Pasha and the two Algerians: Said had offered to hand over to Nasir, as Feisal's representative, the authority he had received the day before, but Nasir, more experienced in desert battles than town-hall politics, had officially requested him to continue in office. The harmony between the Algerian brothers, Shukry and Nasir symbolized the reality of a new Arab administration, loyal to King Hussein, and basing its claim to legitimacy and independence on the 1915 correspondence with Sir Henry McMahon and on President Wilson's Eighth Point.

In this crisis Lawrence was helped by Abdel Kader's impetuous nature. Denouncing the Englishman as an imperialist agent, the Algerian drew a dagger. Auda rushed to Lawrence's defence. The consequent clash between Auda's bedouin and Abdel Kader's retainers gave Nuri the pretext to order the Algerian brothers to withdraw to their house. At the same time he appointed Shukry military governor. When, still later that morning, General Chauvel arrived, not at all pleased by Lawrence's unauthorized dawn disappearance, he found him in a mob of Arabs. Chauvel had received precise, if absurd, instructions at the same Jenin conference where Lawrence had been named his liaison officer: he was to find the Turkish *wali* and order him to carry on. But no Turk, let alone a *wali*, was now in sight. Instead Shukry Pasha was introduced to Chauvel by Lawrence as the military governor elected by a majority of the citizens. Chauvel had no means of knowing that this was untrue. He therefore confirmed Shukry in his post but followed Young's advice that he swiftly take possession of Jemal Pasha's residence, so asserting his own position.[8]

Continuing friction between the bedouin and Abdel Kader's men led to violence next day. A search for hidden weapons developed into the looting of private houses. Al-Umari turned his machine-guns on the looters and, at a cost of twenty-one killed and around thirty wounded, restored the peace.[9]

In an official report Lawrence was to accuse the Algerian brothers of being insane 'as well as pro-Turkish and religious fanatics of the most unpleasant sort.'[10] Furiously angry he visited the tomb of Saladin, whose courtesy to war-prisoners had contrasted with Auda's cruelty, and stayed long enough to remove the banner given Abdel Kader by King Hussein, as well as a satin flag and bronze wreath donated by the Kaiser. The wreath went to the curator of the British War Museum; the Kaiser's flag returned to America with Lowell Thomas; Hussein's banner vanished. Lawrence afterwards admitted that he had intended to kill Abdel Kader and Said,[11] and later, in an early variant of the 'shot while attempting to escape' homicidal formula, Abdel Kader did indeed meet a violent death. 'On the morning of November 7,' stated an official British report, 'the Chief Administrator sent police to arrest them, but Abdel Kadir resisted and after firing at the police, mounted his horse and galloped up the street. The police fired on him and killed him.'[12] By this time Lawrence was back in England.

Abdel Kader's death had as long-lasting repercussions in Syria as the murder of Matteotti in Mussolini's Italy. Al-Umari was to write in 1969: 'The al-Jezairi family and others attribute the crime to Feisal and Ridha Pasha al-Rikabi, who were then in control. The truth is that both were entirely innocent.' As evidence of this al-Umari cited his own experience as officer in charge of security in central Damascus. His detachment was stationed near Arab headquarters in the Hotel Victoria. 'When Nuri al-Said summoned me there, I found Lawrence sitting at his side. Nuri told me: "The Amir Abdel Kader is working against the Arab regime on behalf of the French and he is a danger to public security. I want you to take some of your men and kill him." I was embarrassed by this command and after reflecting a moment replied: "I understand from your order, Sir, that you want me to arrest him—but if he resists, then bring him here dead or alive?" Nuri paused, discussed the matter a moment with Lawrence, then said: "Good. Do that." Then added, "Go to the director of police and ask him urgently for someone to guide you to Abdel Kader's house." I went to the director of police who produced the guide. Before I could accomplish my mission a new message summoned me back to Nuri. When I went in to him I found Lawrence still sitting beside him: "We've changed our opinion about the matter." And some time later we heard the news that Abdel Kader had died at the hands of the police.'[13]

The charges made against Abdel Kader, or his brother Said, were contradictory. Lawrence's first report described him as 'pro-Turkish'; Nuri, as we have seen, told al-Umari that he was 'pro-French'; in a secret report to the Chief Political Officer, G.H.Q., Cairo, of June 1919, Lawrence described Said as 'the only real pan-Islamist, in Damascus.'[14] Such accusations cannot account for the intensity of Lawrence's hatred for Abdel Kader. It was true that the Algerian supported King Hussein: but so did Abdullah, without thereby being marked out for British vengeance. He wished to include Beirut in the Arab state: then so did Shukry Pasha, Lawrence's nominee, who raised the Sharifian flag there in early October and lost his post, not his life. Abdel Kader's outward collaboration with the Turks had been no greater than that of al-Rikabi, whom first Feisal and then Abdullah made their prime minister.

Since Lawrence never adequately explained his hatred for Abdel Kader, a conjectural explanation must fit the facts as we know or deduce them. And the key to this last Arabian puzzle can only be turned by the study of Lawrence's character. He was not an ideologist.* Had Abdel Kader contravened some Allied agreement, this would hardly have worried a man who knew of and understood Feisal's negotiations with the Turks. Nor was he shocked by the abstract notion of political treachery. A few years later he was urging George Bernard Shaw to dramatize the life of Sir Roger Casement, the British traitor and Irish hero. Nor did Lawrence take lasting umbrage at those who hurt him physically. Indeed, one of his earliest British critics, Sir Andrew Macphail, was disgusted that Lawrence (who told the story to Robert Graves) 'allowed himself to be struck in the face by a major in the Army Medical Corps;' the major had been upset by the neglect of Turkish wounded in the Damascus hospital,[16] but Macphail thought Lawrence's acceptance of the slap unmanly. Lawrence had spent only ten days in Abdel Kader's company, on the northward march to Azrak in October 1917, and the seeds of the hatred were undoubtedly sown then. On a caravan 'each member of the party hears all that is said and sees all that is done by his fellows,'[17] and despite the tension between them, Abdel Kader, Sharif Ali and Lawrence could not have ridden from oasis to oasis, camp-fire to camp-fire, in total silence. Turki was with them, later to be joined by his father, Sheikh Mifleh, and it must have been on this journey that Lawrence learnt that the lawless Ali was having an affair with the adolescent Turki: 'the animal in each called to the other, and they wandered about inseparably, taking pleasure in touch and silence.'

In the candour of desert nights, as they sat around flaming camel thorn, Turki probably stirred memories of Dahoum, whom Turki, in Lawrence's description, strikingly resembled. 'He was a fair, open-faced boy of

* In calling him 'perhaps the last right-wing intellectual,' George Orwell was surely off the mark.[15]

perhaps seventeen; not tall, but broad and powerful, with a round freckled face, upturned nose, and very short upper lip, showing his strong teeth, but giving his full mouth rather a sulky look, belied by the happy eyes.'[18] Lawrence may even have mentioned the resemblance to Sharif Ali, and Abdel Kader would inevitably have overheard. Further, the Algerian will surely have observed Lawrence's jealous new attachment to Sharif Ali. Thus, after experiencing the open rebuff of Abdel Kader's desertion at Azrak, it would have been easy for Lawrence, in hallucinatory, self-torturing months, to compound that initial injury by imagining that the Algerian was spreading defamatory insinuations about him. He could even plausibly blame on Abdel Kader's malice emotional losses of great importance: if Abdel Kader had denounced Dahoum, the boy's presumed death in some Turkish prison could thus be explained; Sharif Ali's defection could be attributed to subtler accusations.

Lawrence's bitterness was caught by the camera of an American academic who photographed him surveying the happy city from the balcony of the Victoria Hotel on the day after the liberation of Damascus. He seems an Odysseus who has disembarked on Ithaca—only to find it is the wrong island.

On 3 October Allenby entered Damascus and demanded Feisal, which meant that the Arab leader had to curtail his planned triumphal entry. He arrived instead at the Hotel Victoria accompanied by fewer than fifty bedouin outriders. A conference was at once convened. Present, besides Allenby himself, were Bols, Chief of the General Staff; Chauvel and his Chief of Staff; Feisal and Nuri al-Said; and Cornwallis, representing the Arab Bureau. Lawrence was one of four officers attending from the British Mission to the Hejaz. The others were Joyce, the Mission's chief, Stirling and Young.

The first surprise came when Allenby asked Lawrence to translate an announcement to the effect that the Supreme Allied Council recognized the Arabs as belligerents. The Arabs had assumed such recognition since 1916. Allenby then spelt out British policy. It was in full accord with the Sykes-Picot Agreement: Feisal was to administer inland Syria with French guidance and finance and, for the time being, a French liaison officer would work alongside Lawrence, who was to assist him in every respect.

Feisal, ivory with rage, protested that he knew nothing of France in the matter. He was prepared to accept British assistance; he had understood from the Adviser whom Allenby had sent him [i.e. Lawrence] that the Arabs were to have the whole of Syria, including Lebanon but excluding Palestine. A country without a port was useless to him. He declined to recognize French direction in any manner or to accept a French liaison officer.

Allenby, apparently surprised, turned to Lawrence.

'But surely you told him the French were to have a protectorate over Syria?'

'No, Sir, I did not.'

Bowing to superior force Feisal withdrew from the conference. Lawrence then burst out that he could not possibly work with a French liaison officer. He was due for leave. He thought he had better take it at once and get off to England.

'Yes,' said Allenby, 'I think you had.'

When Lawrence, too, had left them, Allenby regretted his curtness. As a sop, he promised Chauvel he would do his best to arrange a meeting between Lawrence and the King-Emperor he had served.

Next day, the 4th, Lawrence left Damascus. Travelling in a Rolls Royce by way of Palestine, he was in Egypt four days later. His abrupt departure confirmed that his interest in the capture of Damascus had been essentially political, since, for the Arabs, weeks of fighting still lay ahead. Subhi al-Umari, for instance, was to win the British Military Cross for exploits near Aleppo nearly a month after Lawrence left. Al-Umari posed there for a souvenir photograph, dressed up as a bedouin and reclining, barefoot, by his camel. This photograph was to be published all over the world as a portrait of Lawrence in the field, surprised by the perfidy of Harry Chase's camera.

In Cairo, Lawrence wrote a last-minute letter from the Grand Continental Hotel asking to have his rifle sent from Arabia. The weapon, an ordinary short Lee Enfield, had an interesting story. Captured by the Turks at Gallipoli, the trophy had been presented by Enver Pasha to Feisal, when the latter had still seemed a loyal subject. Feisal had presented the rifle to Lawrence his first winter in the Hejaz. 'This old war is closing,' Lawrence now told Major R. H. Scott, the British officer in charge at Akaba, 'and my use is gone.'[19] This was not strictly true. But he saw that the new use for his powers lay in Europe. That it did not yet include authorship was shown by his failure to pack the documents, including his skeleton diary, which he would need if he acted on Lloyd's suggestion that he could write 'a unique book' on the Arabian War. Instead, he told Clayton of the incident involving the Algerian brothers and described the enthusiasm of most of the other Damascenes for Feisal's cause. But 'the volatile Arabs of Syria,' he added in a sombre postscript to Clayton's personal report to the Foreign Office, 'may change their tune at any moment.'[20] He then hastened by way of Italy to London.

BOOK FOUR

1919–1923

A Fourth Karamazov

20

LAWRENCE'S RANK as Colonel enabled him to reach London in time to address the Eastern Committee of the War Cabinet on 29th October 1918, and to be received by the King the following day.* Allenby had kept his word and arranged the private interview through Colonel, later Lord, Wigram.

The impudent, cerebral, young Oxonian who had stood out among regular soldiers for his ability to endure and to fib, for his slovenly khaki and immaculate silk, for his donnish English and fluent if inaccurate Arabic, had become a figure as disturbing as the sun to the level gaze of his contemporaries. The King shared the general difficulty of seeing Lawrence as he was and hearing him as he spoke. Lawrence left George V convinced that his subject had told him that, as he 'might be fighting with the Arabs against British troops, be taken prisoner or killed, "he did not want to be found wearing the ribbons of British decorations." '[1]

Winston Churchill first met Lawrence in the spring of 1919. With his romantic respect for the British ruling house, Churchill had been initially repelled by the story which reached him of Colonel Lawrence's behaviour at the Investiture, when Lawrence was to have been decorated a Commander of the Bath. 'The long queue of recipients of honours was filing past the King. When Colonel Lawrence's turn came and the King took the decoration from the velvet cushion and prepared to hang it on the hook, which officers in these circumstances have attached to their tunics, Lawrence stopped him and in a low voice stated with the utmost respect that it was impossible for him to receive any honour from His Majesty while Britain was about to dishonour the pledges which he had made in her name to the Arabs who had fought so bravely. The scene and the incident were unprecedented. The King was naturally surprised and displeased. The decoration, coveted by so many gallant men, was replaced upon its cushion, Lawrence bowed and passed on, and the ceremony proceeded.'[2]

* In a further instance of his romancing to a regular officer, Lawrence told Liddell Hart that he returned to London just in time for the Armistice.

Lawrence allowed the first post-war edition of *Who's Who*, the standard British reference book, to credit him with his military decorations as well as the title of Prince of Mecca. As he had met the King in a private audience, not a public Investiture, he himself may have been the source from which other garbled accounts derived. He certainly spread the story that he had tied his French decoration round a dog's neck and sent it loping round Oxford. Fortunately the careful Wigram had made a note of what was said the day after the interview with the King, when it was still fresh in his memory: 'During the course of the conversation, Colonel Lawrence said that he had pledged his word to Feisal, and that now the British Government were about to let down the Arabs over the Sykes-Picot Agreement. He was an Amir among the Arabs and intended to stick to them through thick and thin and, if necessary, fight against the French for the recovery of Syria. Colonel Lawrence said that he did not know that he had been gazetted or what the etiquette was in such matters, but he hoped that the King would forgive any want of courtesy on his part in not taking the decorations.'[3]

This account, while repeating his *Who's Who* claim to the princely title of Amir, more of less fits with the guarded version he gave to Robert Graves.*

Despite his virtual dismissal from Damascus and his strong words to the King, in London Lawrence retained the pre-eminence he had won in Arabia. Before the Armistice was signed on 11 November, on his own initiative he drafted a cable urging King Hussein to send Feisal to the Peace Conference, since his splendid victories had given him a personal reputation in Europe. The Foreign Office sent the cable to Wingate in Cairo for him to forward to Mecca. Wingate at once cabled to Balfour explaining that he had decided not to do so, and his reasons: while Allenby approved of Feisal, the problem was Hussein, 'not a little suspicious of Colonel Lawrence's influence with his son.' Yet neither Wingate's position as High Commissioner in Egypt, nor his experience, saved him a Foreign Office reprimand for daring to hold back Lawrence's cable. A note of understandable pique intruded into Wingate's further explanation to Hardinge, Minister of War: 'I have now a fairly intimate knowledge of King Hussein's character and mentality and cannot but think this

* This appeared on page 392, *Lawrence and the Arabs*: 'he explained personally to his Sovereign that the part he had played in the Arab Revolt was dishonourable to himself and to his country and government. He had, by order, fed the Arabs with false hopes and would now be obliged if he might be quietly relieved of the obligation to accept honours for succeeding in his fraud. He said respectfully as a subject, but firmly as an individual, that he intended to fight by straight means or crooked until His Majesty's ministers had conceded to the Arabs a fair settlement of their claims.' It was in reply to this version that the King, through his Secretary, Lord Stamfordham, published his own recollection, with its implication that Lawrence was girding to fight his own countrymen. This was plainly incorrect.

might have been remembered before the rather sharp rebuff in the Foreign Office telegram which was administered.'[4]

In promoting Feisal's cause in London, Lawrence could draw on considerable support; Hogarth assured Clayton at the beginning of November that the War Office and Admiralty, as well as such influential politicians as Robert Cecil, were coming round to the Arab Bureau point of view. 'T.E.L. has put the wind up everybody and done much good, which I don't want him to undo by being here too long and treading too often on corns. He is trying to get the principle accepted that Arabs and Zionists are to be called in to any such "conversations" on the S.P. [Sykes-Picot] business as Cambon [French Foreign Minister] admits must take place eventually. Meanwhile S.P. is considered scrapped here but not so in Paris.'[5]

Into the tired, claustrophobic khaki of late 1918 Lawrence's evocation, in dress and talk, of 'the shades of Arabia, where the Princes ride at noon,' introduced a glittering thread. British politicians, who, with their equivalents in Paris, Rome and Washington, were shortly to plant the seeds for new iron men, could have echoed the words which Hogarth had written earlier in the year: 'How young one is now and how old one will be when the war is over and the strain relaxed.'[6] The lives of the British peacemakers, from Lloyd George and Curzon down to those who carried briefcases and prepared memoranda, would be cruelly bisected by the word 'post-war'. Tired from four years of desk-bound struggle, haunted over evening whiskies by youthful ghosts, ready victims for influenza, they also saw in Lawrence an Open Sesame to the Middle East, whose provinces, like the vague terrains of Africa in the 1880s, were for the grabbing.

At the same time, Lawrence's reputation was spreading beyond Whitehall and Pall Mall. Some time before Christmas 1918, an American publisher, F. N. Doubleday (known to his friends—and made famous by Kipling—as Effendi, from a play on his initials), found himself seated next to a 'young, small, blond gentleman in khaki' at what seems to have been an all-male dinner party given by Sir Evelyn Wrench. The place-card, giving the name 'Colonel Lawrence', signified nothing to the New York visitor. Yet Doubleday, intrigued by his dinner-companion's talk, asked him if he would dine at their hotel, if Mrs. Doubleday wrote him an invitation. Lawrence politely accepted. This done, Doubleday asked Sir Evelyn who the delightful man was that had sat next to him at dinner.

'Why, Effendi, don't you Americans know about Colonel Lawrence of Arabia, who is one of the most sought after men in London?'[7]

Rudyard Kipling—Florence Doubleday described him as her husband's most intimate friend—was staying with his American-born wife at the same Mayfair hotel as the Doubledays. Effendi hastened to ask if the Kiplings would like to meet Lawrence the following Friday. Kipling, to whom Lawrence was the most romantic figure to have come out of the war, readily agreed to cancel a previous engagement. In vain. Lawrence turned up at Brown's, a hotel favoured by the English county, a day early, as the Doubledays were preparing to leave the dining-room. Even so, upstairs in their room, Lawrence captivated Florence as he had already intrigued Effendi. What he later termed the tiring process of 'beginning again from the bottom to make oneself a nest in other people's estimations'[8] in this case proved rewarding. Doubleday became his American publisher as well as devoted friend, and the following month Kipling was corresponding with him over the suggestion that the U.S., not France, might be given a mandate over Syria.[9]

Lawrence threw his new fame and his old energy into the battle for Feisal. That the odds were tilting against Feisal was already clear. On 6 November (the day of Abdel Kader's death in Damascus) Georges-Picot had arrived in Beirut; as 'French High Commissioner in Syria and Armenia' he cabled Paris the same month for 20,000 French and colonial troops to enforce French claims. What remained unclear was the British commitment to their wartime undertakings to Hussein. Yet the Royal Navy sent a warship, the *Gloucester*, to ferry Feisal, duly appointed as his father's representative, from Beirut to Marseilles. Lawrence, in khaki with the Arab headcloth, met him there on the 25th. The French, as suspicious of Lawrence as was King Hussein, curtly informed him that he was welcome in France as an Allied officer; dressed up as an Arab he was not. Lawrence retired to England. Feisal's reception in France was correct but cool. More drained by the war than the British, the French had strong emotional motives for salvaging colonial gains from four ruinous years, and the French government regarded the Arab kingdom, or kingdoms, as structures of British papier maché. Feisal was therefore treated 'only . . . as a person of distinction visiting France.'[10] Shown the battlefields on which France had lost two million sons, made *Grand-Officier* of the *Croix de la Légion d'Honneur*, he was received on the 7th December by President Poincaré at the Elysée Palace. The President restricted the conversation to polite banalities, translated by the same Ben Gabrit who had headed the Algerian pilgrimage in 1916.[11]

By the 10 December a disquieted Feisal was escorted by Lawrence from the English coast to London's Carlton Hotel. He was to stay in Britain for a month until, in January, he and Lawrence moved back to Paris to attend the Peace Conference. Feisal dressed drably in Europe. In his black soutane with high stand-up collar he reminded Hogarth of a youthful priest.[12] But two nights before they returned to Paris, Lawrence attended a party in full Sharifian white and Feisal got into similar array on 6 February when Lawrence translated (fairly accurately, according to an Arabic-speaking friend of Meinertzhagen's) his address to the Peace Conference demanding Arab unity. On that occasion, Lloyd George, one of the more emotional men to have guided British policy, was dazzled by the combined effect of the two men in their surprising robes, and over the coming months he put up a rearguard but diminuendo fight to have the British promises to Feisal's father honoured at least in part.

After a four-year hiatus the glacier-powerful molars of national interest were soon to resume grinding. But briefly Lawrence's legend commanded hearts: intrepid train-basher and Turk-evader, Arabist and expert on every aspect of the East, Feisal's fellow-Prince—the amplitude of the picture owed as much to unconscious British demands as conscious pushing by Lawrence himself. But the demands made and met, Lawrence had to perform oracular functions. Gifted with the ability to say something plausible, and say it quickly, he did so. Perhaps because basically he was uninterested in politics, he lacked, among his formidable talents, political insight. But asked to answer, answer he would, in memoranda to the Cabinet or letters to *The Times*. In retrospect his answers seem often absurd and sometimes dangerous.

His recipe for a post-war settlement (modestly entitled *Reconstruction of Arabia*) was submitted to the Cabinet a week before the guns fell silent.[13]

'The Sharif [Hussein] was ultimately chosen,' he admits, 'because of the rift he would create in Islam, because his geographical position gave him a fair chance of surviving and because his pre-eminence amongst Arabs was based upon the arbitrary and empiric, but in the East unassailable, ground of family prestige.' Lawrence's belief in the Blood of his Hashemite friends was balanced by his ignorance of the Arabian interior. He could thus proceed flippantly to dismiss a man of greater military and diplomatic talent, with a greater future, than any son of Hussein. 'Ibn Saud,' he wrote, 'is now striving to limit the puritan revival becoming too strong for him. If he is carried away by it, and attacks the Holy Places, the orthodox Islam will deal with him, as with his ancestor. If he can control it he will remain Amir of Nejd [the upland steppe of Arabia] after military failure has warned him to recognise the Sharif as his overlord.' This judgement was to be overturned when a few years later Ibn Saud evicted Hussein's eldest son from Mecca, leaving the Hashemite archives a sordid mess in their abandoned palace.

In a secret cable of 18 November, summarizing Lawrence's proposals 'for dealing comprehensively with Arab question,' the Secretary of State for India, the Hon. Edwin Montagu, showed how seriously the Lawrentian oracle was taken. 'He advocates formation of three Councils of Arab States outside Hedjaz and its dependencies, viz.: (1) Lower Mesopotamia, (2) Upper Mesopotamia and (3) Syria, to be placed respectively under Abdullah, Zeid and Feisal, sons of King Hussein. Hussein himself would remain King of Hedjaz and would ultimately be succeeded by his eldest son Ali. He would have no temporal authority in three states above mentioned, and, in fact, no position at all there beyond insertion of his name in Friday prayers in all mosques as Emir-el-Momein [*sic*].'[14]

The last suggestion is interesting. Emir-el-Momein was a telegraphic mangling of the Arabic phrase for Commander of the Faithful, a caliphal title. While Englishmen were thus advocating a Hashemite caliph, Muslims were taking contrary decisions. Having first abolished the sultanate, Atatürk was finally to abolish the Ottoman caliphate in March 1924. Fuad I (in Egypt the titles of Pasha, Khedive and Sultan had culminated in King) then toyed with assuming the mantle himself; but when a young theologian published a book demolishing the notion that the caliphate was essential to Islam, that shrewd ruler quickly dropped the project. Hussein, by then exiled, was to be named Caliph by his son Abdullah from the village of Amman. This claim, hardly taken seriously outside the family circle, was to provoke a wrathful Ibn Saud into his final expulsion of the Hashemites from Arabian soil.

On Palestine, destined to be the most expensive of British promises, Lawrence's Report was equally sweeping. 'In Palestine the Arabs hope that the British will keep what they have conquered. They will not approve Jewish Independence for Palestine but will support as far as they can Jewish infiltration, if it is behind a British, as opposed to an international façade.'

Lawrence, who had hardly had time to consult Palestinian opinion, saw advantages for Britain in the Zionist experiment. He was not a gentile Zionist in the sense that the Rev. Hechler, Theodor Herzl's first disciple, had been, and Meinertzhagen was to become. The metaphysical underpinnings of the movement, whether in its religious or secularized form, meant nothing to him. On the other hand he saw in Lebanese businessmen or Palestinian agriculturalists dangers, not allies, to the bedouin way of life he wished to keep unspoiled.

The bedouin were poor. A subsidy of fifty thousand sovereigns a year could buy Ibn Saud (the notion that Arabia might one day be rich would have made Whitehall laugh) and against bedouin penury Lawrence was highly conscious of Jewish financial strength. A wartime letter from Feisal to his father[15] quotes Lawrence as telling him that 'the Jews are exerting a major influence on the course of the war, particularly in matters of finance, and that all nations need them, and the Arabs might possibly get from fifteen to twenty million pounds, during the war or after, to help them establish a government and organise its affairs.' Sykes had given the Arab prince a similar opinion. 'The Jewish race'—before Hitler, the term was used without embarrassment—'is universal, is all-powerful and cannot be put down . . . And remember these people do not seek to conquer you, do not seek to drive out the Arabs of Palestine . . . they do not desire to go there in millions, what they desire is to be able to feel that in Palestine a Jew may live his life and speak his tongue as he did in ancient times.'[16] Sykes had been confirmed in his statements by Chaim Weizmann, who had told a group of Jerusalem notables on 27 April 1918: 'Do not believe those who insinuate that we intend to take the supreme political power of this country into our hands at the end of the war.' Weizmann had been similarly reassuring when he had met Feisal for forty-five minutes at Wahida, north-west of Akaba, on 4 June. Feisal had been evasive.[17]

But France was to be Feisal's chief preoccupation in 1919. From London he assured his father that the French intended to occupy, not only the coastal area conceded to them in the Sykes-Picot Agreement, but the whole interior.[18] In this mood his emotional dependence on Lawrence —who had provided magical doles of money, stood up to Allenby in Damascus and secured Feisal's presence at the Peace Conference— inclined him to accept his advice almost unexamined. Considering that to a former fellow-officer Lawrence invoked an ultimate and brutal Arab sanction: 'the Arab Govt. is not afraid of them [the Jews] can cut all their throats, or better pull all their teeth out, when it wishes.'[19], he will have been no less reassuring to Feisal.

British motives in promoting such contradictory movements as Arab nationalism and Zionism (for from the start the ninety per cent Arab majority opposed the colonization of their country) were involved with the Suez Canal and the advantage of mounting its defence from a base independent of an unpredictable and restive Egypt. The danger was that the Peace Conference might put Palestine under some international administration but Arab and Jewish support for a British mandate could abort such proposals.

Lawrence was thus promoting a general British brief when he urged Feisal to accept the Zionists as allies against the French. He had earlier shown his sympathy for this brief when he had addressed the Eastern Committee of the War Cabinet under Lord Curzon's chairmanship. On that occasion, he had stated, with apparent seriousness, that Feisal would like to choose his advisers from the ranks of British or American Zionists.[20]

Interpreting for Feisal at a meeting with Weizmann at the Carlton Hotel on 11 December Lawrence had carried this policy one stage further: his interpretation of Feisal's Arabic left Weizmann and Feisal under different impressions as to what had been said.* Weizmann was

* This raises once again the question of how well Lawrence knew Arabic. One Arabic letter was found in the papers of the late Amir Zeid, signed by Lawrence both in English and Arabic. Dated 25 June 1918, it is a military report addressed to Hussein. It is

evidently persuaded that Feisal had promised to support Zionist demands (appropriately softened by such undertakings as that the rights of the Arab peasantry would be respected) in return for Jewish help. Whereas Feisal, dictating his version of what had been said to his secretary, Rustum Haidar, in a letter to King Hussein, wrote that Lawrence had balanced the capital and political influence of the Jews against the danger posed by France. Feisal reported that the Jews did not aim at establishing a government but wanted to invest in useful projects such as railways and roads and to be regarded, in Palestine, as citizens with the right to participate in councils.[21] Since Weizmann wanted something in writing, a joint Feisal-Weizmann statement was issued in early January. The English version spoke (in terms no Arab would have thought of using) of the racial kinship and ancient bonds existing between the Arabs and the Jewish people; it also conceded much of the then limited Zionist demands. At the last moment Feisal insisted on adding a tenth article in his own handwriting. This said that the whole agreement depended on the Arabs obtaining their independence as demanded in a memorandum he had sent to the British government on 4 January 1919: 'But if the slightest modification or departure were to be made, I shall not then be bound by a single word of the present Agreement which shall be deemed void and of no account or validity.'[22]

Feisal's acceptance of Lawrence's view of Zionism (an issue neither his father nor any Arab electorate had authorized him to discuss) was in fact limited and cautious. He had changed Weizmann's 'Jewish State' and 'Jewish Government' to 'Palestine' and 'Palestine Government' in the draft of the agreement;[23] in an interview with a Paris newspaper on 12 February he included Palestine among the Arab countries whose complete independence he was demanding; in another interview on 1 March he said that oppressed Jews would be welcome in Palestine 'on condition that they submit to an Islamic authority, or to a Christian authority delegated by the League of Nations.'[24]* These statements so disturbed Zionist delegates to the Peace Conference (where their influence on President Wilson and the American delegation was considerable) that a letter in Feisal's name, but contrived by Lawrence,

---

plainly not the work of an Arab, being full of grammatical errors, mispellings and Iraqi colloquial expressions. The latter make it probable that Young (who had spent longer in Iraq than Lawrence's few weeks) had a hand in drafting it. If, at the Carlton Hotel conference, Lawrence had failed to catch Feisal's meaning in Arabic, he would have been unlikely to have admitted this in front of Weizmann and might well have blurred some significant detail in a complex discussion.

* Lord Curzon, then Lord President of the Council, had confirmed at a meeting of the War Cabinet's Eastern Committee on 27 November 1918, that 'Palestine was included in the areas to which Great Britain pledged itself that they should be Arab and independent in the future.'[25]

Meinertzhagen, Weizmann and Felix Frankfurter, assured Frankfurter that the Arab delegation found the Zionist proposals to the Peace Conference moderate and proper and that Feisal looked forward 'to a future in which we will help you and you will help us, so that the countries in which we are mutually interested may once again take their place in the comity of civilized peoples of the world.'[26]*

When, ten years[28] later, a copy of this letter was shown to one of the many commissions investigating Palestine, two Arabs who had been with Feisal in Europe at the time were convinced it was a forgery and[29] Feisal himself denied having any memory of writing it.† But Feisal was damaged by even this tepid consideration of a form of colonization which promised to be much more permanent than the French occupation of Tunisia or the British of Egypt. His leadership was further weakened by his dealings with the Syrians (from whom he had absented himself too long) and the French. By Easter 1919, Hogarth reported that he personally doubted Feisal's abilities; when cornered, Lawrence now admitted that he doubted them, too.[30]

* Meinertzhagen published a version of the letter, written from *Délégation Hedjazienne*, 1. iii.1919. 'It was,' he says, 'drafted by Feisal, Lawrence, Weizmann, Frankfurter and myself.'[27]

† *The Jerusalem Post*, in its issue of 16 December 1964, published what was claimed to be a photostat of the original letter, discovered in the files of the Jewish Agency in London. It was in Lawrence's handwriting.

21

If Lawrence had been simply a British agent who had enjoyed 'the life and fun and movement' of exploiting Arab unrest for British purposes and then, on the failure of a plucky fight for his Arabian prince, had ruefully accepted his decorations while planning to fill some Government House with wife and children, he would have resembled other players of Kipling's Great Game. With the officers who had helped win Britain's forty year 'moment' in the Middle East—Wingate, Allenby, Clayton, Lloyd, Stirling, Joyce, Young—he would have joined the secondary game, capricious as roulette, for preferment, high or low. In place of Wingate, suddenly dismissed, Viscount Allenby of Megiddo and Felixstowe became Britain's High Commissioner in Egypt, to be replaced in his turn by George Lloyd, now a Lord. Sir Ronald Storrs governed Cyprus after Jerusalem, losing prized mementoes of his dilettante greatness when Greek Cypriots stormed Government House. Stirling, after governing Sinai and advising King Zog of Albania, became *Times* correspondent in Damascus before dying of cancer in Tangiers. Young governed first Nyasaland (the modern Malawi) and then Northern Rhodesia (the modern Zambia). Like them, Lawrence would have dwindled: into memoirs more or less bad, then obituaries, honorific but fading. Rumours that one famous soldier kept a wardrobe of women's clothes, that another took to drink, would not be enough to galvanize into memorability actors who had outlived a war which was to prove neither the last nor the most ferocious.

Something in Lawrence that was intrinsic to those qualities in him which provoked denigration as well as adulation preserves him as a fabulous monster among named pack-mules.

The five years between his audience with George V on 30 October 1918 and the day in November 1923, when he wrote, 'I hope not again to do anything of my own,'[1] display a texture of surprise, achievement and interest with no equivalent in English fiction, let alone history. Spokesman for Feisal in 1919, he was to move from the disillusionment of his mentor, Hogarth, to the mind-quenching delusion that by rigging Feisal out with another throne in Baghdad, as a substitute for Damascus,

Churchill and he would leave Britain 'with clean hands'.[2] Yet instead of the normal rewards for such conscience-salving, he demanded a hard bed in a barrack hut; instead of a plumed hat, an airman's forage cap. And, most remarkable of all, 'fundamentally fraudulent' as he seemed to others besides Harold Nicolson,[3] in two contrasting books he pursued, with the energy of a schoolboy cyclist, a vision of truth. The first, *Seven Pillars of Wisdom*, attempted to distil his experience of the desert, the Arabs and death into a prose epic; for it he forged a style which one of his most fervent admirers found keyed-up[4] but which testified to the extraordinary background against which he had lived in fact and fantasy. Later, in sharpest contrast, he used plain sentences and short, often ugly words to convert his initial experiences of the Royal Air Force into the first chapters of *The Mint*. In these pages, verbal snapshots, pungent, brief, show the dexterous honesty with which he could synthesize 'spiritual adventure, deliberately sought and stoically endured, in the drabbest physical setting of his own country.'[5] A complex of emotions powered his ambitious and contradictory cerebrations. One was a continuing patriotism. Under its influence he promised to suspend publication of *The Mint* lest it deter recruiting.[6] Another was the ritualization of physical violence: carefully planned ordeals whose regularity and severity make Swinburne's masochistic experiments with Ada Isaacs Mencken resemble the games of children. His quest for an absolute of effort and degradation link him, more than anything in his epic, to the three Karamazov brothers; of whom the only flat statement to be made is that none could have been an Anglo-Saxon.

The gestation of his epic can be traced from Lawrence's letters and from the contemporary diary of Colonel Meinertzhagen.*

As early as 2 September 1917, writing to Colonel Wilson, he had referred to his hopes of writing a book about 'the Hejaz show', which he described as 'quaint', but historically a success. 'All my memories of it are pleasant (largely due to you, of course, for on the face things should not be so), and if ever I can get my book on it out, I'll try to make other people see it.'[8] On Christmas Day 1918, he told Doughty on Carlton Hotel writing paper of meeting some of the old man's Arab acquaintances: 'It has been a wonderful experience, and I have got quite a lot to tell.

* Diaries, while much more valuable to the historian than later recollections, have their perils. Their value depends on the veridicity of the diarist; signs of retrospective editing are more damaging than the errors of fact which few diarists avoid. Meinertzhagen's *Middle East Diary*, edited and published in his old age, has an entry for 13.11.1951 in which, dining at the Israeli Embassy in London, he discusses the possibility of Nasser increasing hostile activities in the Gaza Strip—more than six months before Nasser came to power.[7] But Meinertzhagen's bluff, masculine personality, as well as his dedication to a political movement hardly congruous with the aims with which Lawrence was identified, gives his earlier entries the ring of a different truth from that to be found in such works as *T. E. Lawrence By His Friends*.

'I'm afraid it is not likely to be written for publication, since some of it would give offence to people alive, (including myself!) but I hope to get it put on paper soon.'[9]

Along with Gertrude Bell, Hogarth, Sykes and Lloyd, Meinertzhagen attended the Paris Peace Conference. He seems to have been among the first few people to know of Lawrence's draft and certainly the first to see it. He was also to be one of those whom it would most offend.

In a diary entry for 8 April 1919, Meinertzhagen notes: 'He is writing a book on his Arabian exploits and admitted to me that though it purports to be the truth, a great deal of it is fancy, what might have happened and dull incidents embroidered with hair-breadth escapes. He confesses that he has overdone it and is now terrified lest he is found out and deflated. He told me that ever since childhood he had wanted to be a hero, that he was always fighting between rushing into limelight and hiding in utter darkness but the limelight had always won . . . He hates himself and is having a great struggle with his conscience. Shall he run away and hide, confess his sins and become completely discredited—or carry the myth on into the limelight in the hopes of not being exposed . . . He blames Hogarth, Lowell Thomas, Storrs and many others . . . for making him a little War Hero.'[10]

Meinertzhagen was unaware that the previous day Lawrence had received a telegram with an Oxford postmark: *Father has pneumonia come if possible.* The two Englishmen dined together at the Majestic. The gigantic Meinertzhagen, self-confident, capable of extrovert violence, was puzzled by what he accounted Lawrence's manic depression. 'He is a complex character, his moral barometer jumping about from extreme depression to hilarious practical jokes.' (In one of these he had festooned the central well of the Astoria, where Balfour and Lloyd George were conversing with American and French officials, with uncoiling lavatory paper.) As an instance of his morbidity, Meinertzhagen records that when, upstairs at the Majestic, he had jokingly spanked Lawrence on the bottom, 'he made no attempt to resist and told me later that he could easily understand a woman submitting to rape once a strong man hugged her.' On that night of 8 April, Meinertzhagen persuaded him to drink a little champagne 'to cheer him up', despite his normally teetotal habits.

On that same evening, Thomas Tighe Chapman, the 7th baronet in the eyes of Burke's *Peerage*, lay in his coffin, felled by the pandemic influenza which, seven weeks earlier in Paris, had claimed Sir Mark Sykes. Having stayed to dine with Meinertzhagen, Lawrence arrived too late to see his father.

When Frank Lawrence had been killed in France, Lawrence had found his mother's demands unbearable: then they had travelled by post and were for a brother. 'You *will* never never understand any of us after we are grown up a little,' he had written from Egypt. '*Don't* you ever feel that we love you without our telling you so?—I feel such a contemptible worm for having to write this way about things. If you only knew that if one thinks deeply about anything one would rather die than say anything about it. You know men do nearly all die laughing, because they know death is very terrible, & a thing to be forgotten till after it has come.'[11] In later retrospect Lawrence judged that his mother, 'brought up as a child of sin on the island of Skye by a Bible-thinking Presbyterian, then a nursemaid, then "guilty" (in her own judgment) of taking my father from his wife,'[12] had done to his father what head-hunters do to their trophies. A generous, expansive aristocrat had been shrunk to an abstemious, pence-counting petit bourgeois.

On the shelves at Polstead Road Lawrence may have found *The Singing Caravan*, a volume of verse by one of his father's unacknowledging relations, Sir Robert Vansittart. He certainly had it with him when he returned to France. It was a strange memento of the father who had longed for his son to tell him in person of the more adventurous caravans whose fame was now spreading beyond the circle of Sarah Lawrence and Laura Hogarth. His mother had been left his father's untouched capital; she was not to inherit the alternative love she craved. During all the difficulties of war, Lawrence had written home at least once a month; after April 1919 he was not to write home again until 20 March 1921; and while admittedly he was in England and even Oxford for much of this time, he visited Polstead Road but rarely. After his mother sold the house and accompanied his elder brother to the Chinese mission-field, he was to write barely, briefly, letters that had little to say and less to give.

April 1919 opened the door to a year in most respects bitter. On 21 April Feisal left France for Syria. There was nothing to keep Lawrence in Paris except the slow grind of a Conference which by May had brought Hogarth to despair. Unless His Majesty's Government adopted a firm policy by the end of the month, Hogarth wrote to Clayton, 'I must resign and go back to Oxford sick at heart at all the fiasco and the melancholy consummation of four years work. To think that we are to hand over Feisal and Syria to Senegalese troops and take Palestine with our hands and feet tied!' Hogarth early saw the folly of the scheme, most strongly backed by Lloyd George, for 'the carving up of Asiatic Turkey', but he felt impotent 'in the teeth of ignorance, incuria and national greed at the top.'[13] Lawrence himself felt that Feisal would probably 'bolt it back off to Mecca when he is faced with getting back into the saddle.'[14] That Mecca would not long remain a Sharifian bolt-hole was soon to be evident.

When he still thought to win in Europe what had remained doubtful in Syria, Lawrence had left his notebooks and skeleton diary in Cairo. Now that the Peace Conference had decided to send the first of countless commissions of inquiry to the Middle East, now that Feisal was trying to accommodate the French and the Syrian nationalists, Lawrence decided to fetch the papers he needed for his book.

His prestige easily secured him permission, through General Groves, the British Air delegate at the Peace Conference, to travel to Egypt with a flight of Handley Page bombers. For policing such 'liberated' (but often ungrateful) territories as Iraq, Britain was to rely progressively on aerial power; but the urgency with which this flight was sent east was prompted in part by the worsening relations between King Hussein and his powerful neighbour, Ibn Saud. Britain's larger plans and Lawrence's lesser were on this occasion to go astray. Of the fifty-one bombers which left England in the spring of 1919 only twenty-six had reached Egypt safely by the end of October.

While flying across France, Lawrence used a blank page at the back of *The Singing Caravan* to write the following:

> I wrought for him freedom to lighten his sad eyes: but he had died waiting for me. So I threw my gift away and now not anywhere will I find rest and peace.
>
> Written between Paris and Lyons in Handley Page.

The two writers who first came on these somewhat mysterious words considered them to be a draft of the dedicatory poem with which Lawrence was later to preface *Seven Pillars of Wisdom* and unambiguous proof of the male gender of 'S.A.', Lawrence's equivalent of Shakespeare's equally mysterious Mr. W. H.[15] Yet, written within a few weeks of his father's death, the words were probably inspired by the diminished Irishman who had waited so eagerly to hear his son's exploits from his son's lips. The death of his father is usually a crucial event in a man's maturity. Nothing suggests that in this respect Lawrence was unusual. On the contrary, his post-war interest in such Irish heroes as Casement, his brief dalliance with Irish politics and his acceptance of an Irish honour, were to contrast vividly with his pre-war hostility to the Irish and his identification with England.[16]

At the time he wrote those valedictory words he was planning to use his gratuity and any royalties from his writings to build a house with Vyvyan Richards near Epping Forest; on 1 September he was indeed to buy just over five acres at Pole Hill, Chingford; when he received a further £300, expected in October, he and Richards would contact builders.[17] In this dream house, for which he had preserved timbers rescued long ago from Jesus College, he could have told his father of things which weighed on his mind but which he could never tell his mother in the semi-detached prison in North Oxford. The lines, in no sense a poem, are the first statement of the mood in which, later on the same journey, in the detachment of the air, above the world, he was to rough out four pages of prose—the opening chapter of the published version of *Seven Pillars of Wisdom*—which marked a decisive break with the Uranian ambiguity of his friend Leonard Green.* Lawrence's single first page crowds words and phrases which Green could not have used in an entire book. It is worth extracting them: *evil . . . naked . . . indifferent heaven . . . beating wind . . . stained by dew, and shamed into pettiness . . . ravenous . . . devoured . . . spur and rein . . . slavery, manacled . . . chain-gang . . . serve . . . ill content . . . slaves . . . terrible . . . surrendered . . . overmastering greed . . . drained of morality . . . dead leaves . . . ropes about our necks . . . hideous tortures . . . merciless, merciless . . . bruised feet . . . sag of nerves . . . gusts of cruelty . . . perversions, lusts . . .*

On 17 May, as Lieutenant Prince tried to land his Handley Page in the dusk at Centocelle, near Rome, he misjudged the length of the airfield and the bomber capsized, killing both him and his second pilot, Lieutenant Sprott. Lawrence, seated in the back with two mechanics, escaped, but concussed and with broken ribs.

For Britain it was fortunate that the planes failed to reach Cairo on schedule. In the last week of May the military weakness of King Hussein and his commander-in-chief, his son Abdullah, was revealed. Sent to chase Ibn Saud's *Ikhwan* from the oasis of Khurma, Abdullah's army was surprised by night at Turaba. The Sharifians lost twelve guns, twenty machine-guns, four hundred horses and fifteen hundred camels. By slitting his tent-wall Abdullah escaped in his night clothes. Britain, in turn, had escaped an armed clash with the creator of Saudi Arabia.

For Lawrence, too, the protracted trip to Egypt had advantages. Once he was well enough to leave his Rome hospital, he continued on another Handley Page which, after a delay in Albania, broke down in Crete. He could in the privacy of service travel continue the gestation of his epic since the amplitude of his fame had not reached the Middle East itself. In its Personal and Social column for 23 May the *Egyptian Gazette*, which had reported his Rome misadventure, carried a blurred item:

> Colonel Lawrence, who has now completed his work with the Egyptian Expeditionary Force, will shortly return to Oxford, where he will resume his task of lecturing on history.

* Green published his second slim volume in 1919: *The Youthful Lover and other prose studies*. As delicate and weakly elegiac as *Dream Comrades*, its predecessor, the central story describes the abode of an admired young officer: 'On the walls are pictures of youths as Tuke paints them, as Praxiteles moulded them, as Giorgione and Guercino saw them.'[18]

Colonel Lawrence, who is 29 years of age, was for two years staff officer to the Amir Feisal, Commander-in-chief of the Arab army, and son of the King of Hejaz.

Lawrence, now nearing thirty-one, had never lectured on history at Oxford and was not to do so.

At Souda Bay in Crete the Englishman who had been right all along about Ibn Saud arrived in another bomber. Three years Lawrence's senior, Harry St. John Bridger Philby—on his later 'conversion' to take at Ibn Saud's prompting the name Abdullah and to acquire the honorific title Hajji when he made the pilgrimage—had earlier that year startled the Interdepartmental Committee on the Middle East in London by stating that Ibn Saud could take Mecca whenever he so wished. As Lord Curzon (now Foreign Secretary) had proclaimed at the start of the same meeting, 'Our policy is a Hussein policy', Philby's words had sounded impudent.

Philby was as unlike Lawrence as could be imagined. He was, in his own words, 'more at ease with women and children, flowers and animals, than with the male creatures of his species'; he lacked Lawrence's gift for handling other people through intuiting their desires and pretending to make them his; he tended to antagonize other Englishmen. His son Kim, named after the hero of Kipling's novel, was to have his father's tombstone inscribed: *Greatest of Arabian Explorers*, and the tribute was deserved. By 1919 Philby had already traversed Arabia from east to west; his later distances were to make Lawrence's rides seem excursions. He noted more than mountains, ruined cities and sand seas. He discerned that the Hashemite weakness was moral as well as military. The *Ikhwan*, whom Lawrence's report had belittled, drew their strength from a puritanical conception of Islam whereas the Sharifian rank and file had fought for excitement and gold, their leaders for gold and place.

At Souda Bay, Lawrence was surprised by the stranger's knowledge of Arabia. Then, learning Philby's name, he became laconic. Philby for his part was struck by Lawrence's lack of interest in Arabia proper and his obsessive concentration on securing Feisal a throne in Syria. The two men flew on to Cairo in Philby's aircraft. Thence Philby departed on a placatory mission to Ibn Saud and a career in which he was to write, among many thousands, hardly a living page. Lawrence collected the papers he needed for his epic and within forty-eight hours returned to Paris.

On the eventful journey out, Lawrence had broached to the commander of the luckless flight, Captain Henderson, 'the possibility of his enlisting in the R.A.F.' Knowing his man from Hejaz days, Henderson put this down at the time to 'leg-pulling'. Another characteristic Henderson remembered of Lawrence—his 'marvellous reserve of energy'—was to be displayed in the speed with which, against physical distractions and emotional obstacles he accomplished his first draft of *Seven Pillars of Wisdom* that vexatious summer.[19]

On 17 July Lawrence and Meinertzhagen were staying on different floors of the same Paris hotel; Lawrence's room, which had no bath, was immediately above his senior's. Lawrence lowered his manuscript on a string to Meinertzhagen's window. Three days later, in his diary, Meinertzhagen recorded: 'He surprised me by saying that little of his book was strict truth, though most of it was based on fact; he had intended giving me a copy of his book; I begged him not to as I loathe fakes; he then told me that was also his trouble; he also hated fakes but had been involved in a huge lie—"imprisoned in a lie" was his expression —and that his friends and admirers intended to keep him there.'[20]

Lawrence disclosed to Meinertzhagen two 'facts' which he claimed hitherto to have disclosed to no one: the first was the distress caused him by the circumstances that his parents had never married; the second was 'the indecency and degradation he suffered at the hands of the homosexual Turks.' His family situation has already been discussed; the second 'fact' opens the first window on new and important scenery.

Colonel Meinertzhagen belonged to the profession whose members were the most frequent victims of Lawrence's romancing. What Meinertzhagen heard from Lawrence is evidence, not of what had happened to him at the hands of Turks or anyone else, but of what Lawrence was now saying had happened. It proves that as early as July 1919 he had formulated the psychological climax of his book: the Deraa incident. 'He did not intend', Meinertzhagen continues to quote him, 'to publish the true account of this incident as it was too degrading, "had penetrated his innermost nature" and he lived in constant fear that the true facts would be known. He had been seized, stripped and bound; then sodomized by the Governor of Deraa, followed by similar treatment by the Governor's servants. After this revolting behaviour, he had been flogged.'

In Paris it was now after midnight of 17 July. Lawrence asked if he might have a bath in his friend's bathroom. Meinertzhagen, who had earlier heard of Lawrence's countless wounds and, shortly before, of this 'degrading' experience, took the opportunity of observing him without his clothes on. It was on this occasion that the tattoo-like weals on Lawrence's ribs were seen for the first time by a western witness.

'Good God, what ever are those?'

Lawrence then replied in the terms already quoted:

'A camel accident at Azrak; dragged across barbed wire.'

Meinertzhagen, who knew that bullet marks were normally indelible, noted that, apart from the weals, Lawrence's white skin was unmarked.[21]

After Paris, Lawrence worked on that summer in London and Oxford facing a mountainous problem—how far against the rapid erosion of Feisal's hopes to reveal his personal involvement in the generalized cruelty and degradation described in his first chapter. Home before the end of August (a dead month in Paris then as now), he was later remembered by his mother sitting motionless in evident dejection from breakfast to luncheon. On 1 September he officially became a civilian and as a civilian wrote an unposted letter to Britain's prime minister, Lloyd George (thanking him for not betraying the Arabs), just days before that politician agreed, on 13 September, that British troops would leave Syria, so opening the way for an eventual French occupation. In a process of slow attrition Lloyd George, with troubles in Ireland, Egypt and Iraq, was to be worn down by the French. Already, on 2 July, Balfour had come out for a policy of 'mandates': modish new name for imperial rule over unconsulted peoples. Feisal returned to London where Curzon saw the problem as basically financial: to keep down Egypt, Iraq and Palestine, and fight France as well, would unbearably tax Britain's limited resources. Lawrence coined a phrase: 'My own ambition is that the Arabs should be our first brown dominion,'[22] while Yale (the American who had got into Damascus before him) found, on 30 September, Rustum Haidar, Feisal's secretary, 'possessed with a violent desire to throw bombs at Lloyd George and other British imperialists.'[23] On 18 October Lloyd George made his last rearguard speech for the Arabs. It was thereafter silence. The British withdrew from Damascus on 26 November 1919, and Feisal was out of Syria, a refugee in Palestine, by the following August. In November Lawrence (now a world figure, thanks to Lowell Thomas's lectures, several of which he attended in the dark) was awarded a Fellowship at All Souls, Oxford. It would bring him £200 per annum for the first three years and £50 per annum for the following four. It was intended to provide him with support while he wrote his book on the Arabian War.

These rapidly changing and contrasting events come as prelude to the letter he posted to Doughty from Oxford on 25 November 1919. Eleven months earlier he had told Doughty of his plans to write a book. Now he wrote: 'I have lost the MSS of my own adventures in Arabia: it was stolen from me in the train.'[24]

If Lawrence's first thirty years had given no cause to doubt his truthfulness, and if he had been writing about the French revolution (the subject leaps to mind, since Carlyle's loss of his manuscript resembles Lawrence's), we might take this story as it stands. We would explain later variants in detail as the tricks played by memory. We might even believe that in less than three months, by Herculean labour in Sir Herbert Baker's Westminster attic, he then so exactly recreated the whole vast thing (except for the introduction and two chapters which were not for some reason in the briefcase) that Alan Dawnay, who read the same chapter in the two handwritten versions, found no comma changed. Having swallowed so much, we would not strain at the lack of motive for the theft; the non-reappearance of a manuscript of great commercial value (once *Seven Pillars of Wisdom* had become the decade's most talked about, and least available, book)* would hardly puzzle us.

But the story, in the context of Lawrence's character, seems a smoke-screen behind which he could wrestle with the problem of whether he wished others besides Hogarth, Meinertzhagen and Dawnay to see his book. Problematic material involved separate subjects. Lawrence wrote to Doughty on the eve of the British withdrawal from Damascus. Feisal in November 1919, neither triumphant nor defeated, occupied a limbo highly awkward for an epic in which his discovery by Lawrence and subsequent victories were a central theme. Further, the weight of self-revelation, not only in the first chapter and the Deraa incident but throughout the work, made Lawrence understandably apprehensive as to the effect this would have on his reputation. His desire to bare his wounds was balanced by a desire to hide them. What is surprising and admirable is that despite his puritan upbringing and public idolization he steeled himself to preserve and later publish what he saw as the truth about himself. Doughty, at the time 'greatly concerned & grieved, to hear of the unhappy loss of the MS of your warlike adventures in Arabia',[26] was to be among those most deeply perturbed when he read what Lawrence had 'rewritten'—or, more probably, retained.

* One feeble attempt to puff life into the legend seems to have been made, possibly at Lawrence's instigation. About 1930 a man of indeterminate social class, 'neither a gentleman nor an underling,' called at the bookshop in London run by the Hon. Edward Gathorne Hardy with a partner. The man offered to sell them the original, or 'Reading', manuscript of *Seven Pillars of Wisdom*. Lawrence, at this time serving in England, was known to Mr. Gathorne Hardy's partner, who informed him of the incident. Lawrence arrived at the bookshop and asked the partners to make an appointment with the man and then hold him. The man did not reappear.[25]

22

STANDING ON the fire-fender to increase his height, Lawrence began, early in 1920, to welcome non-military, or ex-military, Oxonians to his dark, oak-panelled rooms at All Souls. Robert Graves, a poet seven years his junior, was then an undergraduate. Through Graves he met Siegfried Sassoon and Edmund Blunden; then the successive Poets Laureate, Robert Bridges and John Masefield, and later, Thomas Hardy. Post-war painting also interested him. At a London Exhibition by Eric Kennington he bought two portraits of soldiers and left his All Souls address. Kennington took the Oxford train and was met at the station by 'a small grinning, hatless kid'—the two men were the same age—'bothered by a lot of untidy hair falling over his eyes.' After an exchange of compliments, Lawrence told the artist that he had written a book, 'a poor thing without illustrations to help it through.'[1] Lawrence was to sit for Kennington, and, with a patience that impressed them, for William Rothenstein and Augustus John, as well. More than vanity was involved. He hoped, he told Graves, that their brushes or chisels could uncover a personality which puzzled its owner as much as anyone. Also, the company of far-from-puritan poets and painters must have helped decide him to preserve the piles of foolscap Graves had noticed on his table.

When, five years later, Graves undertook to portray him in words (*Lawrence and the Arabs* was to be published in 1927), Lawrence told him he had written seven out of the ten books of the first draft of *Seven Pillars of Wisdom* between February and June 1919. This hardly fits with the simultaneous claim that he had written 'the present introduction* in six hours in the Handley Page aeroplane on his way from Paris to collect his belongings in Cairo.' (As we have seen, the flight had left France in May, not June.) He told Graves that these seven books, along with an eighth written in London, had been stolen from him 'about Christmas 1919 while changing trains at Reading. Only the introduction and the drafts of two books remained.' The credulous Graves also retailed the story that 'in less than three months he rewrote a quarter of a million words from memory. He did it in long sittings and probably set a

* Chapter 1 in current edition.

world literary record by writing Book V in twenty-four hours between sunrise and sunrise without a pause. Book V was about 34,000 words in length!'[2]

For once, what he told an army officer, Liddell Hart, makes better sense: that he had barely sketched the outline when his need for diaries and papers drove him to Cairo.[3] This fits with Meinertzhagen's record—that he was speaking of the book in April and had something to show by July. In the Liddell Hart version, after the 'theft', Lawrence 'joyously' tells Hogarth: 'I've lost the damned thing.'[4] Whatever the minor contradictions, Lawrence worked on his original (or if we believe the Reading story, rewritten) version from 1920 to 1922, in the midst of changes in the Middle East and his own position. He had this handwritten version set in print at the offices of the *Oxford Times* in the first part of 1922; eight copies were made, of which five certainly survive. With the flair he had shown when seeking patrons in the world of power, Lawrence then chose his editors: Edward Garnett, author and critic; E. M. Forster, whose *Passage to India* was shortly to appear; and most influential, the playwright George Bernard Shaw. (An approach to Kipling was less fruitful. 'I may as well warn you,' Kipling replied, 'that, if you are a pro-Yid, and think that the present cheap Hell in Palestine is "statesmanship", I shall most likely turn the whole thing back on your hands.'[5]) The non-professional Charlotte Shaw, who encouraged him to print things her husband might have removed, was perhaps his greatest benefactor. But whatever his debts to Garnett, Forster and the Shaws, the final version of *Seven Pillars of Wisdom* belongs, like all works edited with their authors' consent, to its author—Lawrence.

No twentieth-century writer has set out with higher ambitions. As well read as James Joyce, a good deal better read than his namesake D. H. Lawrence, he sought to produce, at whatever cost in hunger, thirst, exhaustion and self-exposure, a masterpiece in the western tradition. He was no *faux naif* or subliterate genius. His literary perspective went back to Homer and Virgil, of whom there are significant echoes in his pages. Along with the *Iliad*'s acceptance of killing as a human activity, Homer's use of repeated epithets suited the authoritarian streak in Lawrence, with his tendency to fix men in uncomplex stereotypes. Although he later earned a considerable sum from translating the *Odyssey*, its echoes are in reverse: for the sea the desert, for an Ithaca with Penelope and waiting hound, a Damascus empty of Sharif Ali and Dahoum. Lawrence, as post-Christian, is closer to the immediately pre-Christian spirit of the 'maidenly' and Celtic Virgil. The *Aeneid*'s structure—the wanderings of a remnant from Troy who eventually establish a new state in Italy—has affinities with Lawrence's ten-book recital of how Arabs, awaking from centuries of neglect, embark on a journey whose end is summed up in the title of Book X: *The House is Perfected.* Lawrence's portrayal of Feisal is as reverent (and lifeless) as the pious Aeneas of Virgil and the mood in which Lawrence subtitled his epic 'A Triumph' is close to Virgil's distinctive blend of imperial confidence and Celtic pessimism. Ostensibly hymning the birth of Rome and, by implication, the genius of Augustus, Virgil gives his last line to the defeated Turnus, whose soul flees *indignata sub umbras*. Lawrence concludes with the author-hero's bitter departure from Damascus.

Lawrence made two lists of modern masterpieces which he admired and alongside which he hoped his book would stand.[6] *Moby Dick* and *The Brothers Karamazov* occur in both lists. *Moby Dick*, accessible to Lawrence in his own language, presents the world as the domain of the hero. Captain Ahab, in fighting the white whale, is Faustus fighting God or western man denying Him. But the most immediate link with Herman Melville is simple, earthy and relevant to the loss, or suppression, of the first draft of Lawrence's book. Melville introduces his alter ego—'Ishmael'—by throwing him, a white Anglo-Saxon male, into the same bed with Queequeg, a dusky, tattooed, Polynesian pagan. Matrimonial turns of phrase—'You had almost thought I had been his wife' . . . and 'his bridegroom clasp' . . . emphasize the surprise.

Lawrence introduces his most startling paragraph even sooner: on page two of the introductory chapter in the version which he first passed for restricted publication and which is now standard:

> The Arab was by nature continent; and the use of universal marriage had nearly abolished irregular courses in his tribes. The public women of the rare settlements we encountered in our months of wandering would have been nothing to our numbers, even had their raddled meat been palatable to a man of healthy parts. In horror of such sordid commerce our youths began indifferently to slake one another's few needs in their own clean bodies—a cold convenience that, by comparison, seemed sexless and even pure. Later, some began to justify this sterile process, and swore that friends quivering together in the yielding sand with intimate hot limbs in supreme embrace, found there hidden in the darkness a sensual co-efficient of the mental passion which was welding our souls and spirits in one flaming effort. Several, thirsting to punish appetites they could not wholly prevent, took a savage pride in degrading the body, and offered themselves fiercely in any habit which promised physical pain or filth.[7]

The generalized statement comes as strangely in the introduction to the history of a military campaign as Ishmael's bedding down at the start of a whaling expedition. But while Melville uses the incident to insinuate a lyrical and, in its original sense, philadelphian note into the conflict between Ahab and Moby Dick, Lawrence is merely expanding the sadic mood of his first page. (He uses *sadic*, a recently minted word, in the same short chapter.) While Ishmael is a projection of Melville, who proclaims himself a participant, Lawrence seems merely to survey these embraces and merely to overhear their justification as 'sexless and pure', thus striking a note which by contrast to Melville's is Olympian and cold. And because his generalized statement about desert amours and the particular instance of them which he later includes are unconvincing, the note is also false.

In Arab cities and towns (as in prisons, armies and boarding schools elsewhere) the separation of men from women has doubtless encouraged the temperamentally bisexual to find relief among themselves. But in the desert, where Arab life is harshest and the moral code sternest, travellers, with the exception of Lawrence, have noted an extreme disapproval of relationships involving males in the feminine role. Explicit as they first seem, Lawrence's sentences leave unclear the important question of who precisely 'our youths' are supposed to be: Auda's Huweitat tribesmen on the march to Akaba? Lawrence's tulip-like bodyguard? or the British soldiers whose white bodies Lawrence remarked as they bathed in one of the oasis pools? Hussein's three eldest sons were already married. Catlike, silent in the starlit night, some bedouin may conceivably have slept with others; they will have done so furtively, obeying the precept that a sin concealed is a sin halved. What is inconceivable is that they should have confided to a Christian stranger activities whose expression was covered by the fierce, hot word of '*aib* or shame. It is equally inconceivable that they will have flaunted such activities before their comrades or have rationalized them in argument. As to the urge to filth: the more extreme perversions involving excreta are found in societies with the cleanest bathrooms.

Brought up in the Oxford classical tradition, a friend of 'Uranian' writers, a devoted reader of the Greek Anthology with its many pederastic poets, Lawrence is imposing the mores of the Theban Band on a group of Arabs. The love idyll between 'Daud' and 'Farraj' similarly reflects the influence of the classical epics.* Once again Lawrence is closer to Virgil than to Homer. The love between the sulky Achilles and the older Patroclus plays a functional role in the *Iliad.* The death of Patroclus rouses Achilles from his anti-Greek inertia. Forgetting his pique over his expropriated courtesan, Briseis, he takes part in the fighting which leads directly to the sack of Troy. The death of Virgil's Nisus and Euryalus, saluted with the lines beginning *Fortunati ambo!* . . . is decorative rather than functional. Lawrence's idyll, playing even less of a role

* From what Lawrence told Graves, the names were invented.[8]

in the motivation of the hero or heroes, and false to the facts of desert life, tells more of the author than of Arabia.

The idyll begins in May 1917 when Lawrence is *en route* for Akaba. Lawrence, dreaming, is woken by a youthful voice: it belongs to 'an anxious Ageyli, a stranger, Daud, squatting by me. His friend Farraj had burned their tent in a frolic, and Saad, captain of Sharraf's Ageyl, was going to beat him in punishment.' Lawrence, despite his later boast that 'Akaba had been taken on my plan by my effort,' apparently lacked the authority to have Farraj reprieved. All Saad would concede for Lawrence's sake 'was to let Daud share the ordained sentence. Daud leaped at the chance, kissing my hand and Saad's, and ran off up the valley; while Saad, laughing, told me stories of the famous pair. They were an instance of the eastern boy and boy affection which the segregation of women made inevitable. Such friendships often led to manly loves of a depth and force beyond our flesh-steeped conceit. When innocent they were hot and unashamed. If sexuality entered, they passed into a give and take, unspiritual relation, like marriage.' Next day, 'two bent figures, with pain in their eyes, but crooked smiles upon their lips, hobbled up and saluted. These were Daud the hasty and his love-fellow, Farraj; a beautiful, soft-framed, girlish creature, with innocent, smooth face and swimming eyes.' Lawrence at first refuses their entreaty to enter his service. Daud, the sterner, refuses to beg, but Farraj 'went over to Nasir and knelt in appeal, all the woman of him evident in his longing.' Lawrence takes them on 'mainly because they looked so young and clean.'[9]

What Lawrence confided, or wrote, about this impossibly overt relationship between two young braves has a tell-tale fluidity of detail. Lowell Thomas: 'Intimate friendships sprang up among Lawrence's personal Followers. Ferraj and Daoud . . . were inseparable pals, and when Daoud died of fever at Akaba [*sic*] during the latter part of the campaign, Ferraj felt so miserable and lonely that he committed suicide by dashing headlong into the Turkish lines on his camel during an engagement.'[10]

This information must derive from one of Lowell Thomas's breakfasts with Lawrence in London just after the war: their meeting in Arabia had taken place well before 'the latter part of the campaign.' It is clear that by 1919 Lawrence had not yet decided on some of the details in his romance, though he had already selected the parties' names. In *Seven Pillars of Wisdom* Daud dies at the Azrak controlled by Sharif Ali; so far from committing suicide, the wounded Farraj dies, in April 1918, Lawrence's bullet sparing him a fate worse then death:

> I knelt down beside him, holding my pistol near the ground by his head, so that he should not see my purpose; but he must have guessed

it, for he opened his eyes, and clutched me with his harsh, scaly hand, the tiny hand of these unripe Nejd fellows. I waited a moment, and he said, 'Daud will be angry with you,' the old smile coming back so strangely to this grey shrinking face. I replied, 'Salute him from me.' He returned the formal answer, 'God will give you peace,' and at last wearily closed his eyes.[11]

When Lawrence sanctioned the publication of a compressed, impersonal version of *Seven Pillars of Wisdom* (he refused to release the complete book to the general public in his lifetime), he retained the fact that Farraj and Daud were frolicsome pals, but the 'death of Farraj is taken out, because it looked awkward, hanging in the air,' he told Edward Garnett, 'where you had kept it.'[12] Garnett replied: 'At present I feel sulky at your suppression of the *best* personal passages. "*I gave you up* Deraa," I say reproachfully, like a sobbing woman! & now you take Farraj's death from me.'[13] Garnett went on: 'I am not sure that you can delete Farraj. You don't seem to see that you are only thinking of *yourself* & preserving intact & secret those moments. What a world it would be if all the great writers had suddenly shied off "wearing their hearts upon their sleeves." ' Garnett was to fret still more, Lawrence to defend still more, when *Revolt in the Desert* (the expurgated abridgement) had appeared. Lawrence then wrote: 'You will not realize the difference between a real book (*The S.P.* being as truthful as I could make it) and an edition for general consumption, put out just to make money, and to stop the mouths of those who were crying for word from me.'[14]

By the arresting word *truthful* Lawrence obviously meant something different and perhaps more important than *historically accurate*. He was also right. *Revolt in the Desert*, as a result of its bowdlerization, is neither a work of literary significance nor historical interest. Lawrence was correct in seeing it as a pot-boiler, right in suspending its sales once they had paid the debts he had incurred in producing and illustrating an expensive, limited edition of the 'real' book. No one interested in the Arab campaign would bother to consult the pot-boiler; those interested in Lawrence will never discard *Seven Pillars of Wisdom*; if only for its effect on his contemporaries it will remain on the library shelves.

After a legible version of his 'real' book existed, in August 1922, Lawrence was to tell Garnett that he had 'collected a shelf of titanic works, those distinguished by greatness of spirit, *Karamazov*, *Zarathustra* and *Moby Dick*. Well, my ambition was to make a fourth.'[15]* Since two of the three are novels, and in the third, Nietzsche attributes his own, nineteenth-century ideas to the historical Zarathustra, the level of truth is plainly that of imaginative literature, not official history.

* A similar list, this time written to E. M. Forster, contained '*Leaves of Grass, War & Peace, The Brothers Karamazoff* [*sic*], *Moby Dick*, Rabelais, *Don Quixote*.'[16]

But if *Seven Pillars of Wisdom* shares elements with two great novels, it does not manifest the usual attributes of successful fiction: character is not delineated in incident and dialogue; the story, as even his greatest admirers have conceded, lacks narrative movement. 'His book was not a great narrative,' André Malraux has written. 'What sort of existence did these people lead?' he asks, qualifying Lawrence's portrayal of the Arabs as scarcely going 'beyond the picturesque, that of the English beyond a crude sketch. What reader, the book closed, "knows" Joyce, Young, Clayton? The most characterized person, Feisal, is he not a sort of official portrait?'[17]

In *Seven Pillars of Wisdom* Lawrence's self-baffling personality plays the role which the philosophy of the Superman plays in Nietzsche's *Zarathustra* or the struggle between man and the absolute in *Moby Dick.** 'Every priest,' once more to quote Malraux, 'knows that confession in the abstract costs little.' Hence the concrete questions from behind the grille: with whom? how many times? in what manner? Yet 'Lawrence's nature was opposed to confession both by the violence of his pride and by that of his modesty.'[19]

To surmount the problem, Lawrence adopts the technique which Perseus used when facing the Medusa. The Greek hero confronted the petrifying monster by looking at her, indirectly, in the mirror of his shield. Lawrence invents myths in whose polished steel he, too, can face the unfaceable. The myths become oblique confessions. And like confessions they look first to the past and then to the future. In the myth of Daud and Farraj he looks back to his own idyllic days in Carchemish and Lebanon with Dahoum; he also looks forward, through the prism of Deraa, to his post-war self. The name Daud was not chosen without care. While having the same initial and vowels as Dahoum, it is also the Arabic for David, a name which gains significance when we read the passage in which Lawrence describes his final parting from Sharif Ali. The parting comes at the end of the period in which Lawrence sets the myth of Deraa. The exchange of clothing is also significant. It repeats, on a different social level, his pre-war game of dressing up as Dahoum.

> He and I took affectionate leave of one another. Ali gave me half his wardrobe: shirts, head-cloths, belts, tunics. I gave him an equivalent half of mine, and we kissed like David and Jonathan, each wearing the other's clothes. Afterwards, with Rahail only, on my two best camels, I struck away southward.[20]

The Deraa incident (omitted along with the idyll from *Revolt in the*

* One bond between Nietzsche and Lawrence is the shared wish to supersede humanity. In a letter to Edward Garnett of 23 October 1922, Lawrence wrote of how few men 'had honestly tried to be greater than mankind.'[18]

Desert) is structurally and emotionally the pivotal incident in the book. Thinking of the *Seven Pillars* as a five-act tragedy, Lawrence told Garnett: 'the bang comes in the third act, properly.'[21] His 'disclosure' to Meinertzhagen of April 1919 was to be amplified to Charlotte Shaw five years later:

> About that night. I shouldn't tell you, because decent men don't talk about such things. I wanted to put it plain in the book, & wrestled for days with my self-respect . . . which wouldn't, hasn't let me. For fear of being hurt, or rather, to earn five minutes' respite from a pain which drove me mad, I gave away the only possession we are born into the world with—our bodily integrity. It's an unforgivable matter, an irrecoverable position: and it's that which has made me forswear decent living, & the exercise of my not-contemptible wits & talents.
>
> You may call this morbid: but think of the offence, and the intensity of my brooding over it for these years. It will hang about me while I live, & afterwards if our personality survives. Consider wandering among the decent ghosts hereafter, crying 'Unclean, unclean!'[22]

Beyond its function in his epic, the Deraa incident is also the most important of Lawrence's myths; in its shield-light he faced the crucial truths about himself. His movements (known at the time to Wingate and Hogarth and recorded in his own skeleton diary and letters) rule out this pointless sortie from Azrak. The myth further conflicts (as has been established by the Arab historian Suleiman Mousa and the authors of *The Secret Lives of Lawrence of Arabia*) with what is known of the Bey of Deraa, as much a historical personage on the Ottoman side as Clayton on the Allied.

The story's internal lack of coherence is a yet more decisive factor for rejecting it as true in the sense of historically accurate.

What is supposed to have happened?

According to the version he had printed at the *Oxford Times*, instead of resting himself and his camels at Azrak for ten days, Lawrence goes off on a reconnaissance mission to the key railway junction between the Hejaz Railway and the spur into Palestine. While he is surveying the aerodrome, a Turkish N.C.O. seizes Lawrence but ignores his Arab companion: he is marched into a compound before a 'fleshy Turkish officer, one leg tucked under him': Lawrence gives his name as Ahmed Ibn Bagr [besides echoing an English synonym for sodomite, the name in Arabic can have connections with the verb to eviscerate] and claims to be a Circassian from Kuneitra [the capital of modern Syria's Jolan province] and thus exempt from military service: [Lawrence had startled Sharif Abdullah by his knowledge of Turkish regiments; he must have known that military service had been obligatory for all Ottoman subjects, whatever their race or religion, since the Young Turk Revolution.] He is led to a guard-room, consoled by Turkish soldiers, fed their food, and told he may be released next day if he fulfils the Bey's pleasures [in this first version Lawrence simply names the governor as Hajjim, or 'my Hajji', a term of respect]; is, after nightfall, conducted across the railway to a somewhat remote, detached and guarded house: is conducted upstairs to the Bey's bedroom: the Bey, who is in bed, fondles Lawrence, 'saying how white and clean I was' [Lawrence had ridden for weeks without a proper bath; was covered with boils and saddle sores]; promises military favours [apparently without checking his papers or military status]; flies into a rage when Lawrence resists: has him stripped: gapes at the bullet-wounds [which had vanished when Meinertzhagen saw him undressed less than eighteen months later]; tries again: gets Lawrence's knee in his groin: shouts for the corporal: has Lawrence pinioned while he slippers his face, bites his neck, kisses, has bayonet-fun; states he knows who Lawrence is; seems not to mean what this implies: [or if he does, sacrifices the chance of a huge reward]; hands the still obdurate Lawrence over to the soldiers: they take him outside, stretch him on the guard-bench [apparently kept outside the Bey's bedroom]; hold him down till the corporal returns with a Circassian riding whip [which Lawrence somehow observes in every detail from his disadvantageous position]; 'a thong of supple black hide, rounded, and tapering from the thickness of a thumb at the grip (which was wrapped in silver) down to a hard point finer than a pencil.'

Four paragraphs are now devoted to the subsequent whipping. Again, despite being held so that his eyes are on the ground (two soldiers grasp his ankles, another two hold his wrists over his head) he can apparently see the area of the flagellation, his back, where 'at the instant of each stroke a hard white mark like a railway, darkening slowly into crimson, leaped over my skin, and a bead of blood swelled up wherever the ridges crossed.' His use of language is revealing: 'they [the blows] hurt more horribly than I had *dreamed of* . . . [this the author's emphasis.]

In the second paragraph he forgets to count the blows after the first twenty.

The third paragraph suggests that the 'men'—squabbling over whose turn would be next, resting, twisting Lawrence's head round to observe their handiwork, easing themselves, playing with him a little—are enjoying the performance. In a supreme display of his command of the language, Lawrence shrieks only in (apparently perfect) Arabic [a high percentage of the Ottoman soldiers in Syria were Arabic speakers].

The fourth paragraph has him lying on the floor 'panting for breath but vaguely comfortable.'

The paragraph that follows is important. The corporal kicks him with his nailed boot, turning 'yellow and lacerated' his whole left side. 'I remembered smiling idly at him, for a delicious warmth, probably sexual, was swelling through me; and then he flung up his arm and hacked with the full length of his whip into my groin.' One soldier giggles; another shows pity. Lawrence is then taken back to the Bey who, disgusted by the results of what one is meant to assume is a normal Deraa evening, rejects him. 'So the crestfallen corporal, as the youngest and best looking on the guard [and as we have seen, the toughest and most sadistic] had to stay behind while the others carried me down the narrow stairs and out into the street.' He is put in a lean-to shed on a pile of quilts; his knife [can it be the gold Sharifian dagger?] is apparently returned to him: an Armenian dresser tends his wounds: a soldier whispers 'in a Druse accent' [whatever that may be, it reveals him as an Arab] 'that the door into the next room was not locked.' Lawrence [with most of his readers] wonders if 'it was not all a dream': he remembers the 'hospital at Khalfati where something of the same kind had happened to me.' In the next room hangs a convenient 'suit of shoddy clothes.' Next morning Lawrence puts them on and in escaping stumbles on a 'hidden approach to Deraa for our future raiding party.' [Deraa was no unmapped mystery town such as Philby looked for in Arabia proper. A railway junction, it appeared in detail on British maps. Local Arabs, who knew every inch of the district, were to support the final assault on Deraa eleven months later. No British officer in the Anglo-Arab forces has mentioned this secret approach.]

For this extraordinary story *Seven Pillars of Wisdom* (in its Oxford and then its edited, published text) remains the only source: along with the supplementary details Lawrence gave to Meinertzhagen, who confided them to his diary, and to Charlotte Shaw, who bequeathed his letters to the British Museum. Had Lawrence so chosen, no one would have known of the myth or been forced to guess what lay behind it.

While the idyll of Daud and Farraj evoked what he described as 'too rich and full a youth', the horror of Deraa looked towards a bleak and penitential future.* Deraa represented the discovery that for him, as for Swinburne before him, pain was the vital ingredient, if not for pleasure, then release. Deraa is not historical in the sense that Allenby's capture of Jerusalem was historical. It embodied an approach to truth which Lawrence shared with such writers as George Borrow, Ford Madox Ford and George Moore. 'Such writers,' David Wright has written, 'take truth as the warp into which a weft of imagination may be woven. The web or embroidery that results is myth, but often an emblematic myth that

* Lawrence told Stirling: 'We should not be happy: and I think I've dodged that sin successfully! The Tank Corps is a hefty penance for too rich and full a youth!'[23]

recreates, makes explicit or at least illuminates some inherent truth or quality that strict fact may sometimes obscure.'[24]

The truth that Lawrence discovered in the War was more than he could totally reveal: only his long concealed post-war actions, his attendance at beating-parties in Chelsea organized by an underworld figure known as Bluebeard, his requests, sporadic but in one case regular, to be birched by soldiers, would uncover a truth as absurd as it was painful. In his predicament, as well as in his fame, Lawrence had a predecessor: the Byron who had dominated the imagination of the Napoleonic generation and whose marriage collapsed in mysterious ruin. Byron's *Don Juan*, like Lawrence's epic, conceals as well as reveals. The scandal in the poet's marriage seems to have been the application to his wife of sexual techniques he had learnt with young men. The legend of incest with his half-sister, as well as *Don Juan*'s portrayal of an obsessive womanizer, help disguise a less acceptable truth. Lawrence disguises the discovery of his physical masochism behind what seems its opposite. Lawrence offsets Deraa—probably the transubstantiation of a genuine experience at Azrak with Sharif Ali—with a plethora of sadic incidents and overtones.[25]

The grisly episode in *Seven Pillars* of Hamed the Moor apparently takes place as early as March 1917, soon after Lawrence first arrayed himself as a Sharif. On the ride to Abdullah's camp Lawrence's companions dispute and an Ageyl is found dead with a bullet through his temples. Hamed the Moor* is then accused of the crime and confesses. 'It must be a formal execution,' Lawrence decides; 'and at last, desperately, I told Hamed that he must die for punishment, and laid the burden of his killing on myself.' What follows has the mesmeric exactitude of fantasy.

> I made him enter a narrow gully of the spur, a dank twilight place overgrown with woods. Its sandy bed had been pitted by trickles of water down the cliffs in the late rain. At the end it shrank to a crack a few inches wide. The walls were vertical. I stood in the entrance and gave him a few moments' delay which he spent crying on the ground. Then I made him rise and shot him through the chest. He fell down on the weeds shrieking, with the blood coming out in spurts over his clothes, and jerked about till he rolled nearly to where I was. I fired again, but was shaking so that I only broke his wrist. He went on calling out, less loudly, now lying on his back with his feet towards me, and I leant forward and shot him for the last time in the thick of

* It is worth observing how Lawrence, a great generalizer, builds his myths round stereotypes. Hamed is a Moor, or North African—perhaps because Abdel Kader was one. The degenerate of Deraa is a Turk; in his post-war versions of what had happened in the latter stages of his student walk the culprits change from Kurds or Arabs to Turks.

his neck under the jaw. His body shivered a little, and I called the Ageyl; who buried him in the gully where he was.[26]

Although serving in Arabia, Lawrence was still bound by King's Regulations. These would have required him to have the man put under arrest until he could be accused, defended and sentenced: presumably, in this case, by officers in Abdullah's army. If he was prepared to forget such niceties, it is inconceivable that Muslims would forget that he was a Christian and would accept him as executioner in the Holy Hejaz. But the story (recalling the opus of Ernest Hemingway) serves to establish Lawrence as a man: i.e. a being who can kill.

If *Seven Pillars of Wisdom* has the prime interest of revealing Lawrence through myth, its deliberate, conscious side must not be overlooked. In two respects Lawrence strives to keep up with his own legend and with the changing realities of the post-war world. Apart from the claim to have singly planned and executed the capture of Akaba, he replenishes his reputation as a military genius. Shortly after the execution of Hamed the Moor, he lies ill with 'the shame' of dysentery in Abdullah's camp. He prefaces a chapter of military theorizing (whose brilliance and coincidence with Liddell Hart's own ideas captivated that expert) with the modest statement: 'In military theory I was tolerably read, my Oxford curiosity having taken me past Napoleon to Clausewitz and his school, to Caemmerer and Moltke, and the recent Frenchmen. They had all seemed to be one-sided; and after looking at Jomini and Willisen, I had found broader principles in Saxe and Guibert and the eighteenth century.'[27] There is good reason, as we have seen, to believe that Lawrence derived his theory of guerilla war from the ideas of Aziz al-Masri, who lived to conspire with Anwar al-Sadat in the Second World War and to know the Nasser of the Egyptian Revolution.

Politically, Lawrence introduces the theme of the betrayal of the Arabs. His guilt over this was stimulated by three factors. We have seen that Hogarth, who joined him at the Paris Conference, had become progressively disillusioned. Still in Cairo on 14 February 1919, Hogarth had written: 'As to the future of the lands and peoples in my special charge all is dark!'[28] Not only was Hogarth's general influence on Lawrence profound; he more than anyone urged him to complete his book. The second factor was the fate of Feisal. By the time Lawrence finished his revised draft, Feisal was on the verge of expulsion from Damascus. The third factor was a mood of general disenchantment to which Lawrence was litmus-reactive. Already evident in the second wave of wartime poets such as Wilfred Owen and Siegfried Sassoon, it was to find prose expression in *All Quiet on the Western Front* and Richard Aldington's *Death of a Hero*.

To forge his myths Lawrence devised a prose style which has probably alienated as many readers as the mysterious dedication to *Seven Pillars of Wisdom* has intrigued. That it was not natural to him is shown by the letters and articles which he published about the Middle East in the British press.*

When the book existed only in the cumbrous print of the *Oxford Times*, Bernard Shaw discussed the literary influences on it with his fellow-Fabian, Sidney Webb. The William Morris who had been the aesthetic idol of Lawrence's youth was too much of the north to have given a model for this epic of the east. With his dislike for latinate words Morris would have condemned such Lawrentian passages as '. . . to Wadi Agida, wherein the Egyptians were taking counsel pavidly with one another.'[29] While Webb discerned Borrow's influence, Shaw was so certain that the influence was Doughty that he took the trouble of reading *Arabia Deserta* the better to appreciate what Lawrence had written. But Shaw was in part misled by Lawrence's admiration for Doughty as a writer and his practical efforts on the old man's behalf. (Lawrence went to commendable lengths to get *Arabia Deserta* reissued and its author awarded a government pension.) There are of course affinities in the background to both works and to a lesser extent in their chief characters: Doughty disguised as the Christian-Arab physician, 'Khalil', and Lawrence as himself. Also, Doughty shared Lawrence's interest in pain, if not his attitude to it. 'Khalil' first puts himself at risk, the third night of the pilgrimage caravan, 'when curiosity led him to the aga's tent to see execution going forward on the person of an Arab thief. Compassion drew from him a hakim's [physician's] protest against further flogging.'[30] Like Lawrence, Doughty subtly changed, in retrospect, his point of view. His contemporary journals reflect none of the prejudice against the pilgrims and their faith evident in the bitter narrative he subsequently published. But Doughty's influence did not lie in his style, whose distinctive tedium, the transliteration of Arabic terms for which English equivalents existed, Lawrence avoided. It lay in Lawrence's acceptance that a carefully wrought style was a necessity. When he had asked Doughty what had prompted him to visit Arabia, the old man gave a reply which has become famous: 'to redeem the English language from the slough into which it had fallen since the time of Spenser.'[31] Lawrence had taken a complete Spenser with him to Carchemish; Malory's *Morte d'Arthur* had accompanied him into the desert.

The influence he missed, not the influences he accepted, constituted Lawrence's misfortune. At a time when he could have been affected by

* These have been conveniently collected and edited by Stanley and Rodelle Weintraub in *Evolution of a Revolt, Early Postwar Writings of T. E. Lawrence*, Pennsylvania State University Press, 1968.

Ezra Pound—whom his brother Will had invited to address an Oxford literary society—Lawrence was still too conformist to see the value of the American's innovatory demands. When Pound did visit Lawrence in his rooms at All Souls, it was too late. *Seven Pillars of Wisdom* had already been written in a style echoing the Butcher and Lang translations of Homer and heavily influenced by the Georgian poets whom Pound demolished.

Georgian poetry, in its now forgotten day linked with Sir John Squire and his friend Eddie Marsh,* represented the anaemic old age of Victorian vigour. How disastrously Lawrence was committed to its values is shown in the handwritten anthology of poems,† 'in a minor key', or 'my box of moral éclairs', which he presented to Charlotte Shaw in 1927. The first half of what finally numbered 112 poems were written down during the four years when he was composing and revising *Seven Pillars of Wisdom.* Apart from poems by such friends as Sassoon and Hardy, Lawrence selected the flowery, the weakly sad. He copied three complete poems by Swinburne, the poet in one respect so close to him. They derive from *Songs Before Sunrise*, composed after the poet had withdrawn to Putney, not from the period of Swinburne's revolutionary and self-revelatory strength.‡

The brutality of Lawrence's material helped to offset the 'faintly Ninetyish-plus-Edwardian flavour' which Cecil Day Lewis, otherwise an admirer, found in his poetic taste.[32] 'The poet's secret', Graves complains, 'Lawrence envisaged as a technical mastery of words rather than as a particular mode of living and thinking.'[33] Yet Lawrence's way of living and thinking gives *Seven Pillars of Wisdom* much of its interest, whether we account him 'one of the greatest beings alive in our time,'§ 'a disgusting little thing',¶ or simply a fascinating human puzzle. If Pound's correcting pencil had deflected him from archaizing diction and the over-use of adjectives, it would surely have been as helpful to him as it was to Eliot and Hemingway. The narrative would have moved

* Edward Howard Marsh, 1872–1953, Private Secretary to Winston Churchill, 1917–1922 and again 1924–9.

† The anthology was published and edited under the title of *Minorities* by J. M. Wilson in 1971.

‡ *The Oblation, The Pilgrims* and *Super Flumina Babylonis.* He also included the Chorus from *Atalanta in Calydon* over two of whose blasphemous lines—*Smiter without sword, and scourger without rod; The supreme evil, God!*—Christina Rossetti had pasted white paper.

§ Winston Churchill, *T. E. Lawrence by His Friends*, p. 202.

¶ Lawrence Durrell to Alan G. Thomas on reading *Seven Pillars of Wisdom*, Corfu, 1935. Durrell, who was to create his own highly wrought style for a work set in the Middle East, found Lawrence's book 'great', but added: 'what a disgusting little thing he was. His own personality decreased as the saga grew. What a little neuter, ripping and goring his body because he loathed it so . . . a sort of nasty child.' Lawrence Durrell, *Spirit of Place, Letters and Essays on Travel*, ed. Alan G. Thomas, E. P. Dutton, New York, 1969, p. 36.

faster; the reader would have lost the sensation of swimming, for much of the time, through fudge. Too late, Lawrence discovered the merits of post-Spenserian prose. On receipt of Hogarth's life of Doughty he was to write: 'He [Doughty] loved Spenser and Chaucer—with so little love of literature and poetry that he loved them for what they did not have in common with the trunk of greatness in English letters.' But Lawrence wrote this when his career as a creative writer was over.[34]

The dedication to *Seven Pillars of Wisdom* has intrigued even those who have failed to read the book. As published, the poem is in part the work of Graves, who changed many of Lawrence's words and phrases. Since Lawrence told Graves that the poem was a cipher, these alterations were perhaps unwise. Lawrence wrote as follows:

To S.A.

I loved you, so I drew these tides of men into my hands
and wrote my will across the sky in stars
To gain you Freedom, the seven-pillared worthy house,
that your eyes might be shining for me
When I came
Death was my servant on the road, till we were near
and saw you waiting:
When you smiled, and in sorrowful envy he outran me and
took you apart:
Into his quietness
So our love's earnings was your cast off body to be
held one moment
Before earth's soft hands would explore your face and
the blind worms transmute
Your failing substance.
Men prayed me to set my work, the inviolate house,
in memory of you.
But for fit monument I shattered it, unfinished: and now
The little things creep out to patch themselves hovels
in the marred shadow
Of your gift.

The earliest reference to the poem had occurred in a letter to Graves dated only 'Sunday' but evidently written some time early in 1922. The full text of his manuscript book was to be set up between February and July 1922, at the *Oxford Times*. Lawrence (as we shall see later) was earning £100 a month, was considering enlisting in the R.A.F. as an airman, and in secret was initiating sado-masochistic rituals with at least one military youth. He had recently told Graves (the twentieth century's greatest idolater of the feminine principle) that 'he had never been able to fall in love: and the hysterical pursuit of him by women who, after listening to Lowell Thomas's lectures, had fallen in love with his fame had made him avoid the society of women even more than he usually did. As a boy he had never had much to do with women, having had no sisters, only brothers, and the habit had stuck. He said, jokingly, that the only settling down he could contemplate was enlistment in the Army or Air Force, where he would be compelled to eat and sleep normally, and have no time to think.'[35]

The statement was qualified in the new letter which accompanied the poem. 'There was an exception who provided a disproportionate share of the motive for the Arabian adventure, and who after it was over dictated the enclosed as preface to the story of it.

'I turned it out a day ago when preparing for a printer . . . '[36]

The new letter had provocative ambiguities: *dictated* and *turned it out*. Dictated could imply that the 'exception' had suggested the terms of the dedicatory poem, or imposed the need to write it; turned it out could mean 'wrote it roughly' or 'discovered it when turning out a drawer.'

Because this, the earliest known reference to S.A., was confided to a friend whose profession Lawrence admired, at a time when his book was still unprinted, it remains, with Lawrence's undoctored text, the most important key to the cipher. For as soon as a printed text existed and could be read—by Vyvyan Richards, for example—Lawrence began to be evasive. On being pressed for clarification, he told Richards, who in turn told Graves, that S.A. was 'a certain Sheikh Achmed, an Arab with whom Lawrence had a sort of blood-brotherhood before the War; that Sheikh Achmed died of typhus in 1918.'[37]* Graves took the suggestion seriously enough to incorporate it in the draft of a biography. Lawrence corrected him in the margin: 'You have taken me too literally. S.A. still exists: but out of my reach, because I have changed.'[39]

Whatever coherence this initial revision may originally have had began to dissolve *after* the text was published and *after* Lawrence had informed his banker friend, R. V. Buxton, that 'S.A. was a person, now dead, regard for whom lay beneath my labour for the Arabic peoples.'[40] Then, in late June 1927, in last-minute corrections to Graves's biography,

* Lawrence could not have seriously described Dahoum as either *Sheikh* or *Achmed*. Sheikh in Arabic means 'old man', or, by extension, tribal leader or venerable person. Arab schoolboys might call each other Sheikh as English boys call each other 'old man' or French boys 'mon vieux', but the relative status of Lawrence and of Dahoum in the Carchemish days would have made it most unlikely that the Englishman would, even in jest, have endowed the Arab youth with that title. Further, Achmed is a form for Ahmed which Lawrence never used, and since the only evidence for supposing that Dahoum's real name was Saleem Ahmed comes from Gunner Beaumont, whose memory on other matters can be faulted,[38] the hypothesis seems untenable.

he offered a third explanation: 'S.A., the subject of the dedication, is rather an idea than a person.'[41] Six years later he further compounded the confusion, this time by splitting S from A: 'One is a person and one is a place.'[42]

At the end of *Seven Pillars of Wisdom* Lawrence declares that 'the strongest motive throughout had been a personal one, not mentioned here, but present to me, I think, every hour of these two years. Active pains and joys might fling up, like towers, among my days: but, refluent as air, this hidden urge re-formed, to be the persisting element of life, till near the end. It was dead, before we reached Damascus.' When Liddell Hart asked him to elaborate on that powerful urge, his answer was that 'the "personal" motive mentioned first in the concluding bit was the "S.A." of the opening poem. But S.A. "croaked" in 1918.'[43] And still later, those significant initials were given yet another interpretation—the sixth: 'S. and A. were two different things, "S" a village in Syria, or property in it, and "A" personal.'[44]*

Out of that jumble of contradictory 'clarifications', one clear fact does emerge. The author of *Seven Pillars of Wisdom* was consistent for more than a decade in attempting to prevent any positive identification of the subject of his dedication. And, in that connection, the actual form of the dedicatory poem—Lawrence's only attempt to practise the art he preferred to all others†—is in itself significant.

Lawrence had spent much of his time with the Arabs on camel-back. Philby, on his much longer travels in Arabia proper, had noted how his camel-companions, even when thirsty or hungry, kept up a constant recitation of poetry, good or banal. Lawrence must have witnessed this addiction. One of the grandest of classical Arabic metres was supposedly modelled on the camel's loping stride, the beat of the final rhyming measures echoing the rhythm of the lurching foot. Thus a poem was an appropriate introduction to a book on an Arab theme, and the phrases *When I came . . . Into his quietness . . . Your failing substance . . .* (and, less successfully) *Of your gift* recall the final lurch of the Arabic metre. (Still highly conscious of typography, as he had been in the days when he looked to a future of making 'beautiful books', Lawrence introduced each phrase with a capital letter.)

The poem certainly contains the ambiguities common to Arabic poetry, and two occur in the first three words: *I loved you.* In everyday English, *I loved you* would mean, 'I used to love you', or 'I loved you over a period of time'; but it may also give the sense of the Arabic perfect

* In a letter in the Bodleian addressed to a Foreign Office official Lawrence listed four motives which had activated him in the 'Arab affair': personal; patriotic; intellectual curiosity; ambition.[45]

† The lines which Lawrence sent to Robert Graves in 1924 or 1925[46] were facetious and not considered by either of them to be poetry.

ḥibbaytek, which would mean, 'I suddenly loved you', or 'I fell for you'. For the sense of 'I loved you over a period of time' an Arab would probably use *kuntu aḥibbek. You* is similarly ambiguous in English, but not in Arabic, where there are separate forms for you singular, you dual and you plural.* Thus Lawrence's three opening words could either refer to someone he had loved over a period of time and for whose sake he had drawn tides of men into his hands; or they could refer to someone with whom he had suddenly fallen in love and for whom he then set out to win Freedom; or conceivably, they could refer to more than one person, or even to things.

Similarly, the 'personal urge' he acknowledges at the end of *Seven Pillars of Wisdom* could refer to a motive that Lawrence had carried with him into the two years, or something that he suddenly discovered and which lasted with him throughout the two years. In deciding which, the term *regard*, which he used to Buxton, should be kept in mind; so should a passage about his motive which he wrote to Graves in 1927: 'The very accident that normally I am empty of motive, helped make the rare motive, when it finally came, overpowering.'[47]

If S.A. was Dahoum, it is strange that Lawrence limits the sovereignty of the 'personal urge' to two years: he could more plausibly have felt the urge after leaving Carchemish, after Turkey's entry into the war, or after the outbreak of the Arab Revolt: in the first case, more than four years, in the second case, four years almost exactly, in the third case, two and a half years would have been involved. If, on the other hand, S.A. was not Dahoum, it could only signify someone whom Lawrence had met at the start of his involvement with bedouin Arabia and who had then dominated his emotions in the two years that followed. His evasive mention of 'Sheikh Achmed' has one value: it indicates that 'S.A.' was associated in his mind with a title. To this conundrum *Seven Pillars of Wisdom* itself is the place to look for a solution.

In Lawrence's first week in the Hejaz, on his ride to meet Feisal, an incident occurred which he was not to forget:

> As we watched, two riders, trotting light and fast on thoroughbred camels, drew towards us from the north. Both were young. One was dressed in rich Cashmere robes and heavy silk embroidered head-cloth. The other was plainer, in white cotton, with a red cotton head-dress. They halted beside the well; and the more splendid one slipped gracefully to the ground without kneeling his camel, and threw his halter to his companion, saying, carelessly, 'Water them while I go over there and rest.' Then he strolled across and sat down under our wall, after glancing at us with affected unconcern. He offered a cigarette, just rolled and licked, saying, 'Your presence is from Syria?'

* And, of course, for you feminine, although an Arab poet conventionally addressed a woman in the masculine form.

I parried politely, suggesting that he was from Mecca, to which he likewise made no distinct reply. We spoke a little of the war and of the leanness of the Masruh she-camels.

Meanwhile the other rider stood by, vacantly holding the halters, waiting perhaps for the Harb to finish watering their herd before taking his turn. The young lord cried, 'What is it, Mustafa? Water them at once.' The servant came up to say dismally, 'They will not let me.' 'God's mercy!' shouted his master furiously, as he scrambled to his feet and hit the unfortunate Mustafa three or four sharp blows about the head and shoulders with his riding stick. 'Go and ask them.' Mustafa looked hurt, astonished, and angry as though he would hit back, but thought better of it, and ran to the well.[48]

It is then revealed to Lawrence that the rider and his servant are in fact two Sharifs, Sharif Ali ibn al-Hussein, and his cousin, Sharif Mohsin, lords of the Harith, blood enemies of the Masruh. They have pretended to be master and servant to disguise their identities.

The scene, impressive in itself, was no casual encounter without a sequel. We have seen that the master, Sharif Ali, was to command (at Lawrence's specific request to Feisal, according to Lawrence), the expedition intended to blow the Yarmuk viaduct. But even as this first incident highlights the phrase in the opening of Lawrence's second stanza—*Death was my servant*—it also raises the question of where to place the emphasis. Presumably, death, an equal, was servant to Lawrence just as an equal had acted as servant to Sharif Ali. Yet this, in turn, generates a new ambiguity: it could mean that death was used by Lawrence (i.e. to kill) or was mastered by him (i.e. in his boasted economy of British and Arab lives).

Ambiguity, to which William Empson drew western attention in a now classical study, the tool of Arab poets for centuries, dominates the rest of the poem. *Saw you waiting* . . . could refer to a vision of Dahoum in prison, or to Sharif Ali, waiting at Azrak, the advance-post on the road to Damascus. *Earth's soft hands* could carry its obvious (and banal) meaning, or could, with an emphasis on *soft*, refer to the hands of women. (We remember how Lawrence stressed the harshness of Farraj's hand.) And again, *the blind worms*: rejecting the obvious (and banal) meaning of subterranean decomposition, we might remember how Lawrence repeatedly used *worms* as a synonym for men and hence argue that men were changing the once noble substance of S.A. to dross.

The last stanza contains an obvious instance of rhetoric (also common in Arabic poetry) rather than ambiguity: *men prayed me to set my work* . . . But the stanza as a whole repeats in poetic form the stringencies of the prefatorv chapter which Shaw persuaded Lawrence to cut:

The morning freshness of the world-to-be intoxicated us. We were wrought up with ideas inexpressible and vaporous, but to be fought for. We lived many lives in those whirling campaigns, never sparing ourselves: yet when we achieved and the new world dawned, the old men came out again and took our victory to re-make in the likeness of the former world they knew.[49]

It is conceivable that S.A. links two people—Sharif Ali *and* Dahoum—and perhaps two places—Seruj, the Syrian village in which he had lost an important piece of property, his camera, and tasted violence—*and* Azrak, where he had spent ten days with Sharif Ali. This would make the kind of involved sense that fits a cipher and fitted Lawrence. In his first reference to Dahoum, he had described the strong, sweet-tempered young wrestler being threatened with a beating by Lawrence and mildly tortured by the administration of a Seidlitz powder; in a letter to the Anonymous Friend with whom he lowered his guard, he reported their last expedition. Crossing to an island near Akaba on a zinc tank buoyed up by air, 'I had tied Dahoum to my tail, since I felt that any intelligent shark would leave me in the cold.'[50]

Between this incident in February 1914 and his farewell to Sharif Ali in November 1917, which he compared to that between David and Jonathan, an evolution in his soul had imposed a change of values. Sharif Ali was the beneficiary, Dahoum the loser. Ali ibn al-Hussein al-Harithi was a pure Arab where Dahoum had been of mixed race; he was a bedouin where Dahoum had come of settled farming stock; he was a noble of the Blood where Dahoum was a donkey-boy or mess-waiter. Sharif Ali was also 'physically splendid: not tall nor heavy'; so that 'no one could see him without the desire to see him again; especially when he smiled, as he did rarely, with both mouth and eyes at once. His beauty was a conscious weapon. He dressed spotlessly, all in black or all in white; and he studied gesture.' Yet, and the prose description echoes the poem's mood, 'despite this richness, there was a constant depression with him, the unknown longing of simple, restless people for abstract thought beyond their minds' supply. His bodily strength grew day by day, and hatefully fleshed over this humble something which he wanted more. His wild mirth was only one sign of the vain wearing-out of his desire.'

Sharif Ali, the pure-blooded, beautiful Arab warrior, is the new reality, reducing Dahoum to the shadowy ghost of a past love. Lawrence's admiration for Sharif Ali's values and vices (nearly all references involve him in some violent role) explains the displacement of Syria in Lawrence's mind. Ali's attachment to the youth, Turki, is openly animal. If Lawrence's own relations with Ali are the reality behind the myth of

Deraa, then the fictitious Bey's admiration for Lawrence's white skin makes sense as an echo of the compliments of Ali, who was dark. It makes no sense in a Turkish context. After the battle of Abu'l Lissan on the way to Akaba Lawrence had seen dead Turks. 'The dead men looked wonderfully beautiful. The night was shining gently down, softening them into new ivory. Turks were white-skinned on their clothed parts, much whiter than the Arabs . . . '[51] If, too, Ali was as brutal as Lawrence admiringly portrays him, some requested punishment to appease an absent, outraged Old Man (to anticipate the ritual worked out after the war) could have aroused the Arab to the point where he subjected Lawrence to the final degradation.

If the internal evidence of the poem and the book strongly suggest that Lawrence's regard was for Sharif Ali (whose initials fit the dedication), external facts reinforce the identification. One also explains why Lawrence had to keep the connection secret.

Once Lawrence had decided that he would publish a limited, lavish, edition of *Seven Pillars of Wisdom*, he commissioned Eric Kennington to portray some of the main English and Arab participants in the Revolt. In 1921 (when Lawrence himself returned to the Middle East as Winston Churchill's adviser on Arab affairs) Kennington visited Cairo, Beirut, Jerusalem and Amman. In Amman he met and painted Sharif Ali, then in the service of Amir Abdullah. On his return to London, Kennington invited Lawrence, back at the Colonial Office, to inspect his Arab portraits. Lawrence passed from one to another. 'There was no sign that the portraits affected him (to which he has owned to several friends).* "Sikeini—he has no self interest. Shakir—few men are loved as he is and deserves to be." At Abdullah, he giggled repeatedly but said nothing. He spent most time on Ali ibn Hussein, and seemed to me to be almost reverential. It was one of the hundred surprises he gave me.'[53] In another surprise, Sharif Ali prompted from Lawrence what Kennington described as 'a blaze of feeling'. Kennington had learnt, what was news to Lawrence, that King Hussein had for some months been holding Ali in gaol. 'He [Lawrence] seemed to double his size. "I'll have him out in a month." ' Kennington's use of the term *reverential* comes close to Lawrence's own term *regard*; neither characterizes Lawrence's attitude to Dahoum.

Like others who had fought in the Revolt, Sharif Ali had become disillusioned with King Hussein and his sons. Although he took part in Feisal's desperate last battle to save Damascus from the French and then worked with Abdullah in Amman, by the time Ibn Saud invaded the

* After concluding *Seven Pillars of Wisdom* and participating with Churchill in the British 'solution' for the Middle East, Lawrence seems to have lost all interest in the Arabs. On his way to India in 1927 he went ashore at Port Said, but only to dine with Stewart Newcombe. At Basra, he did not bother to go ashore.[52]

Hejaz he was ready to change sides. His enthusiastic support for the *Ikhwan* won him royal favour. Some six years later Philby visited him in the company of King Ibn Saud. By this time the desert athlete had settled down and married. His newly constructed mansion stood on a hillock overlooking Wadi Laimun, one of the fertile valleys that interrupt the otherwise desolate Hejaz. Philby and Sharif Ali spent a long, non-alcoholic evening listening to the philogynist monarch discourse on which of his ninety-odd wives he would like, along with the allotted seventy houris, to accompany him in Paradise.* Lawrence would hardly have savoured this conversation, but, more important, Sharif Ali's defection to the Wahhabite cause made it impossible for Lawrence openly to preface his name to an epic whose chief characters were the sons of Hussein and whose hero had selected Feisal as the 'prophet who, if veiled, would give cogent form to the idea behind the activity of the Arab revolt.'[54]

* Ibn Saud, as a champion of orthodox Islam, got round the prohibition against a man having more than four wives at a time by employing a Muslim's right to divorce a wife by simply saying, 'I divorce you', three times. Many of his matches were contracted in order to secure the loyalty of the bride's tribe; some only lasted a matter of hours.

23

LAWRENCE WAS to revise *Seven Pillars of Wisdom* on his salary of £100 a month from a new and important post. On New Years' Day 1921, Winston Churchill had accepted Lloyd George's invitation to succeed Lord Milner as Colonial Secretary. At Churchill's insistence, a new department, responsible to him and not to Curzon, the Secretary of State for Foreign Affairs, was to resolve the conflicting claims of Colonial Office, War Office, India Office and Foreign Office in the Middle East. From 7 January, when Edward Marsh took Lawrence to call on the newly appointed minister, until 20 July 1922, when the *Morning Post* published his letter of resignation, Lawrence worked as Churchill's adviser on Arab affairs. He was thus associated, as persuader, messenger, and mascot, with the arrangements whereby Britain fulfilled some and broke other of her numerous wartime undertakings. Like many a makeshift arrangement, Churchill's settlement was to last longer than might have been predicted. Its basic structure only began to fall apart in the 1950s, when the contradictions between a pro-British and a pro-Arab foreign policy became unbridgeable for most of the rulers in the region. Later in his life Lawrence complained that his first serious biographer minimized the virtuosity and realism of what he called 'my settlement of 1921'. Yet his affirmation that Churchill had fulfilled all Britain's commitments to the Arabs was balanced by the admission that he had secured for his clients 'the half-loaf', not the whole.[1] His admiration for Churchill, his preoccupation with his book, his secret plans for a new existence, help explain the conflicting judgements. Only part of his mind was on the subject.

Winston Spencer Churchill was at first sight a surprising new mentor for Lawrence of Arabia. Chaim Weizmann, later to be first president of Israel, asserted that Churchill 'had a low opinion of the Arab generally'[2]; the use of the generalizing singular, 'the Arab', if not a remembered quotation, was a modish locution, equally employed for 'your working man' or 'the Jew'. And Churchill's career supports Weizmann's assertion. As late as 1918 he had toyed with abandoning Lawrence's Arab comrades to the Turks, should Germany disgorge her Russian conquests. He showed no sympathy for individual Arabs of the class of Dahoum or for eastern Arabs in the mass. When painting near the pyramids, he protested at the admission of Arabs to the Mena House garden, let alone hotel.[3] In 1920, still Secretary of State for War, he had referred to the Iraqis, then in revolt against British occupation, as 'the enemy'. He wanted, his official biographer tells us, 'the Royal Air Force experts to proceed with experimental work on gas bombs; "especially mustard gas," he wrote to Trenchard on August 29, "which would inflict punishment upon recalcitrant natives without inflicting grave injury upon them." '[4]*

Churchill's impatience with the Iraqis (whose revolt cost Britain far more than the Egyptian disturbances of 1919) was linked with his desire to come to terms with Turkey. In admiring the Turks as a warrior race, Churchill took an opposite stance to that of Curzon, who, like Lloyd George, was pro-Greek.†

Lawrence delighted a romantic streak in Churchill's imperialism. The white Prince of Mecca, his glamorous exploits, offset the mud and massacre of Flanders. Impressionable as well as impressive, Churchill could respond to Lawrence's aristocratic or Homeric Arabs. He also saw their usefulness to a Britain controlling the Middle East.

Lawrence had not visited the Arabs since summer 1919, but had yet to lose his interest in them. He wrote letters, signed and unsigned, to *The Times*, *Observer* and less respected papers. His celebrity gave him new importance to old friends. 'Beloved boy,' Gertrude Bell hailed him from the heat of a Baghdad July, 'I've been reading with amusement your articles in the papers; what curious organs [she referred to the *Daily Express*] you choose for self expression! However whatever the organs I'm largely in agreement with what you say.'[5] Lawrence's interventions were directed against Britain's partnership with France and the expense of policing the liberated lands by conventional methods. His debt of honour to the sons of Hussein was a personal burden.

The elimination of France in favour of Jewish capital and Zionist advisers, was not to be achieved. Instead, meeting at San Remo in April 1920 representatives of Britain and France approved a French mandate over Lebanon and Syria. Lawrence's second theme, that

* ' "Mustard gas" produces its chief effects upon the skin, the eyes and the bronchi. A fibrinous exudate forms on the mucosa as a false membrane, which separates as a slough.' *A Textbook of the Practice of Medicine*, ed. Frederick W. Price, Oxford, 1946, p. 1154. The same authority links its use with tracheitis, dermatitis and bronchitis. In the last case the First World War had shown, 'Death not infrequently occurred, much acute suffering was caused, and some permanent damage has resulted in many cases which recovered.'

† Britain's need to strengthen her forces in Iraq had compelled withdrawals from occupied Constantinople, so strengthening the Greek position. The Greek high command used it to the ruin of a Hellenic population settled in Anatolia for longer than the Turks.

aeroplanes should police the liberated territories, suited the British objective of securing imperial communications at the minimum cost. Air bases, not barracks, were to dominate Iraq. 'It is of course infinitely more merciful', so Lawrence described the bombing of villages nine years later, 'than police or military action, as hardly anyone is ever killed—and the killed are as likely to be negligible women and children, as the really important men.'[6] The last words were intended as a joke; Lawrence claimed that the R.A.F. gave ample warning before their strikes.

Iraq could hardly have remained a pro-British monarchy until 1958 if remedies subtler than gas or cautionary bombing had not been discovered. Gertrude Bell, Sir Percy Cox and Sir Arnold Wilson, imperial servants who had stayed in the east, worked hard on a settlement favourable to Britain. Five days after the French seized Damascus from Feisal, Sir Arnold Wilson had proposed that the dispossessed prince should head an all-Arab administration for Iraq. Sir Percy Cox had earlier proposed the Middle East Department which Churchill headed, while Churchill himself, within a month of taking the seats of office, had convened what came to be known as the Cairo Conference. He took his wife to Cairo with him on a journey that was intended to be pleasurable as well as political. Disembarking at Alexandria on 9 March, they visited Aboukir Bay (where Nelson's destruction of Napoleon's fleet had initiated Anglo-French rivalry for the Middle East), then entrained for Cairo. A mob chanting 'Down with Churchill!' outside Shepheard's Hotel marred the holiday atmosphere. Lawrence unpacked his bags at the Semiramis by the quieter Nile. On the 11th he was discussing the expansion of British air facilities with Trenchard and Salmond of the R.A.F.

The conference which opened on 12 March was misnamed, if the word means a gathering of interested parties for consultation. The inhabitants of the area were unrepresented and those who forgathered had either made up their minds already or were there to receive instructions. Iraq was the first subject to be considered. Cox officially advocated the choice of Feisal (whose consent to British conditions had already been secured in England) on the grounds of his proved success in mustering an army. Iraq's first native ruler, Lawrence contributed, should be an active and inspiring personality: Amir Abdullah was lazy and by no means dominating. At the second meeting that day Churchill read the political committee a draft cable to the prime minister, Lloyd George: 'Feisal offers hope of best and cheapest [*sic*] solution.'[7] Next day the R.A.F. was given the task of policing the ungrateful new kingdom, while Sir Percy Cox and Miss Bell were left to eliminate a rival candidate and gerrymander Feisal's election. At midnight on the 16 March Churchill left the ball given by Lord and Lady Allenby at the Residency for urgent discussions with Herbert Samuel, the High Commissioner for Palestine. Samuel had that minute arrived from Jerusalem to urge the inclusion of Transjordan in the Palestine mandate and to express fears that Arab agitation might obstruct the implementation of the Balfour Declaration. In wider discussions the next day Churchill argued that the Sharifians should be used to block Arab nationalism: each promoted prince would be on his best behaviour to preserve his own royal state as well as the interests of his kingly brethren elsewhere. Lawrence neatly defined the ideal ruler for Transjordan: someone not too powerful, not native to the region and dependent on Britain for the retention of his post. He recommended the Abdullah whose sloth he had pilloried five days earlier.

The 'conference' broke up on 22 March; the imperial party then left for Palestine. At Gaza protesting Palestinians obstructed the railway with their bodies, but Lawrence, who understood their gesture, did not press it on Churchill.

Later polemics over Palestine were to centre on the correspondence between Sir Henry McMahon and Sharif Hussein. Long mislaid, then kept secret for many years, this exchange acquired more significance that it perhaps deserved. McMahon's letter on 24 October 1915, was examined like some ancient text to see whether it did or did not envisage Palestine as part of the area inside which Arabs would enjoy independence. Professor Elie Kedourie has argued that what McMahon had told the Sharif 'was so vague and ambiguous that it was compatible with almost anything:'[8] McMahon communicated in needless haste and in terms which exceeded his mandate from the Foreign Office; his letters, the flowery yet sloppy compositions of a Persian scribe, used key terms in imprecise and changing senses. Hussein had been equally elastic in his replies. Both sides used rhetoric more appropriate to the sale of a carpet than the disposition of inhabited countries. Lawrence might have recognized, had not his dislike for the post-feudal world been reinforced by his emotional contacts with the bedouin, that the settled Palestinians had claims to Palestine (in which they constituted nine-tenths of the population) which rested neither on what McMahon conceded nor on what Hussein demanded. A generation earlier the Egyptian leader, Orabi, had told the ruler: 'We are no longer slaves to be handed from one master to another.' The Palestinians sensed that eviction, not enslavement, might be their lot.

Lawrence was sent from Jerusalem to fetch Abdullah from his camp east of the Jordan (whence he threatened to march on Damascus to restore his brother) to discuss a deal. Abdullah at once asked the important question: did the British intend to establish a Jewish kingdom west of the Jordan and to evict the non-Jewish population? 'If so, it would be better to tell the Arabs at once and not to keep them in suspense.' Samuel's protest that the Balfour Declaration embodied pledges to the Palestinians which would be honoured as scrupulously as those to the Jews seems in the light of history a grotesque deception. Yet Theodor Herzl was not the only begetter of the Jewish State; another, also Viennese by adoption, was at this time an unknown ex-serviceman among ten million others—Adolf Hitler. In 1921 there seemed little motive to prompt enough Jews to settle in Palestine to justify Abdullah's apprehensions. Samuel, to his credit, was later to protest when it became clear that the Arab majority was being deprived of political rights. But Abdullah made no further fuss and settled for the post of Amir (later upgraded to King) and a financial subsidy.

Lawrence was given one singlehanded task after he had returned to London. This was to go to Jidda in order to persuade Hussein to follow his two sons' example and accept the French mandate over Syria and the abandonment of Hashemite claims to Palestine. Britain wanted neither conflicts with France (who had got the worse of the Middle East bargain) nor clashes with Ibn Saud, whose central Arabian realm could threaten overland communications with Iraq. Lawrence sailed for Jidda in July. As well as a draft Treaty he carried an impressive document naming him British plenipotentiary. Somewhat mysteriously, it included in his titles the decorations he claimed to have refused.

Hussein received Lawrence on 29 July in the first of a series of futile meetings. Stubborn, vain, ambitious, Hussein also seems to have been the only Arab in the Sharifian movement who, faced with the choice, chose principle, rather than financial betterment or political survival. The Treaty which Lawrence urged him to sign would have confirmed him as King of the Hejaz, would have given him an annual subsidy of £100,000 and have offered protection against his powerful neighbour, Ibn Saud. But Article 17 would have implied his acceptance of the Balfour Declaration and on the issue of Palestine the King refused to yield. 'Had it been simply to free the Hejaz, I would never have revolted. Even under the Turks it was I who dominated the Hejaz.'[9] Lawrence stayed on in the Hejaz until late September while relations between him and the King deteriorated steadily. Lawrence's attempts to jolly or threaten him into signing maddened the old man.

'The only way to escape from you is throw myself out of the window,' he is said to have exclaimed.

Lawrence, in the same story, dispassionately looked out of the window.

'Does Your Majesty realize that it is a four-storey drop? Your Majesty would probably not survive.'[10]

Hussein's refusal was to cost him his throne. After the failure of further negotiations in 1922 and 1923, the British abandoned him to Ibn Saud and in 1924 he abdicated in favour of his eldest son, who, after a reign of months, fled from Mecca to Baghdad to live out his days as a pensioner of Feisal. Hussein himself was exiled to Cyprus. In 1930, after a stroke, he was allowed to leave Famagusta for Amman, where he spent his last months with his cleverest son, Abdullah. Sir Ronald Storrs, as Governor of Cyprus, had personally invested him with the Grand Cross of the Order of the Bath.

Lawrence's business in Jidda prevented him from attending Feisal's August coronation in Baghdad. But in late September he went north to Amman where for some weeks he helped consolidate British control. He also ran through, without careful accounting, some £100,000. Alec Kirkbride, a Lieutenant nine years his junior whose future was to be intimately linked with Palestine and Transjordan, met him on this, his last visit to the desolate landscape in which he had discovered truths about himself which were to scorch his remaining years. During the war, Kirkbride had noted Lawrence's kindness to those younger than himself, his icy hostility to those older or more powerful. 'He wore an ordinary lounge suit,' Kirkbride recorded of their meeting in Amman, 'and had lost his glamour completely.'[11] Kirkbride was clearly unable to read a heart more than usually opaque to strangers. Lawrence's emotional ties to the Arabs were broken. From Arabia he preserved the memory of actions tougher than pew-breaking, and of a few admired individuals lost to him through death, grandeur or marriage; above all a scenery. 'I wake up now, often, in Arabia:' he was to write eight years later, 'the place has stayed with me much more than the men and the deeds. Whenever a landscape or colour in England gets into me deeply, more often than not it is because something of it recalls Arabia. It was a tremendous country and I cared for it far more than I admired my role as man of action. More acting than action, I fancy, there.'[12]

24

'MY DEAR Lawrence' wrote Churchill on 17 July 1922, 'I very much regret your decision to quit our small group in the Middle East Department of the Colonial Office. Your help in all matters and your guidance in many has been invaluable to me and to your colleagues. I should have been glad if you would have stayed with us longer.'[1] Four days later the *Oxford Times* delivered the last chapters of *Seven Pillars of Wisdom*, the bill for printing the eight copies being £175.

His way now clear (for he had been trying to get out since February) Lawrence prepared to do what he had suggested, half humorously, to the commander of the Handley Page bomber force on his 1919 flight to Cairo. In joining the newest of the three armed services he counted on the support of its creator, Hugh Trenchard. Forewarned six months earlier, Trenchard asked Lawrence to call on him any time between 6 and 12 August so that they could discuss the project. After seeing Lawrence, Trenchard *ordered* Oliver Swann (the emphasis comes from Swann, at that time Air Member for Personnel) to arrange for Lawrence's *sub rosa* admission. On 16 August the reluctant Swann sent Lawrence some three hundred words of detailed instructions. In brief, he was to present himself at the R.A.F. recruiting depot in Henrietta Street at 10.30 on the morning of 21 August; he was to ask for a Flight Lieutenant Dexter who would present him with a form; on this he was to write neither the whole truth nor his real name; Dexter would give Lawrence a false age and a false trade. Lawrence must submit to a medical examination but should mention no disability; if he failed it, Dexter would again intervene. He must produce two references as to his character and previous employment and should give his name as John Hume Ross. He would then join a draft of recruits being sent to Uxbridge.[2]

Because of Lawrence's flair for seeming central to any situation, this surprising reversal of career has been examined exclusively in terms of his own mood or whims. Important as these were, they were not the only factors. After the booming of his wartime exploits by Lowell Thomas, after his spectacular appearance at Versailles and his participation in important post-war decisions, Lawrence was in a sense public property.

Those who directed British policy had reasons of their own for accepting what Swann called 'the whole business, with its secrecy and subterfuge.'[3]

No reader of Lawrence's epic could fail to recognize that a central trove of his Arabian adventure had been the recognition that pain could ignite a species of pleasure. To one who had convinced himself as well as others that he was 'sexless', the discovery was momentous. *Seven Pillars of Wisdom* manifests an obsession with pain transcending such episodes as the killing of Hamed the Moor or the ordeal at Deraa. It includes the storms which turn noon to gritty night. 'For my own part, I always rather liked a khamsin, since its torment seemed to fight against mankind with ordered conscious malevolence, and it was pleasant to outface it so directly, challenging its strength, and conquering its extremity. There was pleasure also in the salt sweat-drops which ran singly down the long hair over my forehead, and dripped like ice-water on my cheek.'[4] According to Subhi al-Umari, Arabs avoided walking barefoot on hot sand. Not so Lawrence. He describes himself 'getting by slow degrees the power to walk with little pain over sharp and burning ground.'[5] And fascination with death antedated Lawrence's set-piece on moonlit Turkish corpses. A week before he died in battle, Frank Lawrence had expressed surprise that his brother had sent home photographs of corpses. 'I cannot imagine what he did it for. I could get plenty here if I had a camera and wanted to. The human body after death is a most vile & loathsome thing. The one I helped to pull out of the ditch at the last trench but one absolutely defies description.'[6]

A delight in being subjected to the will of others was the obverse to the world of All Souls, arrogantly pallid in the fierce light of his desert adventures. These had been irresponsible; his fun had been obtained at the cost of other men and another nation; he had done things to trouble what remained of his puritan conscience; he had done other things to outrage conventional morality. Thus, 'It's going to be a brain-sleep,' he told Robert Graves, 'and I'll come out of it less odd than I went in: or at least less odd in other men's eyes.'[7] Graves had first met Lawrence at All Soul's on a sufficiently odd occasion. Lawrence, in full evening dress, was lecturing the Regius Professor of Divinity on the 'influence of the Syrian Greek philosophers on early Christianity, and especially of the importance of the University of Gadara close to the Lake of Galilee. He mentioned that St. James had quoted one of the Gadarene philosophers (I think Mnasalcus) in his Epistle. He went on to speak of Meleager and the other Syrian-Greek contributors to the Greek Anthology, and of their poems in Syrian of which he intended to publish an English translation and which were as good as (or better than) their poems in Greek.'[8] This splendid spoof of academese (which the gullible young Graves took seriously) will hardly have fooled the Regius Professor.

No such University had existed; the influence of the supposed philosophers was non-existent, and Lawrence, who needed a crib to read Greek and who never mastered written Arabic, was ill-equipped to translate such poems, if they existed, from the Syriac. As a joke it hardly deserved Aldington's stern dismantling; but as a mode of conversation it had obvious limits. Lawrence was at All Souls on false pretences. More memorable as a man and a writer than his peers, he was neither an archaeologist nor an intellectual in the Oxonian sense. He was out of place.

At a later stage of his military career he gave a variant account of his motives for joining the R.A.F. to Lionel Curtis, the ideologist of Empire.

> Explaining it to Dawnay I said 'Mind-suicide': but that's only because I'm an incorrigible phraser . . . Seven years of this will make me impossible for anyone to suggest for a responsible position, and that self-degradation is my aim.[9]

And he expanded the implications of that self-degradation in a further letter to Curtis:

> but you know I joined partly to make myself unemployable, or rather impossible, in my old trade: and the burning out of freewill and self-respect and delicacy from a nature as violent as mine is bound to hurt a bit.[10]

Christopher Caudwell, a Marxist critic of the thirties, added to these somewhat abstract explanations. Despite Caudwell's jargon, despite his disregard for the difference between the Air Force, which Lawrence loved, and the Army, which he hated, his viewpoint deserves recording. 'On every manifestation of bourgeois culture he saw the same dreadful slime. Only in the ranks of the Army he found a stunted version of his ideal, barren of fulfilment but at least free from dishonour. In the Army, at least, though men have taken the King's shilling, it is not the search for profit that holds the fabric together; but it is based on a simple social imperative and wields a force that never reckons its dividends. Like a kind of Arabian desert in the heart of the vulgar luxury of bourgeoisdom, the bare tents of the Army shield a simple comradeship, a social existence free from competition or hate. It is both survival and anticipation, for on the one hand it conserves old feudal relations, as they were before bourgeoisdom burst them, and on the other hand it prophesies like a rudimentary symbol the community of to-morrow united by ties of common effort and not of cash.'[11] Lawrence disliked money values; he was nostalgic for the feudal past; Churchill had quarrelled with his admiration for Lenin, pioneer of Caudwell's tomorrow.

An artistic motive was not the least important. Two years earlier he had told Ezra Pound that he wanted to write, and to write for money.[12] He could now use the R.A.F.—a revolutionary form of social life focused on man's conquest of an unsullied element—for a book whose style and content would contrast with those of the *Seven Pillars*. He little understood how reluctant most of his superiors were to have him in the R.A.F. nor foresaw how his writings would upset them. He had hardly donned his blue uniform before he was confiding to Swann 'the special reason for which I came in—there's masses of gorgeous stuff lying about: but the scale of it is heart-rending. I found the Arab Revolt too big to write about, and chose this as a smaller subject to write about: but you'd have to be a man and a half to tackle it at all decently.'[13]

Such motives—self-degradation, a brain-sleep, mind-suicide, writing—were abstract or intellectual. But those who worked for his enlistment had other reasons than collaboration in the satisfaction of masochistic impulses or in the composition of a realistic account of an airman's life.

Lawrence's discovery of his sexual nature had practical as well as theoretical results. When he came to bare his body at the Recruiting Depot it was to display the stigmata of recent flagellation. His Arabian discoveries had been linked to men he liked or admired; but after the war he pursued similar experiences with men less discreet than Arabs. Swinburne once again had anticipated Lawrence in getting himself beaten for money. But there were important differences. Swinburne's masochistic passion, kindled as a boy at Eton, had been directed to masterful women, and as a mere poet the author of 'Dolores' could safely hide behind the curtains of Victorian prudery. Lawrence had made himself enemies as well as admirers. One, inevitably, was Lord Curzon, from whom the Middle East had been snatched by Churchill. Although Lawrence's claim to have reduced the high principled Secretary of State for Foreign Affairs to public tears was absurd, like other myths this clasped its irritant of truth. Lawrence had supported Churchill's pro-Turkish pragmatism and had been ready to abandon Hussein. Curzon was in a position to learn the secret tastes of so conspicuous a servant of his country—even before, as we shall see, Lawrence was forced by fear of a scandal to confess them to a member of the Cabinet.[14] And by a cruel irony Curzon's secretary was one of Lawrence's kinsmen by blood: Robert Gilbert Vansittart, whose intensity of belief or prejudice worried even his friends.[15] Foreign Office officials, Kipling had advised Lawrence in October 1919, 'don't understand deviations from type.'[16] More than twenty years after Lawrence's death, when the secret of his bastardy but not his masochism had been bruited round the world, Vansittart was to record how deeply the legitimate side of the family despised Lawrence's Chapman father, whose mother had been Louisa Vansittart. Among lukewarm references to Lawrence himself Vansittart's autobiography included the observation that 'he had not grown up but grown older, and I was sorry for him since he was sorry for himself.' Vansittart made it his business to scotch stories which Lawrence had retailed to biographers and fellow-rankers. One such story had Churchill offering him Egypt after the assassination of the Sirdar, Sir Lee Stack, by anti-British nationalists. 'Allenby was replaced by my Eton friend George Lloyd. There is no truth in Lawrence's intimation that the job was offered to him,' Vansittart wrote tartly. 'Even less substance is in his claim to have had the chance in 1922. The appointment lay with Curzon. If Winston had ever foolishly proposed Lawrence I should have heard, for Curzon would have laughed him out of court, and the laughter would not have been kind.'[17] This statement, coming from the *éminence grise* of the Foreign Office in the years leading up to the Second World War, deserves examination.

Lawrence, in every respect except height, was immeasurably more distinguished than the Lloyd who had ridden with him to Wadi Rumm and who was conspicuously to fail in Egypt. Unless Vansittart meant that Egypt could only go to a banker and an Etonian (Kitchener, Allenby and Wingate had been neither), his implication is clear; whatever Churchill may have said in an enthusiastic moment, Curzon knew things about Lawrence which ruled him out.

In the event his enlistment went less smoothly than Swann had planned. Lawrence did not turn up at Henrietta Street on the day appointed. Instead he arrived, a week later, to find, not Flight Lieutenant Dexter but Captain W. E. Johns, author of the boys' stories based on a pilot known as 'Biggles'. Johns was assisted by a Sergeant-Major Gee. Experienced at assessing recruits, Gee alerted Johns that there was something fishy about this would-be airman calling himself John Hume Ross. As Lawrence had neglected to provide himself with the requisite references, Johns sent him off to collect these. During his absence he checked with the official repository of Britain's vital statistics: Somerset House had no trace of a John Hume Ross born on the date Lawrence gave. Lawrence returned with a special messenger from the Air Ministry. The R.A.F. doctors observed the evidence of recent punishment on his naked skin,[18] as was confirmed by Lawrence in the notes about the medical examination which he at once began making:

> 'Turn over: get up: stand under here: make yourself as tall as you can: he'll just do five foot six, Mac: chest—say 34. Expansion—by Jove, 38. That'll do. Now jump: higher: lift your right leg: hold it there: cough: all right: on your toes: arms straight in front of you: open your fingers wide: hold them so: turn round: bend over. Hullo,

what the hell's those marks? Punishment?' 'No, Sir, more like persuasion Sir, I think.' Face, neck, chest, getting hot.

'H . . . m . . . m . . . , that would account for the nerves.' His voice sounds softer. 'Don't put them down, Mac. Say *Two parallel scars on ribs*. What were they, boy?'

Superficial wounds, Sir.

'Answer my question.'

A barbed-wire tear, over a fence.[19]

Lawrence had as much right as any other author to compress or otherwise change the subject matter of his book. But, biographically, the account is significant for the details he includes and those he changes. The link with Azrak and barbed wire already made for Meinertzhagen's benefit is repeated. He maintains that the Air Force doctors agreed not to mention his scars in their report, but these doctors were in fact, as Johns put on record, unwilling to pass Lawrence because of them. Only repeated insistence from the Air Ministry got him past their objections and into Uxbridge. It has been plausibly suggested that Swann, resentful of having to stage-manage the enlistment, may have tried to subvert the order which came in his name but at Trenchard's bidding. Certainly Captain Johns was ignorant of Lawrence's identity and of the fact that he was to be enlisted at all costs. Apart from disliking subterfuge, Swann had understandable reasons for not wanting the War's most famous colonel in a squad of raw recruits. A book by Lawrence, a leak to the press, could rend the secrecy in which military institutions prefer to conduct their affairs.

Whatever stage-management was needed to enroll him, Lawrence's first months in the R.A.F. were arduous and fruitful. The letters he wrote to Garnett, Swann and others show the gestation of a book whose title probably derives from A. E. Housman's lines

They carry back bright to the coiner the mintage of man,
The lads that will die in their glory and never be old.

Scribbled between Last Post and lights out, what he called 'rather poor notes'[20] recorded each day's agonies and insights. He filed but did not at the time reread them, because 'the writing was done under difficulties, for I'm awkward anyway at rifle-drill, and when my mind went off truant down the square after a phrase, what remained behind was even more awkward.'[21] In November 1922, he told Garnett that these 'photographs, snap-shots rather, of the places we lived in, and the people we were, and the things we did,' formed 'an iron, rectangular, abhorrent book, one which no man would willingly read.'[22] But about this he was ultimately wrong. Later sections, added during a serener phase of his

Air Force experience, balanced the early chapters in which a hypersensitive, no longer youthful Oxonian endured the routine experience of the working-class recruit. Six years later he was to copy the notes out and present them to Garnett for Christmas. He then recognized the contrast with the *Seven Pillars*, which now seemed prolix, unspontaneous, too consciously an attempt at creating a literary masterpiece. Yet *The Mint*, because of its faithful use of service slang, could not have been published without massive bowdlerization in Lawrence's England. (Even when it finally appeared in 1955, the edition for general sale was potholed with blank spaces.) An extrinsic objection came in an appeal marked 'private and personal' from a friend he could not betray. 'I feel,' wrote Trenchard, Chief of Air Staff from 1918 to 1929, 'I understand everything you put down at the time and your feelings, but I feel it would be unfair to let this loose on a world that likes to blind itself to the ordinary facts that go on day after day. Everything you have written—I can see it happening—the way you have written as if it was happening, but the majority of people will only say, "How awful! how horrible! how terrible! how *bad*!" There are many things you have written which I do feel we know go on and we know should not go on, though what you have written does not hurt me one bit—far from it, and yet, if I saw it in print, if I saw it being published and being misunderstood by the public, I should hate it, and I should feel my particular work of trying to make this force would be irretrievably damaged and that through my own fault.'[23] The then 55-year-old pioneer wrote movingly of his desire that the Air Force should not be for killing only and of his efforts 'in the past three or four years to work on how to improve the careers of the men and officers without it costing too much money.'[23] Although writers he admired reinforced Lawrence's conviction that *The Mint* was his better work, he told his brother, A. W. Lawrence that he would not like it to appear before 1950, and certainly not in his lifetime.[24]

If *The Mint* had been published in the 1920s—perhaps, like *Ulysses* and *Lady Chatterley's Lover*, in France—it could have won Lawrence new fame as a literary innovator. For if *Seven Pillars of Wisdom* looked back, *The Mint* anticipated what the social realists of the 1930s were to attempt with infrequent success. Lawrence had made a writer's most generous sacrifice: it was also the price for continuing a service career which satisfied him and seemed to his prominent male relations a safe way of keeping a deviant hero under control.

BOOK FIVE

1923–1935

The Partitioned Soul

25

LAWRENCE'S PROJECTED 'brain-sleep' was to produce more than most men's cerebration. The notes which became *The Mint*, a translation from the French, a prose version of the *Odyssey*, reviews, essays and prefaces, more than half the letters which David Garnett was to collect and edit after his death, all date from the last dozen years. Far from being a Nijinsky who had ceased to dance, his apparition on a motor cycle would delight a host of friends, leaving such visits among the bright memories of people as different as E. M. Forster and Lady Astor.

Yet admirers were puzzled how to explain Lawrence's withdrawal from the world of power. Some thought him a postulant monk without a faith; untroubled by the lack of a Thou, they saw his military obedience as enforcing the truth in the English hymn:

> Who sweeps a room as for Thy laws
> Makes that and the action fine.

Others tried to equate his final work on speed-boats with his use of dynamite or pen. His choice of careers, others argued, won him an approximation to the English norm. In 1923 he still had 'a slight almost girlish figure';[1] by the early 1930s he had grown stocky, if not plump; his brick-red, open-air complexion recalled neither Oxford dilettante nor tortured guerilla. Undemanding work, a vaunted minimal wage (like his namesake D. H. Lawrence he tended to minimize his funds), working-class comrades, a cottage in which to play the gramophone or eat from cans, a rota of distinguished friends: the solvent to these elements was the series of motor cycles made for him by George Brough.[2] On the pillion he could carry a chosen companion—'who must be a man with a criminal tendency'*—to eat sausages and chips in the neighbouring town; he could visit the Shaws, Thomas Hardy, Churchill or attend an executioner whose penitential services he retained till near the end.

For this apparent peace he paid a price. The attempt at a brain-sleep,

* So Robert Graves originally quoted him: Lawrence toned it down to 'preferably mildly a ruffian.'[3]

however vain, eroded the qualities which had made him famous. Like the Swinburne who retired to Putney Heath or the Wordsworth whose last Sonnets defended hanging, the new, 'normal', Lawrence progressively abandoned the idiosyncracies which had made him, like the island for which he settled, the enigma of the world. From his Oxford years, when his feats and skills impressed contemporaries, through his Middle East decade, an increasing host of admirers had echoed the 1914 poem in which his brother made him the peer of kings. Something, they recognized, set him apart from men of talent like Woolley or Young, from adventurers like Frank Harris or Horatio Bottomley, or from authors like themselves. He had fought a sunlit war of movement. This was much. But it was not enough to explain the admiration of distinguished men. Others had blown up trains or charged on camels. Young spoke better—if imperfect—Arabic; Meinertzhagen set shrewder traps. Lawrence's appeal was linked to the interplay, behind a youthful face, of forces rarely reconciled in a single man. Contradiction enfolded his habits and what passed for his convictions. He hated to be touched yet broke his leg wrestling in a playground, and when Dahoum was in rigor Lawrence sat on his feverish chest. He despised food and said absurd things about water yet worked his way through a French table d'hôte, sipped champagne with an English friend and with an American drank 'wine of various sorts freely.'[4] He felt compelled to lie to officers yet claimed to have been a boy soldier, was apparently painted as such by Tuke and won fame as holder of the King-Emperor's commission. Compassion, a dislike for hand to hand fighting, balanced his own, very British cult of toughness. With 'tastes anything but blood thirsty',[5] he is one of the few English writers to claim to have caused pain and killed. The later francophobe inhabited the same body as the earlier lover of French poets and explorer of French castles. He walked till his socks were in tatters and his feet blistered, then moved to Aleppo's best hotel, possibly paying the bill by selling a camera bought by others. He slept quilted with fleas on a mud floor, then paraded as a Qonsolos in his Magdalen blazer. He recruited Dahoum into British Intelligence and recorded no regrets for the predictable effects on his friend's short future. He ridiculed Arab unity while raiding the Railway, then wrote that if he had been honest he should have advised the Arabs to go home. Known to the world as Lawrence of Arabia, to the post-war *Who's Who* as Prince of Mecca, he took little interest in the kingdom of Iraq or the career of Saad Zaghlul, the Egyptian leader. He would play a record of Dame Clara Butt singing 'Land of Hope and Glory' when depressed, but when it was over would exclaim: 'I'd like to smash every copy of that record.'[6] Contributor to the fantasy life of adolescents, he knew, as Theodor Herzl before him, that dreams backed by will are the stuff of history. Eric Kennington had brought back a trio of dream pictures with his Arab portraits. Of one of them Lawrence wrote:

> I have been pondering since if I meant or thought of cities while I worked: the Arab East to me is always an empty place: and I don't know whether just open country: with perhaps a settlement in the distance: or hills: (*and* hills) I don't know . . . Don't you think it might do if you just scratched out half the windows, or made them fewer houses—or blotted one half of the town out. There was a little bit of land behind the palm tree, leading to the sword, which felt peaceful. The sword was odd. The Arab Movement was one: Feisal another (his name means a flashing sword): then there is the excluded notion, Garden of Eden touch: and the division meaning, like the sword in the bed of mixed sleeping, from the *Morte d'Arthur*. I don't know which was in your mind, but they all came to me—and the sword also means clean-ness, and death.[7]

The last seven words were set in gold letters on the cover of the first popular edition of *Seven Pillars of Wisdom*. Without the comma, they interwove oddity of syntax with enigma. Yet Lawrence wrote with a significant confusion. His words suggest the rapture which Europeans have known, century after century, in encountering the desert, but which in his day was the particular addiction of the British: emptiness, so unlike Clapham Junction with its frequent trains; people, if there must be people, far enough off to be part of the scenery; nature reduced in the palm tree to one forceful symbol, and as close to it as pain to satisfaction, the land 'which felt peaceful'. The sword, besides being amiably archaic, stands for the venture in which only the camels were female; and to emphasize the dreamed of escape from women, the excluding blade bisects 'the bed of mixed sleeping'. In a final assertion, cleanness, the puritan virtue *par excellence*, is made one with non-existence. His only luxury, he once said, was hot baths.

When Lawrence confided to Kennington, he was still undergoing the acerbities behind *The Mint*'s ugly snapshots. 'We dip into a tub of cold water, through its crusted grease, four or five hundred tea-stained mugs and a thousand plates: which afterwards we smooth over with a ball of grease-stiff rag. A stomach-turning smell and feel of muck it is, for hour upon hour: and a chill of water which shrivels our fingers.' Or 'While my mouth is yet hot with it I want to record that some of those who day by day exercise their authority upon us, do it in the lust of cruelty. There is a glitter in their faces when we sob for breath; and evident through their clothes is that tautening of the muscles (and once the actual rise of sexual excitement) which betrays that we are being hurt not for our good, but to gratify a passion.'[8]

Lawrence's reactions were still as confused as Kennington's evocations of dysentery, nightmare and snow. But a year and a month later there had been a change. He wrote to his mother, then on her way to join his missionary brother in China: 'I hope not again to do anything of my own. It is not good for a man to make things.'[9] The same letter told of his taking 'a little cottage (half ruinous) a mile from camp.' It was a different camp and he himself was in a different service. In the interval he had suffered a defeat and accepted a compromise. If, against his words, he again made anything, it was the pattern of his final years. They find no parallel in the lives of British heroes. While he lived, the intensity of his will united strands which his catlike secrecy kept concealed. They can now be unplaited to serve as threads of Ariadne to the compartments of the maze which was his life. When we enter them, we better comprehend the earlier puzzles.

One compartment was his professional life: as aircraftsman, Royal Tank Corps soldier and then aircraftsman again. Another compartment sealed off his military friendships: didactic, platonic, companionable or searing. Outside the service, in his free hours or when he was on leave, friendships with fellow writers, or the social élite from which his secrets barred him, filled another compartment. The small cottage which he first rented, then bought, near Bovington Camp, the work involved in publishing a limited edition of *Seven Pillars of Wisdom* filled two others: the first a rough substitute for the 'hall' he had dreamed of at Oxford, the second, his attempt to produce what he and Richards had understood as the Book Beautiful. One segmented section contains his opinions on everything from music to washing-up. They reflect his moods or the demands made on him. They are preserved in his vast correspondence (despite a disclaimer to Driver Rolls, 'I'm like you—not fond of writing letters,'[10]) or remembered talk. And, at the heart of the maze, the Peer Gynt-like soul which from behind innumerable wrappings asked ultimate questions while surveying what was left of its own existence. The motor cycle enabled him to communicate between the compartments, or escape from one to another.

The partitioning of self was no instantaneous achievement. His letters prove that he initially saw his enlistment as a short-term raid on experience. When he had made enough notes and the *Seven Pillars* had been abridged, he could come to terms with civilian life. Three months after joining up he told Edward Garnett: 'my hankering after flesh-pots is, I fear, too strong to be resisted when there shall be an alternative livelihood, of a workless character, within reach.'[11] Garnett himself had a key role in this consummation. 'Edward Garnett, a critic, has cut it [*Seven Pillars of Wisdom*] to 150,000 words,' he told another correspondent, 'and I'm going to see if a publisher will pay for these miserable orts [remnants of food]. If so I'll become a civilian again. You have no idea how repulsive a barrack is as permanent home.'[12] Four days before Christmas 1922 he was telling Buxton that after the publication of the abridgement, 'I'm quite likely to chuck the R.A.F.'[13]

What decided him to cling to his uniform was a challenge to his granite will. On 27 December the *Daily Express* shouted its discovery that 'the only white man ever made a Prince of Mecca' had become a ranker. The story played into the hands of those who had all along disapproved of the famous Colonel using the newest service as though it were the Foreign Legion. After he was safely dead, an R.A.F. officer was to write that 'T.E., did our service the honour of finding therein many well-acknowledged years of happiness and content,'[14] but in December 1922 Lawrence suspected that an officer had played the role of Judas for £30. At the same time some officers suspected that Lawrence was spying on them. Both suspicions contained truth. Newspapers indeed paid for such information; no commanding officer would welcome so frank an indictment of cruelty and squalor as *The Mint*; Lawrence's implacably active pen wrote reports and suggestions to which his prestige gave unusual push.

The *Daily Express* story could have been the precursor of others more damaging. Lawrence had unwisely attended flagellation parties in Chelsea conducted by an underworld figure known as Bluebeard, and Bluebeard's impending divorce case threatened to release lubricious details concerning Lawrence and one of his aristocratic friends which had already been hinted at in a German scandal-sheet.

Lawrence laid aside other ambitions to meet this challenge to his continued enjoyment of his all-male purgatory. Sacrificing caution, he wrote to the Home Secretary asking for the expulsion of Bluebeard and a ban on the German magazine.[15] To Jonathan Cape, the newly established publisher whose success was underpinned by his link with Lawrence,[16] he wrote urgently in early January countermanding the publication of Garnett's abridgement of *Seven Pillars of Wisdom.* (The abridgement which Cape eventually published as *Revolt in the Desert* was the work of Lawrence aided by service friends.) But these personal and literary sacrifices were in vain. By the end of the month he had been dismissed: 'for the crime of possessing too wide a publicity for a ranker: and as I'm broke as usual the sacking is immediately and physically inconvenient.'[17] His plea to the Secretary to the Chief of the Air Staff that he be transferred to Leuchars in Fife—'whose C.O. is a solid and masterful person'[18]—was disregarded.

Lawrence was less poor than he pretended; his grief was not solely at being crossed. In his four initiatory months he had become strongly attached to a young airman, R. A. M. Guy, described by another of

Lawrence's service friends as 'beautiful, like a Greek god.'[19] A contemporary document testifies to the strength of Lawrence's affection for Guy, and his means. A bill from a London tailor, which Lawrence paid by cheque on 31 March 1923, so securing a fifteen per cent credit discount, survives.* A 'Drab Cheviot overcoat for R. A. M. Guy, Esqr' cost £16.1.0; the bill also included two suits of blue Cashmere, one for Lawrence himself, the other for Guy, together totalling £33.8.0. These were expensive clothes for the early 1920s. Five years later (in a letter to a Labour member of parliament) Lawrence was to explain why he had not bought himself an overcoat: it seemed 'a wicked waste of 3 or 4 pounds, for a mere month',[20] which was an accurate statement of the price of a wearable overcoat in the 1920s.

To the airman who compared Guy's physical attractions to those of a Greek god, Lawrence was to list Guy with such famous friends as Thomas Hardy, E. M. Forster and Air Marshal Salmond.[21] Guy visited the cottage which became the focus of Lawrence's private life,† and to Guy himself (on whom he lavished the pet names of 'Poppet' or 'Rabbit') he wrote ecstatically about their closeness in a letter of Christmas 1923.[22]

But a very different guardian angel—tall, beefy, Scotch—was to overlook the second phase of his post-war military career.

Immediately after Lawrence's dismissal from the Air Force, Trenchard advised him to try the Royal Tank Corps as a Short Service Officer.[23] Lawrence accepted the alternative service but not the status. Under a new pseudonym, 'Shaw', he enlisted as a private at Bovington Camp, Dorset, in March 1923. The sleeper in the adjoining bed was John, or 'Jock', Bruce from Aberdeen. If we are to believe Bruce's account, their arrival in the same hut from different points of departure was facilitated by the British Army. Bruce was to serve Lawrence—who described him as 'inarticulate, excessively uncomfortable'—in the contrasted roles of unofficial batman, bodyguard and periodic flagellant.

Although he was to allocate a portion of his meagre pay to Bruce's mother, and although the elder of Bruce's sons was to receive £4

* Ralph Isham was an American who had joined the British Army as a Lieutenant in 1917 and risen to being a Lieutenant-Colonel by the Armistice. Introduced to Lawrence by Storrs in the summer of 1919, Isham was the bibliophile to whom readers are so much indebted for his rescue of the Boswell papers. He also collected Lawrentiana. After his death, his heir, Jonathan Trumbull Isham, discovered and opened a secret drawer in his father's bureau. A sealed envelope contained the receipted bill from F. P. Scholte of 7, Savile Row. The revelation that Lawrence patronized an expensive tailor must have puzzled Isham. Lawrence had told him in a letter of 11 September 1928: 'I starved in 1922; and don't want to repeat.' The relationship with Guy probably also perplexed Isham.

† The other item in Colonel Isham's sealed envelope was a telegram from Bovington, signed 'Shaw' and dated 30.10.24. Addressed to Guy R.A.F., H.M.S. *Hermes*, Portsmouth, it read: *Saturday quite convenient.*

annually from one of his Trust Funds, Lawrence has left no evidence that his relationship with Bruce was other than functional. It was first publicly aired in an article signed by Bruce but written by a ghost-writer which Bruce sold to the *Scottish Field* in August 1938, after, according to that paper, the B.B.C. had already included him 'in the popular Scottish Regional feature "Queeries" [*sic*]'. Loyal to Lawrence, and laudatory of him, as all Bruce's statements were to be, the article contained fantastic details* which had certainly been added by the writer who ghosted the article. They prove that fantasy, like mannerisms, can be infectious. Bruce also contacted Lawrence's youngest brother after Lawrence's death, and the two met by appointment at a railway station. What Bruce had to tell convinced Arnold Lawrence (who was his brother's literary executor) that there was substance in his story and he alluded to it, though in veiled terms, in the terminal essay to *T. E. Lawrence by his Friends*. Bruce undertook to keep the main secret to himself during the lifetime of Mrs. Lawrence, but after her death, hard up and in poor health, he offered a typescript describing his friendship with Lawrence to the *Sunday Times*. The newspaper agreed to pay him a substantial fee for the right to publish details of this relationship which Bruce saw as an honour to himself and therapeutic for Lawrence. After questioning Bruce closely, two journalists working for the paper, Colin Simpson and Phillip Knightley, began the publication of his story in the *Sunday Times* of 23 June 1968; with some modifications, it was republished in *The Secret Lives of Lawrence of Arabia* the following year. According to the earlier version, Bruce had left his father's dairy, a youth of nineteen, in early 1922. Armed with an introduction from his family doctor and aspiring to employment with Morgan, Grenfell & Co., the London bankers, he contacted in London a Mr. Murray. He was introduced by Murray to a 'Mr. Lawrence' at the Mayfair flat of Francis Rodd, the future Lord Rennel, who was later to be a director of Morgan, Grenfell. (Rodd had visited Lawrence in his Rome hospital after his 1919 crash and brought him to convalesce in the British Embassy where his father was stationed.) The Bank turned Bruce down. He claimed that Lawrence then offered him a regular retainer of £3 a week (more than the average wage at the time) and sent him north to await his call. The services for which he was being retained were not explained, but when Lawrence was discharged from the R.A.F. in January 1923, Bruce was summoned by telegram to London. In exigent agitation Lawrence told him of his

* The unconfirmed and intrinsically improbable statement that Lawrence 'sent for' Bruce when he was in India leads to an adventure story in which Bruce and Lawrence are 'seized by a band of native ruffians and left bound together naked.' Needless to say, Lawrence turns the tables and it is soon the ruffians who are without their clothes. In fact, Lawrence stayed in camp when he was in India, and Bruce was working as a civilian, in Britain.

intention to join the Royal Tank Corps and jumped at Bruce's offer to enlist with him.

The meetings of the obscure, even of those made so by abnegation, are hard to check. Bruce's lack of sophistication and the impression of general truthfulness which he made on two experienced journalists are in favour of his having accurately reported the 1922 London meeting. So is Bruce's reference to it in his 1938 article in the *Scottish Field.*[24] But since no one else has confirmed a meeting prior to Bovington in March 1923, and since Bruce allowed his ghost-writer for the *Scottish Field* article to include inaccurate statements, the question is open.

In any case, whether he met Lawrence in 1922 or 1923 is less important than the role which he began to play in Lawrence's private life and which has not been disputed.

Soon after the pair had enlisted, Lawrence told an extraordinary story which the young Scotsman nevertheless continued to believe for the rest of his life. As a result of it, he was again and again to birch the former Colonel on his bare buttocks. The beatings were savage and formed a routine interrupted only by Lawrence's spell of Indian duty from 1927 to 1929. As late as 1934, the year before Lawrence's departure from the Air Force and the world, Bruce was still fulfilling his curious function. The beatings seem, if anything, to have increased in severity with the passage of time. Nor was Bruce the only executioner, though he is the only one to have put his name to a detailed account.

The story which induced Bruce to perform actions he claims to have found distasteful surprises us less when we approach it from the direction of Azrak.* It ran as follows: a male kinsman, standing in some mysterious way as financial guarantor and moral mentor, had been outraged that Lawrence 'had dragged the family name through the gutters. He had turned his back on God, lost an excellent position at the Colonial Office, become involved financially with "the damned Jews", insulted a Bishop and insulted King George at Buckingham Palace; and ruined the life of a great Foreign Minister, referring to Lord Curzon. The Old Man called him a bastard not fit to live amongst decent people.'[26]

Each charge held its germ of truth. If Lawrence's masochistic practices had become generally known, they would certainly have damaged the Lawrence name and might possibly have revealed his Chapman connections. Lawrence had long abandoned the God in whose service he had

* The suggestion made in *The Secret Lives* that the beatings coincided with the anniversary of Deraa cannot be entertained. The incident at Deraa—or Azrak—took place in November 1917. Lawrence's letter to F. N. Doubleday of 18 September 1930 enables us to date at least one of these rituals.[25] Lawrence was then staying with Bruce—'Jock, the roughest diamond of our Tank Corps hut in 1923'—and another ex-serviceman, who had to witness the beatings, on the coast north of Aberdeen. Lawrence had a fever. The sea was icy. It seems that sea-bathing was included in his punishment.

tramped to St. Aldate's from North Oxford. He had resigned from the Colonial Office. He had urged a pro-Zionist policy on the British and Feisal, invariably justifying it in monetary terms. In one of two drafts of a letter to the Anglican Bishop of Jerusalem (who, along with many Jews, questioned the wisdom of political Zionism) he referred to Weizmann as 'a great man whose boots neither you nor I, my dear Bishop, are fit to black.'* Curzon's career had foundered for reasons not unconnected with the Middle East. Lawrence was illegitimate. His masochistic practices, his desire, as he told Graves, 'to eat dirt till its taste is normal to me,' were activities and attitudes to affright the majority.

The story (which Lawrence took pains to substantiate by various apparently confirmatory happenings) raises important questions:

why, if he simply wanted to be beaten, did he invent and sustain so elaborate a myth?

what made him choose the birch as the instrument of punishment?

who, if anyone, was the reality behind the Old Man?

Sado-masochism can occupy two extremes. At the most dangerous, a sado-masochist, unaware of the sexual roots of his compulsion, may advocate, or practise, performances dangerous to the health of others or himself, or to life itself. At another, post-Freudian extreme, he recognizes, open-eyed, that, for some reason to do with his emotional conditioning, the infliction or acceptance of pain evokes a species of pleasure and then searches for partners who will reciprocate his desires and respect his limits.

As a sado-masochist Lawrence stood somewhere in the middle. His Arabian experience had aroused him sexually, but aspects of the same experience had made him feel the need for physical penance. The story of the Old Man was an explanation which a simple youth could, and did, believe, for complex requirements.

The birches used by Bruce apparently arrived at the nearest railway station, despatched by the vigilant Old Man. Their choice was not accidental. Lawrence's description of the whip used on him at Deraa shows his interest in the details of punishment.

The 1934 publication of *I Claudius* by Robert Graves also prompted the following exchange:

LAWRENCE: 'Were the vine-shoots of the Roman N.C.O.'s really the rods that kill? I envisaged them as light cane-like minor punishments.'

* Whether insulting or merely impolite, the two letters, printed on pages 342–4 in David Garnett's edition of *The Letters of T. E. Lawrence* and indexed under the heading, *JERUSALEM, BISHOP IN. L. disposes of* . . . were hardly fair to Dr. McInnes. The Anglican churchman objected to the attribution to Episcopal dioceses with missionary interests of 'anti-Jewish propaganda'. The charge had been made by Horace M. Kallon in a book entitled *Zionism and World Politics*.

GRAVES: 'The vine-shoots of the centurions *were* used by the mutineers to beat them to death with. "Shoots" is a mistranslation. I would not like to be beaten with a vine stem. They are as tough & pliant as rawhide almost.'[27]

The birch, a bundle of lacerating twigs, was used in the depths and at the heights of English society. A man could be bled by it in prison if he molested a warder, or at Eton if his parents could afford the fees. (On the other hand, Lawrence's headmaster at Oxford High School was remembered for the infrequency with which he administered the cane.) The birch symbolized the abyss Lawrence shared with 'the sort who'd always throw something at any cat they saw'.[28] [He referred to the Royal Tank Corps, not the R.A.F.] It fitted the state of mind in which he told Lionel Curtis that 'he would have got into prison if he could have done so without committing a crime.'[29] It also symbolized the plateau—Eton—from which his bastardy removed him. Curzon, Vansittart and George Lloyd were all Etonians.

Bruce's denial to Simpson and Knightley that Lawrence was sexually aroused is hardly more decisive than the contrary hearsay in Lord Maugham's autobiography. Maugham records that when he joined the Army in 1939, one of the sergeant-instructors produced a bottle of rum in the upstairs room of a local pub. 'He now told me a story which at the time I disbelieved but which has since been partially confirmed. When Colonel T. E. Lawrence was at Bovington under the pseudonym of Shaw, he had made friends with the instructor—who was then a lance-corporal. One evening he had invited the lance-corporal to drink with him. He had then persuaded the lance-corporal to whip him and then to penetrate him. As he gave the unpleasant details of the evening he had spent with Lawrence, the sergeant-instructor became visibly excited. Soon he was stroking my thigh. It was difficult to get out of the room without offending him.'[30] Dr. John E. Mack has asserted that Lawrence 'required that the beatings be severe enough to produce a seminal emission.'[31]

If Lawrence had been young in the pornocratic seventies, within reach of the leather-bars of London or New York, he could have found in publications such as *Drummer*[32] ('the magazine for adult leathermen') proof that his tastes were shared by others. A 1975 advertiser from Dallas, for example, describes himself as: 'Scorpio. 30. 6′ 2″. White. Knowledgeable. Wants masculine guys to paddle bare ass, switch thighs and calves with riding crop. Must be 18–40 and respect limits.' Many of the advertisers proclaim a liking for motor-cycles and military discipline. But Lawrence, whether cyclist, camel-rider or masochist, outdid these others. Rejecting play-acting, he chose to live his fantasy, not at weekends, but in his working life.

According to Bruce, Lawrence identified the Old Man as his senior kinsman on his father's side: Henry Rupert Fetherstonhaugh Frampton, another Old Etonian, who now sleeps, in an unkempt grave thrusting thistle and sorrel, a few yards from Lawrence.

Through his father, Lawrence had a double connection with Frampton, who had been born in 1861 and was to survive until 1955. While Lawrence's paternal great-uncle, Sir Benjamin Chapman, the 4th Baronet, had married Frampton's sister, Maria, their eldest son, Sir Montagu Chapman, the 5th Baronet, had married Lawrence's one paternal aunt. But physically the Old Man was even closer to Lawrence in his barrack room: Bovington Camp constituted a thousand-acre slice of the Frampton estate (bought by the War Office in 1899) and was but a short walk from the manor of Moreton, where Frampton lived as the local squire. On his father's side Frampton derived from Westmeath, the same Irish county which had nurtured the Chapmans. The Frampton name had been added when Rupert Pennefather Fetherston-Haugh, Frampton's father, married the heiress to Dorsetshire lands owned by Framptons since the fourteenth century. (Two of the jurymen who in 1834 had convicted the six Tolpuddle Martyrs for the crime of organizing a primitive trade union were Framptons.) This was the local bigwig who, Bruce was led to believe, had undertaken to guarantee Lawrence's bank account provided Lawrence atoned for his misdeeds by joining the Tank Corps as a private and by submitting to corporal punishment. Bruce had to report on his exertions and Lawrence's reactions to them in letters which he 'posted' through Lawrence.

Lawrence is said to have discovered the cottage at Clouds Hill when on a walk.[33] A mile north of the camp and the eviscerated heath where the men drove their tanks, the cottage stood on a small patch of cleared ground; on all sides except the west (which gave onto the road) a plantation of mauve rhododendrons tightly impacted with the boles of other trees made an impenetrable screen. Built for a woodman or gamekeeper on the Moreton estate, the cottage consisted of one room below and one up. It had been lent rent free to Sergeant Knowles, a veteran of the war still serving at Bovington, on condition he repaired it. Still semi-ruined, Lawrence at first rented it and then bought it from Frampton for £450 in 1929.

It would be wrong to dismiss Lawrence's story of the Old Man as entire fantasy or to accept it as entirely true; as with other of his myths, it was given added plausibility by his skill as a romancer. That Lawrence should have landed up at Bovington, of all the military bases for Britain's still farflung forces, within a short walk of his formidable male relation, will have seemed to Bruce confirmation of the story, not coincidence. That Frampton, a respected paterfamilias, High Sheriff of Dorset in

1929, should have approved the penitential beating of his kinsman seems improbable today, but Frampton and Bruce, however divided by social background, belonged to generations which still believed in the physical correction of the young. Lawrence's other cousin, Vansittart, intruded the topic into the second sentence of his autobiographical account of Eton: 'Fagmasters' canes stung more than the headmaster's birch, whose buds the commercially-minded collected as souvenirs; but we should all have been astonished to hear that corporal punishment ever harmed anybody.'* In the context of Lawrence's peculiarities (which hung like a sword of Damocles over his involuntary cousin) Frampton could have suggested, in exasperation, that ritual beatings might be more prudently effected on an area of the body which would not show each time he took his shirt off, and that a retainer such as Bruce would be a discreeter executioner than the hirelings of Chelsea. So much is of necessity speculation. But other details in the story which Lawrence allegedly told Bruce are plainly incorrect. Lawrence's father did not leave his fortune to Frampton (whose estate was valued at £54,000 on his death) but to Lawrence's mother. Even less credible are the stories which Lawrence told to other military accomplices in his beating ordeals.†

The Old Man was a mythical creation whose features and limbs (like those of the characters in novels) were borrowed from living people. On one level he represented authority and the older generation; on another a fusion of Lawrence's two Etonian kinsmen, Frampton and Vansittart. Both were related to the Anglo-Irish protestants whose Georgian mansions had cradled some of the empire's most resolute soldiers and most ruthless bigots.

* Vansittart was apparently unaware of, or indifferent to, the fate of a more famous Etonian: Swinburne's school experiences distorted his entire personality and accounted for many thousands of obsessive verses on the flogging of schoolboys.

† See John E. Mack's Chapter *Intimacy, Sexuality and Penance* which reproduces three letters from Lawrence in the persona of an uncle accusing his nephew of the theft of £150, and recommending drastic birching without the intervention of clothes.

26

THE DARK little cottage at Clouds Hill from now on catered for Lawrence's emotional needs. His downstairs daybed was covered in leather; two sleeping bags, marked *Meum* and *Tuum*, were for himself and the friend of the night. A large horned gramophone played music from a considerable collection; shelves held his books. He read widely. He was often scathing about the modern writers whose reputations are now most secure and enthusiastic about others who are now forgotten. Three glass bells covered different types of food. He had no refrigerator, or gas stove, and until near the end, a bath.

Away from Clouds Hill, an ordered military life filled his last dozen years. Its only interruptions were the brief interregnum between R.A.F. and Royal Tank Corps in 1923 and his ten weeks of civilian life in 1935.

Alec Dixon, a corporal in the Tank Corps, has described his purposeful walk. 'He walked "all of a piece" as it were, with an air of tidiness; his arms were close to his body and his toes well turned out, though not exaggeratedly so. As he walked he appeared to see no one about him; his head was slightly tilted and the blue-grey eyes steady, looking neither to the right nor to the left.' Dixon supplemented this portrait by an unusual use of a cliché: 'He was surely a man with "ants in his pants", if ever there was one.'[1] He was also increasingly contented. 'Partly because we feel eternal. The army's always aged about 20: no illness; no death: no old or young. All of a sort, all dressed, paid, fed, worked alike. The security of years of sameness before us. The common subjection to arbitrary power, and its assumption of all responsibility.'[2] The first period of his service life, at Uxbridge, had been harsh, almost as though the men who had, understandably, conspired to prevent his enlistment wished somehow to drive him out. His service in the Tank Corps was unpleasant, not because of drill or hardship, but because he found soldiers less congenial than airmen. Miserable and pampered in equal measure, he poured out his disgust in a much quoted series of letters to Lionel Curtis. His dislike for the animality of his new companions was extended to include the continuation of the human species. Lawrence saw the technicians of the R.A.F. as men in love with an abstract new element; his fellow-soldiers were refugees from poverty and unemployment, with nowhere to go but down.

The impressions of C. M. Devers, who served with him at the 1st (Depot) Battalion of the Royal Tank Corps are the more valuable in that Devers was never enrolled in the charmed circle that frequented Clouds Hill. While finding him 'courteous to all, and even distantly popular,' Devers records that he was never seen on parades. 'Indeed, he continued, somehow, to be excused all parades. Perhaps this is because he was on the staff, employed in the Quartermaster's stores as a clerk.'[3]

Devers never recalled seeing 'Shaw' in the mess room. Instead, he would use one or other of the refreshment canteens run by civilians. On occasion he was seen airing his shirt and underwear before the barrack room fire. Occasionally, drunk soldiers demanded the loan of a quid and Bruce would go to his rescue. Otherwise his manner and accent won him the respect due to a gentleman. His motor cycle added to his prestige. 'Possessed of a "permanent" or midnight pass, which concession was allowed men employed on the staff,' he would disappear with a suitcase of civilian clothes, something then unusual in the British army. 'Shaw appeared to dislike discipline. If anything he was careless in most military things. Yet he certainly had some method—some system of his own—His bed would be made, his floor cleaned and his kit, but not by Shaw.'

The contradictions between an undisciplined Private Shaw being waited on by a virtual batman and a penitent Shaw being soundly birched by the selfsame retainer are only apparent. In most sado-masochistic relationships the masochist is in control. Bruce's role as protective disciplinarian is evident in an interesting account of a visit which Lawrence paid to the Kenningtons at Chiswick. Lawrence brought 'a soldier' on his pillion. 'This time—for the first time—he dropped all disguises. There was a wall of pain between him and us . . . Everything was attacked. Life itself. Marriage, parenthood, work, morality, and especially Hope . . . ' Lawrence came close to defining his religious views. 'What I think I heard, in the flow of eloquence', Kennington recalled, 'was a record of process without aim or end, creation followed by dissolution, rebirth, and then decay, to wonder at and to love. But not a hint at a god, certainly none of the Christian God.' Kennington was blinded by a glory 'more of sunset than sunrise or midday'. The soldier was simply angered. 'The young tank man was most positive. He banged his fist on the tea table, and threatened. "Now, none of that. How often have I told you? Look me straight in the face . . . " An animal tamer, and T.E. a wild beast that partially obeyed him . . . Aside, to my wife, the young man revealed his grief at T.E.'s suffering. I don't know who that was, but he had great courage and love for T.E.'[4]

If Lawrence behaved badly so that Bruce should punish him later, he exploited the purgatory of the Tank Corps (whose pains he detailed in letters to powerful friends) as a means to get back into the Air Force. A letter to John Buchan of 5 July expresses gratitude for effective intervention: 'It's like a sudden port, after a voyage all out of reckoning. I owe you the very deepest thanks.'[5] By August 1925 he was at Cranwell, a station where he was employed on the maintenance of planes used in training recruits. Cranwell's comparative comfort and peace inspired the later, more hopeful chapters of *The Mint*. But those who had granted his wish had acted from prudential reasons: they could not afford the suicide of a national hero, and Lawrence had hinted that he might indeed take his life. Equally they could not afford scandal or publicity. He was transferred to India in January 1927.

His stay in India lasted two years and was divided between a depot near Karachi and Miranshah near the North-West Frontier, the smallest and remotest R.A.F. station. Here Lawrence was one of a British contingent of five officers and twenty-one men backed by 700 India Scouts. They lived in a brick and earth fort surrounded by barbed wire and protected by searchlights and machine guns. 'Round us, a few miles off, in a ring are low bare porcelain-coloured hills, with chipped edges and a broken-bottle skyline. Afghanistan is 10 miles off.'[6]

The Lawrence of this period was as different from his brother Will (who had worked in India just before the war) as from his earlier self. Will's letters had shown an intense interest in Indian life as well as pleasure when on occasions he could lead an Englishwoman into dinner. Lawrence neither studied any Indian language nor, despite invitations, visited any archaeological site. He showed no interest in the politics, culture or religion of the sub-continent. His main recreations were reading, writing letters (postage consumed most of his pay), listening to gramophone records and starting a prose translation of the *Odyssey*. This profitable commission (Ralph Isham had secured him the promise of £800) was, before its completion in 1931, to become a tedious chore. His greatest grief was the death of Hogarth.

The proximity of the troubled Frontier, a revolt against the Afghan king, the mythical magic of Lawrence's name, the beginnings of Stalinist hysteria marked by the trial of British engineers, revived the publicity which had damaged the early part of his R.A.F. career. But this time it worked to Lawrence's advantage. He was hurriedly smuggled back to England but was not dismissed. The rest of his service career was devoted to the development of fast light boats for rescuing airmen downed at sea and was exemplary. His ability to put tight compartments between the different sectors of his life served him well. Those who worked with him have testified to his good influence on his comrades. Men who had never been spoken to kindly by a gentleman were made aware of books, which he lent and often lost, and of classical music, which he played them on his gramophone. He was generous with his money and his time, often standing extra duties to enable his more sociable comrades to go on leave.

On his return to England (where he was smuggled past inquisitive pressmen) he had been posted to the maritime station of Cattewater (later renamed Mount Batten) in Lady Astor's constituency of Plymouth. There he was fortunate in his commanding-officer, Wing Commander Sydney Smith. The Smith family home became more or less his own (though for his darker nature Clouds Hill remained a retreat); with Clare Sydney Smith he achieved a platonic relationship which recalls his friendship for Winifred Fontana, the wife of the Consul at Aleppo. But whereas to her he had been a blazered young Oxonian opening windows on highbrow vistas, at Mount Batten he conformed to the middle-class English norm. He apparently cared deeply for Mrs. Smith's daughter, 'Squeak'; he lost the sharp edges, he disguised the contradictions, which in Syria had intrigued the more cosmopolitan Fontanas and Altounyans. The Schneider Trophy replaced *Morte d'Arthur*.

But in jottings for his own eyes, or letters to friends, he expressed an obsessive dislike for women under sixty. The only time he was forcibly thrown into proximity with a large number had been on his journey out to India. A fragment of prose expresses a pathological repulsion:

> *Swish swish* the water goes against the walls of the ship—sounds nearer. Where on earth is that splashing. I tittup along the alley and peep into the lavatory space, at a moment when no woman is there. It's awash with a foul drainage. Tactless posting a sentry over the wives' defaecations, I think. Tactless and useless all our duties aboard. Hullo here's the O.O. [Orderly Officer] visiting. May as well tell him. The grimy-folded face, the hard jaw, toil-hardened hands, bowed and ungainly figure. An ex-naval warrant, I'll bet. No gentleman. He strides boldly to the latrine: 'Excuse me' unshyly to two shrinking women. 'God', he jerked out, 'flooded with shit—where's the trap?' He pulled off his tunic and threw it at me to hold, and with a plumber's quick glance strode over to the far side, bent down, and ripped out a grating. Gazed for a moment, while the ordure rippled over his boots. Up his right sleeve, baring a forearm hairy as a mastiff's grey leg, knotted with veins, and a gnarled hand: thrust it deep in, groped, pulled out a moist white bundle. 'Open that port' and out it splashed into the night. 'You'd think they'd have had some other place for their sanitary towels. Bloody awful show, not having anything fixed up.' He shook his sleeve down as it was over his slowly-drying arm, and huddled on his tunic, while the released liquid gurgled contentedly down its re-opened drain.[7]

Lawrence's horror at female bodily functions extended to the female physique. 'Do you really like naked women?' he asked Kennington. 'They express so little.'[8] To Robert Graves, the poet of *The White Goddess*, he explained his love of machines: 'Being a mechanic cuts one off from all real communication with women.'[9] And he excluded nubile women even from the norms of politeness. Nicolette Devas recalled a Christmas Day he spent at Friern, visiting Augustus John and his entourage. While 'he had a rather cringing, obsequious admiration for Augustus and called him "Master" much to our astonishment,' he rebuffed the writer when she told him how much she admired the *Seven Pillars*. 'He glanced at me, took three quick steps forward and joined Augustus and started to talk to him.' Trying again in John's studio, she joined Lawrence as he looked through a pile of drawings. ' "This is one of the best, don't you think?" After one or two such remarks on my part, he dropped the drawings and moved away. I had never been snubbed quite like that.'[10] Lawrence also excluded women from Parnassus. 'All the women who ever wrote original stuff could have been strangled at birth, & the history of English literature (& my bookshelves) would be unchanged,' he told Cockerell.[11]

Views so clamant and so often repeated, even more than his giggle and posture, impelled the legend-creators to rebut the obvious conclusion. 'In answer to this stupid canard', wrote Lowell Thomas, 'I can say in the first place that anybody who has met thousands of men of all sorts and conditions can recognize a homosexual. If one has any prolonged contact with pathologues [*sic*] they are bound to give themselves away sooner or later by a gesture, a phrase, an inflection, a peculiar fashion of enunciating the sibilants. I have met all sorts and conditions, including several whose endocrine imbalance afflicted them with a sexual inversion. Furthermore, my father is a physician. I passed many hours, weeks, months, in Lawrence's company and never discerned in him the slightest *indicia* of the homosexual.'[12] But Lawrence denied that he had spent more than a few days with this particular champion.

Like many members of a harassed minority, Lawrence could respond to older women who made no sexual demands. Rosina Harrison, Lady Astor's maid, remembered Lawrence arriving at Cliveden on his motorbike and taking her mistress for a turn on the pillion, to the worried embarrassment of his lordship.[13] More importantly, another woman in her sixties filled the role no one had successfully filled before: that of a sympathetic, unpossessive but generous mother. Charlotte Shaw, to whom he 'confided' the Deraa incident, was to receive additional confidences in which he came near to telling the truth about himself; and though she was finally to conclude, in good-tempered irritation, that he was 'an INFERNAL liar!'[14] at Christmas she regularly sent him chocolates and *pâté de foie gras* from London's most expensive shops. Two factors facilitated her maternal role: Lawrence's real mother continued to harvest the Chinese mission field with the son she had entirely conquered; Bernard Shaw was to be the last in the frieze of mentors which had begun with Hogarth.

This vital alliance, destined to yield Charlotte over three hundred letters, began, like broad rivers, all but unnoticed. In early 1922, when Lawrence had been much concerned over the economic plight of his literary hero, Charles Doughty, Sydney Cockerell, curator of the Fitzwilliam Museum in Cambridge, shared this concern. The two men lunched together at a London hotel on 25 March to discuss what could be done to help the author of *Arabia Deserta*. After the meal, Cockerell suggested that Lawrence walk with him by way of Trafalgar Square to Adelphi Terrace, where the Shaws had a flat. The elderly playwright, whose relish for fame lacked Lawrence's ambivalence, was donating an Augustus John portrait of himself to the Fitzwilliam, which Cockerell wished to collect. Though professing a lively admiration for Shaw, Lawrence shrank from what might seem an intrusion. By this hour, Cockerell said to reassure him, both Shaws would have left for their customary long weekend in the Hertfordshire countryside. But thanks to an unexpected delay, the couple were still in London and Shaw bandied a few cordial words with the famous Colonel Lawrence before taking his leave.[15]

There was no further contact until after Lawrence's resignation from the Colonial Office. Then in August he wrote his first letter to Shaw, carrying self-deprecation to Japanese depths. Could England's leading playwright bear to read (it asked) the ugly linotype of an immensely long and probably worthless book but recently completed?

If Lawrence had continued in this vein Shaw might have declined the honour. (He was busy preparing notes for a socialist summer school.) But Lawrence blended his flattery with claims whose modest presentation made them the more titanic: 'after peace came I found I was myself the sole person who knew what had happened in Arabia during the war: and the only literate person in the Arab Army.'*[16] For another four months Lawrence hid the secret of his new service career. Only in December was he to state that poverty had transformed him into 'one of those funny little objects in blue clothes who look forlorn when they walk about the Strand.'[17]

The Shaws had strong motives for adopting the war hero as disciple or son. The repression of militant impulses which his politics demanded

* If Lawrence meant, attached to the Arab Army, he was making an extraordinary judgement on the literacy of comrades-in-arms such as Young, Stirling and Joyce; if he meant in the Sharifian Army (to which he was merely seconded), by literate he must have meant 'literate in English'.

left Shaw peculiarly susceptible to forceful figures. He was to find good words for both Stalin and Hitler. At the same time, in his role as soldier, Lawrence had a distinctive oddness which linked him to St. Joan—or Shaw himself. Affinities antedated their friendship. Shaw had been a pioneer pedal- and motor-cyclist. His preference for vegetarian diets and dislike for alcohol was shared by Lawrence while his exaltation of pure thought as the Omega point of human development complemented Lawrence's disdain for the flesh. Because of Charlotte's insistence that their marriage should not be consummated, Shaw had been denied paternity. To have Lawrence as filial disciple pleased the didactic playwright and how quickly the Shavian approach to the arts could be implanted in the famous young man was shown by his correspondence with Edward Garnett as early as December 1922. 'I didn't call Shakespeare 2nd rate: only his intellect. He's the most consummate master of vowels and consonants: and the greatest poet. As a philosopher and moralist I have no abnormal respect for him: but the Elizabethan age was tempered rather than forged steel.'[18]

Charlotte Shaw had rejected motherhood, not because she lacked maternal feelings, but because of horror at the way in which her own mother had dominated and reduced her father. This experience drove her to the intense if irrational conviction that marriage in the Prayer Book sense was a repulsive institution. Both Shaws had turned their parental urges on to substitute sons, and Lawrence now filled the gap in their lives left by the defection of Harley Granville Barker whose second wife detested the Shaws.

Lawrence showed his acceptance of this new filial role when, in place of his first military pseudonym, he joined the Royal Tank Corps under the name of Shaw. He used this name on his translation of the *Odyssey* and made it legally his own by deed poll in August 1927.* Characteristically, he clouded the issue: the new name was the first monosyllable he chanced on in the London telephone book; beginning with S, it came low down on the service duty list, etc. But no author, however reluctant, selects an already famous name by hazard. Bernard Shaw and his secretary Blanche Patch have both confirmed, though without the acid, Vansittart's claim that Lawrence called himself 'Shaw, after Bernard, also an exhibitionist.'

Lawrence had as strong reasons for wanting to be adopted as the Shaws for adopting. His enlistment had cut him off from the mandarins of All Souls; the sale of his mother's house cut his other Oxford root. The Shaws held an equivocal position in English society which suited his needs. By 1923 he had become a man of four compass points. In his

* Possibly because Squire Frampton, an old-fashioned Tory, disapproved of the Shaws, Lawrence purchased Clouds Hill under the name of T. E. Ross.[19]

avoidance of the centre he accepted barrack room squalor; in recurrent moods of guilt he arranged flagellatory ordeals; he welcomed the company of famous writers and artists; he cultivated the powerful and the rich. The socialism of the Shaws made it hard for them to despise his new working-class friends, though neither approved of what they saw as a talent-wasting masquerade. That they were Irish was also important. Since his father's death the island of extremists had become a magnetic pole, though he was never to set foot there. In the weeks between the Air Force and the Tank Corps he toyed with joining the newly formed army of the Irish Free State; the one post-service honour which he accepted was membership of the Irish Academy of Letters; even his Oxford accent was to slide into an Irish brogue.

But the decisive factor was the timing and intensity of Charlotte's reaction to *Seven Pillars of Wisdom.* Four days after the *Daily Express* publicized his presence in the R.A.F. and set in motion the forces that expelled him, she asked, 'How is it *conceivable, imaginable,* that a man who could write the Seven Pillars can have any doubts about it? If you don't know it is a "great book", what is the use of anyone telling you so.'[20] The inclusion of certain scenes had (if our conclusions are correct) inspired the myth of the manuscript stolen at Reading Station. Now this respectably married Irish gentlewoman implored: *'don't leave out the things an ordinary man would leave out*: the things people will tell you are "too shocking".' Mrs. Shaw referred to precisely the things that made *Seven Pillars of Wisdom* a 'true' book to its author. No male confrère, no Bohemian, could have so buttressed his courage on this sensitive issue. His real mother, if she had had the power, would surely have imitated the Lady Burton who burned her husband's translation of *The Scented Garden.*

Charlotte gave Lawrence much. With her husband the exchange was more equal. From his acquaintance with this enigmatic and complex man Shaw took part of his inspiration for *Saint Joan* and all of Private Napoleon Alexander Trotsky Meek in *Too True to Be Good.* To Lawrence, Shaw's chief service was in the page by page revision of *Seven Pillars.* The semicolons, for what they were worth, were all his. But Shaw's editorial advice was sometimes bad. He persuaded Lawrence to suppress the prefatory chapter* in which the wartime generation's sense of betrayal was poignantly evoked. By paying tribute to other participants in the Revolt it also reduced the egoism of the draft distributed to admirers and friends in 1926 (The price of that first draft was £30; but since Lawrence gave away many of the two hundred or so copies, the sale did not cover the cost of the book's production.)

As a literary critic E. M. Forster was more perceptive than Shaw. His

* First published in *Oriental Assembly*, ed. A. W. Lawrence, 1939.

letters to Lawrence remain among the handful of worthwhile writings on *Seven Pillars of Wisdom* and *The Mint*.[21] But perhaps because Forster's emotional problems in some respects resembled his own, Lawrence accepted his influence less easily. The fervent admiration which he expressed to Forster he questioned in letters about Forster to other friends.[22] He declined an offer to read *Maurice*, the posthumously published novel in which Forster revealed a love for his own sex which he had long managed to conceal from Lionel Trilling, his best critic. For his part, Forster confessed that some of Lawrence's companions had faces he instinctively distrusted.[23]

In regard to Lawrence's chosen way of life Shaw showed the blindness of a cerebral man. As a confirmed busybody, he laboured to extricate Lawrence from the R.A.F., apparently taking seriously his pretense that he was an airman because he was poor.* In his attempt to secure this latterday Belisarius a pension from the prime minister, Stanley Baldwin, Shaw showed an altruism equal to Lawrence's work for Doughty. He seems not to have discerned the subterranean passions of his male Joan of Arc. When he read Charlotte's correspondence with Lawrence after her death, he was shaken.

The motor cycle which brought Lawrence mobility and from whose saddle he was to die was a gift from his adoptive father.

* *The Times* of 9 September 1935, was to disclose that Lawrence 'left estate of the gross value of £7,441,' (or nearly $30,000 by the then exchange). This would have to be multiplied at least ten times to give a rough equivalent in terms of the late 1970s.

27

LAWRENCE LEFT the R.A.F. with a first class testimonial on 26 February 1935. Few of the friends who had given a party for him some days before saw his pedal-cycle leave.[1] His departure from Bridlington meant a break with extended adolescence. The youth hostels at which he stayed for a shilling a night emphasized his sense of age. 'I'm gray-haired and toothless, half blind and shaking at the knees,' was an Irish exaggeration, intended to provoke an encouraging disclaimer.[2] But the death of the Australian writer, Frederic Manning, whom he had planned to visit on his journey south, was a reminder of the mortality which awaits even the eternal boy. ' "You wonder what I am doing?" ' he was to write to Eric Kennington. 'Well, so do I, in truth. Days seem to dawn, suns to shine, evenings to follow, and then I sleep. What I have done, what I am doing, what I am going to do, puzzle me and bewilder me. Have you ever been a leaf and fallen from your tree in autumn and been really puzzled about it? That's the feeling.'[3]

His letters in the remaining weeks reiterate a sense of crisis which for us is thrown into relief by the knowledge of how soon he would be dead. One biographer has gone so far as to suggest not that he committed suicide on the fatal morning of 13 May, but that he was in a mood which made him 'less vigorous in preserving his own life than he might once have been.'[4] But we may reach another conclusion if we examine the Lawrence of 1935 in the light of previous crises. Two such are relevant: the critical Oxford year in which he broke from his dominating mother; the London days preceding his enlistment in the R.A.F. In the first, he spent a doleful Christmas, fasting on the day itself, then trekking through snow. Yet this bitter mood was the prelude to that great surge of life in which he discovered the Levant and became involved with Arabs. Something similar took place in regard to his second crisis. 'The night before his enlistment,' Bruce has stated, 'was spent at Barton Street [where Sir Herbert Baker, the architect, lent him an attic]. He walked the floor most of the night and was in a heck of a state. He kept asking all sorts of questions which I could not answer, like would joining the R.A.F. be degrading? I don't know who was most pleased when morning came.'[5] The mood of anguish is confirmed by the first sentences of *The Mint*:

'God, this is awful. Hesitating for two hours up and down a filthy street, lips and hands and knees tremulously out of control, my heart pounding in fear of that little door through which I must go to join up. Try sitting a moment in the churchyard. That's caused it. The nearest lavatory, now.'

Like the moods which preceded his first visit to the east and the composition of *The Mint*, the gloom of Lawrence's last weeks could have heralded some new phase of action. So, at least, thought two of the writers who knew him best. Although he had often been fibbed to by Lawrence, Robert Graves had come to know him well. In a book first published five years after Lawrence's death, Graves wrote words which deserve remembering as we approach Lawrence's last weeks of life. 'If he had not been killed in a road-accident shortly after his discharge he would have found the temptation to strong political action almost irresistible.'[6]

This strong political action can hardly have been his projected biography of Sir Roger Casement, much though this could have shocked the conventional reader. Sergeant Knowles' son Pat, described the same spring as 'a husky, sun-burned figure, with brawny muscles . . .' who 'guarded him with untiring vigilance,'[7] understood Lawrence to say that he had been offered the job of reorganizing Home Defence. Like the offer of Egypt, this was an exaggeration, if not a myth. The second writer was Henry Williamson, whose *Genius of Friendship* '*T. E. Lawrence*' was to be published in 1941. Williamson believed that Lawrence was about to undertake something creatively eccentric.

On 24 March 1935, an enraptured audience of eight thousand had heard Sir Oswald Mosley address his largest indoor meeting at London's Albert Hall. Williamson had been one of the first to follow Mosley and, unlike other distinguished disciples, was never to leave him. A gallant soldier seared by the pointless carnage of the trenches, Williamson had won a literary reputation for his sensitive descriptions of animals and birds. After the second war, when there was nothing to be gained by flattery, he expressed his hero-worship for Mosley in *The Phasian Bird*, an allegory about an exceptional pheasant.

Williamson's hero was by any standards one of the remarkable men of his age. Heir to a baronetcy created a year earlier than that of the Chapmans of Westmeath, Mosley had piloted a plane in France, been badly wounded and come back, like many others, determined that 'war must never happen again, that we must build a better land for our companions who still lived, that we must conceive a nobler world in memory of those who died.'[8] He had started by making a good marriage, to Lady Cynthia Curzon, the Foreign Secretary's daughter by an

American wife, and by being elected Conservative M.P. for Harrow. Abandoning the Tories for their opponents, he had become the Labour Party's brightest ornament. But Mosley balanced brilliance with inability to work in a humdrum team. Exasperated by his party's failure to implement his economic proposals,* he made the fatal error of trying to transcend, or break, the party system. The first, the New Party, was democratic in form; after its total electoral failure he adopted the black shirt as the classless uniform of a movement designed to gain power in ten years. At his March 1935, Albert Hall meeting Mosley predicted that Britain would be the next Fascist state. He also urged Britain to govern India, not let it drift, and threatened to deport those Jews who refused to put British interests first. Later Mosley was to quote in his autobiography the peroration to this speech. One sentiment anticipated a famous sentence in John F. Kennedy's Inaugural Address:

'We count it a privilege to live in an age when England demands that great things shall be done, a privilege to be of the generation which learns to say what can we give instead of what can we take. For thus our generation learns there are greater things than slothful ease; greater things than safety; more terrible things than death.'[10]

Williamson had first become conscious of Lawrence when he read his account of arriving in Jidda. 'I knew, instantly, after reading the opening paragraph of *Revolt in the Desert*, serialized in the *Daily Telegraph* in the early spring of 1924, that we had similarities of sight and ear.'[11] Might not Lawrence prove the ideal friend he sought? But whereas 'otters and other wild animals knew each other entirely by a glance, an action,'[12] this was not the case with men. Williamson hung back. In the event Lawrence initiated their friendship by writing, in January 1928, a long and appreciative letter about Williamson's *Tarka The Otter* which Edward Garnett forwarded to its delighted author.[13] In the spring of 1935, oppressed by domestic cares and the need to write for money, Williamson contrasted his state with that of Lawrence, whom he pictured building his swimming-pool among the trees and beginning a cottage for 'the use of a friend, a local man [Pat Knowles] who helped with the gardening and work about the house: Crusoe and man Friday.'[14] Williamson had a sudden and astonishing vision. If the British 'irk'† who had been a Colonel and the Austrian corporal who had become German chancellor could meet, together they might prevent another war. 'With Lawrence of

* Of Mosley's policy as a Labour Minister the historian A. J. P. Taylor was to write: 'His proposals were more creative than those of Lloyd George and offered a blueprint for most of the constructive advances in economic policy to the present day. It is impossible to say where Mosley got his ideas from. Perhaps he devised them himself. If so, they were an astonishing achievement, evidence of a superlative talent which was later to be wasted.[9]

† Slang for airman.

Arabia's name to gather a meeting of ex-Service men in the Albert Hall, with his presence and stimulation to cohere into unassailable logic the authentic mind of the war generation come to power of truth and amity, a whirlwind campaign which would end the old fearful thought of Europe (usury-based) for-ever. So that the sun should shine on free men.'

Should he write a letter, or jump into his six-cylinder Alvis and rush to Dorset? Knowing how, more even than most bachelors, Lawrence valued his privacy, 'he wrote a letter saying he would arrive, "unless rainy day".

'The answer came by telegram.

' "11.25 a.m. 13 May 1935.

' "Williamson Shallowford Filleigh

' "Lunch tuesday wet fine cottage 1 mile north

' "Bovington Camp.

' "SHAW." '[15]

Williamson's proposition was evidence of a remarkably personal approach to history. But before we discuss its physical results for Lawrence, it is appropriate to inquire which way his decision would have gone had he survived to eat the lunch Mrs. Knowles was asked to prepare. Williamson's unshakable conviction that the telegram represented Lawrence's acceptance of his plan[16] is not in itself an adequate answer. Nor is its abrupt rejection by other writers.

After the crimes committed in its name and its subsequent defeat, Fascism was to become a term of abuse. We must here limit it to what it had come to mean by the time Lawrence lost consciousness on 13 May 1935. Even by then there was enough to affright liberals such as E. M. Forster; the abolition of press freedom in Italy and Germany; the suppression of other political parties; the murders of Matteotti and Roehm (though Mussolini's responsibility for the first has been disputed); the suppression of Arab resistance in Libya; and the initiation of anti-Jewish measures in Germany. But still for the future were the Italian invasions of Ethiopia, Albania and Greece; Hitler's re-occupation of the Rhineland, Anschluss with Austria and absorption of Czechoslovakia; the bombing of civilians in Spain and elsewhere. The massacre of ethnic groups did not begin before the outbreak of world war in 1939. With some exceptions (and Churchill was not yet one) most members of the ruling Conservative Party saw Fascism as less dangerous than Soviet communism.

Fascism could certainly use an out of work hero: not as leader but as the bestower on the leader and his movement of what the Arabs call *baraka*, or blessedness. This occurred in other Fascist movements. Gabriele d'Annunzio, the poet who had seized Fiume for Italy, irradiated Mussolini; Ludendorff's approval brightened Hitler's Iron Cross; the regime established in France after 1940 required the hero of Verdun. Lawrence's even partial support for the British Union of Fascists would have far outweighed that of intellectuals such as Williamson and Bernard Shaw or of newspaper-owners such as Lord Rothermere.*

Lawrence's admiration for Lenin,[18] the sympathies which Christopher Caudwell considered proletarian, do not decide the issue. Some notable Marxists veered to Fascism† while later the C.I.A. co-opted others. André Malraux has suggested that those who are at once active and pessimistic will inevitably be Fascist unless they have behind them some metaphysical allegiance. In this context Renee Winegarten has perceptively analysed Drieu la Rochelle, a friend of Malraux and an admirer of Lawrence, who eventually killed himself rather than face trial for collaboration with Nazi Germany. 'As he saw it, Fascism was an expression of the innate romanticism of the lower middle class into which he was born. It was a movement aiming to defend a conception of heroic man against encroaching urbanization and the dehumanizing machine. Drieu's views are basically inspired by a romantic dream: the reluctant intellectual's aspiration to be an heroic man of action.'[19]

In this connection we may return to Robert Graves. 'Lawrence was a man of extraordinary powers and with constant temptation to use them experimentally. He both despised and loved the legend that surrounded him, could not be constant either to his friends or himself. He wrote of himself what the man tormented with devils told Jesus: "My name is Legion, for we are many." His long self-humiliation in the R.A.F. made him forget after a time that he was a fellow of All Souls and the son of an Irish baronet. It tempted him to reject deliberately the first rate in literature and art in favour of the second and third rate, as too "inside" and aristocratic. He began to idealize "the little man", in the sense of lower middle class John Citizens of whom R.A.F. mechanics were largely made, and who in Germany and Italy were the backbone of the Fascist and Nazi revolutions; even played with the idea of himself becoming a dictator.'[20]

The Fascist ethos would be more important to a man with Lawrence's blend of the radical and the authoritarian than any specific programme. It exalted the peasant and his soil against the townsman and his shop; it evoked a simpler, or in Lawrence's favourite adjective 'cleaner', past, Mussolini's cult of pagan Rome matching Himmler's interest in nordic runes. French Fascists united in rejecting the Revolution. Nor was Fascism necessarily anti-Semitic: a Zionist group in Israel was to preach a chthonic cult antedating the Prophets. Nostalgia was one element in Lawrence. As an undergraduate he had lamented the end of the feudal

* Shaw extolled the leadership of Sir Oswald Mosley as a desirable substitute for inefficient parliamentary government in a speech to the Fabian Society, *In Praise of Guy Fawkes*.[17] Lord Rothermere's *Daily Mail* organized a beauty competition for women blackshirts.

† Doriot was the classical example in France.

system. The faith which had underpinned the Middle Ages and which could have been the protective allegiance referred to by Malraux meant little to him. His cosmic nihilism thus edged close to the Fascist metaphysic, while his delight in soldiering had obvious affinities to the Fascist love of uniforms and male togetherness. His social position predisposed him to accept the notion of a national community which united rich and poor, boss and underling, against 'the other', however 'the other' was conceived. Despite his connections with the extremes of Burke's *Peerage* and Hut 12, he had been formed in his mother's house: the petit bourgeois were Fascism's essential class. His approach to the arts would also have been approved in Germany and Italy. His boyhood idol, William Morris, had pruned his language of non-Germanic elements long before the Third Reich's professors revived gothic lettering and cut Latin roots The Foro Mussolini, in which giant, naked, male statues symbolized Italy's chief cities, would have appealed to his tastes in sculpture, which were war-memorial homophile. His friend, Eric Kennington, was assessed in a 1936 issue of *The Studio*, in the same volume which carried Bernard Causton's appreciation of Art in Germany under the Nazis. The affinities between Kennington's idealized males and the Discus Thrower of the Prussian Gold Medallist, Eberhard Encke, or Joachim Utech's granite figure for a gravestone, are unmistakable.[21]

Yet however unfairly, Fascism is now remembered almost exclusively for its doctrines on race. Lawrence's attitudes to this subject were not clear-cut. His patriotism could be innocent and Mary Webb-like. 'England is the most beautiful spot on earth,' he told Colonel Isham; 'England is a much bigger place than you think.'[22] But an almost spinsterly chauvinism could infect it. 'I am proudest of my thirty fights in that I did not have any of our own blood shed. All our subject provinces to me were not worth one dead Englishman.'[23] Such chauvinism could inflate into the odd passage about negroes in *Seven Pillars*:

> Their faces, being clearly different from our own, were tolerable; but it hurt [*sic*] that they should possess exact counterparts of all our bodies.[24]

After his death, his executors permitted the publishers of Simon Jesty's *River Niger* to use one of Lawrence's admiring letters as a preface. The opening paragraph of this now forgotten novel shows what Lawrence could tolerate:

> Speaking strictly as a medical man, I don't like niggers. I resent association with the crisp, curly knob, the thick trumpet lips, the shallow receding brow, the mouth first past the winning-post with the rest of the face an abrasion. I don't like the elevation, front or back. Neither do I care for Nature's scheme of *décor*.[25]

But Jews, not negroes, were the 'race' which Fascists of the thirties most disliked and Lawrence never shared the particular bigotry which Adolf Hitler derived from Houston Stewart Chamberlain and Chamberlain's father-in-law, Richard Wagner. In the broadest sense he was pro-Semitic. Brought up with the Bible-Christian's respect for the Hebrews, he had spent his happiest years among the settled Semites of northern Syria and the nomadic Semites of western Arabia. His early letters include hostile references to individual Jews; his writings about Arabs are equally spiced; but such utterances show a naturalness, a lack of constraint, which are the opposite of the suppressed racialist's efforts to be polite. His liking for Arab individuals—the playful Dahoum, the severe Sharif Ali, the noble Feisal—may have been prompted in part by opportunism; his defence of Jews (he was to remove a remark that might have distressed them from Shaw's play about himself)[26] could have owed something to an awareness of Jewish influence in the publishing world. But no disciple of Wagner (whose *Parsifal* was as anti-Arab as it was anti-Jewish) would have bundled up with Dahoum in flea-ridden quilts or have written, 'If I was trying to export the ideal Englishman to an international exhibition, I think I'd like to choose S. S. [Siegfried Sassoon] for chief exhibit.'[27]

There were British Fascists whose obsession was anti-Semitism. Henry Williamson was not of their number, his chief concern being the prevention of another war with Germany. Mosley's policy of a Britain strong yet ready to make peace came closer to Lawrence's expressed opinions (and he left numerous notes as to how the Air Force might be improved) than the ideas of those who simultaneously demanded disarmament and resistance to Hitler. Like the heroine of E. M. Forster's best novel, Lawrence 'hated war but liked soldiers.'

How he would have reacted to Hitler if he had met him remains in doubt.[28] Despite an affinity to Williamson which went further than style, Lawrence's life since 1922 represented a flight from the power which was central to most Fascist daydreams. Hitler was a corporal who had become a warlord; Lawrence was a colonel who had put himself at the beck of corporals. This was a Himalayan difference. The more banal appeals of the Nazi regime would not have tempted him. He might have admired the Hitler Youth: he could hardly have responded to a Nuremberg Rally with Drieu's panegyric: 'I have experienced nothing like it for artistic emotion since the Russian ballet.'[29] Nor would he have condoned what in the defence of another totalitarianism W. H. Auden called 'the necessary murder'. The experiences behind *Seven Pillars of Wisdom* had revealed the roots of cruelty. The icy, snubbing side which he had shown to Nicolette Devas is not mentioned by later witnesses. The truly cruel are the unaware; the author of *The Mint* was of different substance from those who work in concentration camps by day and at dusk return to their budgerigars and Franz Lehár.

In 1935 the question of what Lawrence of Arabia would do next was not academic; nor did it concern himself only, or British Fascists. His military status from 1922 until 1935 had solved the public problem of keeping a hero under control. His re-emergence as a civilian, free to publish his opinions or to join a party, came at a pivotal moment in modern British history. The view that Fascism was a desirable bulwark against Soviet Russia was eroded in 1935 by Italian behaviour. Mussolini's demand for status in Ethiopia similar to Britain's in Egypt, then his invasion, helped prompt a decision to re-arm. In 1935 'the Establishment' (the term was not yet in general use) was virtually the Conservative Party and was split between those who wished to oppose the Fascist Powers and those who wished to appease them. Lawrence's kinsman, Robert Vansittart, was so much of the first school that Vansittartism passed into English usage as a term for extreme hostility to everything German.

In Vansittart's autobiography, unfinished at his death, he had reached this crucial year. 'Among my increasing difficulties,' he wrote, 'was the Cliveden Set. The Astors have publicly denied the existence of any conscious or organized body, and are correct. Its members were not organized, but some were spontaneously inclined to criticize France rather than Germany and to blame me as head of the opposing body in the Foreign Office.... It is nonsensical of commentators like Eddie Winterton [Lord Winterton had campaigned with Lawrence and was to attend his funeral] to call "nonsensical" allegations that the Set was a reality. It is true that Cliveden enjoyed a diversity of visitors. Some came for its view of the Thames, some for its view of the world, and some for talk of that which they knew not. That happens to all of us, if we talk too much . . . Bernard Shaw, for instance, "all intelligence and no brain," said Garvin, also in the ambience. He wrote so often and so loudly that he found something to say for Stalin's Russia as well as Mussolini's Italy and Hitler's Germany.'[30] Vansittart included many of Lawrence's closest friends in the Cliveden Set. Geoffrey Dawson, who had been dismissed from the editorship of *The Times* for his pro-German bias, then reinstated by the Astors when they bought the paper, had secured Lawrence his All Souls fellowship. Lionel Curtis, to whom Lawrence had written poignant letters, also supported appeasement.

These preliminary reflexions may prepare us for Lawrence's death, his last great mystery, if we remember that to those who could follow Lawrence and his movements as closely as Vansittart (whose post gave him access to official secrets) the unpredictable hero was as much a threat as the unpredictable new king was to be in 1936.

Having paid for his telegram to Williamson, he revved up for the short journey home. The road from Bovington Camp had three slight undulations as it pushed north between the moorland churned by tanks. Except in places like Salisbury Plain where he would open up the throttle till he was doing eighty, Lawrence was a careful rider. He had had no more than a couple of spills since he first began riding. George Brough who manufactured his series of bikes, has described him as 'one of the finest riders I have ever met. In the several runs I took with him, I am able to state with conviction that T.E.L. was most considerate to every other road user. I never saw him take a single risk nor put any other rider or driver to the slightest inconvenience.'[31] He was also a creature of habit; Pat Knowles knew exactly at what point on the road home he would change down. He did not wear a crash helmet.

This time he did not reach Clouds Hill. Exactly what happened remains conjecture. None of those who have given evidence observed the precise moment of Lawrence's mishap. Corporal Ernest Catchpole of the Royal Army Ordnance Corps, walking his dog on the rough land to the west of the road, saw parts of the fatal ride; but the road's undulations made it impossible for him to observe Lawrence all the time. From the evidence Catchpole gave later—and from which he refused to budge—it is plain that his eye caught, in sequence, the following: a motor-cyclist, Lawrence, proceeding north in the direction of Clouds Hill; approaching the motor-cyclist from Clouds Hill, a black, private motor car; the motor cycle swerving a moment after it passed the car at a point he could not see; then two pedal-cyclists preceding the motor-cyclist towards Clouds Hill. Finally: 'I saw the bike twisting and turning over and over along the road. I saw nothing of the driver. I ran to the scene and found the motor-cyclist on the road. His face was covered with blood which I tried to wipe away with my handkerchief.'[32]

The other known participants in the drama were Frank Fletcher and Albert Hargreaves, both fourteen, both having just left school, both the sons of serving soldiers. Albert, or 'Bertie', had recently secured a job as a butcher's delivery boy.[33] At the moment of the accident they were cycling in single file towards Lawrence's cottage and the surrounding woods. Their evidence will be discussed when we come to the inquest: at the time, since they were facing in the same direction as Lawrence, they saw nothing, though they apparently heard his engine from behind. Albert, who was following Frank, was described in *The Times* as being concussed;[34] Captain C. P. Allen of the Royal Army Medical Corps who admitted the boy to Bovington Military Hospital between 11.30 and 11.45 a.m. was later to describe him as 'not seriously hurt.'[35] Whether Lawrence's cycle hit Albert Hargreaves as it twisted and turned, or whether Lawrence was still on it, is uncertain. Frank Fletcher, in front, was knocked off his bicycle, 'because Bert's bicycle fell on top of me.'[36]

Lawrence could never tell his side of what had happened. Taken, albeit a civilian, to Bovington Military Hospital, he never regained consciousness.

Bovington Camp reacted to this as something more than an ordinary traffic accident. All ranks were warned that they came under the Official Secrets Act.[37] The boys' fathers were told to keep them silent. Catchpole was cautioned that, since he had not seen the accident, he should not confuse matters by mentioning the black car. Two plain clothes detectives were posted on Lawrence duty: one sat by his bed, while the other rested on a cot outside the door. In permanent coma, Lawrence survived for six days. His brother, Arnold Lawrence, returned from a holiday in Spain to hear reports that officials from the Air Ministry had removed secret papers from Clouds Hill. 'I can only say,' he told a reporter from the *Dorset Daily Echo* 'that a special guard has been sent to the cottage. This has been done to ensure that the sightseers should not bother us and to protect my brother's valuable books, which are in the cottage.'[38] Torn between deference to officialdom (he was to work for Intelligence himself in the Second World War) and anguish for his brother, Arnold Lawrence gave signs of a natural confusion in his statements then and later. The *Dorset Daily Echo* soon reported that the library at Clouds Hill was of no great monetary value since the manuscript of *Seven Pillars of Wisdom* was in the Bodleian Museum. At the inquest Arnold Lawrence was to be unsure of his brother's age,[39] and, more oddly, to declare, despite Lawrence's letter to him about *The Mint*, that he had left no literary work of any value.[40] As late as Friday the 17th he still hoped: 'I think his chances of pulling through are better than those of the average man in a similar condition.'[41] But Lawrence's faculties were wrecked beyond repair; he could have survived only to a vegetative existence. The persistence of his heartbeat until just after 8 a.m. on Sunday the 19th rules out any causal connection between cardiac arrest and his accident.

The notion that their press is freer and their legal system more meticulous than those of all other countries has consoled many Englishmen for their loss of wealth and power. The way the inquiry into Lawrence's death was conducted and reported hardly confirms it. An inquest was hastily arranged for the second morning after his death, the funeral being planned for the same afternoon. No journalist seems to have probed the tangle of contradictions and rumours: perhaps because no newspaper proprietor felt like defying instructions (issued during Lawrence's coma) that all news should come from the War Office.[42] The inquest on Lawrence—who had died, a civilian, on the public highway—was held in a small dining room in the Camp. Few members of the public could gain admittance. Corporal Catchpole was the all-important witness; he was a mature adult, accustomed to responsibility and uninvolved in what had happened. Recalled to repeat his evidence, he persisted in his 'positive' certainty that he had seen a black car moments before the crash. In contradiction, the boys, who had 'spent more time with the army authorities than with the police',[43] denied having seen the black car or any other vehicle. This conflict of evidence was described by one juryman as 'funny'[44] and by the Coroner, Mr. L. E. N. Neville-Jones, when he returned the jury's verdict of accidental death, as 'rather unsatisfactory'.[45]

To consider the boys' evidence first: the intervention of the military and civil police as Lawrence lay in coma had aroused local suspicions that something was being hushed up. To disperse this impression, the authorities allowed a reporter from the *Dorset Daily Echo* to interview Frank Fletcher, described as the son of a bandsman at Bovington Camp. According to what Frank told him, the two friends were cycling to visit a bird's nest at Warwick's Close, two miles from the Camp.

> 'We were riding in single file. I was leading. I heard a motor cycle coming from behind and then I heard a crash. Bertie's cycle hit mine and I fell off.
>
> When I looked up I saw Bertie lying in the road. The motor cycle had skidded on the other side, and the man who had gone over the handle bars had landed with his feet about 5 yards in front of the motor cycle which was about five yards ahead of where I fell. I got up and went to Bertie to see if he was all right. He gave me his butcher's book. I found three pence on the road. I asked Bertie if that was his money but he never answered. He seemed to go to sleep. I waited a minute or two, being afraid to go to the man, because his face was covered with blood. Then a man came up on a cycle and asked me to get the ambulance. But before I could go some soldiers came and he went to get it himself. A lorry came up. The men got two stretchers from some camp at the roadside and the injured man and Bertie were put on them and taken into the lorry.'
>
> The boy said there was no motor car or other vehicle on the road at the time. 'I heard the noise of the motorcycle and then the crash. I did not hear any sound as if possibly a tyre had burst.'[46]

Even on good occasions boys are bad witnesses. (This generalization was confirmed in the police case against Mr. Peter Haine, the Young Liberal leader, in early 1976.) For Frank Fletcher and Bertie Hargreaves the situation could not have been worse. One had been in a state of physical shock; both had an involuntary share in the death of a hero. That the police spoke in terms of 'Lawrence of Arabia' is suggested by Frank Fletcher's reference in his evidence to 'Mr. Lawrence', though Lawrence was locally known as Mr. Shaw. Both boys were under pressure from their fathers, minor cogs in the military machine.*

The black car remains the nub of a mystery which was to prompt friends like Bruce and Williamson to suspect foul play.[48] In rebuttal, it has been suggested that Catchpole mistook a delivery van which passed Clouds Hill every morning except Sundays for the black car. This makes no sense. If the evidence of the boy cyclists disposed of the black car, it also disposed of the van, since they claimed to have seen no vehicle whatsoever, while the local police could easily have located the driver of a familiar delivery van. If Catchpole was right and the black car existed, the failure of its driver to come forward (the news of the accident was in every newspaper and every news bulletin) suggests that he was involved, either accidentally or deliberately, in Lawrence's crash. Everyone who has ridden a motor cycle knows how easily a sudden swerve can be induced; harmless to the driver of a car, on a narrow road it could be fatal to a cyclist without a helmet. Catchpole's evidence of Lawrence's speed—he put it at between fifty and sixty miles an hour—is of less value, since a moving object is hard to time from a hundred yards away. The boys who heard Lawrence's machine approaching from behind described its sound as 'very high powered'. This is not indicative of high speed and Arnold Lawrence said that when his brother's Brough moved fast it was practically soundless. A high-powered noise fits with the evidence of the machine itself, which was carried to the inquest in the back of a truck. The local man who bought it found its gears jammed in second: in this gear the Brough's top speed was thirty-eight miles an hour.

The unsatisfactory nature of the inquest was hardly the fault of the Coroner. He was faced with a paucity of witnesses and an official desire to bury the hero with a minimum of fuss. A student of the case, Mr. Colin Graham, claims that a week before the accident Lawrence and an airman friend, both on motor bikes, noticed a black car apparently being tested on the lonely road leading past his cottage. The road was a good place for such tests: it led to a T junction with the old Dorchester to Wareham road; the only other road of access was through the grounds of Moreton Estate, a rough earth road crossing the Frome by a ford near Moreton

* A useful reminder of the unreliability of youthful evidence as well as of retrospective memory, is given in a version of the accident which Fletcher gave, in his forties, to the Mayor of Wareham. It differs in several respects from the account which he gave at the time to the *Dorset Daily Echo*:
1) Instead of bird-nesting, he had gone with Hargreaves on an errand connected with his job as a butcher's boy; 2) He had seen 'Lawrence go over the handle bars of his bike and land in a sitting position against a tree'; 3) 'When I got over the shock I went over to Lawrence *first*' (this author's emphasis); 4) Dropping all mention of the man on a cycle: 'before I knew it there were soldiers around us. They must have come from the tents on the far side of the road. They put Bert and Lawrence into a lorry and took them to Bovington Military Hospital.'[47]

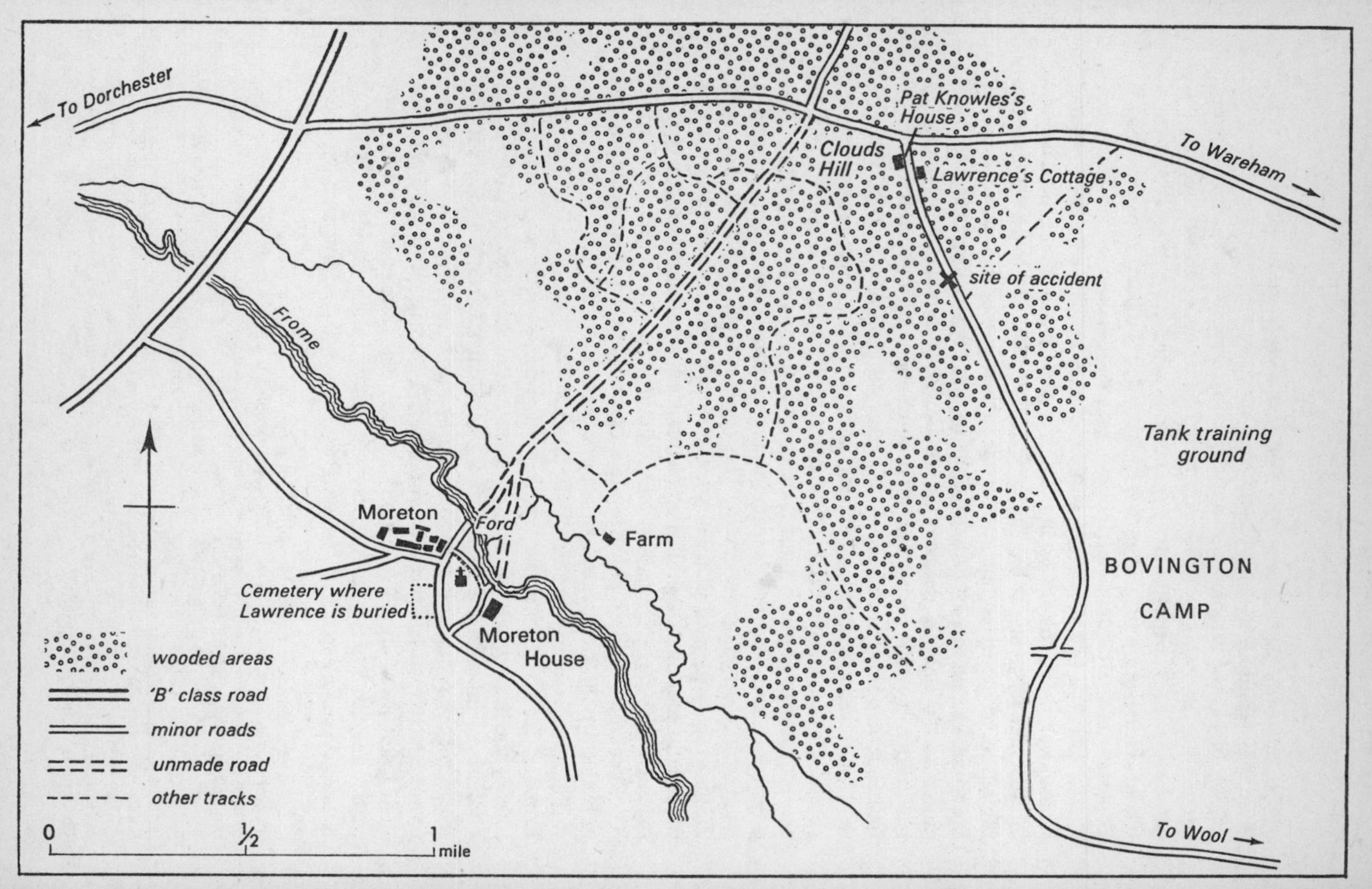
To Dorchester
To Wareham
Pat Knowles's House
Clouds Hill
Lawrence's Cottage
site of accident
Frome
Tank training ground
Moreton
Ford
Farm
Cemetery where Lawrence is buried
Moreton House
BOVINGTON CAMP
wooded areas
'B' class road
minor roads
unmade road
other tracks
0
½
1 mile
To Wool

House and leading through secluded woods to within a short distance of Clouds Hill. Graham asks three questions: 'If it were being tested by a local garage, why didn't the owners come forward? Why couldn't the police trace it? Most of all, why didn't the airman give evidence at the inquest?'[49]

The last question can be answered in the light of what is known. The officials from the Air Ministry or some other body who visited Clouds Hill before Arnold Lawrence got back from Spain will have had no great task in going through the contents of the cottage. We know[50] that these included fifteen letters from Bruce, letters from Lawrence in the persona of the Old Man, as well as a diary in which he recorded the number of lashes administered to him on different occasions by Jock and another serviceman designated by the initial 'G'. An American psychiatrist who has made a close study of Lawrence's masochism has published letters by Lawrence which, apart from birches, mention 'a metal whip,' a 'jute whip' and 'a useful little dogwhip'.[51] Such items would have caught the attention of experienced investigators even if they were not already aware of Lawrence's peculiarities. They probably found, if they were not deliberately seeking, the letter from Henry Williamson to which Lawrence's telegram was the reply. It has never turned up,[52] and just as its disappearance helped to insulate Lawrence of Arabia from a suspect minority, so the evidence of his unusual activities was enough to silence service friends.

These considerations help explain a puzzle involving Bruce. In his first letter to Arnold Lawrence of the 17 May 1935, written from Aberdeen, the Scotsman said that he wished to contact 'Ted's' uncle—the Old Man, in whose existence he still believed, but with whom he had always communicated by way of Lawrence; in his second letter, written on the day of Lawrence's death, he regretted being unable to attend the funeral for financial reasons. Yet in his August 1938 article for the *Scottish Field* Bruce claimed to have seen Lawrence for the last time as he lay unconscious in Bovington Military Hospital; in what he told the *Sunday Times* thirty years later he insisted that he had witnessed his burial and been treated unpleasantly by those conducting the ceremony. While the dating of the letters from Aberdeen makes the first claim, in the ghosted article, implausible, it would have been a simple matter for Bruce to have caught a night train to London and to have gone on to Dorset in good time for the funeral.

For while the jury were reaching their verdict, a special train was bearing distinguished mourners from London. Charlotte and Bernard Shaw were on a South African holiday; Feisal had died in Switzerland two years before; Sharif Ali was entombed in his Saudi marriage. But Siegfried Sassoon, Mrs. Hardy, Lord Winterton and more than a hundred others knelt for a brief service in a church which was to be bombed five years later in the war that happened after all. Under the floor lay Frampton ancestors; across fields stood their house, a substantial mansion with a first-rate collection of third-rate portraits. The chief mourners were the 35-year-old Arnold Lawrence and his wife. But the crowd of villagers, soldiers and navvies working on the Wool road probably recognized no one but Lady Astor and Winston Churchill, though General Wavell was pointed out for having arrived by autogiro. Only the informed will have known that the six pall-bearers represented facets, or phases, of the dead man's life: Sir Ronald Storrs, scholarship; Eric Kennington, art; Aircraftman Bradbury, the Royal Air Force; Private Russell, the Royal Tank Corps; Patrick Knowles, Clouds Hill; Colonel Newcombe, his life in Arabia.

From the church (whose graveyard was full) his friends bore the small coffin to the nearby piece of field which Squire Frampton had recently donated and in which he was to join Lawrence in 1955. Unlike the wreaths, the funerary superlatives were to last undisturbed for twenty years.*

The funeral over, Squire Frampton (whose name *The Times* was not to include in its list of mourners) invited the quality to Moreton House, not in a final acknowledgement of kinship, but in his role as local grandee. Some time later a tombstone was placed above the grave. It renamed the man interred there Lawrence, recalled his All Souls Fellowship and set the symbol of Oxford University above his feet. *To the dear memory of* asserted the possessiveness of a mother who cared so little for her son's essential nature that she added a text from the holy book he disbelieved:

The hour is coming & now is
When the dead shall hear
The voice of the
SON OF GOD
And they that hear
Shall live.[53]

The pilgrim must be dull-souled who does not sense, beneath the green plastic flower pots, a giant spirit writhing in a little frame.

* Richard Aldington published his ungenerous, debunking *Biographical Enquiry* in 1955.

NOTES INCORPORATING BIBLIOGRAPHY

The following abbreviations have been used for the sources which occur most frequently:

TEbF	*T. E. Lawrence by his Friends*, ed. A. W. Lawrence, Jonathan Cape, London, 1937
Ls	*The Letters of T. E. Lawrence*, ed. David Garnett, Jonathan Cape, London, 1938
HLs	*The Home Letters of T. E. Lawrence and his Brothers*, ed. M. R. Lawrence, Basil Blackwell, Oxford, 1954
TEL to RG for Part I, TEL to LH for Part II	T. E. Lawrence/to his Biographers/Robert Graves and Liddell Hart, Cassell, London, 1963
HPs	Hogarth Papers, St. Antony's College, Oxford
SAD	Sudan Archive, School of Oriental Study, University of Durham
BSA	Bonn State Archives
Seven Pillars	*Seven Pillars of Wisdom* by T. E. Lawrence Unless otherwise stated, all quotations are from the accessible, 1962 Penguin Modern Classic Edition

NOTES

Chapter 1

1. Sir John Betjeman has described the social differences in North Oxford: 'Polstead Road and Chalfont Road where I would go for tea, were slightly beyond the pale . . . ' *Victorian and Edwardian Oxford*, Batsford, 1971, p. 7.

2. Mrs. Lawrence's account book, discovered in the attic at 2, Polstead Road, was in 1975 in the possession of Mrs. E. Greening Phillips.

3. A clear photograph of this stall, taken around the time of the Lawrences' move to Oxford, may be found facing page 277 in *Canon Christopher of St. Aldates, Oxford*, John Reynolds, The Abbey Press, Abingdon, 1967.

4. Mrs. Seaton Pringle, a former companion of one of the Chapman daughters, confided this to Dr. John E. Mack, who published it in note 6, p. 472, *A Prince of Our Disorder, The Life of T. E. Lawrence*, Little, Brown and Company, Boston, 1976.

5. Phillip Knightley and Colin Simpson, *The Secret Lives of Lawrence of Arabia*, Nelson, London, 1969, p. 8.

6. John E. Mack, quoting Lady Pansy Lamb, op. cit., p. 472, n. 6.

7. See Reynolds, op. cit., photographs pp. 276 or 350.

8. ibid, pp. 69, 251.

9. *Secret Lives*, p. 11. The authors quote conversations with A. W. Lawrence.

10. I owe this suggestion to the late Dr. Gervase Mathew, O.P.

11. Reynolds, op. cit., p. 232.

12. ibid, p. 286.

13. Vyvyan Richards, TEbF, p. 31.

14. 'Discipline, according to Arnold, was administered in the form of severe whippings on the buttocks and was delivered by his mother because his father was "too gentle, too imaginative—couldn't bring himself to." Arnold remembered receiving only one such beating himself. His mother once told him, "I never had to do it to Bob, once to Frank and frequently to T.E." ' Mack, op. cit., p. 33.

15. Robert Graves, *Lawrence and the Arabs*, Cape, London, 1927, p. 13.

16. Quoted in Appendix to Timothy D'Arch Smith, *Love in Earnest, Some Notes on the Lives and Writings of English 'Uranian' Poets from 1889 to 1930*, Routledge & Kegan Paul, London, 1970, p. 211.

17. HLs, p. 400; Will Lawrence's letter of 11 April 1910.

18. Reynolds, op. cit., p. 233.

19. TEL to LH, p. 78.

20. Letter to Charlotte Shaw, 14.4.1927; B.M. Add. MS. 45903.

Chapter 2

1. TEbF, p. 25.
2. ibid, p. 26.
3. ibid, p. 31.
4. ibid, p. 27.
5. TEL to LH, p. 209.
6. Mack, op. cit., p. 32, quoting Helen J. Cash's interview with Vyvyan Richards, 4.3.1965, in the *Sunday Times* research materials now in the Imperial War Museum, London.
7. TEbF, pp. 30, 31.
8. ibid, pp. 36–7.
9. ibid.
10. T. W. Chaundy, TEbF, p. 41.
11. HLs, under date.
12. TEbF, p. 54.
13. Ls, p. 51.
14. HLs, p. 55.
15. ibid, p. 604, 25.8.1910.
16. ibid, p. 11, 9.8.1906.
17. Canon E. F. Hall, TEbF, p. 46.
18. TEbF, p. 26.
19. Chaundy, TEbF, p. 41.
20. To Mrs. Rieder, 4.7.1909; Ls, p. 115.
21. HLs, p. 31.

Chapter 3

1. *The City of Oxford High School Magazine*, April 1966, p. 37.
2. H. Arnold, C.B.E., quoted in F. C. Lay's *A Contributor School*; published in *Jesus College Record*, 1972.
3. *Jesus College Magazine*, June 1935, article signed J.G.E. [Sir John Goronwy Edwards].
4. TEbF, p. 43.
5. E. H. R. Altounyan, TEbF, p. 115.
6. David Garnett, TEbF, p. 431.
7. See the passage of Robert Graves as amended by Lawrence: 'He took no interest in organised games, ~~which were too tame for him, and has never done so since.~~ [*because they were organised, because they had rules, because they had results. He will never compete—in anything.*'] TEL to RG, p. 61.
8. E. F. Hall, TEbF, p. 48.
9. Ls, p. 101.
10. TEbF, p. 41.
11. ibid, p. 62.
12. ibid, p. 67.
13. ibid, p. 68.
14. For the relationship between E. G. Hardy and Rolfe, see Donald Weeks, *Corvo*, London, 1971, pp. 232–4.
15. 'Cheery and wholesome' was a phrase extracted from one *Times* review by Bradford's publishers.
16. Introductory poem to *The New Chivalry and Other Poems*, Rev. E. E. Bradford, D.D., Kegan Paul, 1918.
17. The two poems were in Lawrence's notebook of favourite short poems

edited as *Minorities*, by J. M. Wilson, with a Preface by C. Day Lewis, Jonathan Cape, London, 1971.

18. 'He was, I remember, most enthusiastic about the work of Augustus John, Henry Tuke and John Nash.' Alec Dixon, TEbF, p. 368.

Chapter 4

1. HLs, p. 75.
2. TEbF, p. 25.
3. TEL to RG, p. 48.
4. The Ashmolean Museum's *Annual Reports*.
5. TEbF, p. 49.
6. See Joan Evans, *Time and Chance*, London, 1943.
7. David G. Hogarth, *A Wandering Scholar in the Levant*, John Murray, London, 1896, p. 94.
8. TEbF, p. 50.
9. Vyvyan Richards, *Portrait of T. E. Lawrence: the Lawrence of the Seven Pillars of Wisdom*, Jonathan Cape, London, 1936, p. 20.
10. TEbF, p. 383.
11. Richards spoke of 'love at first sight' to the authors of *Secret Lives*, p. 29.
12. ibid.
13. TEL to LH, p. 78.
14. TEbF, p. 387.
15. Ls, p. 124.
16. TEbF, p. 385.
17. Mack, op. cit., pp. 64–66.
18. The quotations come in sequence from HLs.
19. HLs, p. 66.
20. Ibid.
21. HLs, p. 70; for Chartres, p. 80–81.
22. The story derives from an Oxford clergyman who claimed to have taken Lawrence for choir-practice. The clergyman, who resigned his cloth on the occasion of his marriage, claimed to have heard the information from Lawrence himself, who had been profoundly disturbed.
23. None of Lawrence's family or friends mentions this experience in their published tributes or letters. Army Records are politely opaque. 'Extensive inquiries', the inquirer is told, 'have been carried out in the past to ascertain whether or not Lawrence of Arabia did actually serve in the Royal Artillery but there is no record of him ever having done so.' Even if it were certain that he had enlisted, and under a false name, and this name was known, Army Records would be unable to confirm this 'as very few records of this period are still in existence.' (Letter dated 1.11.1974.) Lawrence made no mention of the story to his first serious biographer, Robert Graves, but did mention it to his second, Liddell Hart over the weekend of 12 May 1927. Hart made the following note of their conversation: 'Paid for own schooling by scholarships. Took history at Oxford, but studied war since about 16 years of age, because filled with idea of freeing a people and had chosen Arabs as only suitable ones left. Began studies in Risorgimento and the Condottieri. Translated extracts from Procopius and other authors. Interests archaeology, military history etc., and took 1st in history on war questions—originality in treating. Enlisted in artillery about 1906—before going to Oxford— . . . and did 8 months before being bought out.' (TEL to LH, p. 24.)

As Lawrence might have anticipated, this precocious experience of military life caught Hart's attention, who submitted three specific questions: when had it taken place? where had Lawrence served? how had he fared under discipline at that time?

Lawrence's handwritten reply evaded all but the last question. 'This is hush-hush. I should not have told you. I ran away from home . . . and served for six months. No trouble with discipline, I having always been easy; but the other fellows fought all Friday and Saturday nights and frightened me with their roughness. I'd rather keep this out of print, please; the whole episode. It is negligible, militarily, like my subsequent O.T.C. training.' (TEL to LH, p. 51).

Hart then compressed the material into the following draft: 'He was still a schoolboy when . . . he ran off and enlisted in the Artillery. He served some six months before he was brought out.' This did not satisfy Lawrence who bracketed the passage and wrote in substitution: 'In his teens he took a sudden turn for military experience at the urge of some private difficulty, and served for a while in the ranks.' The story appeared in this form in Hart's biography.

The painting signed by Henry Scott Tuke which hangs upstairs at Clouds Hill only adds to the mystery. Not typical of the Painter of Youth at his best (which leaves room to doubt its authenticity), it shows Lawrence as a boy on the beach. He is removing military clothes while a naked friend is already in the water. Tuke made a practice of adding new heads to existing bodies. He may have made this picture towards the end of his life (he died in 1929) having heard the story of Lawrence's enlistment in the Artillery; or the uniform may be that of the Oxford O.T.C. Or alternatively, Tuke may have added the grown-up Lawrence's head to the youthful figure; Lawrence may have seen the picture and as a result invented his fantasy.

24. Records of Oxford City Council.

25. TEbF, p. 28.

26. TEL to LH, p. 79.

27. In her contribution to *T. E. Lawrence by his Friends* Sarah Lawrence countered the statement of Mr. Jane, Lawrence's coach, that he often came for a tutorial between midnight and 4 a.m. by insisting that her son was always home by 11.30.

28. Mack, op. cit., p. 16.

29. TEbF, p. 47.

30. ibid, p. 384.

31. The account of this snowy walk comes from Beeson's contribution to TEbF, p. 57.

Chapter 5

1. Lawrence to Edward Garnett, 22 December 1927; Bodleian; quoted Mack, op. cit., p. 369.

2. Lawrence stressed this to Charlotte Shaw, particularly in his letter of 14.4.1927; B.M. Add. MS. 45903.

3. 'They thought always that they were living in sin, and that we would some day find it out. Whereas I knew it before I was ten.' Letter to Charlotte Shaw, *vide supra*.

4. To Lionel Curtis in a letter of 1926 quoted by authors in *Secret Lives*, p. 16.

5. I owe this description to Miss Mary Lascelles.

6. F.O. 195 2295.

7. *Grande Dizionario Enciclopedico.*
8. Letter to the author from Percival Davies, Esq., O.B.E., dated 6.5.1975.
9. See photograph in TEbF, p. 48.
10. Lord Milner published his *Credo* in *The Times*, London, 27.7.1925.
11. For Will Lawrence's attitude to Boers and Indians, see HLs, pp. 474 and 587.
12. C. H. Firth, *Modern History in Oxford*, Basil Blackwell, Oxford, 1920, p. 43.
13. TEbF, p. 30.
14. Lawrence's *Letters* or *Home Letters* provide most of the evidence for the following pages.
15. Evelyn Waugh described his visit to Port Said in *Labels*, p. 83.
16. TEL to LH, p. 84.
17. ibid, p. 166.
18. HLs, p. 86.
19. ibid, p. 87.
20. ibid, p. 103.
21. For an account of Pirie-Gordon's trip, see Sir Harry Luke, *Cities and Men, an Autobiography*, Vol. 1. Geoffrey Bles, London, 1953.
22. HLs, p. 94.
23. ibid, pp. 88, 97.
24. Letter to author from Miss Nora Harrison, 21.5.1975.
25. HLs, p. 493.
26. ibid, p. 98.
27. ibid, p. 99.
28. L. Oliphant, *Haifa, or Life in Modern Palestine*, London, 1887, pp. 59–60.
29. HLs, p. 105.
30. TEbF, p. 76.
31. HLs, p. 103.
32. Pliny, v. 78; quoted by René Dussaud in *Topographie Historique de la Syrie Antique et Médiévale*, Paris, 1927.
33. HLs, p. 104.
34. ibid, p. 105; Lawrence's emphasis.
35. Ls, p. 77, HLs, p. 105, HLs, p. 133.
36. ibid, p. 105.
37. ibid, p. 106.
38. René Dussaud, op. cit., p. 172.
39. Ls, p. 81.
40. HLs, p. 104.
41. TEbF, p. 62.

Chapter 6

1. TEbF, p. 74.
2. Ls, p. 93.
3. Vyvyan Richards, op. cit., p. 53.
4. *Diary MCMXI*, first published by Corvinus Press, 1937, then reprinted in *Oriental Assembly*, Ed. A. W. Lawrence, Williams and Norgate, London, 1939.
5. Lawrence supplied most of the personal material for Robert Graves's *Lawrence and the Arabs*, Cape, 1927; he then checked the draft text. In this, Lawrence, on his way out to Syria, bought a copper watch at *the Paris Exhibition*. Lawrence (who had gone to Syria by sea through the Straits of Gibraltar) merely

deleted the italicized words. Lawrence also changed, perhaps in a post-war anti-Turkish mood, 'a village of Kurds' to 'a Turkman village'. In the version as passed by Lawrence, a villager stalked him all day believing that the watch was gold. Towards evening the Turkman seized Lawrence's Colt (not a Mauser, as in the contemporary letters) and putting it to the Englishman's head pulled the trigger. The safety catch being on, the Turkman contented himself with battering him about the head with *stones* (the plural was Lawrence's emendation). Next day Lawrence crossed the Euphrates to Birejik, used his *Iradés* to collect 110 men and returned to the Turkman village. Recovering from a brief faint, he found that the elders had surrendered the stolen property and the thief. The latter is said to have worked for Lawrence afterwards at Carchemish: 'not too well, but Lawrence was easy with him.'

Liddell Hart's *'T. E. Lawrence' In Arabia and After* was published by Jonathan Cape, London, in 1934. With Hart, who first met Lawrence in 1927, his memory seemed fitful: he was unable to remember the year of the trip or its details, but he claimed to have got as far as Harran. 'But I was also at Damascus, and I forget how I got there. I saw 60 castles [to Sir John Rhys he had claimed 36], and took 4 months, my route being like a spider's web over Syria.' Lawrence claimed to have had no companions. In this version, which otherwise followed Graves, Lawrence collapsed the trigger guard on his Webley (not a Mauser or Colt) before the Turkman seized it.

Vyvyan Richards (as ignorant of the contemporary accounts in Lawrence's letters as his two predecessors) published his *Portrait of T. E. Lawrence* in 1936: 'he added a little more when he told me the story on his return, for he was struck by the sound Shakespearean way in which he and his assailant by common consent rested between the three bouts.' (p. 54.)

These between-wars fantasies survived into some later biographies. For example, Phillip Knightley and Colin Simpson write: ' . . . what seems to have occurred is that a Turkoman villager attacked him to steal his watch, believing it to be made of gold. A shepherd intervened and saved Lawrence from being severely injured. Lawrence used his irade to persuade a Turkish official to arrest the Turkoman and his watch was recovered.' *Secret Lives*, p. 30.

6. Ls, p. 93.
7. HLs, p. 106.
8. *Diary*, entry for 13 July 1911.
9. ibid, entry for 20 July 1911.
10. ibid, entry for 26 July 1911.
11. Sir Leonard Woolley; TEbF, p. 90.
12. HLs, p. 108.

Chapter 7

1. TEbF, p. 61.
2. *Jesus College Magazine*, June 1935.
3. All quotations come from T. E. Lawrence, Vol. i, *Crusader Castles*, The Golden Cockerel Press, 1936.
4. Ls, p. 68.
5. HLs, p. 109
6. ibid, p. 606.
7. ibid, p. 401.
8. ibid, pp. 605 and 401.

9. British Museum, *Carchemish File.*
10. ibid.
11. TEL to RG, p. 48.

Chapter 8

1. TEL to LH, p. 79.
2. 'I haven't had much kick out of life; those days in Carchemish were the best.' Quoted by E. H. R. Altounyan, TEbF, p. 119.
3. HLs, p. 114.
4. Ls, p. 91.
5. ibid.
6. HLs, p. 119.
7. ibid, p. 90.
8. TEbF, p. 79.
9. TEL to RG, p. 57; TEL to LH, p. 36.
10. The select library possessed by Lawrence at his death, and listed in *T. E. Lawrence by his Friends*, contained some 60 volumes in Greek and more than 40 in or from French. His library possessed neither an Arabic dictionary nor a Koran. From Arabic there was Lady Anne Blunt's translation of *The Stealing of the Mare*, versified by W. S. Blunt; two versions of the *Moallaka*, one by Blunt, the other by F. E. Johnson; one translation of *The Poem of Amriolkais* by Sir William Jones; and Philip Hitti's translation of the *Memoirs* of Usāmah Ibn-Munqidh. For the books he had at Jebail: HLs, pp. 124–5.
11. HLs, p. 125.
12. ibid, pp. 129–131.
13. TEL to RG, p. 49; dated to 28 June 1927.
14. Ls, p. 431.
15. David Garnett reports this in Ls, p. 97.
16. TEL to LH, p. 130.
17. HLs, p. 138.
18. TEbF, p. 79.
19. HLs, p. 136.
20. ibid, p, 137.
21. TEbF, p. 258.
22. TEbF, p. 543.
23. To Ch. Schneegans, 26.11.34; Fellows' Library, Jesus College, Oxford.
24. HLs, p. 138.
25. TEbF, p. 81.
26. British Museum, *Carchemish File.*
27. Quoted in Gordon Waterfield, *Layard of Ninevah*, John Murray, London, 1963.
28. HLs, p. 199, dated 6 April 1912.

Chapter 9

1. TEbF, p. 119.
2. Hogarth to Kenyon, 16.7.1914; British Museum, *Carchemish File.*
3. ibid.
4. Letter dated 15.7.1914 from Woolley to Kenyon, apropos engagement of one Willey; British Museum, *Carchemish File.*
5. Ls, p. 161.

6. British Museum, *Carchemish File.*
7. HLs, p. 140.
8. Ls, pp. 136–7.
9. Ls, p. 99.
10. TEbF, pp. 86–7.
11. HLs, p. 272.
12. Ls, p. 107.
13. Letter from Hogarth to Kenyon, 4.10.1911; British Museum, *Carchemish File.*
14. Ls, pp. 99–100.
15. Introduction to *The Letters of Gertrude Bell*, selected and edited by Lady Bell, D.B.E., Ernest Benn, London, 1927.
16. Letter begun at Urfa, dated Thursday 18 [May 1911], p. 252, ibid.
17. ibid, p. 242.
18. HLs, pp. 161–2.
19. Captain Maxwell H. Coote, TEbF, p. 234.
20. HLs, p. 275.
21. Ls, p. 543.
22. TEbF, p. 90.
23. Ls, p. 104.
24. HLs, p. 162.
25. ibid, p. 163.
26. Captain A. E. Townshend, *A Military Consul in Turkey : The Experiences & Impressions of a British Representative in Asia Minor*, Seeley & Co., London, 1910, p. 244.
27. Leonard Woolley, *Dead Towns and Living Men*, Humphrey Milford, London, 1920, p. 179.
28. Letter dated 31 March 1911; Ls, p. 102.
29. Letter dated 'about June 24th, 1911'; Ls, p. 114.
30. Letter dated 28.7.1912; Ls, p. 145.
31. Louis Mallet to Sir Edward Grey, letter dated 21.11.11; British Museum, *Carchemish File.*
32. Letter dated 13.3.1912; ibid.
33. Letter dated 6.4.1912; HLs, p. 199.
34. TEL to RG, p. 178.
35. *'T. E. Lawrence' In Arabia and After*, p. 34; for revision by Lawrence, see TEL to LH, p. 87.
36. Letter to his mother dated 24.6.1911; printed in *Diary MCMXI.* Corvinus Press, 1937.
37. TEL to LH, p. 85.
38. Suleiman Mousa, *T. E. Lawrence, An Arab View*, tr. Albert Butros, Oxford, 1966, p. 5.
39. ibid, entry for 28 July 1911.

Chapter 10

1. *The Egyptian Gazette*, 3.1.1912, includes Sir John and Lady Maxwell, Sir Paul and Lady Harvey and Lord Edward Cecil among the guests.
2. On 4th February; *The Egyptian Gazette*, 10.2.1912.
3. TEL to RG, p. 68.
4. *The Egyptian Gazette* reported Mrs. Petrie's arrival on the N. German Lloyd's S.S. *Schleswig.*

5. The *Home Letters* were the source for Lawrence's first reactions to Egypt.
6. Hogarth, op. cit., p. 161.
7. HLs, p. 190.
8. *The Egyptian Gazette*; 4.5.1912.
9. HLs, p. 200.
10. David Garnett, in Ls, p. 132.
11. HLs, p. 225.
12. See Wininger, *Crosse Jüdische National-Biographie*, Czernowitz, 1925, and Brockhaus.
13. Leonard Woolley, *Dead Towns and Living Men*, p. 156.
14. Letter dated 2 June 1912; HLs, p. 211.
15. Woolley, op. cit., p. 158.
16. Woolley to Kenyon, 31.3.1912; British Museum, *Carchemish File.*
17. HLs, p. 179.
18. British Museum, *Carchemish File.*
19. Woolley, op. cit., p. 148.
20. HLs, p. 258.
21. HLs, p. 276.
22. Leonard Woolley; TEbF, p. 91.
23. HLs, p. 203.
24. ibid, p. 240.
25. ibid, pp. 180, 243.
26. Woolley; TEbF, p. 91.
27. HLs, p. 238.
28. TEbF, p. 115.
29. ibid, p. 82.
30. ibid, p. 115.
31. Woolley, TEbF, p. 91.
32. Letters dated 24.6.1911, 19.12.1911; HLs, pp. 174, 180.
33. Letter dated 23.6.1912; HLs, p. 218.

Chapter 11

1. Letter dated 13.9.1912; HLs, p. 232.
2. Letter dated 10.12.1913; Ls, p. 161.
3. HLs, p. 170; Ls, p. 114.
4. Ls, p. 115.
5. Letter dated 24.6.1911; HLs, pp. 173–4.
6. Letter conjecturally dated 12 July 1911; HLs, p. 176.
7. HLs, p. 176.
8. To Mrs. Reider; Ls, p. 119.
9. HLs, p. 223.
10. Cf. *Secret Lives*, photograph appearing between pp. 62 and 63.
11. Woolley, op. cit., p. 122.
12. HLs, p. 222.
13. ibid, p. 221.
14. Ali-Haidar al-Rikabi to the author.
15. Subhi al-Umari, *Lorens kama 'areftuhu*, (Lawrence As I Knew Him) Dar al-Nahar, Beirut, 1969, p. 173.
16. TEbF, p. 89.
17. HLs, p. 179.
18. Letter to Arnold Lawrence dated 28.7.1912; HLs, p. 226.

19. Woolley, op. cit., p. 106. Since Woolley states he was away at the time, he must have heard the story from Lawrence.

20. Garnett so describes many of the stories describing Lawrence's practical jokes against the Germans; Ls, p. 126.

21. TEbF, p. 93.

22. Letter dated 20.3.1912; HLs, p. 197.

23. HLs, p. 213.

24. ibid, p. 248.

25. ibid, p. 224.

26. Letter dated July 28 1912; HLs, p. 225.

27. ibid, p. 232.

28. ibid, p. 227.

29. ibid, p. 232.

30. ibid, p. 227.

31. ibid, p. 228.

32. ibid, p. 230.

33. Ls, p. 149.

34. ibid, p. 147.

35. Sir William Rothenstein; TEbF, p. 288.

36. TEL to RG, p. 5.

37. HLs, p. 461.

38. Cf. *Secret Lives*, photograph appearing between pp. 62 and 63.

Chapter 12

1. Gen. Edouard Brémond; *Le Hedjaz dans la Guerre Mondiale*; Paris, 1931, p. 160.

2. *Il parait qui'il fut incorporé trois semaines par les Turcs à Ourfa, avant de pouvoir s'échapper*; ibid.

3. In the first, Oxford, type-set version of *Seven Pillars of Wisdom.*

4. If we assume that Lawrence wore Arab dress, was accompanied by Dahoum and was apprehended on a charge to do with military service, a date earlier than 1912 is impossible. In 1911 Lawrence had yet to wear Arab dress; he was under the supervision of Hogarth, Campbell Thompson and, after he returned to convalesce in Oxford, of his mother. The incident must have occurred when no westerners were at Carchemish, since neither Woolley nor any visitor reports the story. One possible period could be the last week of November and the first week of December 1912: by 23 December Lawrence was back in Oxford for Christmas. A more likely date is between Woolley's departure from Jerablus on 14 June 1913 and mid-July, when Lawrence took Dahoum to England. This would fit with the intensification of his feelings for Dahoum and his discovery of the early, masochistic poems of Swinburne. After mid-July he was either in England or at Carchemish accompanied by visitors and, after 1 October, by Woolley. David Garnett's suggestion (in the 1938 *Letters*) that the Halfati incident belongs to the last period of the 1909 walk is unconvincing, apart from Lawrence's own dating, which put it around 1912–13. In 1909 Lawrence did not wear Arab dress, did not speak convincing Arabic, and had not met Dahoum. The Turks were in a euphoric mood; Lawrence had yet to provoke them.

5. 'And besides we have bought some pottery and a sculpture from outside the digs: the sculpture seems to be a Roman descendant of a Hittite goddess (seated on two lions) and is rather an interesting piece therefore. On the other

hand we are only buying from a photo which Dahoum went & took of it and it *may* be Hittite: very unlikely the latter.' Letter dated 4 November 1912; HLs, p. 241.

6. TEbF, p. 88.

7. Lawrence gave substantially this version to Liddell Hart at Otterbourne, 1 August 1933; TEL to LH, p. 141.

8. The two versions are the Oxford original (*vide supra*) and the 1926 edition limited for distribution to friends and those prepared to pay £30.

9. Lawrence did not mention Dahoum's name to Liddell Hart, but he described the injuries: 'Bruised all up one side. Other man had sprain.'

10. General Hassan Arfa, *Under Five Shahs*, John Murray, London, 1964, p. 31.

11. *Seven Pillars*, p. 455.

12. HLs, p. 261.

13. 'Hospital' in *Seven Pillars*, 'lousy dungeon' in TEL to LH, *vide supra*.

14. HLs, p. 232.

15. ibid.

16. Ls, p. 152.

17. Will Lawrence's 'Altogether rather of the style of Miss Holmes' followed 20 obviously uncharitable words deleted by Bob Lawrence: HLs, p. 451.

18. Ls, p. 139.

19. TEbF, pp. 97, 99.

20. HLs, p. 257.

21. TEbF, p. 98.

22. Sir Ernest Barker's foreword to Will Lawrence's Letters, HLs, p. 397.

23. TEbF, p. 60.

24. Mr. Edwin Slade, St. John's College, Oxford in a communication to Ian Davie, Ampleforth College, 3.12.1974.

25. HLs, p. 610. Frank Lawrence was not in the habit of dating his letters precisely. This letter, which discusses a prospective visit to Camp by Bob and Arnie 'on Monday (Aug. 11)' is dated Tuesday: i.e. 5 August.

26. Ls, p. 157.

27. HLs, p. 442.

28. ibid, p. 443; Ls, p. 158.

29. HLs, p. 447.

30. 'I feel a fundamental, crippling, incuriousness about our officers. Too much body and too little head.' TEL to LH, p. 75. Lawrence's dislike of the Army was known to his family. Cf. Frank's letter to Will of 2.1.1915: 'I know you like the Army and I know also Ned does not. But Ned is so very different from me that I am not putting too much weight on his opinions in this matter.' (HLs.) On public schools: 'It is good news you are not sending him [Noël Rieder] to a public school. I don't like the type they produce.' To Mrs. Rieder, Ls, p. 148.

31. TEbF, p. 122.

32. ibid, p. 89.

33. Sir Richard Burton is quoted by George Allgrove, *Love in the East*, London, 1962, p. 48: 'The references to the people of Lot, and the destruction of Sodom, are, as Burton admits, "rather an instance of Allah's power than a warning against pederasty, which Muhammad seems to have regarded with philosophic indifference." '

34. Letter dated 3.10.1913; HLs, p. 268.

35. Letter dated 2.10.1913; HLs, p. 451.

36. The poem was published in the Corvinus Press edition of Lawrence's *Diary MCMXI*, 1937; also in TEbF, p. 104.

Chapter 13

1. Letter dated 26.12.1913; HLs, p. 278. The editor of HLs, Lawrence's eldest brother, misread Lawrence's hand, transcribing Arabic [for Arabia] Petraea.
2. HLs, p. 280.
3. D.M.O. to Sir Arthur Nicholson; received 19.4.13.
4. TEbF, p. 80.
5. HLs, p. 615.
6. ibid, p. 621.
7. ibid, p. 671.
8. ibid, p. 565.
9. ibid, p. 570.
10. ibid, p. 572.
11. Ls, p. 185.
12. TEL to LH, p. 55.
13. Roger Adelson, *Mark Sykes, Portrait of an Amateur*, Cape, London, 1975, p. 180.
14. HPs, Hogarth to his mother; 20.9.1918.
15. HPs, Hogarth; *Arab Situation*, 1920.
16. TEL to LH, 90–1.
17. ibid, pp. 192–3.
18. Ls, p. 148.
19. Ls, p. 187; letter dated 19 October 1914.
20. Letter postmarked 4 December 1914; Ls, p. 189.
21. Letter dated 20.2.1915; HLs, p. 303.
22. TEbF, p. 132.
23. Ronald Storrs, *Orientations*, Ivor Nicholson and Watson, London, 1937, p. 163.
24. ibid, p. 22.
25. Letter dated 12.2.1915; HLs, p. 302.
26. Ls, p. 197.
27. Letter dated 23.6.1915; from Military Intelligence Office, Cairo; HLs, p. 305.
28. HLs, p. 305.
29. HLs, p. 333.
30. W. F. Stirling, *Cornhill*, April 1933.
31. In a telegram dated 24.12.1914 Clayton reported Lloyd's discussions with Fitzgerald in England to Symes, Khartoum; SAD 134/8.
32. Ls, p. 193.
33. ibid, p. 196.
34. Reports dated 3.1.1915, and 5.1.1915, SAD/134/8.
35. C. H. M. Doughty Wylie, Secret Report from S. S. Magallan; SAD 134/2.
36. Letters to A. B. Watt; Ls, pp. 198, 199.
37. Ls, p. 197.
38. ibid, p. 194.
39. Martin Gilbert; *Winston S. Churchill*; vol. iv: 1917–1922; Heinemann, London, 1975, p. 33.

40. Steuber, Dr., Obergeneralarzt a.D., '*Yilderim*', *Armeearzt 1917/18 in Palästina*; Oldenburg i.O, Berlin; Gerhard Stalling; 1928, p. 110.
41. HPs, Hogarth; *Arab Situation*, 1920.
42. Brémond, op. cit.
43. *Seven Pillars*, p. 579.
44. HLs, p. 718.
45. ibid, p. 303–4.
46. ibid, p. 591.
47. ibid, p. 311.
48. ibid, p. 311.
49. ibid, p. 302.
50. John Buchan, *Memory Hold-The-Door*, Hodder & Stoughton, London, 1940, p. 56.

Chapter 14

1. Roger Adelson, op. cit., p. 190.
2. Storrs, op. cit., p. 67.
3. ibid, p. 52.
4. ibid, p. 219.
5. ibid, p. 142.
6. PRO, FO, 414/461.
7. BSA, WK 11 g Bd. 17, for Stotzingen Mission.
8. 'We are in the Straits now.—Bab el Mandeb—with a splendid Arabia on one side, and a dull damp Persia on the other.' HLs, p. 316.
9. The quotations and many of the details derive from his long letter home, dated 18 May 1916 and composed on the voyage back to Egypt. HLs, pp. 317–327.
10. The contemporary description occurs in the above letter, the later in the suppressed prefatory chapter to *Seven Pillars of Wisdom*; cf *Oriental Assembly*, p. 143.
11. For this quotation and general account of the incident, Sir Arnold Wilson, *Loyalties, Mesopotamia 1914–1917*, Oxford, 1930.
12. John E. Mack, op. cit., p. 139, relies on W. F. Stirling for the description of the Report as 'criticizing every aspect of the campaign'; Mack adds that the Report 'seems not to have survived.' A copy of the Report, headed Intelligence, I.E.F. 'D' SECRET is preserved at the Sudan Archive (137/5), Univ. of Durham. Attached to it is a short, handwritten note dated 12.6.1916: 'My dear General, The attached report was rendered privately to me by Lawrence & will I am sure interest you. Yours very sincerely, G. E. Clayton.' The recipient was presumably General Sir Reginald Wingate. The Report criticizes those aspects of the Iraqi campaign on which Lawrence could write with professional superiority: interrogation of prisoners; mapping and survey work; the state of mind of the local population. Interestingly, in view of the forthcoming Revolt, Lawrence reports a suggestion from the Chief Political Officer, Sir Percy Cox, that the surplus from the Waqf (Muslim religious endowment) should be handed over 'to the Sherif of Mecca, for relief of pilgrims etc.' (*Report*, p. 18) The proposal—whose *etc.* might have included guns—had been vetoed by 'India and home'.
13. TEbF, p. 123.
14. Lawrence was to link Herbert's premature death in 1923 with that of

Hogarth in 1927 and say that both deaths had robbed him and left two empty places which 'no one and nothing can ever fill'. Ls, p. 859.

15. '*T. E. Lawrence*' *In Arabia and after*, p. 98.

16. John Buchan, *Memory Hold-The-Door*, p. 205; *John Buchan by his Wife and Friends*, Hodder & Stoughton, London, 1947, p. 99.

17. John Buchan, *Greenmantle*, Hodder & Stoughton, London, 1916, p. 20.

18. ibid, p. 23.

19. HPs; Hogarth; *Arab Situation*, 1920.

20. B. H. Liddell Hart, *History of the First World War*, Cassell, London, 1930, p. 31.

21. BSA IA Türkei 165 Bd. 38.

22. Von Sanders's comment of 10.7.1916 attached to Germany's Constantinople Embassy report no. 376, 12.7.1916.

23. BSA IA Türkei 165 Bd. 39. Grosses Hauptquartier, 5.8.1916.

24. Speech at literary luncheon, 18.6.1935; Storrs Papers, Middle East Centre, St. Antony's College, Oxford.

25. Preface to *Seven Pillars of Wisdom*.

26. HPs; letter dated 17.8.1916.

27. HLs, p. 330; Lawrence wrote 'sherif's'.

28. HPs; To Clayton from England; 17.8.1916.

29. Storrs, op. cit., p. 192.

30. *Seven Pillars*, p. 56.

31. ibid, p. 65.

32. *Greenmantle*, p. 227.

33. 'The appointment of a titular Governor might arouse Arab and possibly Allied suspicions, while that of a Consul could hardly fail to bring about the arrival of Allied and even neutral colleagues.' Storrs, op. cit., p. 191.

34. *Seven Pillars*, p. 66.

Chapter 15

1. HLs, p. 331; Lawrence wrote 'Sherif Feisul'.

2. SAD/143/1; Wingate to Wilson, 6.11.1916.

3. I owe this information to Dr. Norman Daniel who studied the relevant documents in Khartoum.

4. Wingate gives this estimate in his *Notes for Memoirs* (written like Caesar's in the third person); SAD/219/9. A German report—BSA IA Türkei 165 Bd 39—puts the garrison at 9,000.

5. Suleiman Mousa, op. cit., pp. 21–2.

6. SAD/143/5; Wingate to Grey, 22.11.1916.

7. SAD/143/5; Sirdar 14.12.1916 to Grey. 'The Sirdar with Brémond, whom he has been consulting, is for immediate action and will ask General Murray and the Admiral Commanding in Chief to arrange for the embarkation of the French contingent and a British brigade from Suez.'

8. SAD/143/1 Pt 1; Wilson to Wingate, 17.11.1916.

9. SAD/470/4; Wilson to Clayton, 22.11.1916.

10. SAD/143/1; Telegram of Wingate dated 27.10.1916; Storrs in op. cit., Clayton, SAD/136/6.

11. *Memoirs of King Abdullah*, ed. Philip P. Graves; Cape, London, 1950; p. 171; Martin Gilbert, op. cit., p. 698.

12. Major Sir Hubert Young, *The Independent Arab*, John Murray, London, 1933, p. 150.
13. Gen. Sir Archibald Wavell, *Allenby, a Study in Greatness*, George G. Harrap, London, 1940, p. 286.
14. Storrs, op. cit., p. 206.
15. Confirmed by two enemy witnesses: von Sanders quoted by R. Aldington, in *Lawrence of Arabia: A Biographical Enquiry*, Collins, London, 1955 and Brémond, op. cit., p. 72.
16. SAD/143/1; Wingate to Wilson, 10.11.1916.
17. SAD/143/3; Clayton to Wingate, 19.11.1916.
18. SAD/143/5; Wingate to Wilson, 14.11.1916.
19. Ls, p. 212.
20. SAD/470/8; Wingate to Clayton, 6.3.1918.
21. SAD/139/1; Clayton to Wingate, 3.8.1916.
22. Sir Ronald Wingate, Bart, *Wingate of the Sudan*, John Murray, London, 1955, p. 129.
23. SAD/146/8; Draft Tel. of High Commissioner, 13.11.1917.
24. These are Wingate's figures as given in his already cited *Notes for Memoirs.*
25. Ls, p. 217.
26. ibid.
27. ibid, pp. 219–220.
28. ibid, p. 216.
29. SAD/143/1; Wingate gives it as F.O. Telegram no. 303.
30. HLs, p. 333.
31. This letter was dated 17 January 1917 and written in the Hejaz on Arab Bureau paper. It almost immediately fell into Turkish hands being found in Newcombe's saddlebag, after a resisted attack on the Railway. Ismet Karadogan, then a junior Ottoman officer but later Colonel, preserved it. When Newcombe was captured in November, Ismet Karadogan alleviated his captivity; after the war the two former enemies became personal friends.
32. HLs, p. 335.
33. SAD/143/5; Wingate to Grey, 22.11.1916.
34. Achmed Djemal Pasha, *Erinnerungen*, 1922.
35. SAD/143/3; Wingate to Wilson, 12.11.1916.
36. Ls, p. 222; dated 9.3.1917.
37. SAD/134/1; W. Drury to Wingate, 21.11.1912.
38. SAD/145/1; Wingate to Sir A. Murray, 21.1.1917.
39. SAD/145/1; Arab Bureau communicates High Commissioner's view to Pearson, Jidda. Undated.
40. 'Akaba had been taken on my plan by my effort.' *Seven Pillars*, p. 331.
41. The claims of Feisal and Auda are fully discussed in Suleiman Mousa's *T. E. Lawrence, An Arab View.*
42. SAD/145/1; wherein Feisal sets out the sums he will spend on winning over Auda and other sheikhs preparatory to attacking Akaba.
43. Ls, p. 226.
44. See end pages of *Seven Pillars*.
45. SAD/146/1; Wingate to Wilson, 15.7.1917 and Wingate to Sykes, 16.7.1917.
46. HPs; letter dated 30.9.1917.

Chapter 16

1. Storrs commends General Beach, who assisted Herbert and Lawrence in the negotiations at Kut, 'for a saving admiration for my little genius T. E. Lawrence,' op. cit., p. 260.

2. Wingate to Pearson, 2.3.1917: 'The value of Lawrence in the position which he has made for himself with Feisal is enormous . . .' SAD/145/3; for Clayton, FO/882/7; for Sykes, India Office, L/P and S/10 587; for Lloyd, writing to Wingate, SAD/146/1, 17.8.1917.

3. To V. W. Richards, letter dated End of March [1916]; Ls, p. 201.

4. SAD/143/6; Arab Bureau to Wingate, 17.11.1916.

5. Wavell, op. cit., p. 186.

6. Lawrence denounces Allenby to Winston Churchill, then Colonial Secretary, 24.12.1922; Colonel R. Meinertzhagen, *Middle East Diary 1917–1956*, Cresset Press, London, 1959.

7. Liddel Hart, *History of the First World War*, p. 54.

8. Wavell, op. cit., p. 193; for Lawrence's account, *Seven Pillars*, p. 330.

9. Young, op. cit., p. 155.

10. PRO, FO, 882/25.

11. BSA; IA Türkei 177 Bd. 18.

12. Young, op. cit., p. 146.

13. S. C. Rolls, *Steel Chariots in the Desert*, Jonathan Cape, London, 1937, p. 155.

14. BSA; IA Türkei 165 43 Pera Telegram 22.8.1918 Secret: German Ambassador reports discussion with Talaat Pasha; the latter reports Feisal asking for 'a position like that of Bavaria in the German Empire. The Turkish Government cannot give all that. I replied to Talaat Pasha that Ziya Gökalp, chief literary representative of the National Young Turks had gone further: he had proposed a Turco-Arab dualism on the model of Austria-Hungary.'

15. SAD/146/8; High Commissioner (Wingate) to Foreign Office, draft telegram, 13.11.1917.

16. Adelson, op. cit., p. 229.

17. ibid, p. 231 for sketch.

18. See Wingate's telegram to Foreign Office, 16.6.1918; PRO, CAB, 27/27, tel. 948.

19. SAD/145/6; 21.5.1917.

20. SAD/145/6; note by Sheikh Fuad el-Khatib taken down by Stewart Newcombe, 24.5.1917.

21. Suppressed prefatory chapter to *Seven Pillars*, printed *Oriental Assembly*, by T. E. Lawrence, edited by A. W. Lawrence, Williams and Norgate, London, 1939, p. 145.

22. Subhi al-Umari, op. cit., p. 168.

23. Article 27, from *Twenty-Seven Articles*, PRO, FO, 882/7.

24. Suleiman Mousa has gone to considerable lengths to deny this. Op. cit., pp. 181–2.

25. HLs, pp. 340–1.

26. *Cornhill*, April 1933, p. 496.

27. So remembered by the author's mother, Stirling's first cousin.

28. Letter to W. F. Stirling, 25.9.1917; Bodleian Library, quoted *Secret Lives*.

29. Ls, p. 238.

Chapter 17

1. Abdullah, op. cit., p. 40.
2. Meinertzhagen, op. cit., p. 8.
3. HPs, letter dated 7.11.1917.
4. Amir Said al-Jezairi's recollection, as translated by Suleiman Mousa, op. cit., p. 107.
5. BSA; IA Türkei 165 Bd 41; 'Der Nahre Orient', 17.1.1917, from the Hambürgisches Kolonial-Institut.
6. Lawrence's report to Joyce was published in Ls, pp. 238–40; the report from Akaba, SAD/147/1, 30.11.1917, Cairo to Director of Military Intelligence, War Office, London.
7. The Arab was Sheikh Adhoub al-Zebn; Suleiman Mousa, op. cit., p. 113.
8. BSA; IA Türkei 177 Bd 16.
9. HLs, p. 342.
10. ibid, 343.
11. For Hogarth's letters, see text and notes to chapter 19; Cairo (presumably Wingate) cabled to the Director of Military Intelligence, War Office, London, on 30 November that 'Lawrence himself has been until recently at Azrack but it is believed that he intends to leave today (30 November) for Jauf,' SAD/147/1.
12. Chelib Aslan; BSA; IA Türkei 177 Bd 17 Damascus 7.5.1918; German Consulate.
13. John E. Mack: 'T. E. Lawrence: A study of Heroism and Conflict' *American Journal of Psychiatry*, Feb. 1969, p. 1088. Mack was helped by the Lawrence family.
14. Lawrence attributes an instance of Sharif Ali's adjudication to 5 November 1917, two days before the failure to blow the bridge: 'I referred the case to Ali ibn el Hussein, who set them [two quarrelling tribesmen] at liberty on probation, after sealing their promise with the ancient and curious nomad penance of striking the head sharply with the edge of a weighty dagger again and again till the issuing blood had run down to the waist belt. It caused painful but not dangerous scalp wounds, whose ache at first and whose scars later were supposed to remind the would-be defaulter of the bond he had given.' *Seven Pillars*, p. 425.
15. Rolls, op. cit., p. 249.
16. Meinertzhagen, op. cit., entry for 20.7.1919.

Chapter 18

1. Wavell, op. cit., p. 231.
2. SAD/145/7; telegram dated 6.5.1917 from Foreign Office to Cairo quoting Sykes.
3. *Seven Pillars*, p. 462.
4. HPs; Hogarth to Laura Hogarth, 26.1.1917.
5. HPs; Hogarth to Bill Hogarth, son, 16.12.17.
6. HPs; Hogarth to Laura Hogarth, 13.5.1916.
7. *A Wandering Scholar in the Levant*, pp. 70–1.
8. HPs; Hogarth to Laura Hogarth, 30.1.1918, from Jerusalem.
9. ibid, from Turf Club, Cairo, 30.5.1918.
10. Meinertzhagen, op. cit., p. 28.
11. HPs; letter from Hogarth at Turf Club, 2.1.1919.
12. SAD/146/10; Foreign Office to Wingate, 28.11.1917.
13. SAD/150/11; intercepted cable of 2.9.1918.

14. Young, op. cit., p. 199.
15. Elizabeth Monroe, *Philby of Arabia*, Faber, London, 1973, p. 64.
16. HLs, p. 349.
17. Ls, p. 246.
18. *Cornhill*, April 1933.
19. Martin Gilbert, op. cit., p. 71.
20. BSA; IA, Türkei 177 Bd 18; Telegram 22.8.1918 Grosses Hauptquartier, K. Legations, Sekretär an Auswärtiges Amt.
21. See Lawrence's letter to William Yale, Ls, pp. 670–672. Yale charges that the letter was censored in David Garnett's edition, leaving in that Feisal had negotiated with Jemal Pasha, but minimizing the fact that the British were equally considering a separate peace. See William Yale, *The Near East A Modern History*, Univ. of Michigan Press, 1958, p. 475.
22. SAD/148/10; Note Secret; at top, Sir P. Cox and meeting on 16.6.1918.
23. Subhi al-Umari, op. cit., p. 59.
24. HLs, p. 344.
25. TEbF, p. 206.
26. Lawrence Papers, Middle Eastern Centre, St. Antony' College, Oxford. Letter from Lowell Thomas to Philby, 13.8.1953.
27. Letter to Col. Ralph Isham, dated 10.8.27; Isham Papers.
28. These two quotations from *Strand Magazine*, pp. 258, 255.
29. D. G. Hogarth, *The Life of Charles M. Doughty*, Oxford, 1928, p. 132.
30. Young, op. cit., p. 243.
31. Ls, p. 244.
32. Ls, pp. 246–7.
33. Ls, p. 244.
34. *Seven Pillars*, p. 607.
35. *Secret Lives*, p. 164.
36. *Seven Pillars*, p. 446.
37. ibid, p. 597.
38. Op. cit., p. 306.
39. Young, op. cit., p. 251.
40. *Arab Bulletin*, no. 106; printed in Ls, p. 254.
41. See Henry Chauvel's memorandum to the Director, Australian War Memorial, Canberra, commenting on *Seven Pillars of Wisdom*; here comments on Chapter CXIX. Lawrence Papers, M.E.C., St. Antony's College, Oxford.
42. Hans, Guhr, *Als türkischer Divisionskommandeur in Kleinasien und Pälestina*, Berlin, Mars-Verlag, 1937, p. 265.

Chapter 19

1. For the food situation in Turkey in 1917 and 1918, see BSA; IA Türkei 134 Bd. 39 (reporting on starvation in Constantinople) and IA Türkei Bd. 40 for a July 1918 report from General von Seeckt to Liman von Sanders on the desperate position now that no food was coming from Romania and supplies from the Ukraine were in doubt. Germany herself was unable to send the necessary food.
2. TEL to RG, p. 17.
3. Yale Papers, Middle East Centre, St. Antony's College, Oxford.
4. SAD/150/4; Allenby to Wingate, 1.10.1918.
5. Young, op. cit., p. 229.

6. From Suleiman Mousa's basically pro-Sharifian account, op. cit., p. 209.

7. Ls, p. 256.

8. See Henry Chauvel's report on Lawrence to the Director, Australian War Memorial, Canberra; *vide supra* Note 43 to ch. 18.

9. Al-Umari, op. cit., p. 229.

10. *Arab Bulletin*, reproduced in Ls., p. 257.

11. 'I meant to shoot the two brothers, so interned Abd el Kadir in the Town Hall till I should have caught Mohammed Said. Before I had done so Feisal arrived, and said that like a new sultan he would issue a general amnesty. So Abd el Kadir escaped again.' From a secret report, privately owned, to the Chief Political Officer, G.H.Q., Cairo, dated 28 June 1919; quoted pp. 90–2, *Secret Lives*.

12. PRO, CAB, 27/36. EC 2287; 8.11.1918.

13. Al-Umari, op. cit., pp. 232–3.

14. Secret report; *vide* Note 11 *supra*.

15. In *The Lion and the Unicorn, The Collected Essays, Journalism and Letters of George Orwell*, ed. Sonia Orwell and Ian Angus; vol. 4, Penguin, p. 94.

16. Sir Andrew Macphail, *Three Persons*, John Murray, London, 1929, p. 213.

17. Elizabeth Monroe, op. cit., p. 63.

18. *Seven Pillars*, p. 415.

19. Ls, p. 258.

20. SAD/150/1; Clayton to Foreign Office, 8.10.1918.

Chapter 20

In writing on Versailles, Lawrence and Feisal, I was particularly helped by some pages, unpublished at the time, by the Arab scholar, Suleiman Mousa, who had had access, *inter alia*, to the papers of the late Amir Zeid.

1. Lord Stamfordham's letter to T. E. Lawrence, dated New Year's Day, 1928, was published in *Letters to T. E. Lawrence*, ed. A. W. Lawrence, Cape, London, 1962, p. 185.

2. TEbF, p. 193.

3. See Note 1; Stamfordham's second letter of 17.1.1918, quoted Wigram's memorandum. In the original Amir is spelt Emir.

4. For Lawrence's cable and Wingate's replies to Balfour and Hardinge of 12.11.1918, SAD/150/6.

5. HPs; Hogarth to Clayton, 1.11.1918.

6. Hogarth's letter of 2.2.1918 quoted by C. R. L. Fletcher in his Memoir of Hogarth, *The Geographical Magazine*, April 1928, p. 339.

7. TEbF, p. 314, for Florence Doubleday's recollection. She puts into Sir Evelyn's mouth the further words: 'and whom Lowell Thomas is exploiting in every way which may assist Lawrence in his cause for Arabia.' But as she was remembering second-hand twenty years later, she is almost certainly in error, since Lowell Thomas had yet to start his lectures.

8. Letter to Buxton of 10.5.1928 from Karachi; Fellows Library, Jesus College, Oxford.

9. Letter of 7.1.1919 in *Letters to T. E. Lawrence*.

10. For Foreign Office account of French attitude to Feisal, 29.11.1918, see SAD/150/5; ibid for British Ambassador's memorandum on views of Quai d'Orsay of same date: 'Arab Kingdom or Kingdoms . . . have no real existence.'

11. Poincaré, *Au Service de la France*, vol. X, p. 435.
12. HPs; Hogarth's letter of 26.3.1919.
13. Dated 4 November 1918, *Reconstruction of Arabia* was reprinted in Ls, pp. 265–9. Lawrence wrote 'Sherif' and 'Emir'.
14. Ls, p. 270.
15. Papers of late Amir Zeid; undated.
16. Letter dated 3.3.1918; F.O. 882/3.
17. For text of Weizmann's address, see F.O. 371/3395.
18. Letter dated 12.12.1918; late Amir Zeid's papers.
19. Text of letter to Alan Dawnay, 28.9.1919, in Bodleian Library, first published in *Secret Lives*, p. 120.
20. Cf. *Secret Lives*, p. 110, quoting PRO, CAB, 27/36.
21. Letter dated 12.12.1918; Amir Zeid's papers.
22. George Antonius, *The Arab Awakening*, Hamilton, London, 1938. pp. 437–9.
23. Minute of Arnold Toynbee, quoting Lawrence, 17.1.1919; F.O. 608/98.
24. Interviews in *L'Information* and *Le Matin* respectively.
25. PRO, CAB, 27/24.
26. Suleiman Mousa has pointed out that there are differences of phraseology in the text given in F.O. 608/98 and Wiezmann's *Trial and Error*, pp. 307–8.
27. op. cit., p. 15.
28. To the 1929 Shaw Commission.
29. Awni Abdul Hadi, an Arab lawyer who had been with Feisal; Rustum Haidar by 1929 chief of the Royal Court in Baghdad. His letter stated that Feisal, then King of Iraq, had no remembrance of having signed such a document.
30. HPs; letter dated 'Easter'.

Chapter 21

1. HLs, p. 356; *vide infra*, p. 274.
2. '. . . must put on record my conviction that England is out of the Arab affair with clean hands.' Draft Preface to abridged version of *Seven Pillars of Wisdom*; Ls, pp. 345/6.
3. Harold Nicolson, *Diaries and Letters, 1939–1945*, ed. Nigel Nicolson, Collins, London, 1967, paperback; entry for 8.4.1940, p. 62.
4. Robert Graves, TEbF, p. 327.
5. The tribute, particularly impressive for its source, comes from a paper by H. St J. Philby, *T. E. Lawrence and his Critics*; Lawrence Papers, Middle East Centre, St. Antony's College, Oxford.
6. On hearing of *The Mint*, Marshal of the R.A.F. Sir Hugh Trenchard wrote to Lawrence, 10.4.1928, warning him of the mischief the Press might make if they got hold of the work. Lawrence, in a letter to his brother, A. W. Lawrence, 2.5.1928, said: 'I will not publish these notes (whose present name is *The Mint*) in my day.' See *Letters to T. E. Lawrence*, p. 200 and Ls, p. 600.
7. Storrs, op. cit., p. 441.
8. Ls, p. 236.
9. ibid, p. 271.
10. Meinertzhagen, op. cit., under appropriate dates.
11. HLs, p. 304.
12. B.M. Add. MS. 45903, TEL to Charlotte Shaw, 14.4.1927.
13. HPs; Letter to Clayton, 19.1.1919.

14. HPs; so Hogarth quotes him in a letter to Laura Hogarth, dated 'Easter Sunday'.

15. The authors of *Secret Lives*, given access to the Lawrence Papers in the Bodleian Library, discovered the inscription and drew the conclusion. Op. cit., p. 162.

16. 'Don't go to Ireland,' Lawrence wrote home on 16.10.1913, 'even to play golf. I think the whole place repulsive historically: they should not like English people, and we certainly cannot like them.' HLs, p. 269.

17. Cf. letter to V. W. Richards, Ls, p. 280.

18. Leonard Green, *The Youthful Lover and other prose studies*, Basil Blackwell, Oxford, 1919, p. 28.

19. TEbF, pp. 160, 162.

20. Meinertzhagen, entry, op. cit., for 17.7.1919.

21. ibid.

22. Ls., p. 291.

23. Yale Papers, Middle East Centre, St. Antony's College, Oxford.

24. Ls, p. 296.

25. Information given to the author by the Hon. Edward Gathorne Hardy in Athens, 29.10.1974.

26. *Letters to T. E. Lawrence*, p. 39.

Chapter 22

1. TEbF, p. 262.
2. Robert Graves, *Lawrence and the Arabs*, p. 406.
3. '*T. E. Lawrence*' *In Arabia and After*, p. 398.
4. ibid, p. 400.
5. *Letters to T. E. Lawrence*, letter dated 20.7.1922.
6. To Edward Garnett, 26.8.1922, Ls, p. 360; to E. M. Forster, 29.9.1924, Ls, p. 467.
7. *Seven Pillars*, p. 28.
8. 'The names of the "unhistorical" people, the small fry, English, Arab and Turk in the *Seven Pillars* were fictitious in the MS. and were again changed for the printed text.' TE to RG, p. 55.
9. *Seven Pillars*, p. 244.
10. *The Strand Magazine*, January 1920, p. 260.
11. *Seven Pillars*, p. 529.
12. Letter to Edward Garnett, 20.9.1922, postmarked Farnborough; Ls, p. 383.
13. *Letters to T. E. Lawrence*, letter of 22.11.1922, p. 91.
14. Letter of 22.9.1927, Ls, p. 542.
15. *vide supra*, Note 6.
16. ibid.
17. André Malraux, 'Lawrence and the Demon of the Absolute', *Hudson Review*, Winter 1956.
18. To Edward Garnett, Ls, p. 370.
19. Malraux, *vide supra*.
20. *Seven Pillars*, p. 458.
21. Letter of 22.9.1927; Ls, p. 542.
22. Letter to Charlotte Shaw of 26.3.1924; as printed *Secret Lives*, p. 214.
23. TEbF, p. 157.

24. David Wright, Introduction to *Trelawney's Records of Shelley, Byron, etc.*, Penguin, 1973, pp. 33–4.
25. For a convincing discussion of the relevance of 'Don Juan' to Byron's marriage see G. Wilson Knight, *Lord Byron's Marriage, the Evidence of Asterisks*, Macmillan, New York, 1957.
26. *Seven Pillars*, p. 187.
27. ibid, p. 193.
28. HPs; Hogarth to Laura Hogarth, from Cairo, 14.2.1919.
29. *Seven Pillars*, p. 132.
30. D. G. Hogarth, *The Life of Charles M. Doughty*, Oxford, 1928, p. 39.
31. TEL to RG, p. 4.
32. See Preface to *Minorities*, p. 14.
33. TEbF, p. 327.
34. Letter to W. D. Hogarth from Miranshah, 11.11.1928; Lawrence Papers, Middle East Centre, St. Antony's College, Oxford.
35. TEL to RG, pp. 15–6.
36. ibid.
37. ibid, p. 17.
38. *Vide supra*, p. 201.
39. TEL to RG, p. 17.
40. Letter to R. V. Buxton, 22.9.1923; Ls, p. 431.
41. TEL to RG, p. 55.
42. TEL to LH, p. 64.
43. ibid, p. 68.
44. ibid, p. 143.
45. Quoted in *Secret Lives*, pp. 155–6.
46. TEL to RG, p. 29.
47. ibid, p. 137.
48. *Seven Pillars*, pp. 81–2.
49. *Oriental Assembly*, p. 142; also reprinted in the edition cited throughout this work.
50. Ls, p. 166.
51. *Seven Pillars*, p. 315.
52. Letter of 11.1.1927, from Karachi; HLs, p. 364.
53. TEbF, p. 268.
54. For information on Sharif Ali (apart from Philby's account of his visit to his house in *Arabian Jubilee*, pp. 130–2,) I am indebted to Sayid Tarif Subhi al-Umari and his uncle, Sayid Omar al-Umari. The final quotation comes from *Seven Pillars*, p. 99.

Chapter 23

1. To G. B. Shaw from Karachi, 7.5.1928; Ls, p. 606.
2. Gilbert, op. cit., p. 540.
3. ibid, p. 557; the source being Jessie Crosland, wife of J. B. Crosland and mother of a future Foreign Secretary.
4. ibid, p. 322.
5. *Letters to T. E. Lawrence*, p. 12.
6. Ls, p. 695.
7. For the Cairo Conference, *vide* Gilbert op. cit.
8. Elie Kedourie: *In the Anglo-Arab Labyrinth; The McMahon Correspondence and its Interpretation 1914–1939*; Cambridge University Press, 1976, p. 126.

9. See Z. Gaster 'Lawrence and King Hussein: The 1921 Negotiations', *The National Review*, 15 October 1938, pp. 512–515.
10. ibid.
11. Sir Alec Seath Kirkbride, *A Crackle of Thorns*, John Murray, London, 1956, p. 10.
12. Ls, p. 693.

Chapter 24

1. *Letters to T. E. Lawrence*, p. 23.
2. ibid, pp. 187–8.
3. ibid, p. 188.
4. *Seven Pillars*, p. 254.
5. ibid. p. 175.
6. HLs, p. 713.
7. Ls, p. 379.
8. TEbF, p. 325.
9. Letter from Bovington Camp, 19.3.1923; Ls, p. 410.
10. Letter (wrongly dated to 1922) of 27.6.1923; Ls, p. 419.
11. Christopher Caudwell (Sprigg), *Studies in a Dying Culture*: The Bodley Head, London, 1938, p. 37.
12. Letter from Ezra Pound, 20.4.1920; *Letters to T. E. Lawrence*, p. 149. 'When you say you want to write for money, what do you mean "money"?'
13. Ls, p. 364.
14. See Note 15 in following chapter.
15. See obituary in *The Times*, 15.2.1957.
16. *Letters to T. E. Lawrence*, p. 122.
17. Lord Vansittart, *The Mist Procession*, Hutchinson, London, 1958, p. 327.
18. *Secret Lives*, pp. 180–1.
19. *The Mint*, Jonathan Cape, London, 1955, p. 14.
20. Ls, p. 369.
21. ibid, p. 377.
22. ibid, p. 381.
23. *Letters to T. E. Lawrence*, pp. 202–5.
24. Ls, p. 600.

Chapter 25

1. C. M. Devers, *The World Today*, June 1927.
2. TEbF, p. 565.
3. TEL to RG, p. 126.
4. TEbF, p. 299.
5. Kirkbride, op. cit., p. 8.
6. John Bruce, *The Scottish Field*, August, 1938.
7. Ls, p. 372.
8. *The Mint*, pp. 39 and 102.
9. HLs, p. 356; 22.11.1923.
10. Ls, p. 717.
11. Ls, p. 386.
12. To G. B. Shaw; Ls, p. 388.
13. Ls, p. 389.
14. Squadron-Leader W. M. M. Hurley, TEbF, p. 401.

15. I owe this information to one of the few students of Lawrence's life who have been given access to certain otherwise embargoed papers in the Bodleian Museum.
16. Michael Howard, *Jonathan Cape, Publishers*, Jonathan Cape, London, 1971, p. 82.
17. Ls, p. 395.
18. Ls, p. 394.
19. John E. Mack, *A Prince of our Disorder*, London, p. 324. Mack, quoting an interview with A. E. Chambers, capitalizes God.
20. Ls, p. 649.
21. Letter to A. E. Chambers of 26.4.1926; unembargoed Lawrence Papers in the Bodleian Museum.
22. Mack, op. cit., p. 324.
23. *Letters to T. E. Lawrence*, p. 197.
24. *Scottish Field*, August, 1938; Bruce dates an adventure with Lawrence in Charing Cross Road to some months before their enlistment in the Royal Tank Corps.
25. Ls, p. 700.
26. *Secret Lives*, p. 174.
27. TEL to RG, p. 174; Graves's reply may be found in *Letters to T. E. Lawrence*.
28. Ls, p. 403.
29. TEbF, p. 261.
30. Robin Maugham, *Escape from the Shadows*, Hodder & Stoughton, London, 1972.
31. Mack, op. cit., p. 433.
32. *Drummer*, Vol. 1, August/September, 1975; 5466 Santa Monica Blvd., Los Angeles.
33. Mrs. P. Knowles in verbal communication to author, 9 June 1976.

Chapter 26

1. Mack, op. cit., p. 346.
2. To Charlotte Shaw; BM Add. MS. 45903.4; 9.1.1932.
3. C. M. Devers, *The World Today*, June 1927, pp. 141–4.
4. Eric Kennington, *Atlantic Monthly*, April 1937, p. 413.
5. Ls, p. 478.
6. Ls, p. 614.
7. *Leaves in the Wind*, printed in Ls, p. 502.
8. Ls, p. 524.
9. Ls, p. 853.
10. Nicolette Devas, *Two Flamboyant Fathers*, Collins, London, 1966, p. 91.
11. Ls, p. 450.
12. TEbF, p. 214.
13. *Sunday Times*, 15 June 1975, p. 30.
14. From a handwritten note by G. B. Shaw attached to a copy of *Seven Pillars* in the Arents Collection, N.Y. Public Library; quoted *Secret Lives*, p. 215.
15. For a detailed account of Lawrence's friendship with the Shaws, see Stanley Weintraub, *Private Shaw and Public Shaw*, Jonathan Cape, London, 1963.
16. Ls, p. 356.

17. Ls, p. 388.
18. Ls, p. 385.
19. Communication from The National Trust, Wessex Regional Office, 5 April 1976.
20. Quoted in Weintraub, op. cit., pp. 24–5.
21. See *Letters to T. E. Lawrence*, pp. 58–75.
22. To Forster, Lawrence wrote: 'The truth is of course that you are a very great writer & that it is irredeemably weak of me to envy you . . . ' Ls, p. 462. To Edward Garnett: 'E. M. Forster: very good; but is he quite great? I like him, but a little shamefacedly.' Ls, p. 466.
23. TEbF, p. 285.

Chapter 27

1. Information supplied by H. Montgomery Hyde.
2. Lawrence to 'Walter', a serviceman, 5 April 1935; in a California private collection and quoted by Mack, op. cit., p. 407.
3. Ls, p. 871.
4. Mack, op. cit., p. 411.
5. *Secret Lives*, p. 177.
6. Robert Graves and Alan Hodge, *The Long Week-end*, first published 1940, Penguin, 1971, p. 213.
7. *Dorset Daily Echo*, 20.5.1935.
8. Sir Oswald Mosley, *My Life*, Nelson, London, 1968, p. 71.
9. A. J. P. Taylor, *English History 1914–1945*, Oxford, 1965, p. 285.
10. Mosley, op. cit., p. 315.
11. Henry Williamson, *Genius of Friendship, 'T. E. Lawrence'*, Faber & Faber, London, 1941, p. 12.
12. TEbF, p. 452.
13. See Ls, p. 580.
14. Williamson, op. cit., p. 73.
15. ibid, p. 75.
16. Henry Williamson to the author in 1948, reinforced by a communication to the author from Hon. Lady Mosley, 21 May 1976.
17. Weintraub, op. cit., p. 211.
18. 'One day, when we were talking of Communism, T. E. shocked the troops by remarking, casually: "When history comes to be written, Lenin will probably take his place as the greatest man of our time." ' Alec Dixon, TEbF, p. 375.
19. Renee Winegarten, 'The Fascist Mentality—Drieu la Rochelle', in *Reappraisals of Fascism*, New York, 1976, p. 218.
20. Graves, *vide supra.*
21. *The Studio*, Vol. 112; comprising the six monthly numbers from July to December 1936.
22. TEbF, p. 305.
23. *Oriental Assembly*, p. 144.
24. *Seven Pillars*, p. 176.
25. Simon Jesty, *'River Niger' ; a novel with a prefatory letter by T. E. Lawrence*, Broiswood, London, 1935, p. 21.
26. Weintraub, op. cit., p. 219.
27. To Edward Marsh, 19.3.1929; Ls, p. 644.

28. Victor Meulenyser, who was probably the first to state in print that Lawrence's father was 'un baronnet irlandais', also stated as early as 1939 that Williamson wished Lawrence to meet Hitler: cf. *Le Colonel Lawrence, Agent de l'Intelligence Service*, Editions Rex, Brussels, 1939, p. 231. *Un ami lui demandait un entretien pour lui parler d'un projet de voyage à Berlin afin d'y rencontrer Adolf Hitler.*

29. Quoted by Renee Winegarten, op. cit., p. 220; citing Frederic Grover, *Drieu la Rochelle*, Paris, 1962, p. 84.

30. Vansittart, op. cit., pp. 482–3.

31. TEbF, p. 565.

32. Quoted by Colin Graham in 'The Crash Which Killed Lawrence of Arabia'; Dorset, *The Country Magazine*, Summer 1968.

33. See booklet, *Lawrence of Arabia and Dorset*, compiled by Harry Broughton, formerly Mayor of Wareham, Pictorial Museum, Wareham, 1966.

34. *The Times*, 15 May 1935.

35. *The Times* in its report of the inquest, 22 May 1935.

36. ibid.

37. *Secret Lives*, p. 272.

38. *Dorset Daily Echo*, 16 May 1935.

39. *The Times*, 22 May 1935.

40. 'I do not think, however, that he will be found to have left any work of importance:' *The Times*, 22 May 1976 quoting A. W. Lawrence after the publication of the news that he had been named his brother's literary executor.

41. *The Times*, 18 May 1935.

42. *Secret Lives*, p. 272.

43. ibid.

44. *Dorset Daily Echo*, 21 May 1935.

45. *The Times*, 22 May 1935.

46. *Dorset Daily Echo*, 'The day after the accident military and civil police called on the father and told him that on no account was the boy to be interviewed by anyone without authority.' The interview was published on 16 May 1935.

47. Mayor Broughton's booklet; *vide supra*.

48. *Secret Lives*, p. 274.

49. Graham, op. cit.

50. Mack, op. cit., pp. 431 and 433.

51. ibid, pp. 433, 436.

52. Henry Williamson quoted by John E. Mack, op. cit., p. 409.

53. St. John, v, 25.

ACKNOWLEDGEMENTS

I AM grateful to the Trustees of the Seven Pillars of Wisdom Trust and Jonathan Cape Ltd. for permission to quote from *Seven Pillars of Wisdom*; to the Trustees of the T. E. Lawrence Letters Trust to quote from letters by T. E. Lawrence including those published in *T. E. Lawrence to his Biographers: Robert Graves and Liddell Hart*; to the Trustees of the T. E Lawrence Letters Trust and Jonathan Cape Ltd. to quote from *The Letters of T. E. Lawrence* and *T. E. Lawrence by his Friends*; to the Trustees of the T. E. Lawrence Letters Trust, Mr. A. W. Lawrence and Basil Blackwell Ltd. to quote from *The Home Letters of T. E. Lawrence and his Brothers;* to Mr. A. W. Lawrence and Jonathan Cape Ltd. to quote from *The Mint*; and to Mr. A. W. Lawrence to quote from *Oriental Assembly, Crusader Castles, 1911 Diary,* and the poem 'To S.A.'. Apart from giving these permissions neither Mr. A. W. Lawrence nor the Trustees have given any other assistance in the writing of this book.

Individuals and institutions possessing or guarding documents relating to the life of T. E. Lawrence, as well as libraries and librarians in three continents, have been of cardinal assistance to me in writing this biography and I gratefully record my debts to them.

In Oxford, to Dr. David Rees, Archivist at Jesus College, who allowed me to read the Lawrence papers in the Fellows' Library and to Idris Foster, Jesus Professor of Celtic, who gave me invaluable information about the collegiate background to Lawrence's life as an undergraduate; to Albert Hourani, Fellow of St. Antony's College and University Lecturer in the Modern History of the Middle East, whose general guidance to the documents held at St. Antony's was generously supplemented by Miss D. Grimwood Jones; to Dr. Caroline Barron for permission to quote from The Hogarth Papers at St. Antony's College; to P. R. S. Moorey who gave me access to the Ashmolean Museum's archives while enlightening me on the Hittite background to Lawrence's work at Carchemish; to D. G. Vaisey, Deputy Keeper of the Archives at the Bodleian Museum; to J. C. Everett, City Treasurer, and M. P. M. Crabb of Oxford City Council; and to the late Gervase Mathew, O.P., as whose guest I stayed at Blackfriars, and to the community who made me welcome. In Durham, whose university is the repository of the Sudan

Archive, to Lesley E. Forbes, Keeper of Oriental Books and to Jill Butterworth for their invaluable assistance. In London, to the staff of the British Museum for access to the Carchemish File and the correspondence between Lawrence and Charlotte Shaw and to P. J. Porter, Assistant Keeper, Department of Manuscripts, for drawing up a catalogue of her 1975 *Castles and Sieges* exhibition at the British Library; to the staff of the London Library; to the Goethe Institute for the loan of books and periodicals otherwise unobtainable in England; to Professor Walter Laqueur at the Wiener Library for a bibliographical guide to Clemens Laar. In Dorchester, to Margaret Holmes, County Archivist; in Bovington Camp, to the Curator of the Royal Tank Museum; to Mrs. L. O. Moores of the Ordnance Survey; to the St. Just Town Council in Cornwall and to the National Trust, Wessex Regional Office. In Bonn, to Dr. Gehling of the Politisches Archiv of the Auswärtiges Amt, who facilitated the delivery of hundreds of files in spite of official limitations on numbers and to Dr. W. Hubatsch, Professor of Medieval and Modern History, for advice on the scope and limitations of contemporary German archives. In Stuttgart, to Dr. J. Rohwer, Chief Librarian of the Bibliothek der Zeitgeschichte, and in Freiburg, to Dr. Fleischer, Militärarchiv of the Bundesarchiv, for advice on the memoirs of German soldiers in the 1914–1918 War. For the pursuit of two inconclusive leads, which had nevertheless to be explored, in Berlin to Frau Doktor I. Ritter, Bibliothek Oberamtsratin, Staatsbibliothek, Preussischer Kulturbesitz, for the transmission, gratis, of a photostat of Alistair Crowley's Bekentnisse (with two pages mysteriously extracted); and in Gütersloh to the Bertelsmann Lessering Lektorat; and in Berlin to the Kurschners Deutscher Literatur-Kalendar for investigation of the background to Clemens Laar and his *Kampf in der Wüste*. In Cairo, to the staff of the Geographical Institute and to Richard H. Dewey, Assistant Librarian of the American University; to Dr. Aboul-Enein, editor of the *Egyptian Gazette*, and to Fathi Ghanem, editor of *Rose el-Yussef*. In Istanbul to Dr. Michael Austin, some time lecturer in modern Turkish history at Robert College, for information on the still largely inaccessible Ottoman state archives. In Connecticut, to Jonathan Trumbull Isham, for lordly hospitality at New Canaan and for access to the papers relating to Lawrence in the possession of his late father, Ralph H. Isham, C.B.E. In New York, to the staff of the New York Public Library in general and to the Trustees of the Frederick Lewis Allen Memorial Room in particular.

Nor could the book have been written as it has been written without the help, often considerable, of the following: Sir Philip and Lady Adams; Gillon Aitken; Hugh Auchincloss; Dr. Randall Baker; Captain R. Barlow, R.A.E.C.; Dr. R. L. Bidwell; Carl D. Brandt; Carol Brandt; David Carritt; Dr. Margaret Clarke; Frank Clements; Major-General

S. A. Cook; Dr. Norman Daniel, C.B.E.; Ruth Daniel; Ian Davie; Percival Davies, O.B.E.; Jane Detnon; Rosemary ffolliott; Hon. Edward Gathorne Hardy; Brig.-Gen. Sir John Bagot Glubb, D.S.O.; Hon. Desmond Guinness; Ramez al-Halwani; Norah Harrison; John Haylock; R. E. Holden; Hassan Khamis; F. C. Lay; Mary Lascelles, F.B.A.; Margaret Lenfestey; Captain H. R. Leach, M.B.E.; Abbas Mahrous; Peter Mayne; Tom Metcalfe; Doris Morgan; Hon. Lady Mosley; Suleiman Mousa; Alan Neame; Elinor Greening Phillips; Ivor Powell; Ali-Haidar al-Rikabi; Rev. J. S. Reynolds; Dr. Yusif Sayigh; Anthony Sheil; John Shrive; Colin Simpson; Agnes Stewart; Dr. T. H. M. Stewart; Jean Sulzberger; Christopher Sykes; Sir Herbert Todd; Tarif Subhi al-Umari; Donald Weeks; Henry Williamson; Renee Winegarten.

I thank Frances Lindley for a perceptivity which has left its impress, *splendidior vitro*, on many a page.

I acknowledge the gracious permission of Her Majesty the Queen to quote from two letters from Lord Stamfordham. For permission to quote from other letters and papers I am grateful to Viscount Allenby (Allenby Papers, St. Antony's College, Oxford); Mrs. J. E. Brown (Philby Papers, St. Antony's College, Oxford); Mr. S. W. Clayton (letter from Colonel G. F. Clayton); the Principal and Fellows of Jesus College, Oxford (Lawrence Papers); Lord Lloyd (letter from George Lloyd); The National Trust (letters from Rudyard Kipling); Mrs. Ruth M. Robbins (letter from Charles M. Doughty); Viscount Trenchard (letters from Sir Hugh Trenchard); and Sir Ronald Wingate (letter from General Sir Reginald Wingate). The transcripts of Crown-copyright records in the Public Record Office and Sudan Archive, University of Durham appear by permission of the Controller of H.M. Stationery Office.

The quotations throughout *T. E. Lawrence to his Biographers. Robert Graves and Liddell Hart* are reprinted by permission of Robert Graves and the estate of Liddell Hart; from *The Secret Lives of Lawrence of Arabia* by Phillip Knightley and Colin Simpson by permission of Thomas Nelson & Sons Ltd.; from *The Middle East Diary 1917–1956* by Colonel R. Meinertzhagen by permission of Barrie & Jenkins. The quote from the letter from Ezra Pound from *The Selected Letters of Ezra Pound 1907–1941* ed. D. D. Paige, Copyright 1950 by Ezra Pound, is reprinted by permission of Faber & Faber Ltd. and New Directions Publishing Corporation. The quote from 'Lawrence: An Unofficial Portrait' by Eric Kennington. Copyright © 1937, by The Atlantic Monthly Company, Boston, Mass. is reprinted with permission. The quotes from 'Lawrence and The Demon of the Absolute' by André Malraux are reprinted by permission from *The Hudson Review*, Vol. VIII, No. 4 (Winter, 1956), Copyright © 1956 by The Hudson Review, Inc.

INDEX

BIOGRAPHY

ALBERT EINSTEIN Banesch Hoffmann £1.75
Written with the co-operation of Einstein's personal secretary, this is the most authoritative account of the 20th century's greatest scientist. Illustrated.

ANEURIN BEVAN Vols 1 & 2 Michael Foot £2.50 each
The classic political biography of post-war British politics.

THE BORGIAS Michael Mallett 90p
The rise and fall of one of the most notorious families in European history: legends of poisoning, incest and political contrivance. Illustrated.

CLASSIC LIVES Caroline Silver 75p
The birth, rearing and training of seven thoroughbred horses. 'The straw practically falls out of the pages.' *Jilly Cooper*

CONFUCIUS D. Howard Smith 75p
An introduction to the Way of Confucius – the system of belief which was the inspiration behind one of the richest and noblest civilisations the world has known.

THE DEATH OF LORCA Ian Gibson £1.00
Federico García Lorca, one of the outstanding poets and dramatists of this century, was murdered by Nationalist rebels at the outbreak of the Spanish Civil War in 1936. History enshrines him as a homosexual romantic martyr, but his political convictions are indisputable. 'Lovers of poetry, lovers of truth, lovers of Spain should all read this exemplary piece of literary research.' THE SUNDAY TIMES. Illustrated.

THE FEARFUL VOID Geoffrey Moorhouse £1.25
There is a fearful void out there in the empty quarter of the Sahara Desert, but more terrifying still is the void within our minds – the fear of loneliness and failure. One man's search to conquer his own self-distrust. Illustrated.

MOVING INTO AQUARIUS Sir Michael Tippett 75p
One of our greatest living composers asks: How does music, the most expressive of all communication, relate to a technology-obsessed society in which aggression and acquisitiveness have become an index of personal worth?

BIOGRAPHY

MARIE CURIE Robert Reid £1.95

Widely acclaimed biography of the double Nobel Prize winner. Marie Curie discovered radium and her work has been the basis for much modern chemistry and nuclear physics. A rounded and readable portrait of a brilliant but troubled woman.

THE UNKNOWN ORWELL

Peter Stansky and William Abrahams 90p

The creation of Orwell was an act of will by Eric Blair of Eton. The making of the creator of *1984*.

FLYING Kate Millett £1.50

The extraordinary, frank and stimulating autobiography of Kate Millett, author of *The Prostitution Papers* and *Sexual Politics*.

VIRGINIA WOOLF Vols 1 & 2

Quentin Bell (Vol 1 £1.00; Vol 2 £1.25)

Acclaimed as one of the outstanding literary biographies of the century, these books trace the troubled development of Virginia Woolf as a writer and as a woman. Her Bloomsbury friends are chronicled in parallel.

STRANGER ON THE EARTH Albert Lubin £1.50

A psychological biography of Vincent Van Gogh. Fully illustrated and impeccably researched.

SHAKESPEARE THE MAN A. L. Rowse £1.25

The identity of the dark lady of the sonnets is revealed, and Shakespeare is set in the context of his friends, patrons and contemporaries – not merely of his plays.

MARX David McLellan £2.50

A major new biography by Britain's leading Marxist historian. Marx is shown in his private and family life as well as in his political contexts.

TRAVEL

THE FEARFUL VOID Geoffrey Moorhouse £1.25
There is a fearful void out there in the empty quarter of the Sahara Desert, but more terrifying still is the void within our minds – the fear of loneliness and failure. One man's search to conquer his own self-distrust. Illustrated in full colour.

JOURNEY THROUGH BRITAIN John Hillaby 95p
It was a magical idea to walk through the over-industrialised land of Britain from Land's End to John O'Groats, avoiding all centres of population. Britain's master walker made his reputation with this book. Illustrated.

JOURNEY THROUGH EUROPE John Hillaby £1.00
John Hillaby gives a splendid potpourri of factual account, lively anecdote, mythology and private comment in this account of his walk from the Hook of Holland via the Alps to Nice. Illustrated.

JOURNEY TO THE JADE SEA John Hillaby 95p
Tired of city-living and ashamed of his toleration of boredom, John Hillaby made a three-month safari from the Northern Frontier District of Kenya to the legendary Jade Sea. Illustrated.

JOURNEY THROUGH LOVE John Hillaby £1.25
Hillaby's most recent and possibly most powerful and evocative book concerns a series of several walks, in Yorkshire, Wales, London, the South Downs and North America, and the thread running through the narrative is the story of a great tragedy and loss.

All these books are available at your local bookshop or newsagent, or can be ordered direct from the publisher. Just tick the titles you want and fill in the form below.

Name ....

Address ....

....

Write to Paladin Cash Sales, PO Box 11, Falmouth, Cornwall TR10 9EN.
Please enclose remittance to the value of the cover price plus:
UK: 22p for the first book plus 10p per copy for each additional book ordered to a maximum charge of 82p.
BFPO and EIRE: 22p for the first book plus 10p per copy for the next 6 books, thereafter 3p per book.
OVERSEAS: 30p for the first book and 10p for each additional book.
Granada Publishing reserve the right to show new retail prices on covers, which may differ from those previously advertised in the text or elsewhere.